Hacking Secret Ciphers with Python

By Al Sweigart

Book Version 1

Special thanks to Ari Lacenski. I can't thank her enough. Without her efforts there'd be typos literally on every page.

Thanks to Jason Kibbe. Cover lock photo by "walknboston" http://www.flickr.com/photos/walkn/3859852351/ Romeo & Juliet and other public domain texts from Project Gutenberg. Various image resources from Wikipedia. Wrinkled paper texture by Pink Sherbet Photography http://www.flickr.com/photos/pinksherbet/2978651767/ Computer User icon by Katzenbaer.

If you've downloaded this book from a torrent, it's probably out of date. Go to http://inventwithpython.com/hacking to download the latest version.

ISBN 978-1482614374
1st Edition

Nedroid Picture Diary by Anthony Clark, http://nedroid.com

Movies and TV shows always make hacking look exciting with furious typing and meaningless ones and zeros flying across the screen. They make hacking look like something that you have to be super smart to learn. They make hacking look like magic.

It's not magic. It's based on computers, and everything computers do have logical principles behind them which can be learned and understood. Even when you don't understand or when the computer does something frustrating or mysterious, there is always, always, always a reason why.

And it's not hard to learn. This book assumes you know nothing about cryptography or programming, and helps you learn, step by step, how to write programs that can hack encrypted messages. Good luck and have fun!

100% of the profits from this book are donated
to the Electronic Frontier Foundation, the Creative Commons, and the Tor Project.

Dedicated to Aaron Swartz, 1986 – 2013

"Aaron was part of an army of citizens that believes democracy only works when the citizenry are informed, when we know about our rights—and our obligations. An army that believes we must make justice and knowledge available to all—not just the well born or those that have grabbed the reins of power—so that we may govern ourselves more wisely.

When I see our army, I see Aaron Swartz and my heart is broken. We have truly lost one of our better angels."

- C.M.

About This Book

There are many books that teach beginners how to write secret messages using ciphers. There are a couple books that teach beginners how to hack ciphers. As far as I can tell, there are no books to teach beginners how to write programs to hack ciphers. This book fills that gap.

This book is for complete beginners who do not know anything about encryption, hacking, or cryptography. The ciphers in this book (except for the RSA cipher in the last chapter) are all centuries old, and modern computers now have the computational power to hack their encrypted messages. No modern organization or individuals use these ciphers anymore. As such, there's no reasonable context in which you could get into legal trouble for the information in this book.

This book is for complete beginners who have never programmed before. This book teaches basic programming concepts with the Python programming language. Python is the best language for beginners to learn programming: it is simple and readable yet also a powerful programming language used by professional software developers. The Python software can be downloaded for free from http://python.org and runs on Linux, Windows, OS X, and the Raspberry Pi.

There are two definitions of "hacker". A hacker is a person who studies a system (such as the rules of a cipher or a piece of software) to understand it so well that they are not limited by the original rules of that system and can creatively modify it to work in new ways. "Hacker" is also used to mean criminals who break into computer systems, violate people's privacy, and cause damage. This book uses "hacker" in the first sense. **Hackers are cool. Criminals are just people who think they're being clever by breaking stuff.** Personally, my day job as a software developer pays me way more for less work than writing a virus or doing an Internet scam would.

On a side note, don't use any of the encryption programs in this book for your actual files. They're fun to play with but they don't provide true security. And in general, you shouldn't trust the ciphers that you yourself make. As legendary cryptographer Bruce Schneier put it, "Anyone, from the most clueless amateur to the best cryptographer, can create an algorithm that he himself can't break. It's not even hard. What is hard is creating an algorithm that no one else can break, even after years of analysis. And the only way to prove that is to subject the algorithm to years of analysis by the best cryptographers around."

 The book can be downloaded for free from its website at http://inventwithpython.com/hacking. If you ever have questions about how these programs work, feel free to email me at al@inventwithpython.com.

TABLE OF CONTENTS

Chapter 1

Making Paper Cryptography Tools

Topics Covered In This Chapter:

- What is cryptography?
- Codes and ciphers
- The Caesar cipher
- Cipher wheels
- St. Cyr slides
- Doing cryptography with paper and pencil
- "Double strength" encryption

> "I couldn't help but overhear, probably because I was eavesdropping."
>
> Anonymous

What is Cryptography?

Look at the following two pieces of text:

```
“Zsijwxyfsi niqjsjxx gjyyjw. Ny
nx jnymjw ktqqd tw bnxitr; ny
nx anwyzj ns bjfqym fsi anhj ns
utajwyd. Ns ymj bnsyjw tk tzw
qnkj, bj hfs jsotd ns ujfhj ymj
kwznyx bmnhm ns nyx xuwnsl tzw
nsizxywd uqfsyji. Htzwynjwx tk
lqtwd, bwnyjwx tw bfwwntwx,
xqzrgjw nx ujwrnyyji dtz, gzy
tsqd zuts qfzwjqx.”
```

```
“Flwyt tsytbbnz jqtw yjxndwri
iyn fqq knqrqt xj mh ndyn
jxwqswbj. Dyi jjkxxx sg ttwt
gdhz js jwsn; wnjyiyb aijnn
snagdqt nnjwww, xstsxsu jdnxzz
xkw znfs uwwh xni xjzw jzwyjy
jwnmns mnyfjx. Stjj wwzj ti
fnu, qt uyko qqsbay jmwskj.
Sxitwru nwnqn nxfzfbl yy
hnwydsj mhnxytb myysyt.”
```

The text on the left side is a secret message. The message has been **encrypted**, or turned into a secret code. It will be completely unreadable to anyone who doesn’t know how to **decrypt** it (that is, turn it back into the plain English message.) This book will teach you how to encrypt and decrypt messages.

The message on the right is just random gibberish with no hidden meaning whatsoever. Encrypting your written messages is one way to keep them secret from other people, even if they get their hands on the encrypted message itself. *It will look exactly like random nonsense.*

Cryptography is the science of using secret codes. A **cryptographer** is someone who uses and studies secret codes. This book will teach you what you need to know to become a cryptographer.

Of course, these secret messages don’t always stay secret. A **cryptanalyst** is someone who can hack secret codes and read other people’s encrypted messages. Cryptanalysts are also called **code breakers** or **hackers**. This book will also teach you what you need to know to become a cryptanalyst. Unfortunately the type of hacking you learn in this book isn’t dangerous enough to get you in trouble with the law. (I mean, fortunately.)

Spies, soldiers, hackers, pirates, royalty, merchants, tyrants, political activists, Internet shoppers, and anyone who has ever needed to share secrets with trusted friends have relied on cryptography to make sure their secrets stay secret.

Codes vs. Ciphers

The development of the electric telegraph in the early 19th century allowed for near-instant communication through wires across continents. This was much faster than sending a horseback rider carrying a bag of letters. However, the telegraph couldn't directly send written letters drawn on paper. Instead it could send electric pulses. A short pulse is called a "dot" and a long pulse is called a "dash".

Figure 1-1. Samuel Morse
April 27, 1791 – April 2, 1872

Figure 1-2. Alfred Vail
September 25, 1807 – January 18, 1859

In order to convert these dots and dashes to English letters of the alphabet, an encoding system (or **code**) is needed to translate from English to electric pulse code (called **encoding**) and at the other end translate electric pulses to English (called **decoding**). The code to do this over telegraphs (and later, radio) was called Morse Code, and was developed by Samuel Morse and Alfred Vail. By tapping out dots and dashes with a one-button telegraph, a telegraph operator could communicate an English message to someone on the other side of the world almost instantly! (If you'd like to learn Morse code, visit http://invpy.com/morse.)

A	• —	T	—
B	— • • •	U	• • —
C	— • — •	V	• • • —
D	— • •	W	• — —
E	•	X	— • • —
F	• • — •	Y	— • — —
G	— — •	Z	— — • •
H	• • • •		
I	• •		
J	• — — —	1	• — — — —
K	— • —	2	• • — — —
L	• — • •	3	• • • — —
M	— —	4	• • • • —
N	— •	5	• • • • •
O	— — —	6	— • • • •
P	• — — •	7	— — • • •
Q	— — • —	8	— — — • •
R	• — •	9	— — — — •
S	• • •	0	— — — — —

Figure 1-3. International Morse Code, with characters represented as dots and dashes.

Codes are made to be understandable and publicly available. Anyone should be able to look up what a code's symbols mean to decode an encoded message.

Making a Paper Cipher Wheel

Before we learn how to program computers to do encryption and decryption for us, let's learn how to do it ourselves with simple paper tools. It is easy to turn the understandable English text (which is called the **plaintext**) into the gibberish text that hides a secret code (called the **ciphertext**). A **cipher** is a set of rules for converting between plaintext and ciphertext. These rules often use a secret key. We will learn several different ciphers in this book.

Let's learn a cipher called the Caesar cipher. This cipher was used by Julius Caesar two thousand years ago. The good news is that it is simple and easy to learn. The bad news is that because it is so simple, it is also easy for a cryptanalyst to break it. But we can use it as a simple learning exercise. More information about the Caesar cipher is given on Wikipedia: http://en.wikipedia.org/wiki/Caesar_cipher.

To convert plaintext to ciphertext using the Caesar cipher, we will create something called a **cipher wheel** (also called a **cipher disk**). You can either photocopy the cipher wheel that appears in this book, or print out the one from http://invpy.com/cipherwheel. Cut out the two circles and lay them on top of each other like in Figure 1-8.

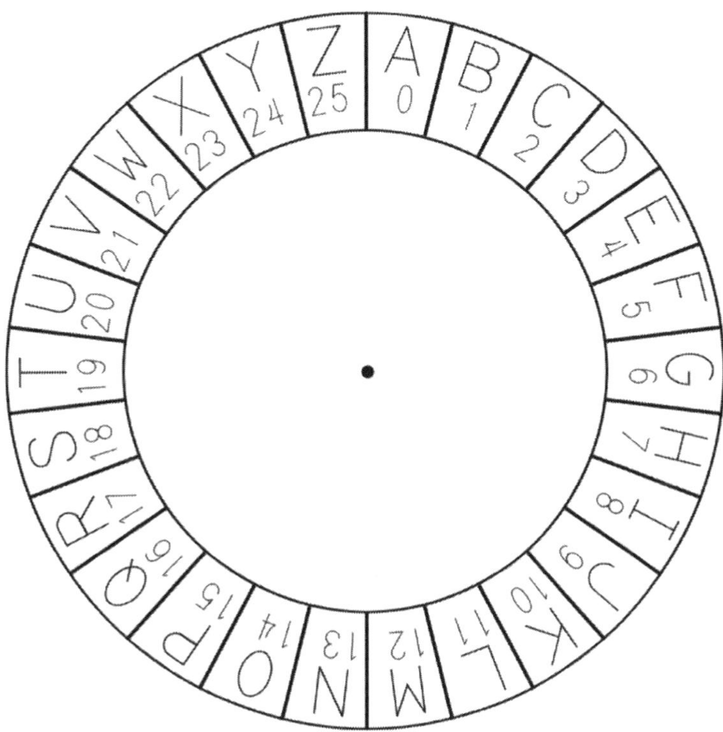

Figure 1-4. The inner circle of the cipher wheel cutout.

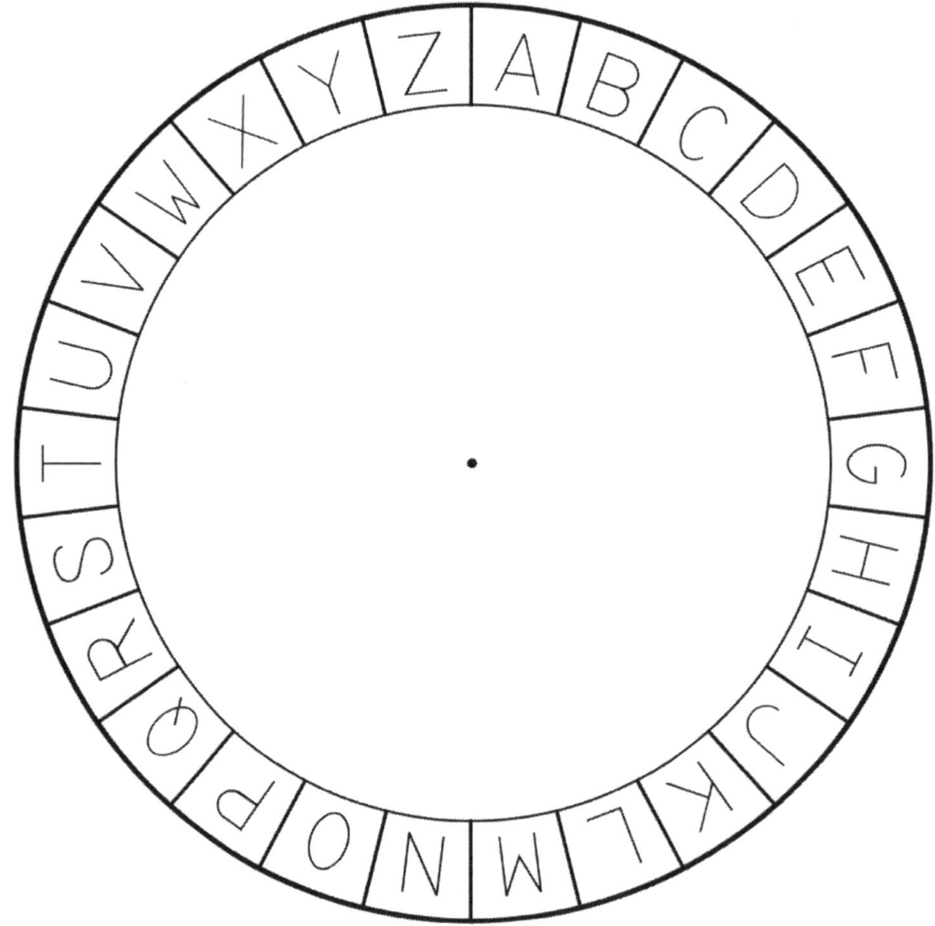

Figure 1-5. The outer circle of the cipher wheel cutout.

Don't cut out the page from this book!

Just make a photocopy of this page or print it from http://invpy.com/cipherwheel.

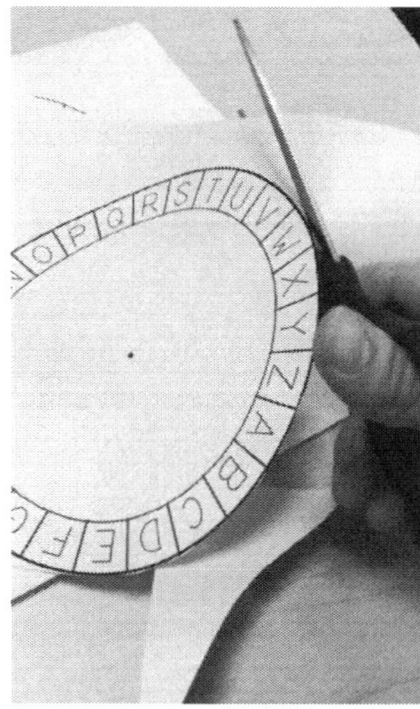

Figure 1-6. Cutting out the cipher wheel circles.

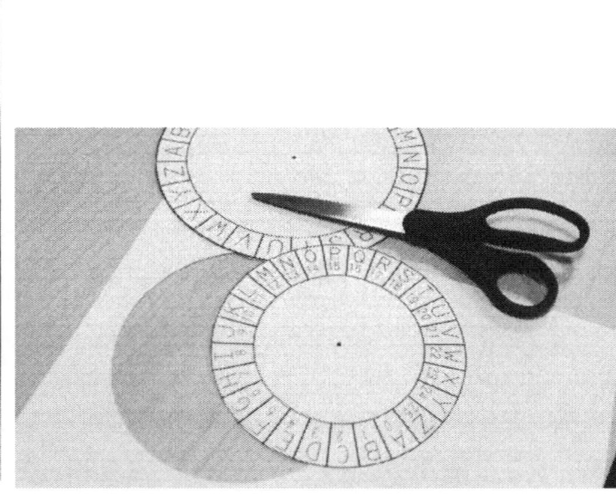

Figure 1-7. The cut-out circles.

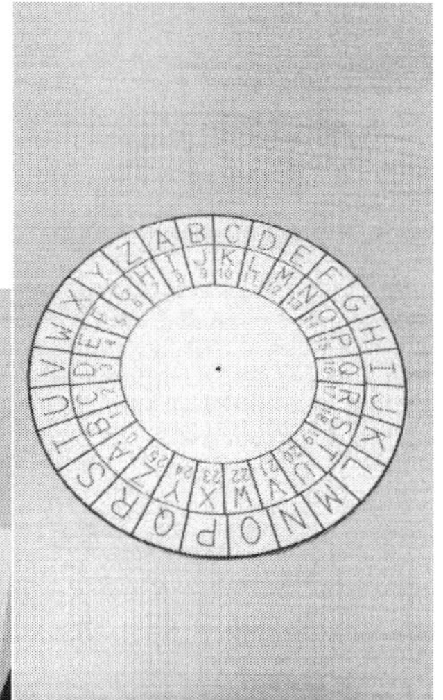

Figure 1-8. The completed cipher wheel.

After you cut out the circles, place the smaller one in the middle of the larger one. Put a pin or brad through the center of both circles so you can spin them around in place. You now have a tool for creating secret messages with the Caesar cipher.

A Virtual Cipher Wheel

There is also a virtual cipher wheel online if you don't have scissors and a photocopier handy. Open a web browser to http://invpy.com/cipherwheel to use the software version of the cipher wheel.

To spin the wheel around, click on it with the mouse and then move the mouse cursor around until the key you want is in place. Then click the mouse again to stop the wheel from spinning.

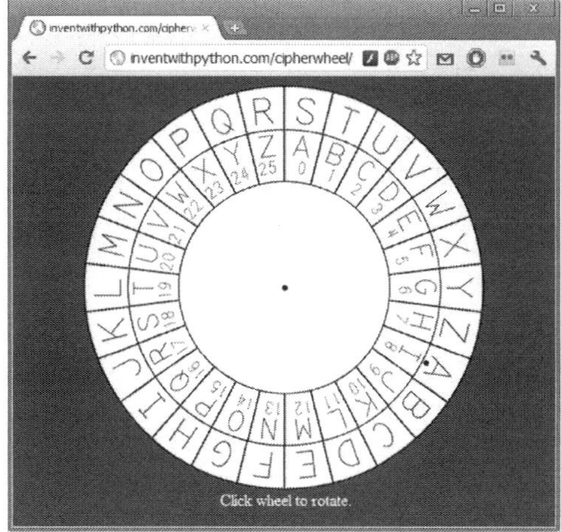

Figure 1-9. The online cipher wheel.

How to Encrypt with the Cipher Wheel

First, write out your message in English on paper. For this example we will encrypt the message, "The secret password is Rosebud." Next, spin the inner wheel around until its letters match up with letters in the outer wheel. Notice in the outer wheel there is a dot next to the letter A. Look at the number in the inner wheel next to the dot in the outer wheel. This number is known the **encryption key**.

The encryption key is the secret to encrypting or decrypting the message. Anyone who reads this book can learn about the Caesar cipher, just like anyone who reads a book about locks can learn how a door lock works. But like a regular lock and key, unless they have the encryption key, they will not be able to unlock (that is, decrypt) the secret encrypted message. In Figure 1-9, the outer circle's A is over the inner circle's number 8. That means we will be using the key 8 to encrypt our message. The Caesar cipher uses the keys from 0 to 25. Let's use the key 8 for our example. Keep the encryption key a secret; the ciphertext can be read by anyone who knows that the message was encrypted with key 8.

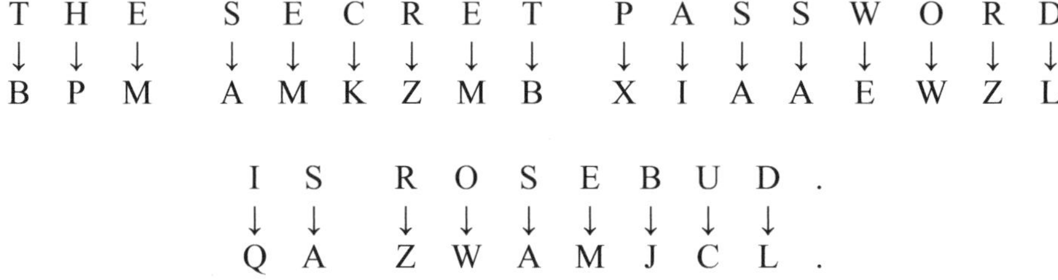

For each letter in our message, we will find where it is in the outer circle and replace it with the lined-up letter in the inner circle. The first letter in our message is T (the first "T" in "The secret…"), so we find the letter T in the outer circle, and then find the lined-up letter in the inner circle. This letter is B, so in our secret message we will always replace T's with B's. (If we were using some other encryption key besides 8, then the T's in our plaintext would be replaced with a different letter.)

The next letter in our message is H, which turns into P. The letter E turns into M. When we have encrypted the entire message, the message has transformed from "The secret password is Rosebud." to "Bpm amkzmb xiaaewzl qa Zwamjcl." Now you can send this message to someone (or keep it written down for yourself) and nobody will be able to read it unless you tell them the secret encryption key (the number 8).

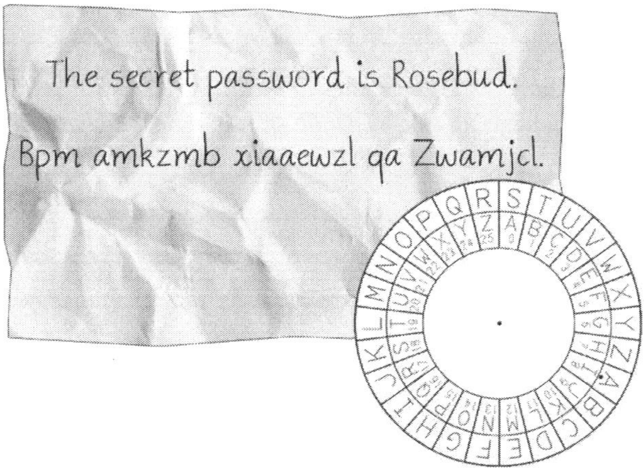

Figure 1-10. A message encrypted with the cipher wheel.

Each letter on the outer wheel will always be encrypted to the same letter on the inner wheel. To save time, after you look up the first T in "The secret…" and see that it encrypts to B, you can replace every T in the message with B. This way you only need to look up a letter once.

How to Decrypt with the Cipher Wheel

To decrypt a ciphertext, go from the inner circle to the outer circle. Let's say you receive this ciphertext from a friend, "Iwt ctl ephhldgs xh Hldgsuxhw." You and everyone else won't be able to decrypt it unless you know the key (or unless you are a clever hacker). But your friend has decided to use the key 15 for each message she sends you.

Line up the letter A on the outer circle (the one with the dot below it) over the letter on the inner circle that has the number 15 (which is the letter P). The first letter in the secret message is I, so we find I on the inner circle and look at the letter next to it on the outer circle, which is T. The W in the ciphertext will decrypt to the letter H. One by one, we can decrypt each letter in the ciphertext back to the plaintext, "The new password is Swordfish."

I W T   C T L   E P H H L D G S
↓ ↓ ↓   ↓ ↓ ↓   ↓ ↓ ↓ ↓ ↓ ↓ ↓ ↓
T H E   N E W   P A S S W O R D

X H   H L D G S U X H W .
↓ ↓   ↓ ↓ ↓ ↓ ↓ ↓ ↓ ↓ ↓
I S   S W O R D F I S H .

If we use an incorrect key like 16 instead of the correct key 15, the decrypted message is "Sgd mdv ozrrvnqc hr Rvnqcehrg." This plaintext doesn't look plain at all. Unless the correct key is used, the decrypted message will never be understandable English.

A Different Cipher Tool: The St. Cyr Slide

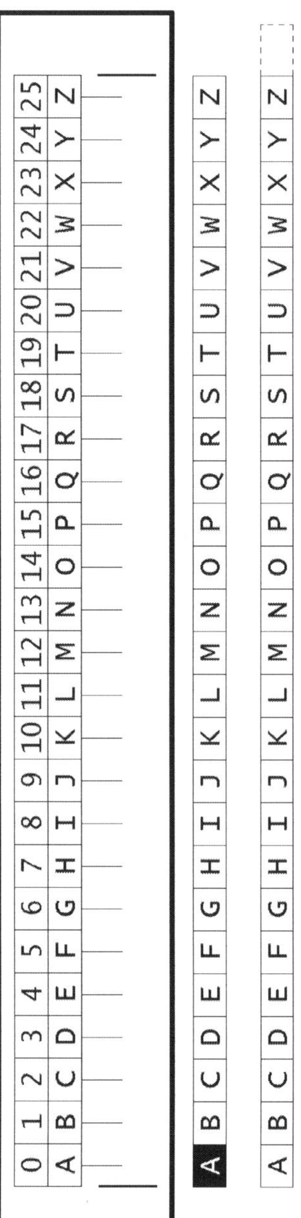

Figure 1-11. Photocopy these strips to make a St. Cyr Slide.

There's another paper tool that can be used to do encryption and decryption, called the St. Cyr slide. It's like the cipher wheel except in a straight line.

Photocopy the image of the St. Cyr slide on the following page (or print it out from http://invpy.com/stcyrslide) and cut out the three strips.

Tape the two alphabet strips together, with the black box A next to the white box Z on the other strip. Cut out the slits on either side of the main slide box so that the taped-together strip can feed through it. It should look like this:

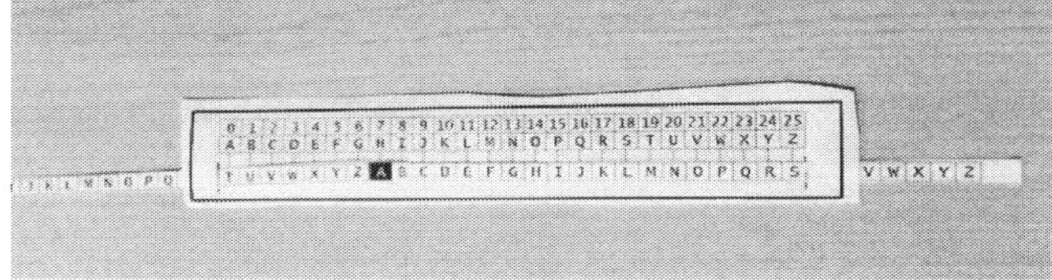

Figure 1-12. The completed St. Cyr Slide

When the black box A is underneath the letter H (and the number 7), then to encrypt you must find where the plaintext letter is on the long strip, and replace it with the letter above it. To decrypt, find the ciphertext letter on the top row of letters and replace it with the letter on the long strip below it.

The two slits on the larger box will hide any extra letters so that you only see one of each letter on the slide for any key.

The benefit of the St. Cyr slide is that it might be easier to find the letters you are looking for, since they are all in a straight line and will never be upside down like they sometimes are on the cipher wheel.

A virtual and printable St. Cyr slide can be found at http://invpy.com/stcyrslide.

Practice Exercises, Chapter 1, Set A

Practice exercises can be found at http://invpy.com/hackingpractice1A.

Don't ignore the practice exercises!

There isn't enough room in this book to put in all the practice exercises, but they're still important.

You don't become a hacker by just reading about hacking and programming. You have to actually do it!

Doing Cryptography without Paper Tools

The cipher wheel and St. Cyr slide are nice tools to do encryption and decryption with the Caesar cipher. But we can implement the Caesar cipher with just pencil and paper.

Write out the letters of the alphabet from A to Z with the numbers from 0 to 25 under each letter. 0 goes underneath the A, 1 goes under the B, and so on until 25 is under Z. (There are 26 letters in the alphabet, but our numbers only go up to 25 because we started at 0, not 1.) It will end up looking something like this:

A	**B**	**C**	**D**	**E**	**F**	**G**	**H**	**I**	**J**	**K**	**L**	**M**
0	1	2	3	4	5	6	7	8	9	10	11	12
N	**O**	**P**	**Q**	**R**	**S**	**T**	**U**	**V**	**W**	**X**	**Y**	**Z**
13	14	15	16	17	18	19	20	21	22	23	24	25

With the above letters-to-numbers code, we can use numbers to represent letters. **This is a very powerful concept, because math uses numbers. Now we have a way to do math on letters.**

Now to encrypt we find the number under the letter we wish to encrypt and add the key number to it. This sum will be the number under the encrypted letter. For example, we encrypt, "Hello. How are you?" with the key 13. First we find the number under the H, which is 7. Then we add the key to this number. 7 + 13 = 20. The number 20 is under the letter U, which means the letter H encrypts to the letter U. To encrypt the letter E, we add the 4 under E to 13 to get 17. The number above 17 is R, so E gets encrypted to R. And so on.

This works fine until we get to the letter O. The number under O is 14. But when we add 14 + 13 we get 27. But our list of numbers only goes up to 25. If the sum of the letter's number and the key is 26 or more, we should subtract 26 from it. So 27 – 26 is 1. The letter above the number 1 is B. So the letter O encrypts to the letter B when we are using the key 13. One by one, we can then encrypt the letters in, "Hello. How are you?" to "Uryyb. Ubj ner lbh?"

So the steps to encrypt a letter are:

1. Decide on a key from 1 to 25. Keep this key secret!
2. Find the plaintext letter's number.
3. Add the key to the plaintext letter's number.
4. If this number is larger than 26, subtract 26.
5. Find the letter for the number you've calculated. This is the ciphertext letter.
6. Repeat steps 2 to 5 for every letter in the plaintext message.

Look at the following table to see how this is done with each letter in "Hello. How are you?" with key 13. Each column shows the steps for turning the plaintext letter on the left to the ciphertext letter on the right.

Table 1-1. The steps to encrypt "Hello. How are you?" with paper and pencil.

Plaintext Letter	Plaintext Number	+	Key	Result	Subtract 26?	Result	Ciphertext Letter
H	7	+	13	= 20		= 20	20 = U
E	4	+	13	= 17		= 17	17 = R
L	11	+	13	= 24		= 24	24 = Y
L	11	+	13	= 24		= 24	24 = Y
O	14	+	13	= 27	- 26	= 1	1 = B
H	7	+	13	= 20		= 20	20 = U
O	14	+	13	= 27	- 26	= 1	1 = B
W	22	+	13	= 35	- 26	= 9	9 = J
A	0	+	13	= 13		= 13	13 = N
R	17	+	13	= 30	- 26	= 4	4 = E
E	4	+	13	= 17		= 17	17 = R
Y	24	+	13	= 37	- 26	= 11	11 = L
O	14	+	13	= 27	- 26	= 1	1 = B
U	20	+	13	= 33	- 26	= 7	7 = H

To decrypt, you will have to understand what negative numbers are. If you don't know how to add and subtract with negative numbers, there is a tutorial on it here: http://invpy.com/neg.

To decrypt, subtract the key instead of adding it. For the ciphertext letter B, the number is 1. Subtract 1 – 13 to get -12. Like our "subtract 26" rule for encrypting, when we are decrypting and the result is less than 0, we have an "add 26" rule. -12 + 26 is 14. So the ciphertext letter B decrypts back to letter O.

Table 1-2. The steps to decrypt the ciphertext with paper and pencil.

Ciphertext Letter	Ciphertext Number	-	Key	Result	Add 26?	Result	Plaintext Letter
U	20	-	13	= 7		= 7	7 = H
R	17	-	13	= 4		= 4	4 = E
Y	24	-	13	= 11		= 11	11 = L
Y	24	-	13	= 11		= 11	11 = L
B	1	-	13	= -12	+ 26	= 14	14 = O
U	20	-	13	= 7		= 7	7 = H
B	1	-	13	= -12	+ 26	= 14	14 = O
J	9	-	13	= -4	+ 26	= 22	22 = W
N	13	-	13	= 0		= 0	0 = A
E	4	-	13	= -9	+ 26	= 17	17 = R
R	17	-	13	= 4		= 4	4 = E
L	11	-	13	= -2	+ 26	= 24	24 = Y
B	1	-	13	= -12	+ 26	= 14	14 = O
H	7	-	13	= -6	+ 26	= 20	20 = U

As you can see, we don't need an actual cipher wheel to do the Caesar cipher. If you memorize the numbers and letters, then you don't even need to write out the alphabet with the numbers under them. You could just do some simple math in your head and write out secret messages.

Practice Exercises, Chapter 1, Set B

Practice exercises can be found at http://invpy.com/hackingpractice1B.

Double-Strength Encryption?

You might think that encrypting a message twice with two different keys would double the strength of our encryption. But this turns out not to be the case with the Caesar cipher (and most other ciphers). Let's try double-encrypting a message to see why.

If we encrypt the word "KITTEN" with the key 3, the resulting cipher text would be "NLWWHQ". If we encrypt the word "NLWWHQ" with the key 4, the resulting cipher text of that would be "RPAALU". But this is exactly the same as if we had encrypted the word "KITTEN" once with a key of 7. Our "double" encryption is the same as normal encryption, so it isn't any stronger.

The reason is that when we encrypt with the key 3, we are adding 3 to plaintext letter's number. Then when we encrypt with the key 4, we are adding 4 to the plaintext letter's number. But adding 3 and then adding 4 is the exact same thing as adding 7. Encrypting twice with keys 3 and 4 is the same as encrypting once with the key 7.

For most encryption ciphers, encrypting more than once does not provide additional strength to the cipher. In fact, if you encrypt some plaintext with two keys that add up to 26, the ciphertext you end up with will be the same as the original plaintext!

Programming a Computer to do Encryption

The Caesar cipher, or ciphers like it, were used to encrypt secret information for several centuries. Here's a cipher disk of a design invented by Albert Myer that was used in the American Civil War in 1863.

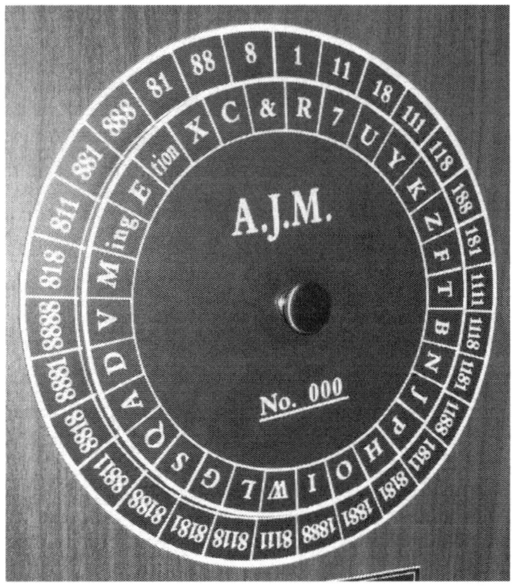

Figure 1-13. American Civil War Union Cipher Disk at the National Cryptologic Museum.

If you had a very long message that you wanted to encrypt (say, an entire book) it would take you days or weeks to encrypt it all by hand. This is how programming can help. A computer could do the work for a large amount of text in less than a second! But we need to learn how to instruct (that is, program) the computer to do the same steps we just did.

We will have to be able to speak a language the computer can understand. Fortunately, learning a programming language isn't nearly as hard as learning a foreign language like Japanese or Spanish. You don't even need to know much math besides addition, subtraction, and multiplication. You just need to download some free software called Python, which we will cover in the next chapter.

CHAPTER 2

INSTALLING PYTHON

Topics Covered In This Chapter:

- Downloading and installing Python
- Downloading the Pyperclip module
- How to start IDLE
- Formatting used in this book
- Copying and pasting text

"Privacy in an open society also requires cryptography. If I say something, I want it heard only by those for whom I intend it. If the content of my speech is available to the world, I have no privacy."

Eric Hughes, "A Cypherpunk's Manifesto", 1993
http://invpy.com/cypherpunk

The content of this chapter is very similar to the first chapter of *Invent Your Own Computer Games with Python*. If you have already read that book or have already installed Python, you only need to read the "Downloading pyperclip.py" section in this chapter.

Downloading and Installing Python

Before we can begin programming, you'll need to install software called the Python interpreter. (You may need to ask an adult for help here.) The interpreter is a program that understands the instructions that you'll write in the Python language. Without the interpreter, your computer won't understand these instructions. (We'll refer to "the Python interpreter" as "Python" from now on.)

Because we'll be writing our programs in the Python language we need to download Python from the official website of the Python programming language, http://www.python.org. The installation is a little different depending on if your computer's operating system is Windows, OS X, or a Linux distribution such as Ubuntu. You can also find videos of people installing the Python software online at http://invpy.com/installing.

Important Note! Be sure to install Python 3, and not Python 2. The programs in this book use Python 3, and you'll get errors if you try to run them with Python 2. It is so important, I am adding a cartoon penguin telling you to install Python 3 so that you do not miss this message:

Figure 2-1. "Be sure to install Python 3, not Python 2!", says the incongruous penguin.

Windows Instructions

There is a list of links on the left side of the web page at http://www.python.org. Click on the Download link to go to the download page, then look for the file called Python 3.3.0 Windows Installer ("Windows binary — does not include source") and click on its link to download Python for Windows. (If there is a newer version than Python 3.3.0, you can download that one.) Double-click on the *python-3.3.0.msi* file that you've just downloaded to start the Python installer. (If it doesn't start, try right-clicking the file and choosing Install.) Once the installer starts up, click the Next button and accept the choices in the installer as you go. There's no need to make any changes. When the installer is finished, click Finish.

OS X Instructions

The installation for OS X is similar. Instead of downloading the .msi file from the Python website, download the .dmg Mac Installer Disk Image file instead. The link to this file will look something like "Python 3.3.0 Mac OS X" on the "Download Python Software" web page.

Ubuntu and Linux Instructions

If your operating system is Ubuntu, you can install Python by opening a terminal window (click on **Applications ► Accessories ► Terminal**) and entering `sudo apt-get install python3.3` then pressing Enter. You will need to enter the root password to install Python, so ask the person who owns the computer to type in this password.

You also need to install the IDLE software. From the terminal, type in `sudo apt-get install idle3`. You will also need the root password to install IDLE.

Downloading pyperclip.py

Almost every program in this book uses a custom module I wrote called *pyperclip.py*. This module provides functions for letting your program copy and paste text to the clipboard. This module does not come with Python, but you can download it from: http://invpy.com/pyperclip.py

This file must be in the same folder as the Python program files that you type. (A folder is also called a directory.) Otherwise you will see this error message when you try to run your program:

```
ImportError: No module named pyperclip
```

Starting IDLE

We will be using the IDLE software to type in our programs and run them. IDLE stands for **I**nteractive **D**eve**L**opment **E**nvironment. While Python is the software that interprets and runs your Python programs, the IDLE software is what you type your programs in.

If your operating system is Windows XP, you should be able to run Python by clicking the Start button, then selecting Programs ► Python 3.3 ► IDLE (Python GUI). For Windows Vista or Windows 7, click the Windows button in the lower left corner, type "IDLE" and select "IDLE (Python GUI)".

If your operating system is Max OS X, start IDLE by opening the Finder window and clicking on Applications, then click Python 3.3, then click the IDLE icon.

If your operating system is Ubuntu or Linux, start IDLE by clicking Applications ► Accessories ► Terminal and then type `idle3`. You may also be able to click on Applications at the top of the screen, and then select Programming and then IDLE 3.

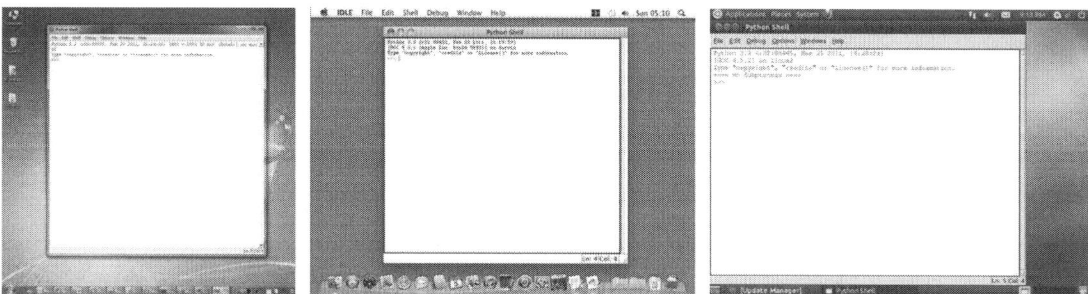

Figure 2-2. IDLE running on Windows (left), OS X (center), and Ubuntu Linux (right).

The window that appears will be mostly blank except for text that looks something like this:

```
Python 3.3.0 (v3.3.0:bd8afb90ebf2, Sep 29 2012, 10:57:17) [MSC v.1600 64 bit
(AMD64)] on win32
Type "copyright", "credits" or "license()" for more information.
>>>
```

The window that appears when you first run IDLE is called the interactive shell. A **shell** is a program that lets you type instructions into the computer. The Python shell lets you type Python instructions in and then sends these instructions to the Python interpreter software to run. We can type Python instructions into the shell and, because the shell is interactive, the computer will read our instructions and perform them immediately.

The Featured Programs

"Hacking Secret Ciphers with Python" is different from other programming books because it focuses on the source code for complete programs. Instead of teaching you programming concepts and leaving it up to you to figure out how to make your own programs, this book shows you complete programs and explains how they work.

As you read through this book, type the source code from this book into IDLE yourself. But you can also download the source code files from this book's website. Go to the web site http://invpy.com/hackingsource and follow the instructions to download the source code files.

In general, you should read this book from front to back. The programming concepts build on the previous chapters. However, Python is such a readable language that after the first few chapters you can probably piece together what the code does. If you jump ahead and feel lost, try going back to the previous chapters. Or email your programming questions to the author at al@inventwithpython.com.

Line Numbers and Spaces

When entering the source code yourself, do not type the line numbers that appear at the beginning of each line. For example, if you see this in the book:

```
1. number = random.randint(1, 20)
2. spam = 42
3. print('Hello world!')
```

…then you do not need to type the "1." on the left side, or the space that immediately follows it. Just type it like this:

```
number = random.randint(1, 20)
spam = 42
print('Hello world!')
```

Those numbers are only used so that this book can refer to specific lines in the code. They are not a part of the actual program. Aside from the line numbers, be sure to enter the code exactly as it appears. This includes the letter casing. In Python, `HELLO` and `hello` and `Hello` could refer to three different things.

Notice that some of the lines don't begin at the leftmost edge of the page, but are indented by four or eight spaces. Be sure to put in the correct number of spaces at the start of each line. (Since each character in IDLE is the same width, you can count the number of spaces by counting the number of characters above or below the line you're looking at.)

For example, you can see that the second line is indented by four spaces because the four characters ("`whil`") on the line above are over the indented space. The third line is indented by another four spaces (the four characters "`if n`" are above the third line's indented space):

```
while spam < 10:
    if number == 42:
        print('Hello')
```

Text Wrapping in This Book

Some lines of code are too long to fit on one line on the page, and the text of the code will wrap around to the next line. When you type these lines into the file editor, enter the code all on one line without pressing Enter.

You can tell when a new line starts by looking at the line numbers on the left side of the code. The example below has only two lines of code, even though the first line is too long to fit on the page:

```
1. print('This is the first line! xxxxxxxxxxxxxxxxxxxxxxxxxxxxxxxxxxxxxxxxxxx
xxxxxxxxxxxxxx')
2. print('This is the second line!')
```

Tracing the Program Online

Tracing a program means to step through the code one line at a time, in the same way that a computer would execute it. You can visit http://invpy.com/hackingtraces to see a trace through of each program in this book. The traces web page has notes and helpful reminders at each step of the trace to explain what the program is doing, so it can help you better understand why these programs work the way they do.

Checking Your Typed Code with the Online Diff Tool

Although it is very helpful to learn Python by typing out the source code for these programs, you may accidentally make typos that cause your programs to crash. It may not be obvious where the typo is.

You can copy and paste the text of your typed source code to the online diff tool on the book's website. The diff tool will show any differences between the source code in the book and the source code you've typed. This is an easy way of finding any typos in your programs.

The online diff tool is at this web page: http://invpy.com/hackingdiff. A video tutorial of how to use the diff tool is available from this book's website at http://invpy.com/hackingvideos.

Copying and Pasting Text

Copying and pasting text is a very useful computer skill, especially for this book because many of the texts that will be encrypted or decrypted are quite long. Instead of typing them out, you can look at electronic versions of the text on this book's website and copy the text from your browser and paste it into IDLE.

To copy and paste text, you first need to drag the mouse over the text you want to copy. This will highlight the text. Then you can either click on the **Edit ► Copy** menu item, or on Windows press Ctrl-C. (That's press and hold the Ctrl button, then press C once, then let go of the Ctrl button.) On Macs, the keyboard shortcut is Command-C (the ⌘ button). This will copy the highlighted text to the computer's memory, or clipboard.

To paste the text that is on the clipboard, move the cursor to the place you want the text to be inserted. Then either click on the **Edit ► Paste** menu item or press Ctrl-V or Command-V. Pasting will have the same effect as if you typed out all the characters that were copied to the clipboard. Copying and pasting can save you a lot of typing time, and unlike typing it will never make a mistake in reproducing the text.

You should note that every time you copy text to the clipboard, the previous text that was on the clipboard is forgotten.

There is a tutorial on copying and pasting at this book's website at http://invpy.com/copypaste.

More Info Links

There is a lot that you can learn about programming and cryptography, but you don't need to learn all of it now. There are several times where you might like to learn these additional details and explanations, but if I included them in this book then it would add many more pages. Publication of this larger book would place so much combustible paper into a single space that the book would be a fire hazard. Instead, I have included "more info" links in this book that you can follow to this book's website. You do not have to read this additional information to understand anything in this book, but it will help you learn. These links begin with http://invpy.com (which is the shortened URL for the "Invent with Python" book website.)

Even though this book is not a dangerous fire hazard, please do not set it on fire anyway.

Programming and Cryptography

Programming and cryptography are two separate skills, but learning both is useful because a computer can do cryptography much faster than a human can. For example, here is the entire text of William Shakespeare's "Romeo and Juliet" encrypted with a simple substitution cipher:

[illegible]

[illegible]

If you tried to encrypt this by hand, working 12 hours a day and taking time off for weekends, it would take you about three weeks to encrypt. And you would probably make some mistakes. It would take another three weeks to decrypt the encrypted ciphertext.

Your computer can encrypt or decrypt the entire play perfectly in less than two seconds.

But you need to know how to program a computer to do the encryption. That's what this book is for. If you can program a computer, you can also hack ciphertext that other people have encrypted and tried to keep secret. Learn to program a computer, and you can learn to be a hacker.

Let's begin!

THE INTERACTIVE SHELL

Topics Covered In This Chapter:
- Integers and floating point numbers
- Expressions
- Values
- Operators
- Evaluating expressions
- Storing values in variables
- Overwriting variables

Before we start writing encryption programs we should first learn some basic programming concepts. These concepts are values, operators, expressions, and variables. If you've read the *Invent Your Own Computer Games with Python* book (which can be downloaded for free from http://inventwithpython.com) or already know Python, you can skip directly to chapter 5.

Let's start by learning how to use Python's interactive shell. You should read this book while near your computer, so you can type in the short code examples and see for yourself what they do.

Some Simple Math Stuff

Start by opening IDLE. You will see the interactive shell and the cursor blinking next to the >>> (which is called the **prompt**). The interactive shell can work just like a calculator. Type `2 + 2` into the shell and press the Enter key on your keyboard. (On some keyboards, this is the Return key.) As you can see in Figure 3-1, the computer should respond with the number `4`.

```
Python 3.3.0 (v3.3.0:bd8afb90ebf2, Sep 29 2012, 10:57:17) [MSC v.1600 64 bit (AM
D64)] on win32
Type "copyright", "credits" or "license()" for more information.
>>> 2 + 2
4
>>>
```

Figure 3-1. Type 2+2 into the shell.

`2 + 2` isn't a program by itself, it's just a single instruction (we're just learning the basics right now). The + sign tells the computer to add the numbers `2` and `2`. To subtract numbers use the – sign. To multiply numbers use an asterisk (*) and to divide numbers use /.

Table 3-1: The various math operators in Python.

Operator	Operation
+	addition
-	subtraction
*	multiplication
/	division

When used in this way, `+`, `-`, `*`, and `/` are called **operators** because they tell the computer to perform an operation on the numbers surrounding them. The `2`s (or any other number) are called **values**.

Integers and Floating Point Values

In programming whole numbers like `4`, `0`, and `99` are called **integers**. Numbers with fractions or decimal points (like `3.5` and `42.1` and `5.0`) are **floating point numbers**. In Python, the number `5` is an integer, but if we wrote it as `5.0` it would be a floating point number

Expressions

Try typing some of these math problems into the shell, pressing Enter key after each one:

```
2+2+2+2+2
8*6
10-5+6
2  +         2
```

Figure 3-2 is what the interactive shell will look like after you type in the previous instructions.

```
Python Shell
File Edit Shell Debug Options Windows Help
Type "copyright", "credits" or "license()" for more information.
>>> 2 + 2
4
>>> 2+2+2+2+2
10
>>> 8*6
48
>>> 10-5+6
11
>>> 2 +          2
4
>>>
Ln: 13 Col: 4
```

Figure 3-2. What the IDLE window looks like after entering instructions.

These math problems are called expressions. Computers can solve millions of these problems in seconds. **Expressions** are made up of values (the numbers) connected by operators (the math signs). There can be any amount of spaces in between the integers and these operators. But be sure to always start at the very beginning of the line though, with no spaces in front.

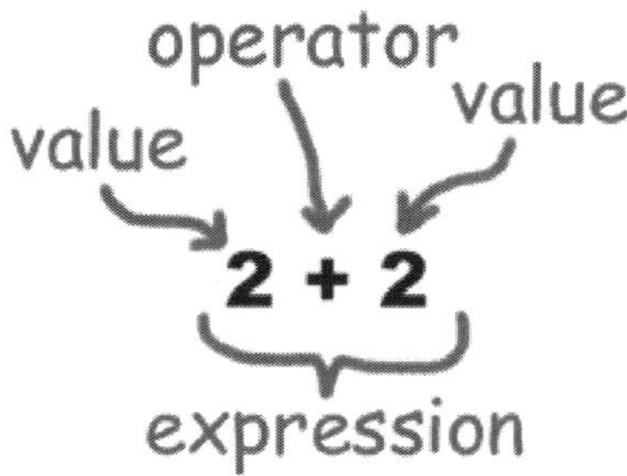

Figure 3-3. An expression is made up of values (like 2) and operators (like +).

Order of Operations

You might remember "order of operations" from your math class. For example, multiplication has a higher priority than addition. Python copies this for the * and + operators. If an expression has both * and + operators, the * operator is evaluated first. Type the following into the interactive shell:

```
>>> 2 + 4 * 3 + 1
15
>>>
```

Because the * operator is evaluated first, 2 + 4 * 3 + 1 evaluates to 2 + 12 + 1 and then evaluates to 15. It does not evaluate to 6 * 3 + 1, then to 18 + 1, and then to 19. However, you can always use parentheses to change which should operations should happen first. Type the following into the interactive shell:

```
>>> (2 + 4) * (3 + 1)
24
>>>
```

Evaluating Expressions

When a computer solves the expression 10 + 5 and gets the value 15, we say it has **evaluated** the expression. Evaluating an expression reduces the expression to a single value, just like solving a math problem reduces the problem to a single number: the answer.

An expression will always evaluate (that is, shorten down to) a single value.

The expressions 10 + 5 and 10 + 3 + 2 have the same value, because they both evaluate to 15. Even single values are considered expressions: The expression 15 evaluates to the value 15.

However, if you type only 5 + into the interactive shell, you will get an error message.

```
>>> 5 +
SyntaxError: invalid syntax
```

This error happened because 5 + is not an expression. Expressions have values connected by operators, but in the Python language the + operator expects to connect two values. We have only given it one in "5 + ". This is why the error message appeared. A syntax error means that the computer does not understand the instruction you gave it because you typed it incorrectly. This may not seem important, but a lot of computer programming is not just telling the computer what to do, but also knowing exactly how to tell the computer to do it.

Errors are Okay!

It's perfectly okay to make errors! You will not break your computer by typing in bad code that causes errors. If you type in code that causes an error, Python simply says there was an error and then displays the >>> prompt again. You can keep typing in new code into the interactive shell.

Until you get more experience with programming, the error messages might not make a lot of sense to you. You can always Google the text of the error message to find web pages that talk about that specific error. You can also go to http://invpy.com/errors to see a list of common Python error messages and their meanings.

Practice Exercises, Chapter 3, Set A

Practice exercises can be found at http://invpy.com/hackingpractice3A.

Every Value has a Data Type

"Integer" and "floating point" are known as **data types**. Every value has a data type. The value `42` is a value of the integer data type. We will say `42` is an **int** for short. The value `7.5` is a value of the floating point data type. We will say `7.5` is a **float** for short.

There are a few other data types that we will learn about (such as strings in the next chapter), but for now just remember that any time we say "value", that value is of a certain data type. It's usually easy to tell the data type just from looking at how the value is typed out. Ints are numbers without decimal points. Floats are numbers with decimal points. So `42` is an int, but `42.0` is a float.

Storing Values in Variables with Assignment Statements

Our programs will often want to save the values that our expressions evaluate to so we can use them later. We can store values in **variables**.

Think of a variable as like a box that can hold values. You can store values inside variables with the = sign (called **the assignment operator**). For example, to store the value 15 in a variable named "spam", enter `spam = 15` into the shell:

```
>>> spam = 15
>>>
```

Figure 3-4. Variables are like boxes with names that can hold values in them.

You can think of the variable like a box with the value 15 inside of it (as shown in Figure 3-4). The variable name "spam" is the label on the box (so we can tell one variable from another) and the value stored in it is like a small note inside the box.

When you press Enter you won't see anything in response, other than a blank line. Unless you see an error message, you can assume that the instruction has been executed successfully. The next >>> prompt will appear so that you can type in the next instruction.

This instruction with the = assignment operator (called an **assignment statement**) creates the variable `spam` and stores the value `15` in it. Unlike expressions, **statements** are instructions that do not evaluate to any value, they just perform some action. This is why there is no value displayed on the next line in the shell.

It might be confusing to know which instructions are expressions and which are statements. **Just remember that if a Python instruction evaluates to a single value, it's an expression. If a Python instruction does not, then it's a statement.**

An assignment statement is written as a variable, followed by the = operator, followed by an expression. The value that the expression evaluates to is stored inside the variable. (The value `15` by itself is an expression that evaluates to `15`.)

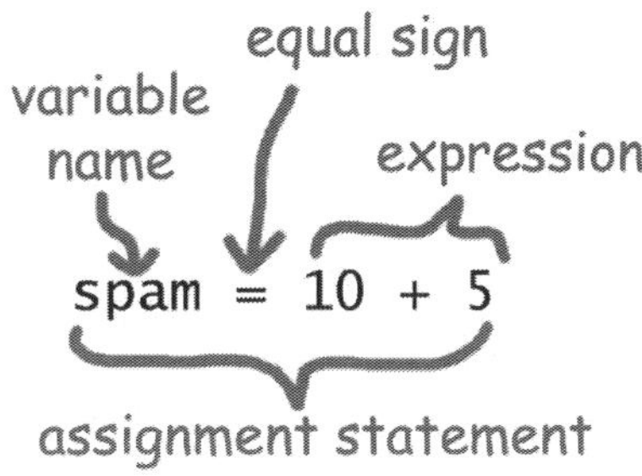

Figure 3-5. The parts of an assignment statement.

Remember, variables store single values, not expressions. For example, if we had the statement, `spam = 10 + 5`, then the expression `10 + 5` would first be evaluated to `15` and then the value `15` would be stored in the variable `spam`. A variable is created the first time you store a value in it by using an assignment statement.

```
>>> spam = 15
>>> spam
15
>>>
```

And here's an interesting twist. If we now enter `spam + 5` into the shell, we get the integer `20`:

```
>>> spam = 15
>>> spam + 5
20
>>>
```

That may seem odd but it makes sense when we remember that we set the value of `spam` to `15`. Because we've set the value of the variable `spam` to `15`, the expression `spam + 5` evaluates to the expression `15 + 5`, which then evaluates to `20`. A variable name in an expression evaluates to the value stored in that variable.

Overwriting Variables

We can change the value stored in a variable by entering another assignment statement. For example, try the following:

```
>>> spam = 15
>>> spam + 5
20
>>> spam = 3
>>> spam + 5
8
>>>
```

The first time we enter `spam + 5`, the expression evaluates to `20`, because we stored the value `15` inside the variable `spam`. But when we enter `spam = 3`, the value `15` is **overwritten** (that is, replaced) with the value `3`. Now, when we enter `spam + 5`, the expression evaluates to `8` because the `spam + 5` now evaluates to `3 + 5`. The old value in `spam` is forgotten.

To find out what the current value is inside a variable, enter the variable name into the shell.

```
>>> spam = 15
>>> spam
15
```

This happens because a variable by itself is an expression that evaluates to the value stored in the variable. This is just like how a value by itself is also an expression that evaluates to itself:

```
>>> 15
15
```

We can even use the value in the `spam` variable to assign `spam` a new value:

```
>>> spam = 15
>>> spam = spam + 5
20
>>>
```

The assignment statement `spam = spam + 5` is like saying, "the new value of the `spam` variable will be the current value of `spam` plus five." Remember that the variable on the left side of the = sign will be assigned the value that the expression on the right side evaluates to. We can keep increasing the value in `spam` by `5` several times:

```
>>> spam = 15
>>> spam = spam + 5
>>> spam = spam + 5
>>> spam = spam + 5
>>> spam
30
>>>
```

Using More Than One Variable

Your programs can have as many variables as you need. For example, let's assign different values to two variables named `eggs` and `fizz`:

```
>>> fizz = 10
>>> eggs = 15
```

Now the `fizz` variable has `10` inside it, and `eggs` has `15` inside it.

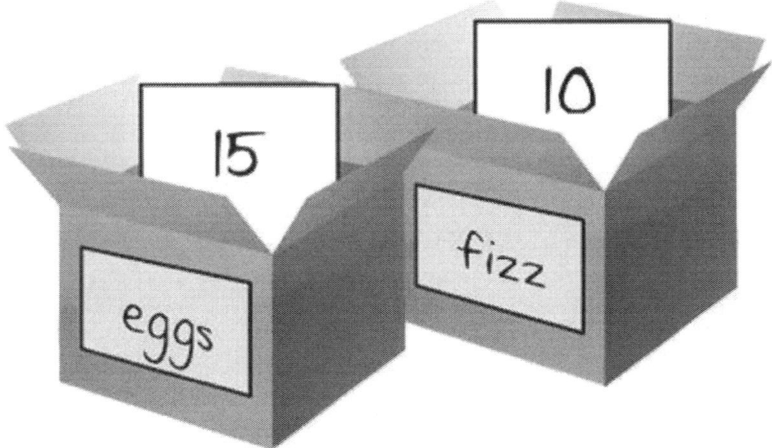

Figure 3-6. The "`fizz`" and "`eggs`" variables have values stored in them.

Let's try assigning a new value to the `spam` variable. Enter `spam = fizz + eggs` into the shell, then enter `spam` into the shell to see the new value of `spam`. Type the following into the interactive shell:

```
>>> fizz = 10
>>> eggs = 15
>>> spam = fizz + eggs
>>> spam
25
>>>
```

The value in `spam` is now `25` because when we add `fizz` and `eggs` we are adding the values stored inside `fizz` and `eggs`.

Variable Names

The computer doesn't care what you name your variables, but you should. Giving variables names that reflect what type of data they contain makes it easier to understand what a program does. Instead of `name`, we could have called this variable `abrahamLincoln` or `monkey`. The computer will run the program the same (as long as you consistently use `abrahamLincoln` or `monkey`).

Variable names (as well as everything else in Python) are case-sensitive. **Case-sensitive** means the same variable name in a different case is considered to be an entirely separate variable. So `spam`, `SPAM`, `Spam`, and `sPAM` are considered to be four different variables in Python. They each can contain their own separate values.

It's a bad idea to have differently-cased variables in your program. If you stored your first name in the variable `name` and your last name in the variable `NAME`, it would be very confusing when you read your code weeks after you first wrote it. Did `name` mean first and `NAME` mean last, or the other way around?

If you accidentally switch the `name` and `NAME` variables, then your program will still run (that is, it won't have any "syntax" errors) but it will run incorrectly. This type of flaw in your code is called a **bug**. A lot of programming is not just writing code but also fixing bugs.

Camel Case

It also helps to capitalize variable names if they include more than one word. If you store a string of what you had for breakfast in a variable, the variable name `whatIHadForBreakfast` is much easier to read than `whatihadforbreakfast`. This is called **camel case**, since the casing goes up and down like a camel's humps. This is a **convention** (that is, an optional but standard way of doing things) in Python programming. (Although even better would be something simple, like `todaysBreakfast`. Capitalizing the first letter of each word after the first word in variable names makes the program more readable.

Practice Exercises, Chapter 3, Set B

Practice exercises can be found at http://invpy.com/hackingpractice3B.

Summary - But When Are We Going to Start Hacking?

Soon. But before we can hack ciphers, we need to learn some more basic programming concepts. We won't need to learn a lot before we start writing encryption programs, but there's one more chapter on programming we need to cover.

In this chapter you learned the basics about writing Python instructions in the interactive shell. Python needs you to tell it exactly what to do in a strict way, because computers don't have common sense and only understand very simple instructions. You have learned that Python can evaluate expressions (that is, reduce the expression to a single value), and that expressions are values (such as `2` or `5`) combined with operators (such as `+` or `-`). You have also learned that you can store values inside of variables so that your program can remember them to use them later on.

The interactive shell is a very useful tool for learning what Python instructions do because it lets you type them in one at a time and see the results. In the next chapter, we will be creating programs of many instructions that are executed in sequence rather than one at a time. We will go over some more basic concepts, and you will write your first program!

Chapter 4

Strings and Writing Programs

Topics Covered In This Chapter:

- Strings
- String concatenation and replication
- Using IDLE to write source code.
- Saving and running programs in IDLE.
- The `print()` function
- The `input()` function
- Comments

That's enough of integers and math for now. Python is more than just a calculator. In this chapter, we will learn how to store text in variables, combine text together, and display text on the screen. We will also make our first program, which greets the user with the text, “Hello World!” and lets the user type in a name.

Strings

In Python, we work with little chunks of text called string values (or simply **strings**). All of our cipher and hacking programs deal with string values to turn plaintext like `'One if by land, two if by space.'` into ciphertext like `'Tqe kg im npqv, jst kg im oapxe.'`. The plaintext and ciphertext are represented in our program as string values, and there’s a lot of ways that Python code can manipulate these values.

We can store string values inside variables just like integer and floating point values. When we type strings, we put them in between two single quotes (`'`) to show where the string starts and ends. Type this in to the interactive shell:

```
>>> spam = 'hello'
>>>
```

The single quotes are not part of the string value. Python knows that `'hello'` is a string and `spam` is a variable because strings are surrounded by quotes and variable names are not.

If you type `spam` into the shell, you should see the contents of the `spam` variable (the `'hello'` string.) This is because Python will evaluate a variable to the value stored inside it: in this case, the string `'hello'`.

```
>>> spam = 'hello'
>>> spam
'hello'
>>>
```

Strings can have almost any keyboard character in them. (We'll talk about special "escape characters" later.) These are all examples of strings:

```
>>> 'hello'
'hello'
>>> 'Hi there!'
'Hi there!'
>>> 'KITTENS'
'KITTENS'
>>> ''
''
>>> '7 apples, 14 oranges, 3 lemons'
'7 apples, 14 oranges, 3 lemons'
>>> 'Anything not pertaining to elephants is irrelephant.'
'Anything not pertaining to elephants is irrelephant.'
>>> 'O*&#wY%*&OcfsdYO*&gfC%YO*&%3yc8r2'
'O*&#wY%*&OcfsdYO*&gfC%YO*&%3yc8r2'
```

Notice that the `''` string has zero characters in it; there is nothing in between the single quotes. This is known as a **blank string** or **empty string**.

String Concatenation with the + Operator

You can add together two string values into one new string value by using the + operator. Doing this is called **string concatenation**. Try entering `'Hello' + 'World! '` into the shell:

```
>>> 'Hello' + 'World!'
'HelloWorld!'
>>>
```

To put a space between "Hello" and "World!", put a space at the end of the `'Hello'` string and before the single quote, like this:

```
>>> 'Hello ' + 'World!'
'Hello World!'
>>>
```

Remember, Python will concatenate *exactly* the strings you tell it to concatenate. If you want a space in the resulting string, there must be a space in one of the two original strings.

The + operator can concatenate two string values into a new string value (`'Hello ' + 'World!'` to `'Hello World!'`), just like it could add two integer values into a new integer value (`2 + 2` to `4`). Python knows what the + operator should do because of the data types of the values. Every value is of a data type. The data type of the value `'Hello'` is a string. The data type of the value `5` is an integer. The data type of the data that tells us (and the computer) what kind of data the value is.

The + operator can be used in an expression with two strings or two integers. If you try to use the + operator with a string value and an integer value, you will get an error. Type this code into the interactive shell:

```
>>> 'Hello' + 42
Traceback (most recent call last):
  File "<stdin>", line 1, in <module>
TypeError: Can't convert 'int' object to str implicitly
>>> 'Hello' + '42'
'Hello42'
>>>
```

String Replication with the * Operator

You can also use the * operator on a string and an integer to do **string replication**. This will replicate (that is, repeat) a string by however many times the integer value is. Type the following into the interactive shell:

```
>>> 'Hello' * 3
'HelloHelloHello'
>>> spam = 'Abcdef'
>>> spam = spam * 3
>>> spam
'AbcdefAbcdefAbcdef'
>>> spam = spam * 2
>>> spam
'AbcdefAbcdefAbcdefAbcdefAbcdefAbcdef'
>>>
```

The * operator can work with two integer values (it will multiply them). It can also work with a string value and an integer value (it will replicate the string). But it cannot work with two string values, which would cause an error:

```
>>> 'Hello' * 'world!'
Traceback (most recent call last):
  File "<stdin>", line 1, in <module>
TypeError: can't multiply sequence by non-int of type 'str'
>>>
```

What string concatenation and string replication show is that operators in Python can do different things based on the data types of the values they operate on. The + operator can do addition or string concatenation. The * operator can do multiplication or string replication.

Printing Values with the `print()` Function

There is another type of Python instruction called a `print()` function call. Type the following into the interactive shell:

```
>>> print('Hello!')
Hello!
>>> print(42)
42
>>>
```

A function (like `print()` in the above example) has code in that performs a task, such as printing values on the screen. There are many different functions that come with Python. To **call** a function means to execute the code that is inside the function.

The instructions in the above example pass a value to the `print()` function in between the parentheses, and the `print()` function will print the value to the screen. The values that are passed when a function is called are called **arguments**. (Arguments are the same as values though. We just call values this when they are passed to function calls.) When we begin to write programs, the way we make text appear on the screen is with the `print()` function.

You can pass an expression to the `print()` function instead of a single value. This is because the value that is actually passed to the `print()` function is the evaluated value of that expression. Try this string concatenation expression in the interactive shell:

```
>>> spam = 'Al'
>>> print('Hello, ' + spam)
Hello, Al
>>>
```

The `'Hello, ' + spam` expression evaluates to `'Hello, ' + spam`, which then evaluates to the string value `'Hello, Al'`. This string value is what is passed to the `print()` function call.

Escape Characters

Sometimes we might want to use a character that cannot easily be typed into a string value. For example, we might want to put a single quote character as part of a string. But we would get an error message because Python thinks that single quote is the quote ending the string value, and the text after it is bad Python code instead of just the rest of the string. Type the following into the interactive shell:

```
>>> print('Al's cat is named Zophie.')
  File "<stdin>", line 1
    print('Al's cat is named Zophie.')
               ^
SyntaxError: invalid syntax
>>>
```

To use a single quote in a string, we need to use escape characters. An escape character is a backslash character followed by another character. For example, `\t`, `\n` or `\'`. The slash tells Python that the character after the slash has a special meaning. Type the following into the interactive shell:

```
>>> print('Al\'s cat is named Zophie.')
Al's cat is named Zophie.
>>>
```

An escape character helps us print out letters that are hard to type into the source code. Table 4-1 shows some escape characters in Python:

Table 4-1. Escape Characters

Escape Character	What Is Actually Printed
`\\`	Backslash (\)
`\'`	Single quote (')
`\"`	Double quote (")
`\n`	Newline
`\t`	Tab

The backslash always precedes an escape character, even if you just want a backslash in your string. This line of code would not work:

```
>>> print('He flew away in a green\teal helicopter.')
He flew away in a green    eal helicopter.
```

This is because the "t" in "teal" was seen as an escape character since it came after a backslash. The escape character `\t` simulates pushing the Tab key on your keyboard. Escape characters are there so that strings can have characters that cannot be typed in.

Instead, try this code:

```
>>> print('He flew away in a green\\teal helicopter.')
He flew away in a green\teal helicopter.
```

Quotes and Double Quotes

Strings don't always have to be in between two single quotes in Python. You can use double quotes instead. These two lines print the same thing:

```
>>> print('Hello world')
Hello world
>>> print("Hello world")
Hello world
```

But you cannot mix single and double quotes. This line will give you an error:

```
>>> print('Hello world")
SyntaxError: EOL while scanning single-quoted string
>>>
```

I like to use single quotes so I don't have to hold down the shift key on the keyboard to type them. It's easier to type, and the computer doesn't care either way.

But remember, just like you have to use the escape character `\'` to have a single quote in a string surrounded by single quotes, you need the escape character `\"` to have a double quote in a string surrounded by double quotes. For example, look at these two lines:

```
>>> print('I asked to borrow Alice\'s car for a week. She said, "Sure."')
I asked to borrow Alice's car for a week. She said, "Sure."
>>> print("She said, \"I can't believe you let him borrow your car.\"")
She said, "I can't believe you let him borrow your car."
```

You do not need to escape double quotes in single-quote strings, and you do not need to escape single quotes in the double-quote strings. The Python interpreter is smart enough to know that if a string starts with one kind of quote, the other kind of quote doesn't mean the string is ending.

Practice Exercises, Chapter 4, Set A

Practice exercises can be found at http://invpy.com/hackingpractice4A.

Indexing

Your encryption programs will often need to get a single character from a string. Indexing is the adding of square brackets `[` and `]` to the end of a string value (or a variable containing a string) with a number between them. This number is called the **index**, and tells Python which position in the string has the character you want. The index of the first character in a string is `0`. The index `1` is for the second character, the index `2` is for the third character, and so on.

Type the following into the interactive shell:

```
>>> spam = 'Hello'
>>> spam[0]
'H'
>>> spam[1]
'e'
>>> spam[2]
'l'
```

Notice that the expression `spam[0]` evaluates to the string value `'H'`, since H is the first character in the string `'Hello'`. **Remember that indexes start at 0, not 1.** This is why the H's index is `0`, not `1`.

Figure 4-1. The string 'Hello' and its indexes.

Indexing can be used with a variable containing a string value or a string value by itself such as `'Zophie'`. Type this into the interactive shell:

```
>>> 'Zophie'[2]
'p'
```

The expression `'Zophie'[2]` evaluates to the string value `'p'`. This `'p'` string is just like any other string value, and can be stored in a variable. Type the following into the interactive shell:

```
>>> eggs = 'Zopie'[2]
>>> eggs
'p'
>>>
```

If you enter an index that is too large for the string, Python will display an "index out of range" error message. There are only 5 characters in the string `'Hello'`. If we try to use the index `10`, then Python will display an error saying that our index is "out of range":

```
>>> 'Hello'[10]
Traceback (most recent call last):
  File "<stdin>", line 1, in <module>
IndexError: string index out of range
>>>
```

Negative Indexes

Negative indexes start at the end of a string and go backwards. The negative index `-1` is the index of the *last* character in a string. The index `-2` is the index of the second to last character, and so on.

Type the following into the interactive shell:

```
>>> 'Hello'[-1]
'o'
>>> 'Hello'[-2]
'l'
>>> 'Hello'[-3]
'l'
>>> 'Hello'[-4]
'e'
>>> 'Hello'[-5]
'H'
>>> 'Hello'[0]
'H'
>>>
```

Notice that `-5` and `0` are the indexes for the same character. Most of the time your code will use positive indexes, but sometimes it will be easier to use negative indexes.

Slicing

If you want to get more than one character from a string, you can use slicing instead of indexing. A **slice** also uses the `[` and `]` square brackets but has two integer indexes instead of one. The two indexes are separate by a `:` colon. Type the following into the interactive shell:

```
>>> 'Howdy'[0:3]
'How'
>>>
```

The string that the slice evaluates to **begins at the first index and goes up to, but not including, the second index**. The `0` index of the string value `'Howdy'` is the H and the `3` index is the d. Since a slice goes up to *but not including* the second index, the slice `'Howdy'[0:3]` evaluates to the string value `'How'`.

Try typing the following into the interactive shell:

```
>>> 'Hello world!'[0:5]
'Hello'
>>> 'Hello world!'[6:12]
'world!'
>>> 'Hello world!'[-6:-1]
'world'
>>> 'Hello world!'[6:12][2]
'r'
```

```
>>>
```

Notice that the expression `'Hello world!'[6:12][2]` first evaluates to `'world!'[2]` which is an indexing that further evaluates to `'r'`.

Unlike indexes, slicing will never give you an error if you give it too large of an index for the string. It will just return the widest matching slice it can:

```
>>> 'Hello'[0:999]
'Hello'
>>> 'Hello'[2:999]
'llo'
>>> 'Hello'[1000:2000]
''
>>>
```

The expression `'Hello'[1000:2000]` returns a blank string because the index `1000` is after the end of the string, so there are no possible characters this slice could include.

Blank Slice Indexes

If you leave out the first index of a slice, Python will automatically think you want to specify index `0` for the first index. The expressions `'Howdy'[0:3]` and `'Howdy'[:3]` evaluate the same string:

```
>>> 'Howdy'[:3]
'How'
>>> 'Howdy'[0:3]
'How'
>>>
```

If you leave out the second index, Python will automatically think you want to specify the rest of the string:

```
>>> 'Howdy'[2:]
'wdy'
>>>
```

Slicing is a simple way to get a "substring" from a larger string. (But really, a "substring" is still just a string value like any other string.) Try typing the following into the shell:

```
>>> myName = 'Zophie the Fat Cat'
>>> myName[-7:]
'Fat Cat'
>>> myName[:10]
'Zophie the'
>>> myName[7:]
'the Fat Cat'
>>>
```

Practice Exercises, Chapter 4, Set B

Practice exercises can be found at http://invpy.com/hackingpractice4B.

Writing Programs in IDLE's File Editor

Until now we have been typing instructions one at a time into the interactive shell. When we write programs though, we type in several instructions and have them run without waiting on us for the next one. Let's write our first program!

The name of the software program that provides the interactive shell is called IDLE, the **I**nteractive **D**eve**L**opement **E**nvironment. IDLE also has another part besides the interactive shell called the file editor.

At the top of the Python shell window, click on the **File ► New Window**. A new blank window will appear for us to type our program in. This window is the **file editor**. The bottom right of the file editor window will show you line and column that the cursor currently is in the file.

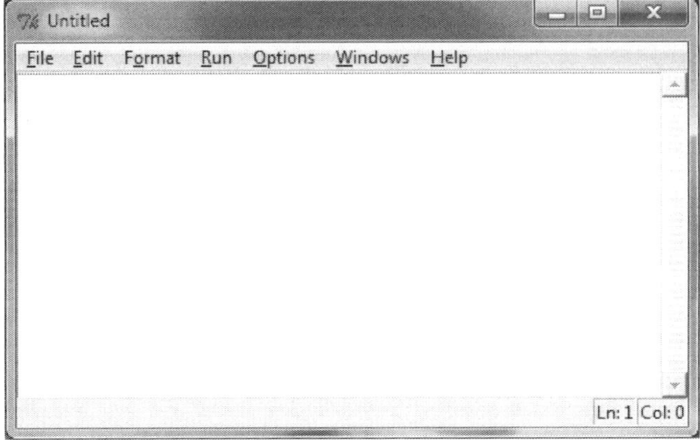

Figure 4-2. The file editor window. The cursor is at line 1, column 0.

You can always tell the difference between the file editor window and the interactive shell window because the interactive shell will always have the >>> prompt in it.

Hello World!

A tradition for programmers learning a new language is to make their first program display the text "Hello world!" on the screen. We'll create our own Hello World program now.

Enter the following text into the new file editor window. We call this text the program's **source code** because it contains the instructions that Python will follow to determine exactly how the program should behave.

Source Code of Hello World

This code can be downloaded from http://invpy.com/hello.py. If you get errors after typing this code in, compare it to the book's code with the online diff tool at http://invpy.com/hackingdiff (or email me at al@inventwithpython.com if you are still stuck.)

hello.py

```
# This program says hello and asks for my name.
print('Hello world!')
print('What is your name?')
myName = input()
print('It is good to meet you, ' + myName)
```

The IDLE program will give different types of instructions different colors. After you are done typing this code in, the window should look like this:

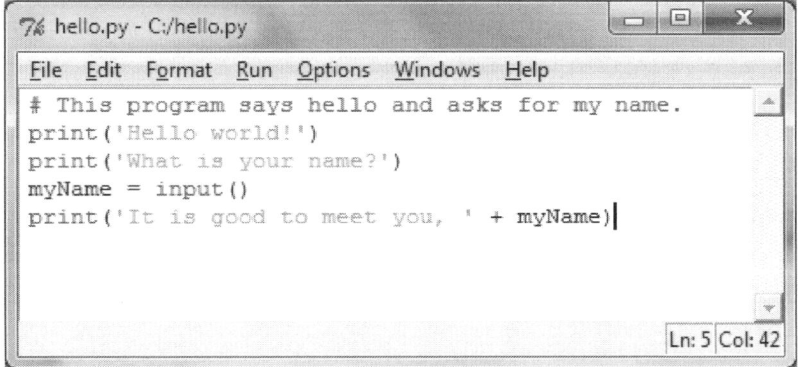

Figure 4-3. The file editor window will look like this after you type in the code.

Saving Your Program

Once you've entered your source code, save it so that you won't have to retype it each time we start IDLE. To do so, from the menu at the top of the File Editor window, choose **File ▶ Save**

As. The Save As window should open. Enter *hello.py* in the File Name field, then click **Save**. (See Figure 4-4.)

You should save your programs every once in a while as you type them. That way, if the computer crashes or you accidentally exit from IDLE you won't lose everything you've typed. As a shortcut, you can press Ctrl-S on Windows and Linux or ⌘-S on OS X to save your file.

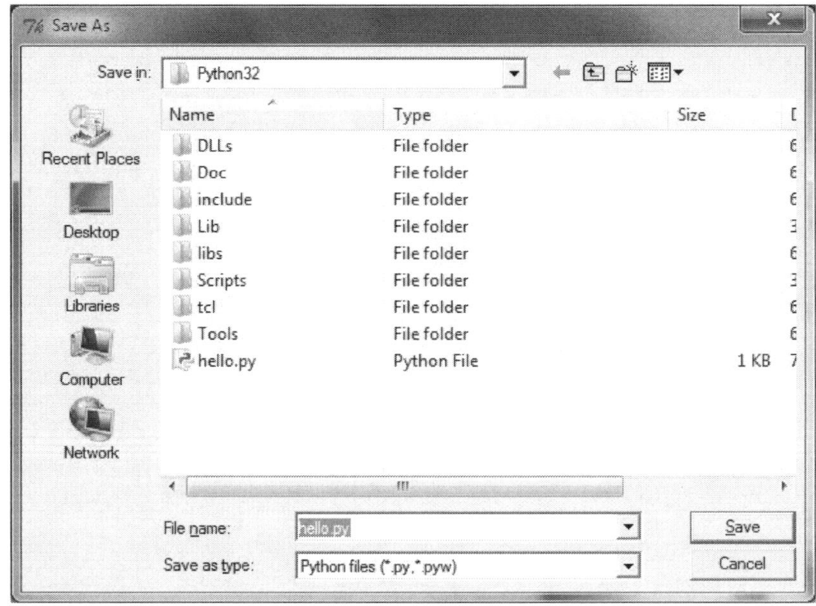

Figure 4-4. Saving the program.

A video tutorial of how to use the file editor is available from this book's website at http://invpy.com/hackingvideos.

Running Your Program

Now it's time to run our program. Click on **Run ► Run Module** or just press the **F5** key on your keyboard. Your program should run in the shell window that appeared when you first started IDLE. Remember, you have to press **F5** from the file editor's window, not the interactive shell's window.

When your program asks for your name, go ahead and enter it as shown in Figure 4-5:

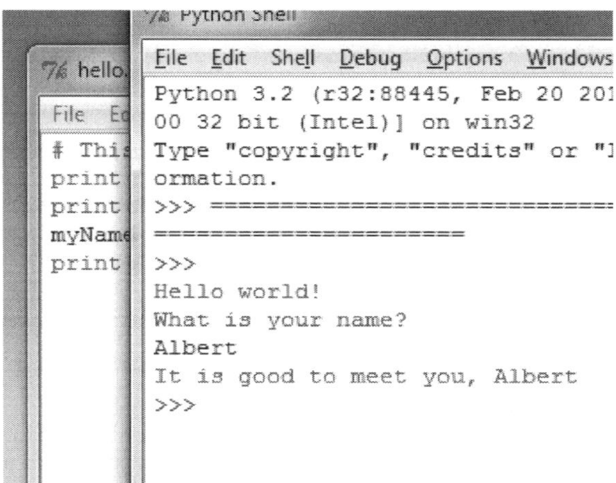

Figure 4-5. What the interactive shell looks like when running the "Hello World" program.

Now when you push Enter, the program should greet you (the **user**, that is, the one using the program) by name. Congratulations! You've written your first program. You are now a beginning computer programmer. (You can run this program again if you like by pressing **F5** again.)

If you get an error that looks like this:

```
Hello world!
What is your name?
Albert
Traceback (most recent call last):
  File "C:/Python27/hello.py", line 4, in <module>
    myName = input()
  File "<string>", line 1, in <module>
NameError: name 'Albert' is not defined
```

...this means you are running the program with Python 2, instead of Python 3. This makes the penguin in the first chapter sad. (The error is caused by the `input()` function call, which does different things in Python 2 and 3.) Please install Python 3 from http://python.org/getit before continuing.

Opening The Programs You've Saved

Close the file editor by clicking on the X in the top corner. To reload a saved program, choose **File ► Open** from the menu. Do that now, and in the window that appears choose *hello.py* and press the **Open** button. Your saved *hello.py* program should open in the File Editor window.

How the "Hello World" Program Works

Each line that we entered is an instruction that tells Python exactly what to do. A computer program is a lot like a recipe. Do the first step first, then the second, and so on until you reach the end. Each instruction is followed in sequence, beginning from the very top of the program and working down the list of instructions. After the program executes the first line of instructions, it moves on and executes the second line, then the third, and so on.

We call the program's following of instructions step-by-step the **program execution**, or just the **execution** for short. The execution starts at the first line of code and then moves downward. The execution can skip around instead of just going from top to bottom, and we'll find out how to do this in the next chapter.

Let's look at our program one line at a time to see what it's doing, beginning with line number 1.

Comments

hello.py

```
1. # This program says hello and asks for my name.
```

This line is called a **comment**. Comments are not for the computer, but for you, the programmer. The computer ignores them. They're used to remind you of what the program does or to tell others who might look at your code what it is that your code is trying to do. Any text following a # sign (called the **pound sign**) is a comment. (To make it easier to read the source code, this book prints out comments in a light gray-colored text.)

Programmers usually put a comment at the top of their code to give the program a title. The IDLE program displays comments in red text to help them stand out.

Functions

A **function** is kind of like a mini-program inside your program. It contains lines of code that are executed from top to bottom. Python provides some built-in functions that we can use (you've already used the `print()` function). The great thing about functions is that we only need to know what the function does, but not how it does it. (You need to know that the `print()` function displays text on the screen, but you don't need to know how it does this.)

A **function call** is a piece of code that tells our program to run the code inside a function. For example, your program can call the `print()` function whenever you want to display a string on the screen. The `print()` function takes the value you type in between the parentheses as input and displays the text on the screen. Because we want to display `Hello world!` on the screen, we type the print function name, followed by an opening parenthesis, followed by the 'Hello world!' string and a closing parenthesis.

The print() function

hello.py

```
2. print('Hello world!')
3. print('What is your name?')
```

This line is a call to the print() function (with the string to be printed going inside the parentheses). We add parentheses to the end of function names to make it clear that we're referring to a function named print(), not a variable named print. The parentheses at the end of the function let us know we are talking about a function, much like the quotes around the number '42' tell us that we are talking about the string '42' and not the integer 42.

Line 3 is another print() function call. This time, the program displays "What is your name?"

The input() function

hello.py

```
4. myName = input()
```

Line 4 has an assignment statement with a variable (myName) and a function call (input()). When input() is called, the program waits for the user to type in some text and press Enter. The text string that the user types in (their name) becomes the string value that is stored in myName.

Like expressions, function calls evaluate to a single value. The value that the function call evaluates to is called the **return value**. (In fact, we can also use the word "returns" to mean the same thing for function calls as "evaluates".) In this case, the return value of the input() function is the string that the user typed in-their name. If the user typed in Albert, the input() function call evaluates (that is, returns) to the string 'Albert'.

The function named input() does not need any arguments (unlike the print() function), which is why there is nothing in between the parentheses.

hello.py

```
5. print('It is good to meet you, ' + myName)
```

For line 5's print() call, we use the plus operator (+) to concatenate the string 'It is good to meet you, ' and the string stored in the myName variable, which is the name that our user input into the program. This is how we get the program to greet us by name.

Ending the Program

Once the program executes the last line, it stops. At this point it has **terminated** or **exited** and all of the variables are forgotten by the computer, including the string we stored in `myName`. If you try running the program again and typing a different name it will print that name.

```
Hello world!
What is your name?
Alan
It is good to meet you, Alan
```

Remember, the computer only does exactly what you program it to do. In this program it is programmed to ask you for your name, let you type in a string, and then say hello and display the string you typed.

But computers are dumb. The program doesn't care if you type in your name, someone else's name, or just something silly. You can type in anything you want and the computer will treat it the same way:

```
Hello world!
What is your name?
poop
It is good to meet you, poop
```

Practice Exercises, Chapter 4, Set C

Practice exercises can be found at http://invpy.com/hackingpractice4C.

Summary

Writing programs is just about knowing how to speak the computer's language. While you learned a little bit of this in the last chapter, in this chapter you've put together several Python instructions to make a complete program that asks for the user's name and then greets them.

All of our programs later in this book will be more complex and sophisticated, but don't worry. The programs will all be explained line by line. And you can always enter instructions into the interactive shell to see what they do before they are all put into a complete program.

Now let's start with our first encryption program: the reverse cipher.

CHAPTER 5

THE REVERSE CIPHER

Topics Covered In This Chapter:

- The `len()` function
- `while` loops
- The Boolean data type
- Comparison operators
- Conditions
- Blocks

> "Every man is surrounded by a neighborhood of voluntary spies."
>
> Jane Austen

The Reverse Cipher

The reverse cipher encrypts a message by printing it in reverse order. So "Hello world!" encrypts to "!dlrow olleH". To decrypt, you simply reverse the reversed message to get the original message. The encryption and decryption steps are the same.

The reverse cipher is a very weak cipher. Just by looking at its ciphertext you can figure out it is just in reverse order. .syas ti tahw tuo erugif llits ylbaborp nac uoy ,detpyrcne si siht hguoht neve ,elpmaxe roF

But the code for the reverse cipher program is easy to explain, so we'll use it as our first encryption program.

Source Code of the Reverse Cipher Program

In IDLE, click on **File ► New Window** to create a new file editor window. Type in the following code, save it as *reverseCipher.py*, and press **F5** to run it: (Remember, don't type in the line numbers at the beginning of each line.)

Source code for reverseCipher.py

```
 1. # Reverse Cipher
 2. # http://inventwithpython.com/hacking (BSD Licensed)
 3.
 4. message = 'Three can keep a secret, if two of them are dead.'
 5. translated = ''
 6.
 7. i = len(message) - 1
 8. while i >= 0:
 9.     translated = translated + message[i]
10.     i = i - 1
11.
12. print(translated)
```

Sample Run of the Reverse Cipher Program

When you run this program the output will look like this:

```
.daed era meht fo owt fi ,terces a peek nac eerhT
```

To decrypt this message, copy the ".daed era meht fo owt fi ,terces a peek nac eerhT" text to the clipboard (see http://invpy.com/copypaste for instructions on how to copy and paste text) and paste it as the string value stored in `message` on line 4. Be sure to have the single quotes at the beginning and end of the string. The new line 4 will look like this (with the change in **bold**):

reverseCipher.py

```
 4. message = '.daed era meht fo owt fi ,terces a peek nac eerhT'
```

Now when you run the *reverseCipher.py* program, the output will decrypt to the original message:

```
Three can keep a secret, if two of them are dead.
```

Checking Your Source Code with the Online Diff Tool

Even though you could copy and paste or download this code from this book's website, it is very helpful to type in this program yourself. This will give you a better idea of what code is in this program. However, you might make some mistakes while typing it in yourself.

To compare the code you typed to the code that is in this book, you can use the book's website's online diff tool. Copy the text of your code and open http://invpy.com/hackingdiff in your web browser. Paste your code into the text field on this web page, and then click the Compare button. The diff tool will show any differences between your code and the code in this book. This is an easy way to find typos that are causing errors.

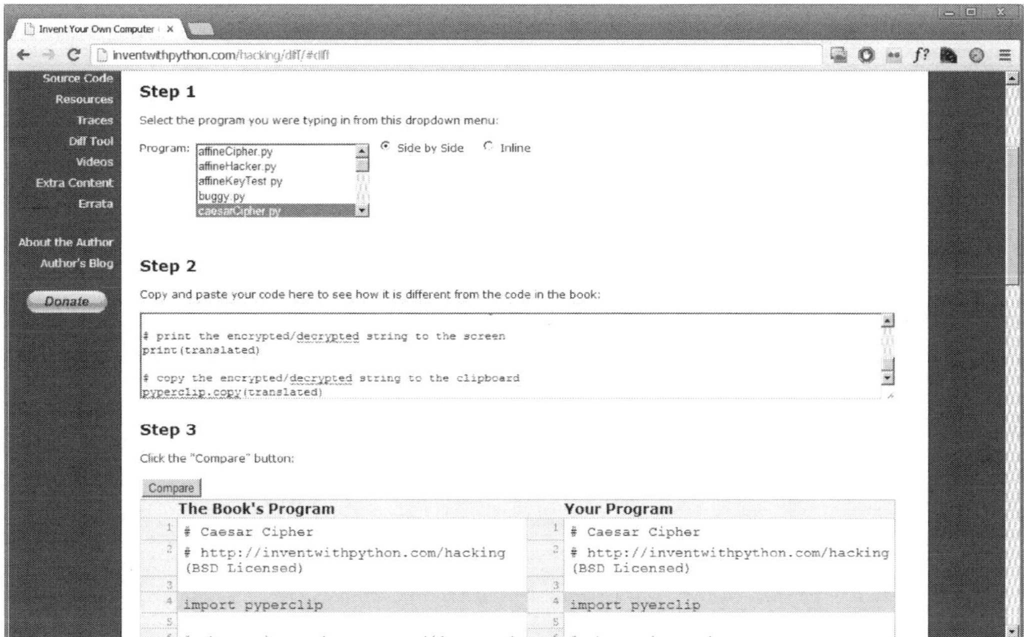

Figure 5-1. The online diff tool at http://invpy/hackingdiff

How the Program Works

reverseCipher.py

```
# Reverse Cipher
# http://inventwithpython.com/hacking (BSD Licensed)
```

The first two lines are comments explaining what the program is, and also the website where you can find it. The "BSD Licensed" part means that this program is free to copy and modify by anyone as long as the program retains the credits to the original author (in this case, the book's website at http://inventwithpython.com/hacking) (The full text of the Berkeley Software

Distribution license can be seen at http://invpy.com/bsd) I like to have this info in the file so if it gets copied around the Internet, a person who downloads it will always know where to look for the original source. They'll also know this program is open source software and free to distribute to others.

reverseCipher.py

```
4. message = 'Three can keep a secret, if two of them are dead.'
```

Line 4 stores the string we want to encrypt in a variable named `message`. Whenever we want to encrypt or decrypt a new string we will just type the string directly into the code on line 4. (The programs in this book don't call `input()`, instead the user will type in the message into the source code. You can just change the source directly before running the program again to encrypt different strings.)

reverseCipher.py

```
5. translated = ''
```

The `translated` variable is where our program will store the reversed string. At the start of the program, it will contain the blank string. (Remember that the blank string is two single quote characters, not one double quote character.)

The `len()` Function

reverseCipher.py

```
7. i = len(message) - 1
```

Line 6 is just a blank line, and Python will simply skip it. The next line of code is on line 7. This code is just an assignment statement that stores a value in a variable named `i`. The expression that is evaluated and stored in the variable is `len(message) - 1`.

The first part of this expression is `len(message)`. This is a function call to the `len()` function. The `len()` function accepts a string value argument (just like the `print()` function does) and returns an integer value of how many characters are in the string (that is, the length of the string). In this case, we pass the `message` variable to `len()`, so `len(message)` will tell us how many characters are in the string value stored in `message`.

Let's experiment in the interactive shell with the `len()` function. Type the following into the interactive shell:

```
>>> len('Hello')
5
>>> len('')
```

```
0
>>> spam = 'Al'
>>> len(spam)
2
>>> len('Hello' + ' ' + 'world!')
12
>>>
```

From the return value of `len()`, we know the string `'Hello'` has five characters in it and the blank string has zero characters in it. If we store the string `'Al'` in a variable and then pass the variable to `len()`, the function will return `2`. If we pass the expression `'Hello' + ' ' + 'world!'` to the `len()` function, it returns `12`. This is because `'Hello' + ' ' + 'world!'` will evaluate to the string value `'Hello world!'`, which has twelve characters in it. (The space and the exclamation point count as characters.)

Line 7 finds the number of characters in message, subtracts one, and then stores this number in the `i` variable. This will be the index of the last character in the `message` string.

Introducing the `while` Loop

reverseCipher.py

```
8. while i >= 0:
```

This is a new type of Python instruction called a `while` loop or `while` statement. A `while` loop is made up of four parts:

1. The `while` keyword.
2. An expression (also called a condition) that evaluates to the Boolean values `True` or `False`. (Booleans are explained next in this chapter.)
3. A : colon.
4. A block (explained later) of indented code that comes after it, which is what lines 9 and 10 are. (Blocks are explained later in this chapter.)

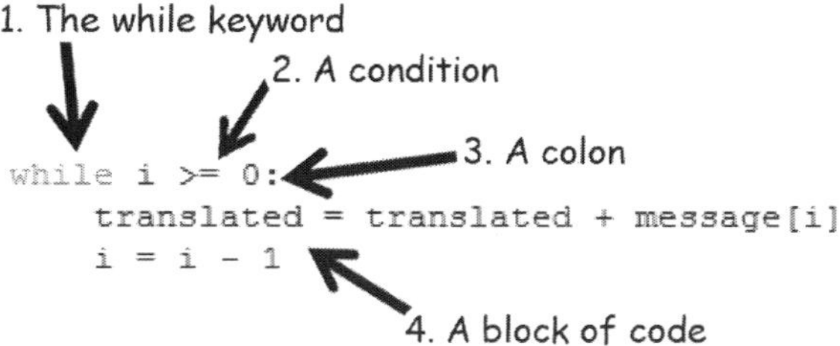

Figure 5-2. The parts of a `while` loop statement.

To understand while loops, we will first need to learn about Booleans, comparison operators, and blocks.

The Boolean Data Type

The Boolean data type has only two values: True or False. These values are case-sensitive (you always need to capitalize the T and F, and leave the rest in lowercase). They are not string values. You do not put a ' quote character around True or False. We will use Boolean values (also called **bools**) with comparison operators to form conditions. (Explained later after Comparison Operators.)

Like a value of any other data type, bools can be stored in variables. Type this into the interactive shell:

```
>>> spam = True
>>> spam
True
>>> spam = False
>>> spam
False
>>>
```

Comparison Operators

In line 8 of our program, look at the expression after the while keyword:

reverseCipher.py

```
8. while i >= 0:
```

The expression that follows the while keyword (the i >= 0 part) contains two values (the value in the variable i, and the integer value 0) connected by an operator (the >= sign, called the "greater than or equal" operator). The >= operator is called a **comparison operator**.

The comparison operator is used to compare two values and evaluate to a True or False Boolean value. Table 5-1 lists the comparison operators.

Table 5-1. Comparison operators.

Operator Sign	Operator Name
<	Less than
>	Greater than
<=	Less than or equal to
>=	Greater than or equal to
==	Equal to
!=	Not equal to

Enter the following expressions in the interactive shell to see the Boolean value they evaluate to:

```
>>> 0 < 6
True
>>> 6 < 0
False
>>> 50 < 10.5
False
>>> 10.5 < 11.3
True
>>> 10 < 10
False
```

The expression `0 < 6` returns the Boolean value `True` because the number `0` is less than the number `6`. But because `6` is not less than `0`, the expression `6 < 0` evaluates to `False`. `50` is not less than `10.5`, so `50 < 10.5` is `False`. `10.5` is less than `11.3`, so `10 < 11.3` evaluates to `True`.

Look again at `10 < 10`. It is `False` because the number `10` is not smaller than the number `10`. They are exactly the same size. If Alice was the same height as Bob, you wouldn't say that Alice is shorter than Bob. That statement would be false.

Try typing in some expressions using the other comparison operators:

```
>>> 10 <= 20
True
>>> 10 <= 10
True
>>> 10 >= 20
False
>>> 20 >= 20
True
>>>
```

Remember that for the "less than or equal to" and "greater than or equal to" operators, the < or > sign always comes **before** the = sign.

Type in some expressions that use the == (equal to) and != (not equal to) operators into the shell to see how they work:

```
>>> 10 == 10
True
>>> 10 == 11
False
>>> 11 == 10
False
>>> 10 != 10
False
>>> 10 != 11
True
>>> 'Hello' == 'Hello'
True
>>> 'Hello' == 'Good bye'
False
>>> 'Hello' == 'HELLO'
False
>>> 'Good bye' != 'Hello'
True
```

Notice the difference between the assignment operator (=) and the "equal to" comparison operator (==). The equal (=) sign is used to assign a value to a variable, and the equal to (==) sign is used in expressions to see whether two values are the same. If you're asking Python if two things are equal, use ==. If you are telling Python to set a variable to a value, use =.

String and integer values will always be not-equal to each other. For example, try entering the following into the interactive shell:

```
>>> 42 == 'Hello'
False
>>> 42 == '42'
False
>>> 10 == 10.0
True
```

Just remember that every expression with comparison operators always evaluates to the value `True` or the value `False`.

Conditions

A **condition** is another name for an expression when it is used in a `while` or `if` statement. (`if` statements aren't used in the reverse cipher program, but will be covered in the next chapter.) Conditions usually have comparison operators, but conditions are still just expressions.

Blocks

A block is one or more lines of code grouped together with the same minimum amount of **indentation** (that is, the number of spaces in front of the line). You can tell where a block begins and ends by looking at the line's indentation.

A block begins when a line is indented by four spaces. Any following line that is also indented by at least four spaces is part of the block. When a line is indented with another four spaces (for a total of eight spaces in front of the line), a new block begins inside the block. A block ends when there is a line of code with the same indentation before the block started.

Let's look at some imaginary code (it doesn't matter what the code is, we are only paying attention to the indentation of each line). We will replace the indenting spaces with black squares to make them easier to count:

```
1. codecodecodecodecodecodecode # zero spaces of indentation
2. ▪▪▪▪codecodecodecodecodecodecodecodecode # four spaces of indentation
3. ▪▪▪▪codecodecodecodecodecodecode # four spaces of indentation
4. ▪▪▪▪▪▪▪▪codecodecodecodecodecodecodecodecode # eight spaces of indentation
5. ▪▪▪▪codecodecodecodecode # four spaces of indentation
6.
7. ▪▪▪▪codecodecodecodecodecode # four spaces of indentation
8. codecodecodecodecodecodecodecodecodecodecode # zero spaces of indentation
```

You can see that line 1 has no indentation, that is, there are zero spaces in front of the line of code. But line 2 has four spaces of indentation. Because this is a larger amount of indentation than the previous line, we know a new block has begun. Line 3 also has four spaces of indentation, so we know the block continues on line 3.

Line 4 has even more indentation (8 spaces), so a new block has begun. This block is inside the other blocks. In Python, you can have blocks-within-blocks.

On line 5, the amount of indentation has decreased to 4, so we know that the block on the previous line has ended. Line 4 is the only line in that block. Since line 5 has the same amount of indentation as the block from line 3, we know that the block has continue on to line 5.

Line 6 is a blank line, so we just skip it.

Line 7 has four spaces on indentation, so we know that the block that started on line 2 has continued to line 7.

Line 8 has zero spaces of indentation, which is less indentation than the previous line. This decrease in indentation tells us that the previous block has ended.

There are two blocks in the above make-believe code. The first block goes from line 2 to line 7. The second block is just made up of line 4 (and is inside the other block).

(As a side note, it doesn't always have to be four spaces. The blocks can use any number of spaces, but the convention is to use four spaces.)

The `while` Loop Statement

reverseCipher.py

```
 8. while i >= 0:
 9.     translated = translated + message[i]
10.     i = i - 1
11.
12. print(translated)
```

Let's look at the `while` statement on line 8 again. What a `while` statement tells Python to do is first check to see what the condition (which on line 8 is `i >= 0`) evaluates to. If the condition evaluates to `True`, then the program execution enters the block following the `while` statement. From looking at the indentation, this block is made up of lines 9 and 10.

If the `while` statement's condition evaluates to `False`, then the program execution will skip the code inside the following block and jump down to the first line after the block (which is line 12).

If the condition was `True`, the program execution starts at the top of the block and executes each line in turn going down. When it reaches the bottom of the block, the program execution jumps back to the `while` statement on line 8 and checks the condition again. If it is still `True`, the execution jumps into the block again. If it is `False`, the program execution will skip past it.

You can think of the `while` statement `while i >= 0:` as meaning, "while the variable `i` is greater than or equal to zero, keep executing the code in the following block".

"Growing" a String

Remember on line 7 that the `i` variable is first set to the length of the `message` minus one, and the `while` loop on line 8 will keep executing the lines inside the following block until the condition `i >= 0` is `False`.

reverseCipher.py

```
 7. i = len(message) - 1
 8. while i >= 0:
 9.     translated = translated + message[i]
10.     i = i - 1
11.
12. print(translated)
```

There are two lines inside the `while` statement's block, line 9 and line 10.

Line 9 is an assignment statement that stores a value in the `translated` variable. The value that is stored is the current value of `translated` concatenated with the character at the index `i` in `message`. In this way, the string value stored in `translated` "grows" until it becomes the fully encrypted string.

Line 10 is an assignment statement also. It takes the current integer value in `i` and subtracts one from it (this is called **decrementing** the variable), and then stores this value as the new value of `i`.

The next line is line 12, but since this line has less indentation, Python knows that the `while` statement's block has ended. So rather than go on to line 12, the program execution jumps back to line 8 where the `while` loop's condition is checked again. If the condition is `True`, then the lines inside the block (lines 9 and 10) are executed again. This keeps happening until the condition is `False` (that is, when `i` is less than `0`), in which case the program execution goes to the first line after the block (line 12).

Let's think about the behavior of this loop. The variable `i` starts off with the value of the last index of `message` and the `translated` variable starts off as the blank string. Then inside the loop, the value of `message[i]` (which is the last character in the `message` string, since `i` will have the value of the last index) is added to the end of the `translated` string.

Then the value in `i` is decremented (that is, reduced) by `1`. This means that `message[i]` will be the second to last character. So while `i` as an index keeps moving from the back of the string in `message` to the front, the string `message[i]` is added to the end of `translated`. This is what causes `translated` to hold the reverse of the string in the `message`. When `i` is finally set to `-1`, then the `while` loop's condition will be `False` and the execution jumps to line 12.

reverseCipher.py

```
12. print(translated)
```

At the end of our program on line 12, we print out the contents of the `translated` variable (that is, the string `'.daed era meht fo owt fi ,terces a peek nac eerhT'`) to the screen. This will show the user what the reversed string looks like.

If you are still having trouble understanding how the code in the `while` loop reverses the string, try adding this new line inside the `while` loop:

reverseCipher.py

```
 8. while i >= 0:
 9.     translated = translated + message[i]
10.     print(i, message[i], translated)
11.     i = i - 1
12.
13. print(translated)
```

This will print out the three expressions `i`, `message[i]`, and `translated` each time the execution goes through the loop (that is, on each **iteration** of the loop). The commas tell the `print()` function that we are printing three separate things, so the function will add a space in between them. Now when you run the program, you can see how the `translated` variable "grows". The output will look like this:

```
48 . .
47 d .d
46 a .da
45 e .dae
44 d .daed
43   .daed
42 e .daed e
41 r .daed er
40 a .daed era
39   .daed era
38 m .daed era m
37 e .daed era me
36 h .daed era meh
35 t .daed era meht
34   .daed era meht
33 f .daed era meht f
32 o .daed era meht fo
31   .daed era meht fo
30 o .daed era meht fo o
29 w .daed era meht fo ow
28 t .daed era meht fo owt
27   .daed era meht fo owt
26 f .daed era meht fo owt f
25 i .daed era meht fo owt fi
24   .daed era meht fo owt fi
23 , .daed era meht fo owt fi ,
```

```
22 t .daed era meht fo owt fi ,t
21 e .daed era meht fo owt fi ,te
20 r .daed era meht fo owt fi ,ter
19 c .daed era meht fo owt fi ,terc
18 e .daed era meht fo owt fi ,terce
17 s .daed era meht fo owt fi ,terces
16   .daed era meht fo owt fi ,terces
15 a .daed era meht fo owt fi ,terces a
14   .daed era meht fo owt fi ,terces a
13 p .daed era meht fo owt fi ,terces a p
12 e .daed era meht fo owt fi ,terces a pe
11 e .daed era meht fo owt fi ,terces a pee
10 k .daed era meht fo owt fi ,terces a peek
9   .daed era meht fo owt fi ,terces a peek
8 n .daed era meht fo owt fi ,terces a peek n
7 a .daed era meht fo owt fi ,terces a peek na
6 c .daed era meht fo owt fi ,terces a peek nac
5   .daed era meht fo owt fi ,terces a peek nac
4 e .daed era meht fo owt fi ,terces a peek nac e
3 e .daed era meht fo owt fi ,terces a peek nac ee
2 r .daed era meht fo owt fi ,terces a peek nac eer
1 h .daed era meht fo owt fi ,terces a peek nac eerh
0 T .daed era meht fo owt fi ,terces a peek nac eerhT
.daed era meht fo owt fi ,terces a peek nac eerhT
```

The first line, which shows "`48 . .`", is showing what the expressions `i`, `message[i]`, and `translated` evaluate to after the string `message[i]` has been added to the end of `translated` but before `i` is decremented. You can see that the first time the program execution goes through the loop, `i` is set to `48`, and so `message[i]` (that is, `message[48]`) is the string `'.'`. The `translated` variable started as a blank string, but when `message[i]` was added to the end of it on line 9, it became the string value `'.'`.

On the next iteration of the loop, the `print()` call displays "`47 . .d`". You can see that `i` has been decremented from `48` to `47`, and so now `message[i]` is `message[47]`, which is the `'d'` string. (That's the second "d" in "dead".) This `'d'` gets added to the end of `translated` so that translated is now set to `'.d'`.

Now you can see how the `translated` variable's string is slowly "grown" from a blank string to the reverse of the string stored in `message`.

Tracing Through the Program, Step by Step

The previous explanations have gone through what each line does, but let's go step by step through the program the same way the Python interpreter does. The interpreter starts at the very top, executes the first line, then moves down a line to execute the next instruction. The blank lines and comments are skipped. The `while` loop will cause the program execution will loop back to the start of the loop after it finishes.

Here is a brief explanation of each line of code in the same order that the Python interpreter executes it. Follow along with to see how the execution moves down the lines of the program, but sometimes jumps back to a previous line.

reverseCipher.py

```
 1. # Reverse Cipher
 2. # http://inventwithpython.com/hacking (BSD Licensed)
 3.
 4. message = 'Three can keep a secret, if two of them are dead.'
 5. translated = ''
 6.
 7. i = len(message) - 1
 8. while i >= 0:
 9.     translated = translated + message[i]
10.     i = i - 1
11.
12. print(translated)
```

Step 1	Line 1	This is a comment, so the Python interpreter skips it.
Step 2	Line 2	This is a comment, and skipped.
Step 3	Line 4	The string value `'Three can keep a secret, if two of them are dead.'` is stored in the `message` variable.
Step 4	Line 5	The blank string `''` is stored in the `translated` variable.
Step 5	Line 7	`len(message) - 1` evaluates to `48`. The integer `48` is stored in the `i` variable.
Step 6	Line 8	The `while` loop's condition `i >= 0` evaluates to `True`. Since the condition is `True`, the program execution moves inside the following block.
Step 7	Line 9	`translated + message[i]` to `'.'`. The string value `'.'` is stored in the `translated` variable.
Step 8	Line 10	`i - 1` evaluates to `47`. The integer `47` is stored in the `i` variable.
Step 9	Line 8	When the program execution reaches the end of the block, the execution moves back to the `while` statement and rechecks the condition. `i >= 0` evaluates to `True`, the program execution moves inside the block again.
Step 10	Line 9	`translated + message[i]` evaluates `'.d'`. The string value `'.d'` is stored in the `translated` variable.
Step 11	Line 10	`i - 1` evaluates to `46`. The integer `46` is stored in the `i` variable.
Step 12	Line 8	The `while` statement rechecks the condition. Since `i >= 0` evaluates to `True`, the program execution will move inside the block again.

Step 13 to Step 149		...The lines of the code continue to loop. We fast-forward to when `i` is set to `0` and `translated` is set to `' .daed era meht fo owt fi ,terces a peek nac eerh'`...
Step 150	Line 8	The `while` loop's condition is checked, and 0 >= 0 evaluates to True.
Step 151	Line 9	`translated + message[i]` evaluates to `'.daed era meht fo owt fi ,terces a peek nac eerhT'`. This string is stored in the `translated` variable.
Step 152	Line 10	`i - 1` evaluates to `0 - 1`, which evaluates to `-1`. `-1` is stored in the `i` variable.
Step 153	Line 8	The `while` loop's condition is `i >= 0`, which evaluates to `-1 >= 0`, which evaluates to `False`. Because the condition is now `False`, the program execution skips the following block of code and goes to line 12.
Step 154	Line 12	`translated` evaluates to the string value `'.daed era meht fo owt fi ,terces a peek nac eerhT'`. The `print()` function is called and this string is passed, making it appear on the screen.
		There are no more lines after line 12, so the program terminates.

Using `input()` In Our Programs

The programs in this book are all designed so that the strings that are being encrypted or decrypted are typed directly into the source code. You could also modify the assignment statements so that they call the `input()` function. You can pass a string to the `input()` function to appear as a prompt for the user to type in the string to encrypt. For example, if you change line 4 in *reverseCipher.py* to this:

reverseCipher.py

```
4. message = input('Enter message: ')
```

Then when you run the program, it will print the prompt to the screen and wait for the user to type in the message and press Enter. The message that the user types in will be the string value that is stored in the `message` variable:

```
Enter message: Hello world!
!dlrow olleH
```

Practice Exercises, Chapter 5, Section A

Practice exercises can be found at http://invpy.com/hackingpractice5A.

Summary

Now that we have learned how to deal with text, we can start making programs that the user can run and interact with. This is important because text is the main way the user and the computer will communicate with each other.

Strings are just a different data type that we can use in our programs. We can use the + operator to concatenate strings together. We can use indexing and slicing to create a new string from part of a different string. The `len()` function takes a string argument and returns an integer of how many characters are in the string.

The Boolean data type has only two values: `True` and `False`. Comparison operators ==, `!=`, <, >, <=, and >= can compare two values and evaluate to a Boolean value.

Conditions are expression that are used in several different kinds of statements. A `while` loop statement keeps executing the lines inside the block that follows it as long as its condition evaluates to `True`. A block is made up of lines with the same level of indentation, including any blocks inside of them.

A common practice in programs is to start a variable with a blank string, and then concatenate characters to it until it “grows” into the final desired string.

Chapter 6

The Caesar Cipher

Topics Covered In This Chapter:

- The `import` statement
- Constants
- The `upper()` string method
- `for` loops
- `if`, `elif`, and `else` statements
- The `in` and `not in` operators
- The `find()` string method

"BIG BROTHER IS WATCHING YOU."

"1984" by George Orwell

Implementing a Program

In Chapter 1, we used a cipher wheel, a St. Cyr slide, and a chart of letters and numbers to implement the Caesar cipher. In this chapter, we will use a computer program to implement the Caesar cipher.

The reverse cipher always encrypts the same way. But the Caesar cipher uses keys, which encrypt the message in a different way depending on which key is used. The keys for the Caesar cipher are the integers from `0` to `25`. Even if a cryptanalyst knows that the Caesar cipher was used, that alone does not give her enough information to break the cipher. She must also know the key.

Source Code of the Caesar Cipher Program

Type in the following code into the file editor, and then save it as *caesarCipher.py*. Press **F5** to run the program. Note that first you will need to download the *pyperclip.py* module and place this file in the same directory (that is, folder) as the *caesarCipher.py* file. You can download this file from http://invpy.com/pyperclip.py

Source code for caesarCipher.py

```
# Caesar Cipher
# http://inventwithpython.com/hacking (BSD Licensed)

import pyperclip

# the string to be encrypted/decrypted
message = 'This is my secret message.'

# the encryption/decryption key
key = 13

# tells the program to encrypt or decrypt
mode = 'encrypt' # set to 'encrypt' or 'decrypt'

# every possible symbol that can be encrypted
LETTERS = 'ABCDEFGHIJKLMNOPQRSTUVWXYZ'

# stores the encrypted/decrypted form of the message
translated = ''

# capitalize the string in message
message = message.upper()

# run the encryption/decryption code on each symbol in the message string
for symbol in message:
    if symbol in LETTERS:
        # get the encrypted (or decrypted) number for this symbol
        num = LETTERS.find(symbol) # get the number of the symbol
        if mode == 'encrypt':
            num = num + key
        elif mode == 'decrypt':
            num = num - key

        # handle the wrap-around if num is larger than the length of
        # LETTERS or less than 0
        if num >= len(LETTERS):
            num = num - len(LETTERS)
```

```
        elif num < 0:
            num = num + len(LETTERS)

        # add encrypted/decrypted number's symbol at the end of translated
        translated = translated + LETTERS[num]

    else:
        # just add the symbol without encrypting/decrypting
        translated = translated + symbol

# print the encrypted/decrypted string to the screen
print(translated)

# copy the encrypted/decrypted string to the clipboard
pyperclip.copy(translated)
```

Sample Run of the Caesar Cipher Program

When you run this program, the output will look like this:

```
GUVF VF ZL FRPERG ZRFFNTR.
```

The above text is the string `'This is my secret message.'` encrypted with the Caesar cipher with key `13`. The Caesar cipher program you just ran will automatically copy this encrypted string to the clipboard so you can paste it in an email or text file. This way you can easily take the encrypted output from the program and send it to another person.

To decrypt, just paste this text as the new value stored in the `message` variable on line 7. Then change the assignment statement on line 13 to store the string `'decrypt'` in the variable `mode`:

caesarCipher.py

```
 6. # the string to be encrypted/decrypted
 7. message = 'GUVF VF ZL FRPERG ZRFFNTR.'
 8.
 9. # the encryption/decryption key
10. key = 13
11.
12. # tells the program to encrypt or decrypt
13. mode = 'decrypt' # set to 'encrypt' or 'decrypt'
```

When you run the program now, the output will look like this:

```
THIS IS MY SECRET MESSAGE.
```

If you see this error message when running the program:

```
Traceback (most recent call last):
  File "C:\Python32\caesarCipher.py", line 4, in <module>
    import pyperclip
ImportError: No module named pyperclip
```

…then you have not downloaded the `pyperclip` module into the right folder. If you still cannot get the module working, just delete lines 4 and 52 (which have the text "pyperclip" in them) from the program. This will get rid of the code that depends on the `pyperclip` module.

Checking Your Source Code with the Online Diff Tool

To compare the code you typed to the code that is in this book, you can use the online diff tool on this book's website. Open http://invpy.com/hackingdiff in your web browser. Copy and paste your code into the text field on this web page, and then click the Compare button. The diff tool will show any differences between your code and the code in this book. This can help you find any typos you made when typing out the program.

Practice Exercises, Chapter 6, Set A

Practice exercises can be found at http://invpy.com/hackingpractice6A.

How the Program Works

Let's go over exactly what each of the lines of code in this program does.

Importing Modules with the `import` Statement

caesarCipher.py

```
1. # Caesar Cipher
2. # http://inventwithpython.com/hacking (BSD Licensed)
3.
4. import pyperclip
```

Line 4 is a new kind of statement called an `import` statement. While Python includes many built-in functions, some functions exist in separate programs called modules. **Modules** are Python programs that contain additional functions that can be used by your program. In this case, we're importing a module named `pyperclip` so that we can call the `pyperclip.copy()` function later in this program.

The `import` statement is made up of the `import` keyword followed by the module name. Line 4 is an `import` statement that imports the `pyperclip` module, which contains several functions related to copying and pasting text to the clipboard.

caesarCipher.py

```
# the string to be encrypted/decrypted
message = 'This is my secret message.'

# the encryption/decryption key
key = 13

# tells the program to encrypt or decrypt
mode = 'encrypt' # set to 'encrypt' or 'decrypt'
```

The next few lines set three variables: `message` will store the string to be encrypted or decrypted, `key` will store the integer of the encryption key, and `mode` will store either the string `'encrypt'` (which will cause code later in the program to encrypt the string in `message`) or `'decrypt'` (which will tell the program to decrypt rather than encrypting).

Constants

caesarCipher.py

```
# every possible symbol that can be encrypted
LETTERS = 'ABCDEFGHIJKLMNOPQRSTUVWXYZ'
```

We also need a string that contains all the capital letters of the alphabet in order. It would be tiring to type the full `'ABCDEFGHIJKLMNOPQRSTUVWXYZ'` string value each time we use it in the program (and we might make typos when typing it, which would cause errors in our program). So instead we will type the code for the string value once and place it in a variable named `LETTERS`. This string contains all the letters that our cipher program can possibly encrypt. This set of letters (which don't have to be just letters but can also be numbers, punctuation, or any other symbol) is called the cipher's **symbol set**. The end of this chapter will tell you how to expand this program's symbol set to include other characters besides letters.

The `LETTERS` variable name is in all capitals. This is the programming convention for constant variables. **Constants** are variables whose values are not meant to be changed when the program runs. Although we *can* change `LETTERS` just like any other variable, the all-caps reminds the programmer to not write code that does so.

Like all conventions, we don't *have* to follow it. But doing it this way makes it easier for other programmers to understand how these variables are used. (It even can help you if you are looking at code you wrote yourself a long time ago.)

The upper() and lower() String Methods

caesarCipher.py

```
18. # stores the encrypted/decrypted form of the message
19. translated = ''
20.
21. # capitalize the string in message
22. message = message.upper()
```

On line 19, the program stores a blank string in a variable named `translated`. Just like in the reverse cipher from last chapter, by the end of the program the `translated` variable will contain the completely encrypted (or decrypted) message. But for now it starts as a blank string.

Line 22 is an assignment statement that stores a value in a variable named `message`, but the expression on the right side of the = operator is something we haven't seen before: `message.upper()`.

This is a method call. **Methods** are just like functions, except they are attached to a non-module value (or in the case of line 22, a variable containing a value) with a period. The name of this method is `upper()`, and it is being called on the string value stored in the `message` variable.

A function is not a method just because it is in a module. You will see on line 52 that we call `pyperclip.copy()`, but `pyperclip` is a module that was imported on line 4, so `copy()` is not a method. It is just a function that is inside the `pyperclip` module. If this is confusing, then you can always call methods and functions a "function" and people will know what you're talking about.

Most data types (such as strings) have methods. Strings have a method called `upper()` and `lower()` which will evaluate to an uppercase or lowercase version of that string, respectively. Try typing the following into the interactive shell:

```
>>> 'Hello world!'.upper()
'HELLO WORLD!'
>>> 'Hello world!'.lower()
'hello world!'
>>>
```

Because the `upper()` method returns a string value, you can call a method on *that* string as well. Try typing `'Hello world!'.upper().lower()` into the shell:

```
>>> 'Hello world!'.upper().lower()
'hello world!'
```

```
>>>
```

`'Hello world!'.upper()` evaluates to the string `'HELLO WORLD!'`, and then we call the `lower()` method on *that* string. This returns the string `'hello world!'`, which is the final value in the evaluation. The order is important. `'Hello world!'.lower().upper()` is not the same as `'Hello world!'.upper().lower()`:

```
>>> 'Hello world'.lower().upper()
'HELLO WORLD!'
>>>
```

If a string is stored in a variable, you can call any string method (such as `upper()` or `lower()`) on that variable. Look at this example:

```
>>> fizz = 'Hello world!'
>>> fizz.upper()
'HELLO WORLD!'
>>> fizz
'Hello world!'
```

Calling the `upper()` or `lower()` method on a string value in a variable does not change the value inside a variable. Methods are just part of expressions that evaluate to a value. (Think about it like this: the expression `fizz + 'ABC'` would not change the string stored in `fizz` to have `'ABC'` concatenated to the end of it, unless we used it in an assignment statement like `fizz = fizz + 'ABC'`.)

Different data types have different methods. You will learn about other methods as you read this book. A list of common string methods is at http://invpy.com/stringmethods.

The `for` Loop Statement

caesarCipher.py
```
# run the encryption/decryption code on each symbol in the message string
for symbol in message:
```

The `for` loop is very good at looping over a string or list of values (we will learn about lists later). This is different from the `while` loop, which loops as long as a certain condition is `True`. A `for` statement has six parts:

1. The for keyword.
2. A variable name.
3. The in keyword.
4. A string value (or a variable containing a string value).
5. A colon.
6. A block of code.

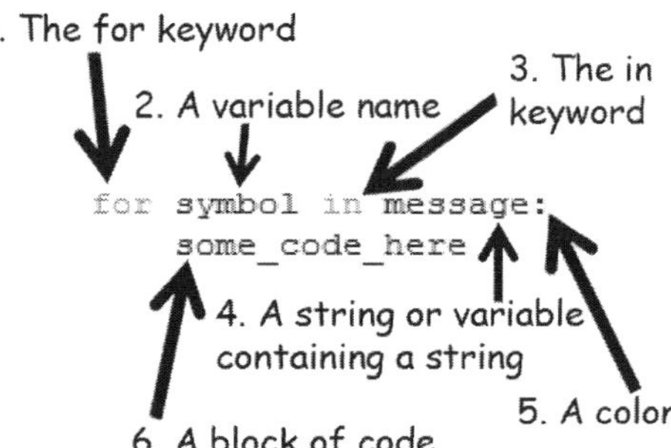

Figure 6-1. The parts of a for loop statement.

Each time the program execution goes through the loop (that is, on each iteration through the loop) the variable in the for statement takes on the value of the next character in the string.

For example, type the following into the interactive shell. Note that after you type the first line, the >>> prompt will turn into ... (although in IDLE, it will just print three spaces) because the shell is expecting a block of code after the for statement's colon. In the interactive shell, the block will end when you enter a blank line:

```
>>> for letter in 'Howdy':
...     print('The letter is ' + letter)
...
The letter is H
The letter is o
The letter is w
The letter is d
The letter is y
>>>
```

A while Loop Equivalent of a for Loop

The for loop is very similar to the while loop, but when you only need to iterate over characters in a string, using a for loop is much less code to type. You can make a while loop that acts the same way as a for loop by adding a little extra code:

```
>>> i = 0
>>> while i < len('Howdy'):
...     letter = 'Howdy'[i]
...     print('The letter is ' + letter)
...     i = i + 1
...
The letter is H
The letter is o
The letter is w
```

```
The letter is d
The letter is y
>>>
```

Notice that this `while` loop does the exact same thing that the `for` loop does, but is not as short and simple as the `for` loop.

Before we can understand lines 26 to 32 of the Caesar cipher program, we need to first learn about the `if`, `elif`, and `else` statements, the `in` and `not in` operators, and the `find()` string method.

Practice Exercises, Chapter 6, Set B

Practice exercises can be found at http://invpy.com/hackingpractice6B.

The `if` Statement

An `if` statement can be read as "If this condition is `True`, execute the code in the following block. Otherwise if it is `False`, skip the block." Open the file editor and type in the following small program. Then save the file as *password.py* and press **F5** to run it.

Source code for password.py

```
print('What is the password?')
password = input()
if password == 'rosebud':
    print('Access granted.')
if password != 'rosebud':
    print('Access denied.')
print('Done.')
```

When the `password = input()` line is executed, the user can type in anything she wants and it will be stored as a string in the variable `password`. If she typed in "rosebud" (in all lowercase letters), then the expression `password == 'rosebud'` will evaluate to `True` and the program execution will enter the following block to print the `'Access granted.'` string.

If `password == 'rosebud'` is `False`, then this block of code is skipped. Next, the second `if` statement will have its condition also evaluated. If this condition, `password != 'rosebud'` is `True`, then the execution jumps inside of the following block to print out `'Access denied.'`. If the condition is `False`, then this block of code is skipped.

The `else` Statement

Often we want to test a condition and execute one block of code if it is `True` and another block of code if it is `False`. The previous *password.py* example is like this, but it used two `if` statements.

An `else` statement can be used after an `if` statement's block, and its block of code will be executed if the `if` statement's condition is `False`. You can read the code as "if this condition is true, execute this block, or else execute this block.

Type in the following program and save it as *password2.py*. Notice that it does the same thing as the previous *password.py* program, except it uses an `if` and `else` statement instead of two `if` statements:

Source code for password2.py

```
print('What is the password?')
password = input()
if password == 'rosebud':
    print('Access granted.')
else:
    print('Access denied.')
print('Done.')
```

The `elif` Statement

There is also an "else if" statement called the `elif` statement. Like an `if` statement, it has a condition. Like an `else` statement, it follows an `if` (or another `elif`) statement and executes if the previous `if` (or `elif`) statement's condition was `False`. You can read `if`, `elif` and `else` statements as, "If this condition is true, run this block. Or else, check if this next condition is true. Or else, just run this last block." Type in this example program into the file editor and save it as *elifeggs.py*:

Source code for elifeggs.py

```
numberOfEggs = 12
if numberOfEggs < 4:
    print('That is not that many eggs.')
elif numberOfEggs < 20:
    print('You have quite a few eggs.')
elif numberOfEggs == 144:
    print('You have a lot of eggs. Gross!')
else:
    print('Eat ALL the eggs!')
```

When you run this program, the integer `12` is stored in the variable `numberOfEggs`. Then the condition `numberOfEggs < 4` is checked to see if it is `True`. If it isn't, the execution skips the block and checks `numberOfEggs < 20`. If it isn't `True`, execution skips that block and checks if `numberOfEggs == 144`. If all of these conditions have been `False`, then the `else` block is executed.

Notice that one and only one of these blocks will be executed. You can have zero or more `elif` statements following an `if` statement. You can have zero or one `else` statements, and the `else` statement always comes last.

The `in` and `not in` Operators

An expression of two strings connected by the `in` operator will evaluate to `True` if the first string is inside the second string. Otherwise the expression evaluates to `False`. Notice that the `in` and `not in` operators are case-sensitive. Try typing the following in the interactive shell:

```
>>> 'hello' in 'hello world!'
True
>>> 'ello' in 'hello world!'
True
>>> 'HELLO' in 'hello world!'
False
>>> 'HELLO' in 'HELLO world!'
True
>>> '' in 'Hello'
True
>>> '' in ''
True
>>> 'D' in 'ABCDEF'
True
>>>
```

The `not in` operator will evaluate to the opposite of `in`. Try typing the following into the interactive shell:

```
>>> 'hello' not in 'hello world!'
False
>>> 'ello' not in 'hello world!'
False
>>> 'HELLO' not in 'hello world!'
True
>>> 'HELLO' not in 'HELLO world!'
False
>>> '' not in 'Hello'
```

```
False
>>> '' not in ''
False
>>> 'D' not in 'ABCDEF'
False
>>>
```

Expressions using the `in` and `not in` operators are handy for conditions of `if` statements so that we can execute some code if a string exists inside of another string.

Also, the `in` keyword used in `for` statements is not the same as the `in` operator used here. They are just typed the same.

The `find()` String Method

Just like the `upper()` method can be called on a string values, the `find()` method is a string method. The `find()` method takes one string argument and returns the integer index of where that string appears in the method's string. Try typing the following into the interactive shell:

```
>>> 'hello'.find('e')
1
>>> 'hello'.find('o')
4
>>> fizz = 'hello'
>>> fizz.find('h')
0
>>>
```

If the string argument cannot be found, the `find()` method returns the integer `-1`. Notice that the `find()` method is case-sensitive. Try typing the following into the interactive shell:

```
>>> 'hello'.find('x')
-1
>>> 'hello'.find('H')
-1
>>>
```

The string you pass as an argument to `find()` can be more than one character. The integer that `find()` returns will be the index of the first character where the argument is found. Try typing the following into the interactive shell:

```
>>> 'hello'.find('ello')
1
```

```
>>> 'hello'.find('lo')
3
>>> 'hello hello'.find('e')
1
>>>
```

The `find()` string method is like a more specific version of using the `in` operator. It not only tells you if a string exists in another string, but also tells you where.

Practice Exercises, Chapter 6, Set C

Practice exercises can be found at http://invpy.com/hackingpractice6C.

Back to the Code

Now that we understand how `if`, `elif`, `else` statements, the `in` operator, and the `find()` string method works, it will be easier to understand how the rest of the Caesar cipher program works.

caesarCipher.py

```
26.     if symbol in LETTERS:
27.         # get the encrypted (or decrypted) number for this symbol
28.         num = LETTERS.find(symbol) # get the number of the symbol
```

If the string in `symbol` (which the `for` statement has set to be only a single character) is a capital letter, then the condition `symbol in LETTERS` will be `True`. (Remember that on line 22 we converted `message` to an uppercase version with `message = message.upper()`, so `symbol` cannot possibly be a lowercase letter.) The only time the condition is `False` is if `symbol` is something like a punctuation mark or number string value, such as `'?'` or `'4'`.

We want to check if `symbol` is an uppercase letter because our program will only encrypt (or decrypt) uppercase letters. Any other character will be added to the `translated` string without being encrypted (or decrypted).

There is a new block that starts after the `if` statement on line 26. If you look down the program, you will notice that this block stretches all the way to line 42. The `else` statement on line 44 is paired to the `if` statement on line 26.

caesarCipher.py

```
29.             if mode == 'encrypt':
30.                 num = num + key
31.             elif mode == 'decrypt':
32.                 num = num - key
```

Now that we have the current symbol's number stored in `num`, we can do the encryption or decryption math on it. The Caesar cipher adds the key number to the letter's number to encrypt it, or subtracts the key number from the letter's number to decrypt it.

The `mode` variable contains a string that tells the program whether or not it should be encrypting or decrypting. If this string is `'encrypt'`, then the condition for line 29's `if` statement will be `True` and line 30 will be executed (and the block after the `elif` statement will be skipped). If this string is any other value besides `'encrypt'`, then the condition for line 29's `if` statement is `False` and the program execution moves on to check the `elif` statement's condition.

This is how our program knows when to encrypt (where it is adding the key) or decrypt (where it is subtracting the key). If the programmer made an error and stored `'pineapples'` in the `mode` variable on line 13, then both of the conditions on lines 29 and 31 would be `False` and nothing would happen to the value stored in `num`. (You can try this yourself by changing line 13 and re-running the program.)

caesarCipher.py

```
34.         # handle the wrap-around if num is larger than the length of
35.         # LETTERS or less than 0
36.         if num >= len(LETTERS):
37.             num = num - len(LETTERS)
38.         elif num < 0:
39.             num = num + len(LETTERS)
```

Remember that when we were implementing the Caesar cipher with paper and pencil, sometimes the number after adding or subtracting the key would be greater than or equal to 26 or less than 0. In those cases, we had to add or subtract 26 to the number to "wrap-around" the number. This "wrap-around" is what lines 36 to 39 do for our program.

If `num` is greater than or equal to `26`, then the condition on line 36 is `True` and line 37 is executed (and the `elif` statement on line 38 is skipped). Otherwise, Python will check if `num` is less than `0`. If that condition is `True`, then line 39 is executed.

The Caesar cipher adds or subtracts 26 because that is the number of letters in the alphabet. If English only had 25 letters, then the "wrap-around" would be done by adding or subtracting 25.

Notice that instead of using the integer value `26` directly, we use `len(LETTERS)`. The function call `len(LETTERS)` will return the integer value `26`, so this code works just as well. But the reason that we use `len(LETTERS)` instead of `26` is that the code will work no matter what characters we have in `LETTERS`.

We can modify the value stored in LETTERS so that we encrypt and decrypt more than just the uppercase letters. How this is done will be explained at the end of this chapter.

caesarCipher.py
```
41.         # add encrypted/decrypted number's symbol at the end of translated
42.         translated = translated + LETTERS[num]
```

Now that the integer in num has been modified, it will be the index of the encrypted (or decrypted) letter in LETTERS. We want to add this encrypted/decrypted letter to the end of the translated string, so line 42 uses string concatenation to add it to the end of the current value of translated.

caesarCipher.py
```
44.     else:
45.         # just add the symbol without encrypting/decrypting
46.         translated = translated + symbol
```

Line 44 has four spaces of indentation. If you look at the indentation of the lines above, you'll see that this means it comes after the if statement on line 26. There's a lot of code in between this if and else statement, but it all belongs in the block of code that follows the if statement on line 26. If that if statement's condition was False, then the block would have been skipped and the program execution would enter the else statement's block starting at line 46. (Line 45 is skipped because it is a comment.)

This block has just one line in it. It adds the symbol string as it is to the end of translated. This is how non-letter strings like ' ' or '.' are added to the translated string without being encrypted or decrypted.

Displaying and Copying the Encrypted/Decrypted String

caesarCipher.py
```
48. # print the encrypted/decrypted string to the screen
49. print(translated)
50.
51. # copy the encrypted/decrypted string to the clipboard
52. pyperclip.copy(translated)
```

Line 49 has no indentation, which means it is the first line after the block that started on line 26 (the for loop's block). By the time the program execution reaches line 49, it has looped through each character in the message string, encrypted (or decrypted) the characters, and added them to translated.

Line 49 will call the `print()` function to display the `translated` string on the screen. Notice that this is the only `print()` call in the entire program. The computer does a lot of work encrypting every letter in `message`, handling wrap-around, and handling non-letter characters. But the user doesn't need to see this. The user just needs to see the final string in `translated`.

Line 52 calls a function that is inside the `pyperclip` module. The function's name is `copy()` and it takes one string argument. Because `copy()` is a function in the `pyperclip` module, we have to tell Python this by putting `pyperclip.` in front of the function name. If we type `copy(translated)` instead of `pyperclip.copy(translated)`, Python will give us an error message.

You can see this error message for yourself by typing this code in the interactive shell:

```
>>> copy('Hello')
Traceback (most recent call last):
  File "<stdin>", line 1, in <module>
NameError: name 'copy' is not defined
>>>
```

Also, if you forget the `import pyperclip` line before trying to call `pyperclip.copy()`, Python will give an error message. Try typing this into the interactive shell:

```
>>> pyperclip.copy('Hello')
Traceback (most recent call last):
  File "<stdin>", line 1, in <module>
NameError: name 'pyperclip' is not defined
>>>
```

That's the entire Caesar cipher program. When you run it, notice how your computer can execute the entire program and encrypt the string in less than a second. Even if you type in a very, very long string for the value to store in the `message` variable, your computer can encrypt or decrypt a message within a second or two. Compare this to the several minutes it would take to do this with a cipher wheel or St. Cyr slide. The program even copies the encrypted text to the clipboard so the user can simply paste it into an email to send to someone.

Encrypt Non-Letter Characters

One problem with the Caesar cipher that we've implemented is that it cannot encrypt non-letters. For example, if you encrypt the string `'The password is 31337.'` with the key 20, it will encrypt to `'Dro zkccgybn sc 31337.'` This encrypted message doesn't keep the password in the message very secret. However, we can modify the program to encrypt other characters besides letters.

If you change the string that is stored in `LETTERS` to include more than just the uppercase letters, then the program will encrypt them as well. This is because on line 26, the condition `symbol in LETTERS` will be `True`. The value of `num` will be the index of symbol in this new, larger `LETTERS` constant variable. The "wrap-around" will need to add or subtract the number of characters in this new string, but that's already handled because we use `len(LETTERS)` instead of typing in `26` directly into the code. (This is why we programmed it this way.)

The only changes you have to make are to the `LETTERS` assignment statement on line 16 and commenting out line 22 which capitalizes all the letters in `message`.

caesarCipher.py

```
15. # every possible symbol that can be encrypted
16. LETTERS = ' !"#$%&\'()*+,-./0123456789:;<=>?@ABCDEFGHIJKLMNOPQRSTUVWXYZ[\\]^_`a bcdefghijklmnopqrstuvwxyz{|}~'
17.
18. # stores the encrypted/decrypted form of the message
19. translated = ''
20.
21. # capitalize the string in message
22. #message = message.upper()
```

Notice that this new string has the escape characters `\'` and `\\` in it. You can download this new version of the program from http://invpy.com/caesarCipher2.py.

This modification to our program is like if we had a cipher wheel or St. Cyr slide that had not only uppercase letters but numbers, punctuation, and lowercase letters on it as well.

Even though the value for `LETTERS` has to be the same when running the program for decryption as when it encrypted the message, this value doesn't have to be secret. Only the key needs to be kept secret, while the rest of program (including the code for the Caesar cipher program) can be shared with the world.

Summary

You've had to learn several programming concepts and read through quite a few chapters to get to this point, but now you have a program that implements a secret cipher. And more importantly, you can understand how this code works.

Modules are Python programs that contain useful functions we can use. To use these functions, you must first import them with an `import` statement. To call functions in an imported module, put the module name and a period before the function name, like: `module.function()`.

Constant variables are by convention written in UPPERCASE. These variables are not meant to have their value changed (although nothing prevents the programmer from writing code that does this). Constants are helpful because they give a "name" to specific values in your program.

Methods are functions that are attached to a value of a certain data type. The `upper()` and `lower()` string methods return an uppercase or lowercase version of the string they are called on. The `find()` string method returns an integer of where the string argument passed to it can be found in the string it is called on.

A `for` loop will iterate over all the characters in string value, setting a variable to each character on each iteration. The `if`, `elif`, and `else` statements can execute blocks of code based on whether a condition is `True` or `False`.

The `in` and `not in` operators can check if one string is or isn't in another string, and evaluates to `True` or `False` accordingly.

Knowing how to program gives you the power to take a process like the Caesar cipher and put it down in a language that a computer can understand. And once the computer understands how to do it, it can do it much faster than any human can and with no mistakes (unless there are mistakes in your programming.) This is an incredibly useful skill, but it turns out the Caesar cipher can easily be broken by someone who knows computer programming. In the next chapter we will use our skills to write a Caesar cipher "hacker" so we can read ciphertext that other people encrypted. So let's move on to the next chapter, and learn how to hack encryption.

CHAPTER 7

HACKING THE CAESAR CIPHER WITH THE BRUTE-FORCE TECHNIQUE

Topics Covered In This Chapter:

- Kerckhoffs's Principle and Shannon's Maxim
- The brute-force technique
- The `range()` function
- String formatting (string interpolation)

Hacking Ciphers

We can hack the Caesar cipher by using a cryptanalytic technique called "brute-force". Because our code breaking program is so effective against the Caesar cipher, you shouldn't use it to encrypt your secret information.

Ideally, the ciphertext would never fall into anyone's hands. But **Kerckhoffs's Principle** (named after the19th-century cryptographer Auguste Kerckhoffs) says that a cipher should still be secure even if everyone else knows how the cipher works and has the ciphertext (that is, everything except the key). This was restated by the 20th century mathematician Claude Shannon as **Shannon's Maxim**: "The enemy knows the system."

Figure 7-1. Auguste Kerckhoffs
January 19, 1835 - August 9, 1903

"A cryptosystem should be secure even if everything about the system, except the key, is public knowledge."

Figure 7-2. Claude Shannon
April 30, 1916 - February 24, 2001

"The enemy knows the system."

The Brute-Force Attack

Nothing stops a cryptanalyst from guessing one key, decrypting the ciphertext with that key, looking at the output, and if it was not the correct key then moving on to the next key. The technique of trying every possible decryption key is called a **brute-force attack**. It isn't a very sophisticated hack, but through sheer effort (which the computer will do for us) the Caesar cipher can be broken.

Source Code of the Caesar Cipher Hacker Program

Open a new file editor window by clicking on **File ► New Window**. Type in the following code into the file editor, and then save it as *caesarHacker.py*. Press **F5** to run the program. Note that first you will need to download the *pyperclip.py* module and place this file in the same directory as the *caesarHacker.py* file. You can download this file from http://invpy.com/pyperclip.py.

Source code for caesarHacker.py

```
# Caesar Cipher Hacker
# http://inventwithpython.com/hacking (BSD Licensed)

message = 'GUVF VF ZL FRPERG ZRFFNTR.'
```

```
LETTERS = 'ABCDEFGHIJKLMNOPQRSTUVWXYZ'

# loop through every possible key
for key in range(len(LETTERS)):

    # It is important to set translated to the blank string so that the
    # previous iteration's value for translated is cleared.
    translated = ''

    # The rest of the program is the same as the original Caesar program:

    # run the encryption/decryption code on each symbol in the message
    for symbol in message:
        if symbol in LETTERS:
            num = LETTERS.find(symbol) # get the number of the symbol
            num = num - key

            # handle the wrap-around if num is 26 or larger or less than 0
            if num < 0:
                num = num + len(LETTERS)

            # add number's symbol at the end of translated
            translated = translated + LETTERS[num]

        else:
            # just add the symbol without encrypting/decrypting
            translated = translated + symbol

    # display the current key being tested, along with its decryption
    print('Key #%s: %s' % (key, translated))
```

You will see that much of this code is the same as the code in the original Caesar cipher program. This is because the Caesar cipher hacker program does the same steps to decrypt the key.

Sample Run of the Caesar Cipher Hacker Program

Here is what the Caesar cipher program looks like when you run it. It is trying to break the ciphertext, "GUVF VF ZL FRPERG ZRFFNTR." Notice that the decrypted output for key 13 is plain English, so the original encryption key must have been 13.

```
Key #0: GUVF VF ZL FRPERG ZRFFNTR.
Key #1: FTUE UE YK EQODQF YQEEMSQ.
Key #2: ESTD TD XJ DPNCPE XPDDLRP.
Key #3: DRSC SC WI COMBOD WOCCKQO.
Key #4: CQRB RB VH BNLANC VNBBJPN.
```

```
Key #5: BPQA QA UG AMKZMB UMAAIOM.
Key #6: AOPZ PZ TF ZLJYLA TLZZHNL.
Key #7: ZNOY OY SE YKIXKZ SKYYGMK.
Key #8: YMNX NX RD XJHWJY RJXXFLJ.
Key #9: XLMW MW QC WIGVIX QIWWEKI.
Key #10: WKLV LV PB VHFUHW PHVVDJH.
Key #11: VJKU KU OA UGETGV OGUUCIG.
Key #12: UIJT JT NZ TFDSFU NFTTBHF.
Key #13: THIS IS MY SECRET MESSAGE.
Key #14: SGHR HR LX RDBQDS LDRRZFD.
Key #15: RFGQ GQ KW QCAPCR KCQQYEC.
Key #16: QEFP FP JV PBZOBQ JBPPXDB.
Key #17: PDEO EO IU OAYNAP IAOOWCA.
Key #18: OCDN DN HT NZXMZO HZNNVBZ.
Key #19: NBCM CM GS MYWLYN GYMMUAY.
Key #20: MABL BL FR LXVKXM FXLLTZX.
Key #21: LZAK AK EQ KWUJWL EWKKSYW.
Key #22: KYZJ ZJ DP JVTIVK DVJJRXV.
Key #23: JXYI YI CO IUSHUJ CUIIQWU.
Key #24: IWXH XH BN HTRGTI BTHHPVT.
Key #25: HVWG WG AM GSQFSH ASGGOUS.
```

How the Program Works

caesarHacker.py

```
# Caesar Cipher Hacker
# http://inventwithpython.com/hacking (BSD Licensed)

message = 'GUVF VF ZL FRPERG ZRFFNTR.'
LETTERS = 'ABCDEFGHIJKLMNOPQRSTUVWXYZ'
```

The hacker program will create a `message` variable that stores the ciphertext string the program tries to decrypt. The `LETTERS` constant variable contains every character that can be encrypted with the cipher. The value for `LETTERS` needs to be exactly the same as the value for `LETTERS` used in the Caesar cipher program that encrypted the ciphertext we are trying to hack, otherwise the hacker program won't work.

The `range()` Function

caesarHacker.py

```
# loop through every possible key
for key in range(len(LETTERS)):
```

Line 8 is a `for` loop that does not iterate over a string value, but instead iterates over the return value from a call to a function named `range()`. The `range()` function takes one integer argument and returns a value of the range data type. These range values can be used in `for` loops to loop a specific number of times. Try typing the following into the interactive shell:

```
>>> for i in range(4):
...     print('Hello')
...
Hello
Hello
Hello
Hello
>>>
```

More specifically, the range value returned from the `range()` function call will set the `for` loop's variable to the integers `0` up to, but not including, the argument passed to `range()`. Try typing the following into the interactive shell:

```
>>> for i in range(6):
...     print(i)
...
0
1
2
3
4
5
>>>
```

Line 8 is a `for` loop that will set the `key` variable with the values `0` up to (but not including) `26`. Instead of hard-coding the value `26` directly into our program, we use the return value from `len(LETTERS)` so that if we modify `LETTERS` the program will still work. See the "Encrypt Non-Letter Characters" section in the last chapter to read why.

So the first time the program execution goes through this loop, `key` will be set to `0` and the ciphertext in `message` will be decrypted with key `0`. (The code inside the `for` loop does the decrypting.) On the next iteration of line 8's `for` loop, `key` will be set to `1` for the decryption.

You can also pass two integer arguments to the `range()` function instead of just one. The first argument is where the range should start and the second argument is where the range should stop (up to but not including the second argument). The arguments are separated by a comma:

```
>>> for i in range(2, 6):
...   print(i)
...
2
3
4
5
>>>
```

The `range()` call evaluates to a value of the "range object" data type.

Back to the Code

caesarHacker.py

```
 7. # loop through every possible key
 8. for key in range(len(LETTERS)):
 9.
10.     # It is important to set translated to the blank string so that the
11.     # previous iteration's value for translated is cleared.
12.     translated = ''
```

On line 12, `translated` is set to the blank string. The decryption code on the next few lines adds the decrypted text to the end of the string in `translated`. It is important that we reset translated to the blank string at the beginning of this `for` loop, otherwise the decrypted text will be added to the decrypted text in `translated` from the last iteration in the loop.

caesarHacker.py

```
14.     # The rest of the program is the same as the original Caesar program:
15.
16.     # run the encryption/decryption code on each symbol in the message
17.     for symbol in message:
18.         if symbol in LETTERS:
19.             num = LETTERS.find(symbol) # get the number of the symbol
```

Lines 17 to 31 are almost exactly the same as the code in the Caesar cipher program from the last chapter. It is slightly simpler, because this code only has to decrypt instead of decrypt or encrypt.

First we loop through every symbol in the ciphertext string stored in `message` on line 17. On each iteration of this loop, line 18 checks if `symbol` is an uppercase letter (that is, it exists in the `LETTERS` constant variable which only has uppercase letters) and, if so, decrypts it. Line 19 locates where `symbol` is in `LETTERS` with the `find()` method and stores it in a variable called `num`.

caesarHacker.py

```
20.             num = num - key
21.
22.             # handle the wrap-around if num is 26 or larger or less than 0
23.             if num < 0:
24.                 num = num + len(LETTERS)
```

Then we subtract the key from `num` on line 20. (Remember, in the Caesar cipher, subtracting the key decrypts and adding the key encrypts.) This may cause `num` to be less than zero and require "wrap-around". Line 23 checks for this case and adds `26` (which is what `len(LETTERS)` returns) if it was less than `0`.

caesarHacker.py

```
26.             # add number's symbol at the end of translated
27.             translated = translated + LETTERS[num]
```

Now that `num` has been modified, `LETTERS[num]` will evaluate to the decrypted symbol. Line 27 adds this symbol to the end of the string stored in `translated`.

caesarHacker.py

```
29.         else:
30.             # just add the symbol without encrypting/decrypting
31.             translated = translated + symbol
```

Of course, if the condition for line 18's condition was `False` and `symbol` was not in `LETTERS`, we don't decrypt the symbol at all. If you look at the indentation of line 29's `else` statement, you can see that this `else` statement matches the `if` statement on line 18.

Line 31 just adds `symbol` to the end of `translated` unmodified.

String Formatting

caesarHacker.py

```
33.     # display the current key being tested, along with its decryption
34.     print('Key #%s: %s' % (key, translated))
```

Although line 34 is the only `print()` function call in our Caesar cipher hacker program, it will print out several lines because it gets called once per iteration of line 8's `for` loop.

The argument for the `print()` function call is something we haven't used before. It is a string value that makes use of **string formatting** (also called **string interpolation**). String formatting with the `%s` text is a way of placing one string inside another one. The first `%s` text in the string gets replaced by the first value in the parentheses after the `%` at the end of the string.

Type the following into the interactive shell:

```
>>> 'Hello %s!' % ('world')
'Hello world!'
>>> 'Hello ' + 'world' + '!'
'Hello world!'
>>> 'The %s ate the %s that ate the %s.' % ('dog', 'cat', 'rat')
'The dog ate the cat that ate the rat.'
>>>
```

String formatting is often easier to type than string concatenation with the + operator, especially for larger strings. And one benefit of string formatting is that, unlike string concatenation, you can insert non-string values such as integers into the string. Try typing the following into the interactive shell:

```
>>> '%s had %s pies.' % ('Alice', 42)
'Alice had 42 pies.'
>>> 'Alice' + ' had ' + 42 + ' pies.'
Traceback (most recent call last):
  File "<stdin>", line 1, in <module>
TypeError: Can't convert 'int' object to str implicitly
>>>
```

Line 34 uses string formatting to create a string that has the values in both the `key` and `translated` variables. Because `key` stores an integer value, we'll use string formatting to put it in a string value that is passed to `print()`.

Practice Exercises, Chapter 7, Set A

Practice exercises can be found at http://invpy.com/hackingpractice7A.

Summary

The critical failure of the Caesar cipher is that there aren't that many different possible keys that can be used to encrypt a message. Any computer can easily decrypt with all 26 possible keys, and it only takes the cryptanalyst a few seconds to look through them to find the one that is in English. To make our messages more secure, we will need a cipher that has more possible keys. That transposition cipher in the next chapter can provide this for us.

ENCRYPTING WITH THE TRANSPOSITION CIPHER

Topics Covered In This Chapter:

- Creating functions with `def` statements.
- `main()` functions
- Parameters
- The global and local scope, and global and local variables
- The `global` statement
- The list data type, and how lists and strings are similar
- The `list()` function
- Lists of lists
- Augmented assignment operators (+=, -=, *=, /=)
- The `join()` string method
- Return values and the `return` statement
- The special `__name__` variable

The Caesar cipher isn't secure. It doesn't take much for a computer to brute-force through all twenty-six possible keys. The transposition cipher has many more possible keys to make a brute-force attack more difficult.

Encrypting with the Transposition Cipher

Instead of replacing characters with other characters, the transposition cipher jumbles up the message's symbols into an order that makes the original message unreadable. Before we start writing code, let's encrypt the message "Common sense is not so common." with pencil and paper. Including the spaces and punctuation, this message has 30 characters. We will use the number 8 for the key.

The first step is to draw out a number of boxes equal to the key. We will draw 8 boxes since our key for this example is 8:

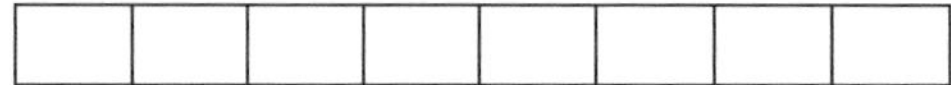

The second step is to start writing the message you want to encrypt into the boxes, with one character for each box. Remember that spaces are a character (this book marks the boxes with (s) to indicate a space so it doesn't look like an empty box).

C	o	m	m	o	n	(s)	s

We only have 8 boxes but there are 30 characters in the message. When you run out of boxes, draw another row of 8 boxes under the first row. Keep creating new rows until you have written out the full message:

1st	2nd	3rd	4th	5th	6th	7th	8th
C	o	m	m	o	n	(s)	s
e	n	s	e	(s)	i	s	(s)
n	o	t	(s)	s	o	(s)	c
o	m	m	o	n	.		

We shade in the two boxes in the last row to remind us to ignore them. The ciphertext is the letters read from the top left box going down the column. "C", "e", "n", and "o" are from the 1st column. When you get to the last row of a column, move to the top row of the next column to the right. The next characters are "o", "n", "o", "m". Ignore the shaded boxes.

The ciphertext is "Cenoonommstmme oo snnio. s s c", which is sufficiently scrambled to keep someone from figuring out the original message by looking at it.

The steps for encrypting are:

1. Count the number of characters in the message and the key.
2. Draw a number of boxes equal to the key in a single row. (For example, 12 boxes for a key of 12.)
3. Start filling in the boxes from left to right, with one character per box.
4. When you run out of boxes and still have characters left, add another row of boxes.

5. Shade in the unused boxes in the last row.
6. Starting from the top left and going down, write out the characters. When you get to the bottom of the column, move to the next column to the right. Skip any shaded boxes. This will be the ciphertext.

Practice Exercises, Chapter 8, Set A

Practice exercises can be found at http://invpy.com/hackingpractice8A.

A Transposition Cipher Encryption Program

Encrypting with paper and pencil involves a lot of work and it's easy to make mistakes. Let's look at a program that can implement transposition cipher encryption (a decryption program will be demonstrated later in this chapter).

Using the computer program has a slight problem, however. If the ciphertext has space characters at the end, then it is impossible to see them since a space is just empty… well, space. To fix this, the program adds a `|` character at the end of the ciphertext. (The `|` character is called the "pipe" character and is above the Enter key on your keyboard.) For example:

```
Hello|   # There are no spaces at the end of the message.
Hello |  # There is one space at the end of the message.
Hello  | # There are two spaces at the end of the message.
```

Source Code of the Transposition Cipher Encryption Program

Open a new file editor window by clicking on **File ► New Window**. Type in the following code into the file editor, and then save it as *transpositionEncrypt.py*. Press **F5** to run the program. Note that first you will need to download the *pyperclip.py* module and place this file in the same directory as the *transpositionEncrypt.py* file. You can download this file from http://invpy.com/pyperclip.py.

Source code for transpositionEncrypt.py

```
# Transposition Cipher Encryption
# http://inventwithpython.com/hacking (BSD Licensed)

import pyperclip

def main():
    myMessage = 'Common sense is not so common.'
    myKey = 8

    ciphertext = encryptMessage(myKey, myMessage)
```

```

    # Print the encrypted string in ciphertext to the screen, with
    # a | (called "pipe" character) after it in case there are spaces at
    # the end of the encrypted message.
    print(ciphertext + '|')

    # Copy the encrypted string in ciphertext to the clipboard.
    pyperclip.copy(ciphertext)


def encryptMessage(key, message):
    # Each string in ciphertext represents a column in the grid.
    ciphertext = [''] * key

    # Loop through each column in ciphertext.
    for col in range(key):
        pointer = col

        # Keep looping until pointer goes past the length of the message.
        while pointer < len(message):
            # Place the character at pointer in message at the end of the
            # current column in the ciphertext list.
            ciphertext[col] += message[pointer]

            # move pointer over
            pointer += key

    # Convert the ciphertext list into a single string value and return it.
    return ''.join(ciphertext)


# If transpositionEncrypt.py is run (instead of imported as a module) call
# the main() function.
if __name__ == '__main__':
    main()
```

Sample Run of the Transposition Cipher Encryption Program

When you run the above program, it produces this output:

```
Cenoonommstmme oo snnio. s s c|
```

This ciphertext (without the pipe character at the end) is also copied to the clipboard, so you can paste it into an email to someone. If you want to encrypt a different message or use a different key, change the value assigned to the `myMessage` and `myKey` variables on lines 7 and 8. Then run the program again.

How the Program Works

transpositionEncrypt.py

```
1. # Transposition Cipher Encryption
2. # http://inventwithpython.com/hacking (BSD Licensed)
3.
4. import pyperclip
```

The transposition cipher program, like the Caesar cipher program, will copy the encrypted text to the clipboard. So first we will import the `pyperclip` module so it can call `pyperclip.copy()`.

Creating Your Own Functions with `def` Statements

transpositionEncrypt.py

```
6. def main():
7.     myMessage = 'Common sense is not so common.'
8.     myKey = 8
```

A function (like `print()`) is a sort of mini-program in your program. When the function is called, the execution moves to the code inside that function and then returns to the line after the function call. You can create your own functions with a `def` statement like the one on line 6.

The `def` statement on line 6 isn't a call to a function named `main()`. Instead, the `def` statement means we are creating, or **defining**, a new function named `main()` that we can call later in our program. When the execution reaches the `def` statement Python will *define* this function. We can then call it the same way we call other functions. When we *call* this function, the execution moves inside of the block of code following the `def` statement.

Open a new file editor window and type the following code into it:

Source code for helloFunction.py

```
def hello():
    print('Hello!')
    total = 42 + 1
    print('42 plus 1 is %s' % (total))
print('Start!')
hello()
print('Call it again.')
hello()
```

```
9. print('Done.')
```

Save this program with the name *helloFunction.py* and run it by pressing **F5**. The output looks like this:

```
Start!
Hello!
42 plus 1 is 43
Call it again.
Hello!
42 plus 1 is 43
Done.
```

When the *helloFunction.py* program runs, the execution starts at the top. The first line is a `def` statement that defines the `hello()` function. The execution skips the block after the `def` statement and executes the `print('Start!')` line. This is why `'Start!'` is the first string printed when we run the program.

The next line after `print('Start!')` is a function call to our `hello()` function. The program execution jumps to the first line in the `hello()` function's block on line 2. This function will cause the strings `'Hello!'` and `'42 plus 1 is 43'` to be printed to the screen.

When the program execution reaches the bottom of the `def` statement, the execution will jump back to the line after the line that originally called the function (line 7). In *helloFunction.py*, this is the `print('Call it again.')` line. Line 8 is *another* call to the `hello()` function. The program execution will jump back into the `hello()` function and execute the code there again. This is why `'Hello!'` and `'42 plus 1 is 43'` are displayed on the screen two times.

After that function returns to line 9, the `print('Done.')` line executes. This is the last line in our program, so the program exits.

The Program's `main()` Function

transpositionEncrypt.py

```
def main():
    myMessage = 'Common sense is not so common.'
    myKey = 8
```

The rest of the programs in this book have a function named `main()` which is called at the start of program. The reason is explained at the end of this chapter, but for now just know that the `main()` function in the programs in this book are always called soon after the programs are run.

On lines 7 and 8, the variables `myMessage` and `myKey` will store the plaintext message to encrypt and the key used to do the encryption.

transpositionEncrypt.py
```
10.     ciphertext = encryptMessage(myKey, myMessage)
```

The code that does the actual encrypting will be put into a function we define on line 21 named `encryptMessage()`. This function will take two arguments: an integer value for the key and a string value for the message to encrypt. When passing multiple arguments to a function call, separate the arguments with a comma.

The return value of `encryptMessage()` will be a string value of the encrypted ciphertext. (The code in this function is explained next.) This string will be stored in a variable named `ciphertext`.

transpositionEncrypt.py
```
12.     # Print the encrypted string in ciphertext to the screen, with
13.     # a | (called "pipe" character) after it in case there are spaces at
14.     # the end of the encrypted message.
15.     print(ciphertext + '|')
16.
17.     # Copy the encrypted string in ciphertext to the clipboard.
18.     pyperclip.copy(ciphertext)
```

The ciphertext message is printed to the screen on line 15 and copied to the clipboard on line 18. The program prints a | character (called the "pipe" character) at the end of the message so that the user can see any empty space characters at the end of the ciphertext.

Line 18 is the last line of the `main()` function. After it executes, the program execution will return to the line after the line that called it. The call to `main()` is on line 45 and is the last line in the program, so after execution returns from `main()` the program will exit.

Parameters

transpositionEncrypt.py
```
21. def encryptMessage(key, message):
```

The code in the `encryptMessage()` function does the actual encryption. The `key` and `message` text in between the parentheses next to `encryptMessage()`'s `def` statement shows that the `encryptMessage()` function takes two parameters.

Parameters are the variables that contain the arguments passed when a function is called. Parameters are automatically deleted when the function returns. (This is just like how variables are forgotten when a program exits.)

When the `encryptMessage()` function gets called from line 10, two argument values are passed (on line 10, they are the values in `myKey` and `myMessage`). These values get assigned to the parameters `key` and `message` (which you can see on line 21) when the execution moves to the top of the function.

A parameter is a variable name in between the parentheses in the `def` statement. An argument is a value that is passed in between the parentheses for a function call.

Python will raise an error message if you try to call a function with too many or too few arguments for the number of parameters the function has. Try typing the following into the interactive shell:

```
>>> len('hello', 'world')
Traceback (most recent call last):
  File "<stdin>", line 1, in <module>
TypeError: len() takes exactly one argument (2 given)
>>> len()
Traceback (most recent call last):
  File "<stdin>", line 1, in <module>
TypeError: len() takes exactly one argument (0 given)
>>>
```

Changes to Parameters Only Exist Inside the Function

Look at the following program, which defines and then calls a function named `func()`:

```
def func(param):
    param = 42
spam = 'Hello'
func(spam)
print(spam)
```

When you run this program, the `print()` call on the last line will print out `'Hello'`, not `42`. When `func()` is called with `spam` as the argument, the `spam` variable is not being sent into the `func()` function and having `42` assigned to it. Instead, the value inside `spam` is being copied and assigned to `param`. Any changes made to `param` inside the function will **not** change the value in the `spam` variable.

(There is an exception to this rule when you are passing something called a list or dictionary value, but this will be explained in chapter 10 in the "List References" section.)

This is an important idea to understand. The argument value that is "passed" in a function call is *copied* to the parameter. So if the parameter is changed, the variable that provided the argument value is not changed.

Variables in the Global and Local Scope

You might wonder why we even have the `key` and `message` parameters to begin with, since we already have the variables `myKey` and `myMessage` from the `main()` function. The reason is because `myKey` and `myMessage` are in the `main()` function's local scope and can't be used outside of the `main()` function.

Every time a function is called, a **local scope** is created. Variables created during a function call exist in this local scope. Parameters always exist in a local scope. When the function returns, the local scope is destroyed and the local variables are forgotten. A variable in the local scope is still a separate variable from a global scope variable even if the two variables have the same name.

Variables created outside of every function exist in the **global scope**. When the program exits, the global scope is destroyed and all the variables in the program are forgotten. (All the variables in the reverse cipher and Caesar cipher programs were global.)

The `global` Statement

If you want a variable that is assigned inside a function to be a global variable instead of a local variable, put a `global` statement with the variable's name as the first line after the `def` statement.

Here are the rules for whether a variable is a global variable (that is, a variable that exists in the global scope) or local variable (that is, a variable that exists in a function call's local scope):

1. Variables outside of all functions are always global variables.
2. If a variable in a function is never used in an assignment statement, it is a global variable.
3. If a variable in a function is not used in a `global` statement and but is used in an assignment statement, it is a local variable.
4. If a variable in a function is used in a `global` statement, it is a global variable when used in that function.

For example, type in the following short program, save it as *scope.py*, and press **F5** to run it:

Source code for scope.py

```
 1. spam = 42
 2.
 3. def eggs():
 4.     spam = 99 # spam in this function is local
 5.     print('In eggs():', spam)
 6.
 7. def ham():
 8.     print('In ham():', spam) # spam in this function is global
 9.
10. def bacon():
11.     global spam # spam in this function is global
12.     print('In bacon():', spam)
13.     spam = 0
14.
15. def CRASH():
16.     print(spam) # spam in this function is local
17.     spam = 0
18.
19. print(spam)
20. eggs()
21. print(spam)
22. ham()
23. print(spam)
24. bacon()
25. print(spam)
26. CRASH()
```

The program will crash when Python executes line 16, and the output will look like this:

```
42
In eggs(): 99
42
In ham(): 42
42
In bacon(): 42
0
Traceback (most recent call last):
  File "C:\scope.py", line 27, in <module>
    CRASH()
  File "C:\scope.py", line 16, in CRASH
    print(spam)
UnboundLocalError: local variable 'spam' referenced before assignment
```

When the spam variable is used on lines 1, 19, 21, 23, 25 it is outside of all functions, so this is the global variable named spam. In the eggs() function, the spam variable is assigned the integer 99 on line 4, so Python regards this spam variable as a local variable named spam. Python considers this local variable to be completely different from the global variable that is also named spam. Being assigned 99 on line 4 has no effect on the value stored in the global spam variable since they are different variables (they just happen to have the same name).

The spam variable in the ham() function on line 8 is never used in an assignment statement in that function, so it is the global variable spam.

The spam variable in the bacon() function is used in a global statement, so we know it is the global variable named spam. The spam = 0 assignment statement on line 13 will change the value of the global spam variable.

The spam variable in the CRASH() function is used in an assignment statement (and not in a global statement) so the spam variable in that function is a local variable. However, notice that it is used in the print() function call on line 16 before it is assigned a value on line 17. This is why calling the CRASH() function causes our program to crash with the error, UnboundLocalError: local variable 'spam' referenced before assignment.

It can be confusing to have global and local variables with the same name, so even if you remember the rules for how to tell global and local variables apart, you would be better off using different names.

Practice Exercises, Chapter 8, Set B

Practice exercises can be found at http://invpy.com/hackingpractice8B.

The List Data Type

transpositionEncrypt.py

```
22.     # Each string in ciphertext represents a column in the grid.
23.     ciphertext = [''] * key
```

Line 23 uses a new data type called the **list** data type. A list value can contain other values. Just like how strings begin and end with quotes, a list value begins with a [open bracket and ends with] close bracket. The values stored inside the list are typed within the brackets. If there is more than one value in the list, the values are separated by commas.

Type the following into the interactive shell:

```
>>> animals = ['aardvark', 'anteater', 'antelope', 'albert']
>>> animals
['aardvark', 'anteater', 'antelope', 'albert']
>>>
```

The `animals` variable stores a list value, and in this list value are four string values. The individual values inside of a list are also called **items**. Lists are very good when we have to store lots and lots of values, but we don't want variables for each one. Otherwise we would have something like this:

```
>>> animals1 = 'aardvark'
>>> animals2 = 'anteater'
>>> animals3 = 'antelope'
>>> animals4 = 'albert'
>>>
```

This makes working with all the strings as a group very hard, especially if you have hundreds, thousands, or millions of different values that you want stored in a list.

Many of the things you can do with strings will also work with lists. For example, indexing and slicing work on list values the same way they work on string values. Instead of individual characters in a string, the index refers to an item in a list. Try typing the following into the interactive shell:

```
>>> animals = ['aardvark', 'anteater', 'antelope', 'albert']
>>> animals[0]
'aardvark'
>>> animals[1]
'anteater'
>>> animals[2]
'antelope'
>>> animals[3]
'albert'
>>> animals[1:3]
['anteater', 'antelope']
>>>
```

Remember, the first index is `0` and not `1`. While using slices with a string value will give you a string value of part of the original string, using slices with a list value will give you a list value of part of the original list.

A `for` loop can also iterate over the values in a list, just like it iterates over the characters in a string. The value that is stored in the `for` loop's variable is a single value from the list. Try typing the following into the interactive shell:

```
>>> for spam in ['aardvark', 'anteater', 'antelope', 'albert']:
...   print('For dinner we are cooking ' + spam)
...
For dinner we are cooking aardvark
For dinner we are cooking anteater
For dinner we are cooking antelope
For dinner we are cooking albert
>>>
```

Using the `list()` Function to Convert Range Objects to Lists

If you need a list value that has increasing integer amounts, you could have code like this to build up a list value using a `for` loop:

```
>>> myList = []
>>> for i in range(10):
...   myList = myList + [i]
...
>>> myList
[0, 1, 2, 3, 4, 5, 6, 7, 8, 9]
>>>
```

However, it is simpler to directly make a list from a range object that the `range()` function returned by using the `list()` function:

```
>>> myList = list(range(10))
>>> myList
[0, 1, 2, 3, 4, 5, 6, 7, 8, 9]
>>>
```

The `list()` function can also convert strings into a list value. The list will have several single-character strings that were in the original string:

```
>>> myList = list('Hello world!')
>>> myList
['H', 'e', 'l', 'l', 'o', ' ', 'w', 'o', 'r', 'l', 'd', '!']
>>>
```

We won't be using the `list()` function on strings or range objects in this program, but it will come up in later in this book.

Reassigning the Items in Lists

The items inside a list can also be modified. Use the index with a normal assignment statement. Try typing the following into the interactive shell:

```
>>> animals = ['aardvark', 'anteater', 'antelope', 'albert']
>>> animals
['aardvark', 'anteater', 'antelope', 'albert']
>>> animals[2] = 9999
>>> animals
['aardvark', 'anteater', 9999, 'albert']
>>>
```

Reassigning Characters in Strings

While you can reassign items in a list, you cannot reassign a character in a string value. Try typing the following code into the interactive shell to cause this error:

```
>>> 'Hello world!'[6] = 'x'
Traceback (most recent call last):
  File "<stdin>", line 1, in <module>
TypeError: 'str' object does not support item assignment
>>>
```

To change a character in a string, use slicing instead. Try typing the following into the interactive shell:

```
>>> spam = 'Hello world!'
>>> spam = spam[:6] + 'x' + spam[7:]
>>> spam
'Hello xorld!'
>>>
```

Lists of Lists

List values can even contain other list values. Try typing the following into the interactive shell:

```
>>> spam = [['dog', 'cat'], [1, 2, 3]]
>>> spam[0]
['dog', 'cat']
>>> spam[0][0]
```

```
'dog'
>>> spam[0][1]
'cat'
>>> spam[1][0]
1
>>> spam[1][1]
2
>>>
```

The double index brackets used for `spam[0][0]` work because `spam[0]` evaluates to `['dog', 'cat']` and `['dog', 'cat'][0]` evaluates to `'dog'`. You could even use another set of index brackets, since string values also use them:

```
>>> spam = [['dog', 'cat'], [1, 2, 3]]
>>> spam[0][1][1]
'a'
>>>
```

Say we had a list of lists stored in a variable named `x`. Here are the indexes for each of the items in `x`. Notice that `x[0]`, `x[1]`, `x[2]`, and `x[3]` refer to list values:

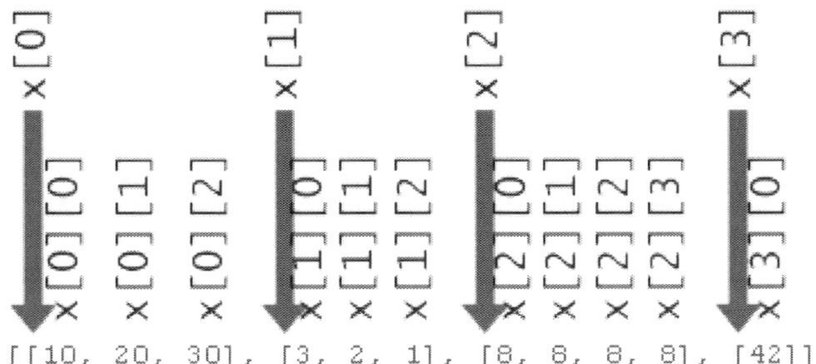

Figure 8-1. A list of lists with every item's index labeled.

Practice Exercises, Chapter 8, Set C

Practice exercises can be found at http://invpy.com/hackingpractice8C.

Using `len()` and the `in` Operator with Lists

We've used the `len()` function to tell us how many characters are in a string (that is, the length of the string). The `len()` function also works on list values and returns an integer of how many items are in the list.

Try typing the following into the interactive shell:

```
>>> animals = ['aardvark', 'anteater', 'antelope', 'albert']
>>> len(animals)
4
>>>
```

We've used the `in` operator to tell us if a string exists inside another string value. The `in` operator also works for checking if a value exists in a list. Try typing the following into the interactive shell:

```
>>> animals = ['aardvark', 'anteater', 'antelope', 'albert']
>>> 'anteater' in animals
True
>>> 'anteater' not in animals
False
>>> 'anteat' in animals
False
>>> 'delicious spam' in animals
False
>>>
```

Just like how a set of quotes next to each other represents the blank string value, a set of brackets next to each other represents a blank list. Try typing the following into the interactive shell:

```
>>> animals = []
>>> len(animals)
0
>>>
```

List Concatenation and Replication with the + and * Operators

Just like how the + and * operators can concatenate and replicate strings, the same operators can concatenate and replicate lists. Try typing the following into the interactive shell:

```
>>> ['hello'] + ['world']
['hello', 'world']
>>> ['hello'] * 5
['hello', 'hello', 'hello', 'hello', 'hello']
>>>
```

That's enough about the similarities between strings and lists. Just remember that most things you can do with string values will also work with list values.

Practice Exercises, Chapter 8, Set D

Practice exercises can be found at http://invpy.com/hackingpractice8D.

The Transposition Encryption Algorithm

We need to translate these paper-and-pencil steps into Python code. Let's take a look at encrypting the string `'Common sense is not so common.'` with the key `8`. If we wrote out the boxes with pencil and paper, it would look like this:

C	o	m	m	o	n	(s)	s
e	n	s	e	(s)	i	s	(s)
n	o	t	(s)	s	o	(s)	c
o	m	m	o	n	.		

Add the index of each letter in the string to the boxes. (Remember, indexes begin with `0`, not `1`.)

C 0	o 1	m 2	m 3	o 4	n 5	(s) 6	s 7
e 8	n 9	s 10	e 11	(s) 12	i 13	s 14	(s) 15
n 16	o 17	t 18	(s) 19	s 20	o 21	(s) 22	c 23
o 24	m 25	m 26	o 27	n 28	. 29		

We can see from these boxes that the first column has the characters at indexes `0`, `8`, `16`, and `24` (which are `'C'`, `'e'`, `'n'`, and `'o'`). The next column has the characters at indexes `1`, `9`, `17`, and `25` (which are `'o'`, `'n'`, `'o'` and `'m'`). We can see a pattern emerging: The nth column will have all the characters in the string at indexes 0 + n, 8 + n, 16 + n, and 24 + n:

C 0+0=0	o 1+0=1	m 2+0=2	m 3+0=3	o 4+0=4	n 5+0=5	(s) 6+0=6	s 7+0=7
e 0+8=8	n 1+8=9	s 2+8=10	e 3+8=11	(s) 4+8=12	i 5+8=13	s 6+8=14	(s) 7+8=15
n 0+16=16	o 1+16=17	t 2+16=18	(s) 3+16=19	s 4+16=20	o 5+16=21	(s) 6+16=22	c 7+16=23
o 0+24=24	m 1+24=25	m 2+24=26	o 3+24=27	n 4+24=28	. 5+24=29		

There is an exception for the 6th and 7th columns, since 24 + 6 and 24 + 7 are greater than 29, which is the largest index in our string. In those cases, we only use 0, 8, and 16 to add to n (and skip 24).

What's so special about the numbers 0, 8, 16, and 24? These are the numbers we get when, starting from 0, we add the key (which in this example is 8). 0 + 8 is 8, 8 + 8 is 16, 16 + 8 is 24. 24 + 8 would be 32, but since 32 is larger than the length of the message, we stop at 24.

So, for the nth column's string we start at index n, and then keep adding 8 (which is the key) to get the next index. We keep adding 8 as long as the index is less than 30 (the message length), at which point we move to the next column.

If we imagine a list of 8 strings where each string is made up of the characters in each column, then the list value would look like this:

```
['Ceno', 'onom', 'mstm', 'me o', 'o sn', 'nio.', ' s ', 's c']
```

This is how we can simulate the boxes in Python code. First, we will make a list of blank strings. This list will have a number of blank strings equal to the key because each string will represent a column of our paper-and-pencil boxes. (Our list will have 8 blank strings since we are using the key 8 in our example.) Let's look at the code.

transpositionEncrypt.py

```
    # Each string in ciphertext represents a column in the grid.
    ciphertext = [''] * key
```

The `ciphertext` variable will be a list of string values. Each string in the `ciphertext` variable will represent a column of the grid. So `ciphertext[0]` is the leftmost column, `ciphertext[1]` is the column to the right of that, and so on.

The string values will have all the characters that go into one column of the grid. Let's look again at the grid from the "Common sense is not so common." example earlier in this chapter (with column numbers added to the top):

0	1	2	3	4	5	6	7
C	o	m	m	o	n	(s)	s
e	n	s	e	(s)	i	s	(s)
n	o	t	(s)	s	o	(s)	c
o	m	m	o	n	.		

The `ciphertext` variable for this grid would look like this:

```
>>> ciphertext = ['Ceno', 'onom', 'mstm', 'me o', 'o sn', 'nio.', ' s ', 's c']
>>> ciphertext[0]
'Ceno'
```

The first step to making this list is to create as many blank strings in the `ciphertext` list as there are columns. Since the number of columns is equal to the key, we can use list replication to multiply a list with one blank string value in it by the value in `key`. This is how line 23 evaluates to a list with the correct number of blank strings.

transpositionEncrypt.py

```
25.     # Loop through each column in ciphertext.
26.     for col in range(key):
27.         pointer = col
```

The next step is to add text to each string in `ciphertext`. The `for` loop on line 26 will iterate once for each column, and the `col` variable will have the correct integer value to use for the index to `ciphertext`. The `col` variable will be set to `0` for the first iteration through the `for` loop, then `1` on the second iteration, then `2` and so on. This way the expression `ciphertext[col]` will be the string for the `col`th column of the grid.

Meanwhile, the `pointer` variable will be used as the index for the string value in the `message` variable. On each iteration through the loop, `pointer` will start at the same value as `col` (which is what line 27 does.)

Augmented Assignment Operators

Often when you are assigning a new value to a variable, you want it to be based off of the variable's current value. To do this you use the variable as the part of the expression that is evaluated and assigned to the variable, like this example in the interactive shell:

```
>>> spam = 40
>>> spam = spam + 2
>>> print(spam)
42
>>>
```

But you can instead use the += augmented assignment operator as a shortcut. Try typing the following into the interactive shell:

```
>>> spam = 40
>>> spam += 2
>>> print(spam)
42
>>> spam = 'Hello'
>>> spam += ' world!'
>>> print(spam)
Hello world!
```

```
>>> spam = ['dog']
>>> spam += ['cat']
>>> print(spam)
['dog', 'cat']
>>>
```

The statement `spam += 2` does the *exact same thing* as `spam = spam + 2`. It's just a little shorter to type. The += operator works with integers to do addition, strings to do string concatenation, and lists to do list concatenation. Table 8-1 shows the augmented assignment operators and what they are equivalent to:

Table 8-1. Augmented Assignment Operators

Augmented Assignment	Equivalent Normal Assignment
`spam += 42`	`spam = spam + 42`
`spam -= 42`	`spam = spam - 42`
`spam *= 42`	`spam = spam * 42`
`spam /= 42`	`spam = spam / 42`

Back to the Code

transpositionEncrypt.py

```
29.         # Keep looping until pointer goes past the length of the message.
30.         while pointer < len(message):
31.             # Place the character at pointer in message at the end of the
32.             # current column in the ciphertext list.
33.             ciphertext[col] += message[pointer]
34.
35.             # move pointer over
36.             pointer += key
```

Inside the `for` loop that started on line 26 is a `while` loop that starts on line 30. For each column, we want to loop through the original `message` variable and pick out every `key`th character. (In the example we've been using, we want every 8th character since we are using a key of `8`.) On line 27 for the first iteration of the `for` loop, `pointer` was set to `0`.

While the value in `pointer` is less than the length of the `message` string, we want to add the character at `message[pointer]` to the end of the `col`th string in `ciphertext`. We add `8` (that is, the value in `key`) to `pointer` each time through the loop on line 36. The first time it is `message[0]`, the second time `message[8]`, the third time `message[16]`, and the fourth time `message[24]`. Each of these single character strings are concatenated to the end of `ciphertext[col]` (and since `col` is `0` on the first time through the loop, this is `ciphertext[0]`).

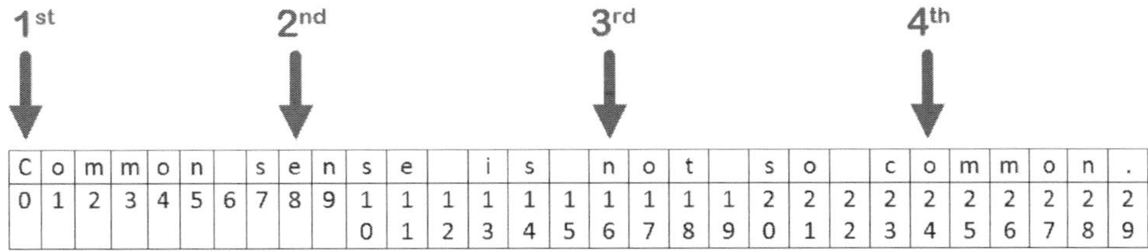

Figure 8-2. Arrows pointing to what `message[pointer]` refers to during the first iteration of the for loop when col is set to `0`.

Figure 8-2 shows the characters at these indexes, they will be concatenated together to form the string `'Ceno'`. Remember that we want the value in ciphertext to eventually look like this:

```
>>> ciphertext = ['Ceno', 'onom', 'mstm', 'me o', 'o sn', 'nio.', ' s ', 's c']
>>> ciphertext[0]
'Ceno'
>>>
```

Storing `'Ceno'` as the first string in the `ciphertext` list is our first step.

On the next iteration of the `for` loop, `col` will be set to `1` (instead of `0`) and `pointer` will start at the same value as `col`. Now when we add `8` to `pointer` on each iteration of line 30's `while` loop, the indexes will be `1`, `9`, `17`, and `25`.

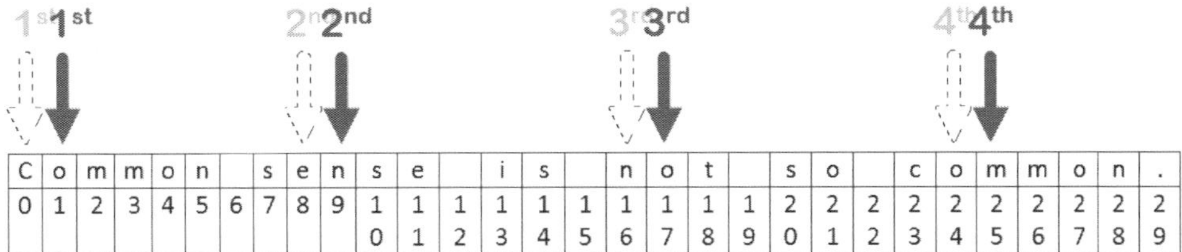

Figure 8-3. Arrows pointing to to what `message[pointer]` refers to during the second iteration of the for loop when col is set to `1`.

As `message[1]`, `message[9]`, `message[17]`, and `message[25]` are concatenated to the end of `ciphertext[1]`, they form the string `'onom'`. This is the second column of our grid.

Once the `for` loop has finished looping for the rest of the columns, the value in `ciphertext` will be `['Ceno', 'onom', 'mstm', 'me o', 'o sn', 'nio.', ' s ', 's c']`. We will use the `join()` string method to convert this list of strings into a single string.

The `join()` String Method

The `join()` method is used later on line 39. The `join()` method takes a list of strings and returns a single string. This single string has all of the strings in the list concatenated (that is, joined) together. The string that the `join()` method gets called on will be placed in between the strings in the list. (Most of the time, we will just use a blank string for this.) Try typing the following into the interactive shell:

```
>>> eggs = ['dogs', 'cats', 'moose']
>>> ''.join(eggs)
'dogscatsmoose'
>>> ' '.join(eggs)
'dogs cats moose'
>>> 'XYZ'.join(eggs)
'dogsXYZcatsXYZmoose'
>>> ''.join(eggs).upper().join(eggs)
'dogsDOGSCATSMOOSEcatsDOGSCATSMOOSEmoose'
>>>
```

That last expression, `''.join(eggs).upper().join(eggs)`, looks a little tricky, but if you go through the evaluation one step at a time, it will look like this:

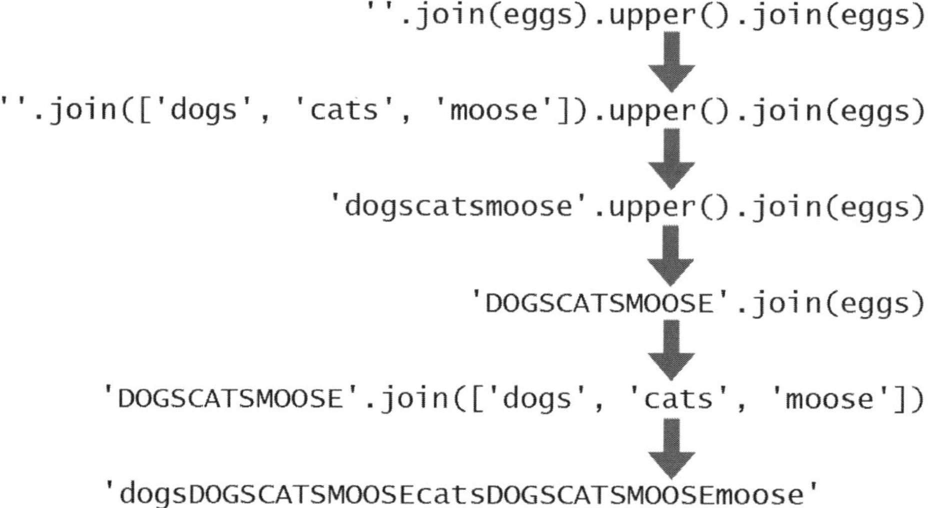

Figure 8-4. The steps of evaluation for `''.join(eggs).upper().join(eggs)`

This is why `''.join(eggs).upper().join(eggs)` returns the string, `'dogsDOGSCATSMOOSEcatsDOGSCATSMOOSEmoose'`.

Whew!

Remember, no matter how complicated an expression looks, you can just evaluate it step by step to get the single value the expression evaluates to.

Return Values and `return` Statements

transpositionEncrypt.py

```
    # Convert the ciphertext list into a single string value and return it.
    return ''.join(ciphertext)
```

Our use of the `join()` method isn't nearly as complicated as the previous example. We just want to call `join()` on the blank string and pass `ciphertext` as the argument so that the strings in the `ciphertext` list are joined together (with nothing in between them).

Remember that a function (or method) call always evaluates to a value. We say that this is the value *returned* by the function or method call, or that it is the *return value* of the function. When we create our own functions with a `def` statement, we use a `return` statement to tell what the return value for our function is.

A `return` statement is the `return` keyword followed by the value to be returned. We can also use an expression instead of a value. In that case the return value will be whatever value that expression evaluates to. Open a new file editor window and type the following program in and save it as *addNumbers.py*, then press **F5** to run it:

Source code for addNumbers.py

```
1. def addNumbers(a, b):
2.     return a + b
3.
4. spam = addNumbers(2, 40)
5. print(spam)
```

When you run this program, the output will be:

```
42
```

That's because the function call `addNumbers(2, 40)` will evaluate to `42`. The `return` statement in `addNumbers()` will evaluate the expression `a + b` and then return the evaluated value. That is why `addNumbers(2, 40)` evaluates to `42`, which is the value stored in `spam` on line 4 and next printed to the screen on line 5.

Practice Exercises, Chapter 8, Set E

Practice exercises can be found at http://invpy.com/hackingpractice8E.

Back to the Code

transpositionEncrypt.py

```
    # Convert the ciphertext list into a single string value and return it.
    return ''.join(ciphertext)
```

The encryptMessage() function's return statement returns a string value that is created by joining all of the strings in the ciphertext list. This final string is the result of our encryption code.

The great thing about functions is that a programmer only has to know what the function does, but not how the function's code does it. A programmer can understand that if she calls the encryptMessage() function and pass it an integer and a string for the key and message parameters, the function call will evaluate to an encrypted string. She doesn't need to know anything about how the code in encryptMessage() actually does this.

The Special __name__ Variable

transpositionEncrypt.py

```
42. # If transpositionEncrypt.py is run (instead of imported as a module) call
43. # the main() function.
44. if __name__ == '__main__':
45.     main()
```

We can turn our transposition encryption program into a module with a special trick involving the main() function and a variable named __name__.

When a Python program is run, there is a special variable with the name __name__ (that's two underscores before "name" and two underscores after) that is assigned the string value '__main__' (again, two underscores before and after "main") even before the first line of your program is run.

At the end of our script file (and, more importantly, after all of our def statements), we want to have some code that checks if the __name__ variable has the '__main__' string assigned to it. If so, we want to call the main() function.

This if statement on line 44 ends up actually being one of the first lines of code executed when we press **F5** to run our transposition cipher encryption program (after the import statement on line 4 and the def statements on lines 6 and 21).

The reason we set up our code this way is although Python sets __name__ to '__main__' when the program is run, it sets it to the string 'transpositionEncrypt' if our program is imported by a different Python program. This is how our program can know if it is being run as a program or imported by a different program as a module.

Just like how our program imports the `pyperclip` module to call the functions in it, other programs might want to import *transpositionEncrypt.py* to call its `encryptMessage()` function. When an `import` statement is executed, Python will look for a file for the module by adding ".py" to the end of the name. (This is why `import pyperclip` will import the *pyperclip.py* file.)

When a Python program is imported, the `__name__` variable is set to the filename part before ".py" and then runs the program. When our *transpositionEncrypt.py* program is imported, we want all the `def` statements to be run (to define the `encryptMessage()` function that the importing program wants to use), but we don't want it to call the `main()` function because that will execute the encryption code for `'Common sense is not so common.'` with key `8`.

That is why we put that part of the code inside a function (which by convention is named `main()`) and then add code at the end of the program to call `main()`. If we do this, **then our program can both be run as a program on its own and also imported as a module by another program.**

Key Size and Message Length

Notice what happens when the message length is less than twice the key size:

C	o	m	m	o	n	(s)	s	e	n	s	e	(s)	i	s	(s)	n	o	t	(s)	s	o	(s)	c	o
m	m	o	n	.																				

When using a key of 25, the "Common sense is not so common." message encrypts to "Cmommomno.n sense is not so co". Part of the message isn't encrypted! This happens whenever key size becomes more than twice the message length, because that causes there to only be one character per column and no characters get scrambled for that part of the message.

Because of this, the transposition cipher's key is limited to half the length of the message it is used to encrypt. The longer a message is, the more possible keys that can be used to encrypt it.

Summary

Whew! There were a lot of new programming concepts introduced in this chapter. The transposition cipher program is much more complicated (but much more secure) than the Caesar cipher program in the last chapter. The new concepts, functions, data types, and operators we've learned in this chapter let us manipulate data in much more sophisticated ways. Just remember that much of understanding a line of code is just evaluating it step by step the way Python will.

We can organize our code into groups called functions, which we create with `def` statements. Argument values can be passed to functions for the function's parameters. Parameters are local variables. Variables outside of all functions are global variables. Local variables are different from global variables, even if they have the same name as the global variable.

List values can store multiple other values, including other list values. Many of the things you can do with strings (such as indexing, slicing, and the `len()` function) can be used on lists. And augmented assignment operators provide a nice shortcut to regular assignment operators. The `join()` method can join a list that contains multiple strings to return a single string.

Feel free to go over this chapter again if you are not comfortable with these programming concepts. In the next chapter, we will cover decrypting with the transposition cipher.

CHAPTER 9

DECRYPTING WITH THE TRANSPOSITION CIPHER

Topics Covered In This Chapter:

- Decrypting with the transposition cipher
- The `math.ceil()`, `math.floor()` and `round()` functions
- The `and` and `or` boolean operators
- Truth tables

"When stopping a terrorist attack or seeking to recover a kidnapped child, encountering encryption may mean the difference between success and catastrophic failures."

Attorney General Janet Reno, September 1999

"Even the Four Horsemen of Kid Porn, Dope Dealers, Mafia and Terrorists don't worry me as much as totalitarian governments. It's been a long century, and we've had enough of them."

Bruce Sterling, 1994 Computers, Freedom, and Privacy conference

Unlike the Caesar cipher, the decryption process for the transposition cipher is very different from the encryption process. In this chapter we will create a separate program, *transpositionDecrypt.py*, to handle decryption.

Decrypting with the Transposition Cipher on Paper

Let's pretend we send the ciphertext "Cenoonommstmme oo snnio. s s c" to a friend (and she already knows that the secret key is 8). The first step for her to decrypt the ciphertext is to calculate how many boxes she needs to draw. To find this amount, divide the length of the ciphertext message by the key and round up. The length of our ciphertext is 30 characters (exactly the same as the plaintext) and the key is 8. So calculate 30 divided by 8 to get 3.75.

3.75 rounds up to 4. This means we want to draw a grid of boxes with 4 columns (the number we just calculated) and 8 rows (the key). It will look like this:

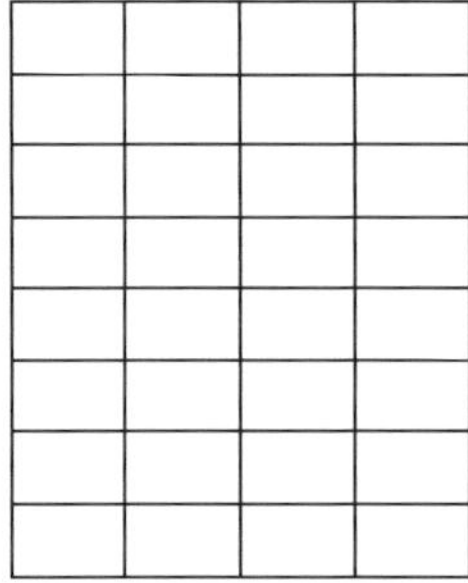

(Note that if the length divided by the key was a whole number, like in 30 / 5 = 6.0, then 6.0 would not "round up" to 7.)

The second thing we need to calculate is how many boxes on the rightmost column to shade in. Take the total number of boxes (32) and subtract the length of the ciphertext (30). 32 – 30 = 2, so shade in the *bottom* 2 boxes on the *rightmost* column:

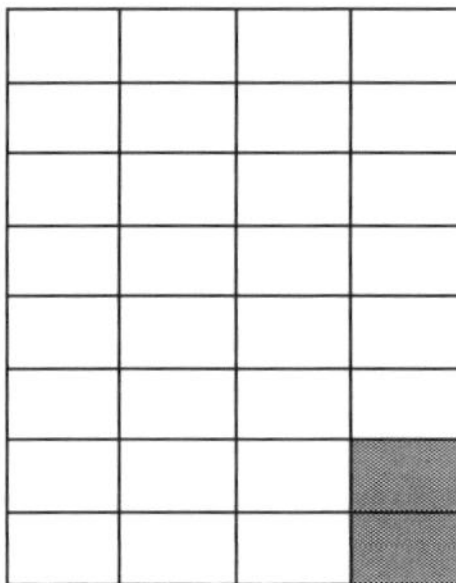

Then start filling in the boxes with one character of the ciphertext per box. Start at the top left and go right, just like we did when we were encrypting. The ciphertext is "Cenoonommstmme oo snnio. s s c", and so "Ceno" goes in the first row, then "onom" in the second row, and so on. After we are done, the boxes will look like this (where the (s) represents a space):

C	e	n	o
o	n	o	m
m	s	t	m
m	e	(s)	o
o	(s)	s	n
n	i	o	.
(s)	s	(s)	
s	(s)	c	

Our friend who received the ciphertext will see that if she reads the text going down the columns, the original plaintext has been restored: "Common sense is not so common."

The steps for decrypting are:

1. Calculate the number of columns you will have by taking the length of the message and dividing by the key, then rounding up.
2. Draw out a number of boxes. The number of columns was calculated in step 1. The number of rows is the same as the key.
3. Calculate the number of boxes to shade in by taking the number of boxes (this is the number of rows and columns multiplied) and subtracting the length of the ciphertext message.
4. Shade in the number of boxes you calculated in step 3 at the bottom of the rightmost column.
5. Fill in the characters of the ciphertext starting at the top row and going from left to right. Skip any of the shaded boxes.
6. Get the plaintext by reading from the leftmost column going from top to bottom, and moving over to the top of the next column.

Note that if you use a different key, you will be drawing out the wrong number of rows. Even if you follow the other steps in the decryption process correctly, the plaintext will come out looking like random garbage (just like when you use the wrong key with the Caesar cipher).

Practice Exercises, Chapter 9, Set A

Practice exercises can be found at http://invpy.com/hackingpractice9A.

A Transposition Cipher Decryption Program

Open a new file editor window and type out the following code in it. Save this program as *transpositionDecrypt.py*.

Source Code of the Transposition Cipher Decryption Program

Open a new file editor window by clicking on **File ► New Window**. Type in the following code into the file editor, and then save it as *transpositionDecrypt.py*. Press **F5** to run the program. Note that first you will need to download the *pyperclip.py* module and place this file in the same directory as the *transpositionDecrypt.py* file. You can download this file from http://invpy.com/pyperclip.py.

Source code for transpositionDecrypt.py

```
# Transposition Cipher Decryption
# http://inventwithpython.com/hacking (BSD Licensed)

import math, pyperclip

def main():
    myMessage = 'Cenoonommstmme oo snnio. s s c'
    myKey = 8

    plaintext = decryptMessage(myKey, myMessage)

    # Print with a | (called "pipe" character) after it in case
    # there are spaces at the end of the decrypted message.
    print(plaintext + '|')

    pyperclip.copy(plaintext)


def decryptMessage(key, message):
    # The transposition decrypt function will simulate the "columns" and
    # "rows" of the grid that the plaintext is written on by using a list
    # of strings. First, we need to calculate a few values.

    # The number of "columns" in our transposition grid:
    numOfColumns = math.ceil(len(message) / key)
    # The number of "rows" in our grid will need:
    numOfRows = key
    # The number of "shaded boxes" in the last "column" of the grid:
    numOfShadedBoxes = (numOfColumns * numOfRows) - len(message)

    # Each string in plaintext represents a column in the grid.
```

```
32.     plaintext = [''] * numOfColumns
33.
34.     # The col and row variables point to where in the grid the next
35.     # character in the encrypted message will go.
36.     col = 0
37.     row = 0
38.
39.     for symbol in message:
40.         plaintext[col] += symbol
41.         col += 1 # point to next column
42.
43.         # If there are no more columns OR we're at a shaded box, go back to
44.         # the first column and the next row.
45.         if (col == numOfColumns) or (col == numOfColumns - 1 and row >=
numOfRows - numOfShadedBoxes):
46.             col = 0
47.             row += 1
48.
49.     return ''.join(plaintext)
50.
51.
52. # If transpositionDecrypt.py is run (instead of imported as a module) call
53. # the main() function.
54. if __name__ == '__main__':
55.     main()
```

When you run the above program, it produces this output:

```
Common sense is not so common.|
```

If you want to decrypt a different message, or use a different key, change the value assigned to the `myMessage` and `myKey` variables on lines 5 and 6.

How the Program Works

transpositionDecrypt.py

```
1. # Transposition Cipher Decryption
2. # http://inventwithpython.com/hacking (BSD Licensed)
3.
4. import math, pyperclip
5.
6. def main():
7.     myMessage = 'Cenoonommstmme oo snnio. s s c'
8.     myKey = 8
9.
```

```
    plaintext = decryptMessage(myKey, myMessage)

    # Print with a | (called "pipe" character) after it in case
    # there are spaces at the end of the decrypted message.
    print(plaintext + '|')

    pyperclip.copy(plaintext)
```

The first part of the program is very similar to the first part of *transpositionEncrypt.py*. The `pyperclip` module is imported along with a different module named `math`. If you separate the module names with commas, you can import multiple modules with one `import` statement.

The `main()` function creates variables named `myMessage` and `myKey`, and then calls the decryption function `decryptMessage()`. The return value of this function is the decrypted plaintext of the ciphertext and key that we passed it. This is stored in a variable named `plaintext`, which is then printed to the screen (with a pipe character at the end in case there are spaces at the end of the message) and copied to the clipboard.

transpositionDecrypt.py

```
def decryptMessage(key, message):
```

Look at the six steps to decrypting from earlier in this chapter. For example, if we are decrypting "Cenoonommstmme oo snnio. s s c" (which has 30 characters) with the key 8, then the final set of boxes will look like this:

C	e	n	o
o	n	o	m
m	s	t	m
m	e	(s)	o
o	(s)	s	n
n	i	o	.
(s)	s	(s)	
s	(s)	c	

The `decryptMessage()` function implements each of the decryption steps as Python code.

The `math.ceil()`, `math.floor()` and `round()` Functions

When you divide numbers using the `/` operator, the expression returns a floating point number (that is, a number with a decimal point). This happens even if the number divides evenly. For example, `21 / 7` will evaluate to `3.0`, not `3`.

```
>>> 21 / 7
3.0
>>>
```

This is useful because if a number does not divide evenly, the numbers after the decimal point will be needed. For example, `22 / 5` evaluates to `4.4`:

```
>>> 22 / 5
4.4
>>>
```

(If the expression `22 / 5` evaluates to `4` instead of `4.4`, then you are using version 2 of Python instead of version 3. Please go to the http://python.org website and download and install Python 3.)

If you want to round this number to the nearest integer, you can use the `round()` function. Type the following into the interactive shell:

```
>>> round(4.2)
4
>>> round(4.5)
4
>>> round(4.9)
5
>>> round(5.0)
5
>>> round(22 / 5)
4
>>>
```

If you only want to round up then use the `math.ceil()` function, which stands for "ceiling". If you only want to round down then use the `math.floor()` function. These functions exist in the `math` module, so you will need to import the `math` module before calling them. Type the following into the interactive shell:

```
>>> import math
>>> math.floor(4.0)
4
>>> math.floor(4.2)
4
>>> math.floor(4.9)
4
>>> math.ceil(4.0)
```

```
4
>>> math.ceil(4.2)
5
>>> math.ceil(4.9)
5
>>>
```

The `math.ceil()` function will implement step 1 of the transposition decryption.

transpositionDecrypt.py

```
19. def decryptMessage(key, message):
20.     # The transposition decrypt function will simulate the "columns" and
21.     # "rows" of the grid that the plaintext is written on by using a list
22.     # of strings. First, we need to calculate a few values.
23.
24.     # The number of "columns" in our transposition grid:
25.     numOfColumns = math.ceil(len(message) / key)
26.     # The number of "rows" in our grid will need:
27.     numOfRows = key
28.     # The number of "shaded boxes" in the last "column" of the grid:
29.     numOfShadedBoxes = (numOfColumns * numOfRows) - len(message)
```

Line 25 calculates the number of columns (step 1 of decrypting) by dividing `len(message)` by the integer in `key`. This value is passed to the `math.ceil()` function, and that return value is stored in `numOfColumns`.

Line 27 calculates the number of rows (step 2 of decrypting), which is the integer stored in `key`. This value gets stored in the variable `numOfRows`.

Line 29 calculates the number of shaded boxes in the grid (step 3 of decrypting), which will be the number of columns times rows, minus the length of the message.

If we are decrypting "Cenoonommstmme oo snnio. s s c" with key 8, `numOfColumns` will be set to `4`, `numOfRows` will be set to `8`, and `numOfShadedBoxes` will be set to `2`.

transpositionDecrypt.py

```
31.     # Each string in plaintext represents a column in the grid.
32.     plaintext = [''] * numOfColumns
```

Just like the encryption program had a variable named `ciphertext` that was a list of strings to represent the grid of ciphertext, the `decryptMessage()` function will have a variable named `plaintext` that is a list of strings. These strings start off as blank strings, and we will need one string for each column of the grid. Using list replication, we can multiply a list of one blank string by `numOfColumns` to make a list of several blank strings.

(Remember that each function call has its own local scope. The `plaintext` in `decryptMessage()` exists in a different local scope than the `plaintext` variable in `main()`, so they are two different variables that just happen to have the same name.)

Remember that the grid for our `'Cenoonommstmme oo snnio. s s c'` example looks like this:

C	e	n	o
o	n	o	m
m	s	t	m
m	e	(s)	o
o	(s)	s	n
n	i	o	.
(s)	s	(s)	
s	(s)	c	

The `plaintext` variable will have a list of strings. Each string in the list is a single column of this grid. For this decryption, we want `plaintext` to end up with this value:

```
>>> plaintext = ['Common s', 'ense is ', 'not so c', 'ommon.']
>>> plaintext[0]
'Common s'
```

That way, we can join all the list's strings together to get the `'Common sense is not so common.'` string value to return.

transpositionDecrypt.py

```
34.     # The col and row variables point to where in the grid the next
35.     # character in the encrypted message will go.
36.     col = 0
37.     row = 0
38.
39.     for symbol in message:
```

The `col` and `row` variables will track the column and row where the next character in `message` should go. We will start these variables at `0`. Line 39 will start a `for` loop that iterates over the characters in the `message` string. Inside this loop the code will adjust the `col` and `row` variables so that we concatenate `symbol` to the correct string in the `plaintext` list.

transpositionDecrypt.py

```
40.         plaintext[col] += symbol
41.         col += 1 # point to next column
```

As the first step in this loop we concatenate `symbol` to the string at index `col` in the `plaintext` list. Then we add `1` to `col` (that is, we **increment** `col`) on line 41 so that on the next iteration of the loop, `symbol` will be concatenated to the next string.

The `and` and `or` Boolean Operators

The Boolean operators `and` and `or` can help us form more complicated conditions for `if` and `while` statements. The `and` operator connects two expressions and evaluates to `True` if both expressions evaluate to `True`. The `or` operator connects two expressions and evaluates to `True` if one or both expressions evaluate to `True`. Otherwise these expressions evaluate to `False`. Type the following into the interactive shell:

```
>>> 10 > 5 and 2 < 4
True
>>> 10 > 5 and 4 != 4
False
>>>
```

The first expression above evaluates to `True` because the two expressions on the sides of the `and` operator both evaluate to True. This means that the expression `10 > 5 and 2 < 4` evaluates to `True and True`, which in turn evaluates to `True`.

However, for the second above expression, although `10 > 5` evaluates to `True` the expression `4 != 4` evaluates to `False`. This means the whole expression evaluates to `True and False`. Since both expressions have to be `True` for the `and` operator to evaluate to `True`, instead they evaluate to `False`.

Type the following into the interactive shell:

```
>>> 10 > 5 or 4 != 4
True
>>> 10 < 5 or 4 != 4
False
>>>
```

For the `or` operator, only one of the sides must be `True` for the `or` operator to evaluate them both to `True`. This is why `10 > 5 or 4 != 4` evaluates to `True`. However, because both the expression `10 < 5` and the expression `4 != 4` are both `False`, this makes the second above expression evaluate to `False or False`, which in turn evaluates to `False`.

The third Boolean operator is `not`. The `not` operator evaluates to the opposite Boolean value of the value it operates on. So `not True` is `False` and `not False` is `True`. Type the following into the interactive shell:

```
>>> not 10 > 5
False
>>> not 10 < 5
True
>>> not False
True
>>> not not False
False
>>> not not not not not False
True
>>>
```

Practice Exercises, Chapter 9, Set B

Practice exercises can be found at http://invpy.com/hackingpractice9B.

Truth Tables

If you ever forget how the Boolean operators work, you can look at these charts, which are called **truth tables**:

Table 6-1: The `and` operator's truth table.

A	and	B	is	Entire statement
True	and	True	is	True
True	and	False	is	False
False	and	True	is	False
False	and	False	is	False

Table 6-2: The `or` operator's truth table.

A	and	B	is	Entire statement
True	and	True	is	True
True	and	False	is	False
False	and	True	is	False
False	and	False	is	False

Table 6-3: The `not` operator's truth table.

not A	is	Entire statement
not True	is	False
not False	is	True

The `and` and `or` Operators are Shortcuts

Just like `for` loops let us do the same thing as `while` loops but with less code, the `and` and `or` operators let us shorten our code also. Type in the following into the interactive shell. Both of these bits of code do the same thing:

```
>>> if 10 > 5:
...     if 2 < 4:
...         print('Hello!')
...
Hello!
>>>
>>> if 10 > 5 and 2 < 4:
...     print('Hello!')
...
Hello!
>>>
```

So you can see that the `and` operator basically takes the place of two `if` statements (where the second `if` statement is inside the first `if` statement's block.)

You can also replace the `or` operator with an `if` and `elif` statement, though you will have to copy the code twice. Type the following into the interactive shell:

```
>>> if 4 != 4:
...     print('Hello!')
... elif 10 > 5:
...     print('Hello!')
...
Hello!
>>>
>>> if 4 != 4 or 10 > 5:
...     print('Hello!')
...
Hello!
>>>
```

Order of Operations for Boolean Operators

Just like the math operators have an order of operations, the `and`, `or`, and `not` operators also have an order of operations: first `not`, then `and`, and then `or`. Try typing the following into the interactive shell:

```
>>> not False and True    # not False evaluates first
True
>>> not (False and True)  # (False and True) evaluates first
False
>>>
```

Back to the Code

transpositionDecrypt.py

```
        # If there are no more columns OR we're at a shaded box, go back to
        # the first column and the next row.
        if (col == numOfColumns) or (col == numOfColumns - 1 and row >= numOfRows - numOfShadedBoxes):
            col = 0
            row += 1
```

There are two cases where we want to reset `col` back to `0` (so that on the next iteration of the loop, symbol is added to the first string in the list in `plaintext`). The first is if we have incremented `col` past the last index in `plaintext`. In this case, the value in `col` will be equal to `numOfColumns`. (Remember that the last index in `plaintext` will be `numOfColumns` minus one. So when `col` is equal to `numOfColumns`, it is already past the last index.)

The second case is if both `col` is at the last index and the `row` variable is pointing to a row that has a shaded box in the last column. Here's the complete decryption grid with the column indexes along the top and the row indexes down the side:

	0	1	2	3
0	C 0	e 1	n 2	o 3
1	o 4	n 5	o 6	m 7
2	m 8	s 9	t 10	m 11
3	m 12	e 13	(s) 14	o 15
4	o 16	(s) 17	s 18	n 19
5	n 20	i 21	o 22	. 23
6	(s) 24	s 25	(s) 26	
7	s 27	(s) 28	c 29	

You can see that the shaded boxes are in the last column (whose index will be `numOfColumns - 1`) and rows 6 and 7. To have our program calculate which row indexes are shaded, we use the expression `row >= numOfRows - numOfShadedBoxes`. If this expression is `True`, and `col` is equal to `numOfColumns - 1`, then we know that we want to reset `col` to `0` for the next iteration.

These two cases are why the condition on line 45 is `(col == numOfColumns) or (col == numOfColumns - 1 and row >= numOfRows - numOfShadedBoxes)`. That looks like a big, complicated expression but remember that you can break it down into smaller parts. The block of code that executes will change `col` back to the first column by setting it to `0`. We will also increment the `row` variable.

transpositionDecrypt.py

```
49.     return ''.join(plaintext)
```

By the time the `for` loop on line 39 has finished looping over every character in `message`, the `plaintext` list's strings have been modified so that they are now in the decrypted order (if the correct key was used, that is). The strings in the `plaintext` list are joined together (with a blank string in between each string) by the `join()` string method. The string that this call to `join()` returns will be the value that our `decryptMessage()` function returns.

For our example decryption, plaintext will be `['Common s', 'ense is ', 'not so c', 'ommon.']`, so `''.join(plaintext)` will evaluate to `'Common sense is not so common.'`.

transpositionDecrypt.py

```
52. # If transpositionDecrypt.py is run (instead of imported as a module) call
53. # the main() function.
54. if __name__ == '__main__':
55.     main()
```

The first line that our program runs after importing modules and executing the `def` statements is the `if` statement on line 54. Just like in the transposition encryption program, we check if this program has been run (instead of imported by a different program) by checking if the special `__name__` variable is set to the string value `'__main__'`. If so, we execute the `main()` function.

Practice Exercises, Chapter 9, Set C

Practice exercises can be found at http://invpy.com/hackingpractice9C.

Summary

That's it for the decryption program. Most of the program is in the `decryptMessage()` function. We can see that our programs can encrypt and decrypt the message "Common sense is not so common." with the key 8. But we should try several other messages and keys to see that a message that is encrypted and then decrypted will result in the same thing as the original message. Otherwise, we know that either the encryption code or the decryption code doesn't work.

We could start changing the `key` and `message` variables in our *transpositionEncrypt.py* and *transpositionDecrypt.py* and then running them to see if it works. But instead, let's automate this by writing a program to test our program.

CHAPTER 10

PROGRAMMING A PROGRAM TO TEST OUR PROGRAM

Topics Covered In This Chapter:

- The `random.seed()` function
- The `random.randint()` function
- List references
- The `copy.deepcopy()` Functions
- The `random.shuffle()` function
- Randomly scrambling a string
- The `sys.exit()` function

"It is poor civic hygiene to install technologies that could someday facilitate a police state."

Bruce Schneier, cryptographer

We can try out the transposition encryption and decryption programs from the previous chapter by encrypting and decrypting a few messages with different keys. It seems to work pretty well. But does it *always* work?

You won't know unless you test the `encryptMessage()` and `decryptMessage()` functions with different values for the `message` and `key` parameters. This would take a lot of time. You'll have to type out a message in the encryption program, set the key, run the encryption program, paste the ciphertext into the decryption program, set the key, and then run the decryption program. And you'll want to repeat that with several different keys and messages!

That's a lot of boring work. Instead we can write a program to test the cipher programs for us. This new program can generate a random message and a random key. It will then encrypt the message with the `encryptMessage()` function from *transpositionEncrypt.py* and then pass the ciphertext from that to the `decryptMessage()` in *transpositionDecrypt.py*. If the plaintext returned by `decryptMessage()` is the same as the original message, the program can know that the encryption and decryption messages work. This is called **automated testing**.

There are several different message and key combinations to try, but it will only take the computer a minute or so to test thousands different combinations. If all of those tests pass, then we can be much more certain that our code works.

Source Code of the Transposition Cipher Tester Program

Open a new file editor window by clicking on **File ► New Window**. Type in the following code into the file editor, and then save it as *transpositionTest.py*. Press **F5** to run the program. Note that first you will need to download the *pyperclip.py* module and place this file in the same directory as the *transpositionTest.py* file. You can download this file from http://invpy.com/pyperclip.py.

Source code for transpositionTest.py

```
# Transposition Cipher Test
# http://inventwithpython.com/hacking (BSD Licensed)

import random, sys, transpositionEncrypt, transpositionDecrypt

def main():
    random.seed(42) # set the random "seed" to a static value

    for i in range(20): # run 20 tests
        # Generate random messages to test.

        # The message will have a random length:
        message = 'ABCDEFGHIJKLMNOPQRSTUVWXYZ' * random.randint(4, 40)

        # Convert the message string to a list to shuffle it.
        message = list(message)
        random.shuffle(message)
```

```
        message = ''.join(message) # convert list to string

        print('Test #%s: "%s..."' % (i+1, message[:50]))

        # Check all possible keys for each message.
        for key in range(1, len(message)):
            encrypted = transpositionEncrypt.encryptMessage(key, message)
            decrypted = transpositionDecrypt.decryptMessage(key, encrypted)

            # If the decryption doesn't match the original message, display
            # an error message and quit.
            if message != decrypted:
                print('Mismatch with key %s and message %s.' % (key, message))
                print(decrypted)
                sys.exit()

    print('Transposition cipher test passed.')


# If transpositionTest.py is run (instead of imported as a module) call
# the main() function.
if __name__ == '__main__':
    main()
```

Sample Run of the Transposition Cipher Tester Program

When you run this program, the output will look like this:

```
Test #1: "KQDXSFQDBPMMRGXFKCGIQUGWFFLAJIJKFJGSYOSAWGYBGUNTQX..."
Test #2: "IDDXEEWUMWUJPJSZFJSGAOMFIOWWEYANRXISCJKXZRHMRNCFYW..."
Test #3: "DKAYRSAGSGCSIQWKGARQHAOZDLGKJISQVMDFGYXKCRMPCMQWJM..."
Test #4: "MZIBCOEXGRDTFXZKVNFQWQMWIROJAOKTWISTDWAHZRVIGXOLZA..."
Test #5: "TINIECNCBFKJBRDIUTNGDINHULYSVTGHBAWDQMZCNHZOTNYHSX..."
Test #6: "JZQIHCVNDWRDUFHZFXCIASYDSTGQATQOYLIHUFPKEXSOZXQGPP..."
Test #7: "BMKJUERFNGIDGWAPQMDZNHOQPLEOQDYCIIWRKPVEIPLAGZCJVN..."
Test #8: "IPASTGZSLPYCORCVEKWHOLOVUFPOMGQWZVJNYQIYVEOFLUWLMQ..."
Test #9: "AHRYJAPTACZQNNFOTONMIPYECOORDGEYESYFHROZDASFIPKSOP..."
Test #10: "FSXAAPLSQHSFUPQZGTIXXDLDMOIVMWFGHPBPJROOSEGPEVRXSX..."
Test #11: "IVBCXBIHLWPTDHGEGANBGXWQZMVXQPNJZQPKMRUMPLLXPAFITN..."
Test #12: "LLNSYMNRXZVYNPRTVNIBFRSUGIWUJREMPZVCMJATMLAMCEEHNW..."
Test #13: "IMWRUJJHRWAABHYIHGNPSJUOVKRRKBSJKDHOBDLOUJDGXIVDME..."
Test #14: "IZVXWHTIGKGHKJGGWMOBAKTWZWJPHGNEQPINYZIBERJPUNWJMX..."
Test #15: "BQGFNMGQCIBOTRHZZOBHZFJZVSRTVHIUJFOWRFBNWKRNHGOHEQ..."
Test #16: "LNKGKSYIPHMCDVKDLNDVFCIFGEWQGUJYJICUYIVXARMUCBNUWM..."
```

```
Test #17: "WGNRHKIQZMOPBQTCRYPSEPWHLRDXZMJOUTJCLECKEZZRRMQRNI..."
Test #18: "PPVTELDHJRZFPBNMJRLAZWRXRQVKHUUMRPNFKXJCUKFOXAGEHM..."
Test #19: "UXUIGAYKGLYUQTFBWQUTFNSOPEGMIWMQYEZAVCALGOHUXJZPTY..."
Test #20: "JSYTDGLVLBCVVSITPTQPHBCYIZHKFOFMBWOZNFKCADHDKPJSJA..."
Transposition cipher test passed.
```

Our testing program works by importing the *transpositionEncrypt.py* and *transpositionDecrypt.py* programs as modules. This way, we can call the `encryptMessage()` and `decryptMessage()` functions in these programs. Our testing program will create a random message and choose a random key. It doesn't matter that the message is just random letters, we just need to check that encrypting and then decrypting the message will result in the original message.

Our program will repeat this test twenty times by putting this code in a loop. If at any point the returned string from `transpositionDecrypt()` is not the exact same as the original message, our program will print an error message and exit.

How the Program Works

transpositionTest.py

```
# Transposition Cipher Test
# http://inventwithpython.com/hacking (BSD Licensed)

import random, sys, transpositionEncrypt, transpositionDecrypt

def main():
```

First our program imports two modules that come with Python, `random` and `sys`. We also want to import the transposition cipher programs we've written: *transpositionEncrypt.py* and *transpositionDecrypt.py*. Note that we don't put the .py extension in our `import` statement.

Pseudorandom Numbers and the `random.seed()` Function

transpositionTest.py

```
    random.seed(42) # set the random "seed" to a static value
```

Technically, the numbers produced by Python's `random.randint()` function are not really random. They are produced from a pseudorandom number generator algorithm, and this algorithm is well known and the numbers it produces are predictable. We call these random-*looking* (but predictable) numbers **pseudorandom numbers** because they are not truly random.

The pseudorandom number generator algorithm starts with an initial number called the **seed**. All of the random numbers produced from a seed are predictable. You can reset Python's random seed by calling the `random.seed()` function. Type the following into the interactive shell:

```
>>> import random
>>> random.seed(42)
>>> for i in range(5):
...   print(random.randint(1, 10))
...
7
1
3
3
8
>>> random.seed(42)
>>> for i in range(5):
...   print(random.randint(1, 10))
...
7
1
3
3
8
>>>
```

When the seed for Python's pseudorandom number generator is set to `42`, the first "random" number between `1` and `10` will **always** be `7`. The second "random" number will **always** be `1`, and the third number will **always** be `3`, and so on. When we reset the seed back to 42 again, the same set of pseudorandom numbers will be returned from `random.randint()`.

Setting the random seed by calling `random.seed()` will be useful for our testing program, because we want predictable numbers so that the same pseudorandom messages and keys are chosen each time we run the automated testing program. Our Python programs only seem to generate "unpredictable" random numbers because the seed is set to the computer's current clock time (specifically, the number of seconds since January 1st, 1970) when the `random` module is first imported.

It is important to note that not using truly random numbers is a common security flaw of encryption software. If the "random" numbers in your programs can be predicted, then this can provide a cryptanalyst with a useful hint to breaking your cipher. More information about generating truly random numbers with Python using the `os.urandom()` function can be found at http://invpy.com/random.

The random.randint() Function

transpositionTest.py

```
 9.     for i in range(20): # run 20 tests
10.         # Generate random messages to test.
11.
12.         # The message will have a random length:
13.         message = 'ABCDEFGHIJKLMNOPQRSTUVWXYZ' * random.randint(4, 40)
```

The code that does a single test will be in this `for` loop's block. We want this program to run multiple tests since the more tests we try, the more certain that we know our programs work.

Line 13 creates a random message from the uppercase letters and stores it in the `message` variable. Line 13 uses string replication to create messages of different lengths. The `random.randint()` function takes two integer arguments and returns a random integer between those two integers (including the integers themselves). Type the following into the interactive shell:

```
>>> import random
>>> random.randint(1, 20)
20
>>> random.randint(1, 20)
18
>>> random.randint(1, 20)
3
>>> random.randint(1, 20)
18
>>> random.randint(100, 200)
107
>>>
```

Of course, since these are pseudorandom numbers, the numbers you get will probably be different than the ones above. Line 13 creates a random message from the uppercase letters and stores it in the `message` variable. Line 13 uses string replication to create messages of different lengths.

References

Technically, variables do not store list values in them. Instead, they store reference values to list values. Up until now the difference hasn't been important. But storing list references instead of lists becomes important if you copy a variable with a list reference to another variable. Try entering the following into the shell:

```
>>> spam = 42
>>> cheese = spam
>>> spam = 100
>>> spam
100
>>> cheese
42
>>>
```

This makes sense from what we know so far. We assign `42` to the `spam` variable, and then we copy the value in `spam` and assign it to the variable `cheese`. When we later change the value in `spam` to `100`, this doesn't affect the value in `cheese`. This is because `spam` and `cheese` are different variables that each store their own values.

But lists don't work this way. When you assign a list to a variable with the = sign, you are actually assigning a list reference to the variable. A **reference** is a value that points to some bit of data, and a **list reference** is a value that points to a list. Here is some code that will make this easier to understand. Type this into the shell:

```
>>> spam = [0, 1, 2, 3, 4, 5]
>>> cheese = spam
>>> cheese[1] = 'Hello!'
>>> spam
[0, 'Hello!', 2, 3, 4, 5]
>>> cheese
[0, 'Hello!', 2, 3, 4, 5]
```

This looks odd. The code only changed the `cheese` list, but it seems that both the `cheese` and `spam` lists have changed.

Notice that the line `cheese = spam` copies the list *reference* in `spam` to `cheese`, instead of copying the list value itself. This is because the value stored in the `spam` variable is a list reference, and not the list value itself. This means that the values stored in both `spam` and `cheese` refer to the same list. There is only one list because the list was not copied, the reference to the list was copied. So when you modify `cheese` in the `cheese[1] = 'Hello!'` line, you are modifying the same list that `spam` refers to. This is why `spam` seems to have the same list value that `cheese` does.

Remember that variables are like boxes that contain values. List variables don't actually contain lists at all, they contain references to lists. Here are some pictures that explain what happens in the code you just typed in:

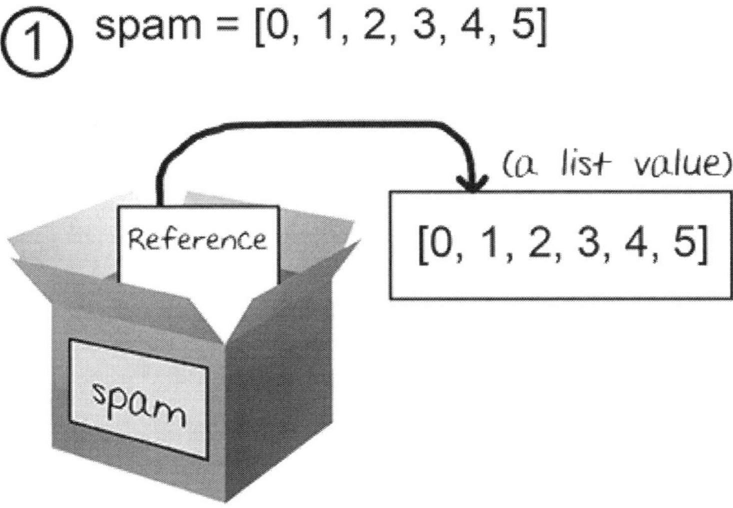

Figure 10-1. Variables do not store lists, but rather references to lists.

On the first line, the actual list is not contained in the `spam` variable but a reference to the list. The list itself is not stored in any variable.

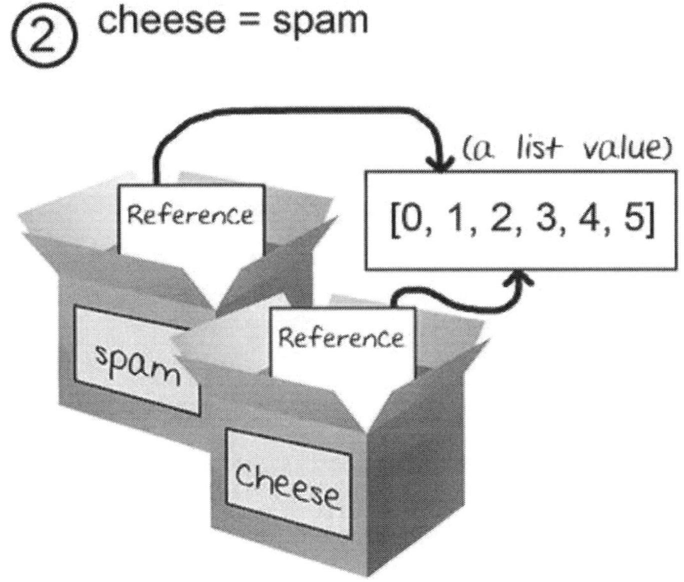

Figure 10-2. Two variables store two references to the same list.

When you assign the reference in spam to cheese, the cheese variable contains a copy of the reference in spam. Now both cheese and spam refer to the same list.

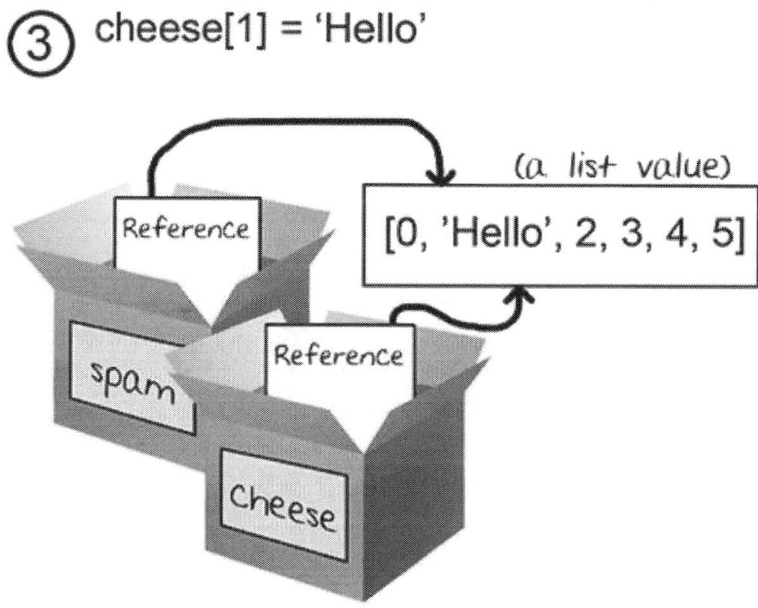

Figure 10-3. Changing the list changes all variables with references to that list.

When you alter the list that cheese refers to, the list that spam refers to is also changed because they refer to the same list. If you want spam and cheese to store two different lists, you have to create two different lists instead of copying a reference:

```
>>> spam = [0, 1, 2, 3, 4, 5]
>>> cheese = [0, 1, 2, 3, 4, 5]
```

In the above example, spam and cheese have two different lists stored in them (even though these lists are identical in content). Now if you modify one of the lists, it will not affect the other because spam and cheese have references to two different lists:

```
>>> spam = [0, 1, 2, 3, 4, 5]
>>> cheese = [0, 1, 2, 3, 4, 5]
>>> cheese[1] = 'Hello!'
>>> spam
[0, 1, 2, 3, 4, 5]
>>> cheese
[0, 'Hello!', 2, 3, 4, 5]
```

Figure 10-4 shows how the two references point to two different lists:

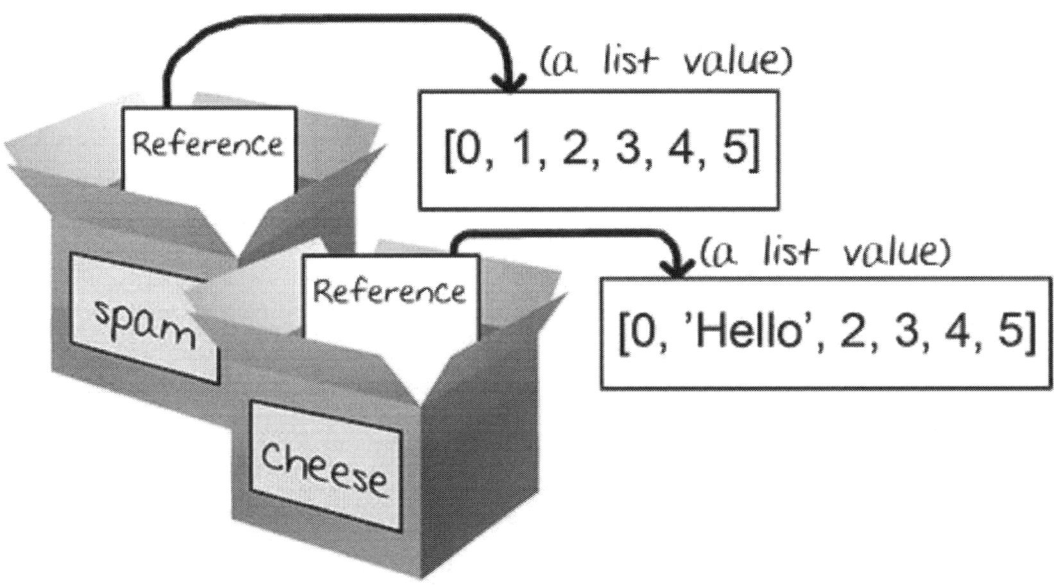

Figure 10-4. Two variables each storing references to two different lists.

The `copy.deepcopy()` Functions

As we saw in the previous example, the following code only copies the reference value, not the list value itself:

```
>>> spam = [0, 1, 2, 3, 4, 5]
>>> cheese = spam    # copies the reference, not the list
```

If we want to copy the list value itself, we can import the `copy` module to call the `copy.deepcopy()` function, which will return a separate copy of the list it is passed:

```
>>> spam = [0, 1, 2, 3, 4, 5]
>>> import copy
>>> cheese = copy.deepcopy(spam)
>>> cheese[1] = 'Hello!'
>>> spam
[0, 1, 2, 3, 4, 5]
>>> cheese
[0, 'Hello!', 2, 3, 4, 5]
>>>
```

The copy.deepcopy() function isn't used in this chapter's program, but it is helpful when you need to make a duplicate list value to store in a different variable.

Practice Exercises, Chapter 10, Set A

Practice exercises can be found at http://invpy.com/hackingpractice10A.

The random.shuffle() Function

The random.shuffle() function is also in the random module. It accepts a list argument, and then randomly rearranges items in the list. Type the following into the interactive shell:

```
>>> import random
>>> spam = [0, 1, 2, 3, 4, 5, 6, 7, 8, 9]
>>> spam
[0, 1, 2, 3, 4, 5, 6, 7, 8, 9]
>>> random.shuffle(spam)
>>> spam
[3, 0, 5, 9, 6, 8, 2, 4, 1, 7]
>>> random.shuffle(spam)
>>> spam
[1, 2, 5, 9, 4, 7, 0, 3, 6, 8]
>>>
```

An important thing to note is that shuffle() **does not return a list value**. Instead, it changes the list value that is passed to it (because shuffle() modifies the list directly from the list reference value it is passed.) We say that the shuffle() function modifies the list **in-place**. This is why we only need to execute random.shuffle(spam) instead of spam = random.shuffle(spam).

Remember that you can use the list() function to convert a string or range object to a list value. Type the following into the interactive shell:

```
>>> import random
>>> eggs = list('Hello')
>>> eggs
['H', 'e', 'l', 'l', 'o']
>>> random.shuffle(eggs)
>>> eggs
 ['o', 'H', 'l', 'l', 'e']
>>>
```

And also remember you can use the join() string method to pass a list of strings and return a single string:

```
>>> eggs
['o', 'H', 'l', 'l', 'e']
>>> eggs = ''.join(eggs)
>>> eggs
'oHlle'
>>>
```

Randomly Scrambling a String

transpositionTest.py

```
        # Convert the message string to a list to shuffle it.
        message = list(message)
        random.shuffle(message)
        message = ''.join(message) # convert list to string
```

In order to shuffle the characters in a string value, first we convert the string to a list with `list()`, then shuffle the items in the list with `shuffle()`, and then convert back to string value with the `join()` string method. Try typing the following into the interactive shell:

```
>>> import random
>>> spam = 'Hello world!'
>>> spam = list(spam)
>>> random.shuffle(spam)
>>> spam = ''.join(spam)
>>> spam
'wl delHo!orl'
>>>
```

We use this technique to scramble the letters in the `message` variable. This way we can test many different messages just in case our transposition cipher can encrypt and decrypt some messages but not others.

Back to the Code

transpositionTest.py

```
20.         print('Test #%s: "%s..."' % (i+1, message[:50]))
```

Line 20 has a `print()` call that displays which test number we are on (we add one to `i` because `i` starts at `0` and we want the test numbers to start at `1`). Since the string in `message` can be very long, we use string slicing to show only the first 50 characters of `message`.

Line 20 uses string interpolation. The value that `i+1` evaluates to will replace the first `%s` in the string and the value that `message[:50]` evaluates to will replace the second `%s`. When using string interpolation, be sure the number of `%s` in the string matches the number of values that are in between the parentheses after it.

transpositionTest.py

```
22.         # Check all possible keys for each message.
23.         for key in range(1, len(message)):
```

While the key for the Caesar cipher could be an integer from `0` to `25`, the key for the transposition cipher can be between `1` and the length of the message. We want to test every possible key for the test message, so the `for` loop on line 23 will run the test code with the keys `1` up to (but not including) the length of the message.

transpositionTest.py

```
24.             encrypted = transpositionEncrypt.encryptMessage(key, message)
25.             decrypted = transpositionDecrypt.decryptMessage(key, encrypted)
```

Line 24 encrypts the string in `message` using our `encryptMessage()` function. Since this function is inside the *transpositionEncrypt.py* file, we need to add `transpositionEncrypt.` (with the period at the end) to the front of the function name.

The encrypted string that is returned from `encryptMessage()` is then passed to `decryptMessage()`. We use the same key for both function calls. The return value from `decryptMessage()` is stored in a variable named `decrypted`. If the functions worked, then the string in `message` should be the exact same as the string in `decrypted`.

The `sys.exit()` Function

transpositionTest.py

```
27.             # If the decryption doesn't match the original message, display
28.             # an error message and quit.
29.             if message != decrypted:
30.                 print('Mismatch with key %s and message %s.' % (key,
message))
31.                 print(decrypted)
32.                 sys.exit()
33.
34.     print('Transposition cipher test passed.')
```

Line 29 tests if `message` and `decrypted` are equal. If they aren't, we want to display an error message on the screen. We print the `key`, `message`, and `decrypted` values. This information could help us figure out what happened. Then we will exit the program.

Normally our programs exit once the execution reaches the very bottom and there are no more lines to execute. However, we can make the program exit sooner than that by calling the `sys.exit()` function. When `sys.exit()` is called, the program will immediately end.

But if the values in `message` and `decrypted` are equal to each other, the program execution skips the `if` statement's block and the call to `sys.exit()`. The next line is on line 34, but you can see from its indentation that it is the first line after line 9's `for` loop.

This means that after line 29's `if` statement's block, the program execution will jump back to line 23's `for` loop for the next iteration of that loop. If it has finished looping, then instead the execution jumps back to line 9's `for` loop for the next iteration of that loop. And if it has finished looping for that loop, then it continues on to line 34 to print out the string `'Transposition cipher test passed.'`.

transpositionTest.py

```
# If transpositionTest.py is run (instead of imported as a module) call
# the main() function.
if __name__ == '__main__':
    main()
```

Here we do the trick of checking if the special variable `__name__` is set to `'__main__'` and if so, calling the `main()` function. This way, if another program imports *transpositionTest.py*, the code inside `main()` will not be executed but the `def` statements that create the `main()` function will be.

Testing Our Test Program

We've written a test program that tests our encryption programs, but how do we know that the test program works? What if there is a bug with our test program, and it is just saying that our transposition cipher programs work when they really don't?

We can test our test program by purposefully adding bugs to our encryption or decryption functions. Then when we run the test program, if it does not detect a problem with our cipher program, then we know that the test program is not correctly testing our cipher programs.

Change *transpositionEncrypt.py*'s line 36 from this:

transpositionEncrypt.py

```
35.             # move pointer over
36.             pointer += key
```

…to this:

transpositionEncrypt.py

```
            # move pointer over
            pointer += key + 1
```

Now that the encryption code is broken, when we run the test program it should give us an error:

```
Test #1: "JEQLDFKJZWALCOYACUPLTRRMLWHOBXQNEAWSLGWAGQQSRSIUIQ..."
Mismatch with key 1 and message
JEQLDFKJZWALCOYACUPLTRRMLWHOBXQNEAWSLGWAGQQSRSIUIQTRGJHDVCZECRESZJARAVIPFOBWZXX
TBFOFHVSIGBWIBBHGKUWHEUUDYONYTZVKNVVTYZPDDMIDKBHTYJAHBNDVJUZDCEMFMLUXEONCZXWAWG
XZSFTMJNLJOKKIJXLWAPCQNYCIQOFTEAUHRJODKLGRIZSJBXQPBMQPPFGMVUZHKFWPGNMRYXROMSCEE
XLUSCFHNELYPYKCNYTOUQGBFSRDDMVIGXNYPHVPQISTATKVKM.
JQDKZACYCPTRLHBQEWLWGQRIITGHVZCEZAAIFBZXBOHSGWBHKWEUYNTVNVYPDIKHYABDJZCMMUENZWW
XSTJLOKJLACNCQFEUROKGISBQBQPGVZKWGMYRMCELSFNLPKNTUGFRDVGNPVQSAKK
```

Summary

We can use our programming skills for more than just writing programs. We can also program the computer to test those programs to make sure they work for different inputs. It is a common practice to write code to test code.

This chapter covered a few new functions such as the `random.randint()` function for producing pseudorandom numbers. Remember, pseudorandom numbers aren't random enough for cryptography programs, but they are good enough for this chapter's testing program. The `random.shuffle()` function is useful for scrambling the order of items in a list value.

The `copy.deepcopy()` function will create copies of list values instead of reference values. The difference between a list and list reference is explained in this chapter as well.

All of our programs so far have only encrypted short messages. In the next chapter, we will learn how to encrypt and decrypt entire files on your hard drive.

CHAPTER 11

ENCRYPTING AND DECRYPTING FILES

Topics Covered In This Chapter:

- Reading and writing files
- The `open()` function
- The `read()` file object method
- The `close()` file object method
- The `write()` file object method
- The `os.path.exists()` function
- The `startswith()` string method
- The `title()` string method
- The `time` module and `time.time()` function

"Why do security police grab people and torture them? To get their information. If you build an information management system that concentrates information from dozens of people, you've made that dozens of times more attractive. You've focused the repressive regime's attention on the hard disk. And hard disks put up no resistance to torture. You need to give the hard disk a way to resist. That's cryptography."

Patrick Ball

Up until now our programs have only worked on small messages that we type directly into the source code as string values. The cipher program in this chapter will use the transposition cipher to encrypt and decrypt entire files, which can be millions of characters in size.

Plain Text Files

This program will encrypt and decrypt plain text files. These are the kind of files that only have text data and usually have the .txt file extension. Files from word processing programs that let you change the font, color, or size of the text do not produce plain text files. You can write your own text files using Notepad (on Windows), TextMate or TextEdit (on OS X), or gedit (on Linux) or a similar plain text editor program. You can even use IDLE's own file editor and save the files with a .txt extension instead of the usual .py extension.

For some samples, you can download the following text files from this book's website:

- http://invpy.com/devilsdictionary.txt
- http://invpy.com/frankenstein.txt
- http://invpy.com/siddhartha.txt
- http://invpy.com/thetimemachine.txt

These are text files of some books (that are now in the public domain, so it is perfectly legal to download them.) For example, download Mary Shelley's classic novel "Frankenstein" from http://invpy.com/frankenstein.txt. Double-click the file to open it in a text editor program. There are over 78,000 words in this text file! It would take some time to type this into our encryption program. But if it is in a file, the program can read the file and do the encryption in a couple seconds.

If you get an error that looks like "`UnicodeDecodeError: 'charmap' codec can't decode byte 0x90 in position 148: character maps to <undefined>`" then you are running the cipher program on a non-plain text file, also called a "binary file".

To find other public domain texts to download, go to the Project Gutenberg website at http://www.gutenberg.org/.

Source Code of the Transposition File Cipher Program

Like our transposition cipher testing program, the transposition cipher file program will import our *transpositionEncrypt.py* and *transpositionDecrypt.py* files so we can use the `encryptMessage()` and `decryptMessage()` functions in them. This way we don't have to re-type the code for these functions in our new program.

Open a new file editor window by clicking on **File ► New Window**. Type in the following code into the file editor, and then save it as *transpositionFileCipher.py*. Press **F5** to run the program. Note that first you will need to download *frankenstein.txt* and place this file in the same directory as the *transpositionFileCipher.py* file. You can download this file from http://invpy.com/frankenstein.txt.

Source code for transpositionFileCipher.py

```
# Transposition Cipher Encrypt/Decrypt File
# http://inventwithpython.com/hacking (BSD Licensed)

import time, os, sys, transpositionEncrypt, transpositionDecrypt

def main():
    inputFilename = 'frankenstein.txt'
    # BE CAREFUL! If a file with the outputFilename name already exists,
    # this program will overwrite that file.
    outputFilename = 'frankenstein.encrypted.txt'
    myKey = 10
    myMode = 'encrypt' # set to 'encrypt' or 'decrypt'

    # If the input file does not exist, then the program terminates early.
    if not os.path.exists(inputFilename):
        print('The file %s does not exist. Quitting...' % (inputFilename))
        sys.exit()

    # If the output file already exists, give the user a chance to quit.
    if os.path.exists(outputFilename):
        print('This will overwrite the file %s. (C)ontinue or (Q)uit?' % (outputFilename))
        response = input('> ')
        if not response.lower().startswith('c'):
            sys.exit()

    # Read in the message from the input file
    fileObj = open(inputFilename)
    content = fileObj.read()
    fileObj.close()

    print('%sing...' % (myMode.title()))

    # Measure how long the encryption/decryption takes.
    startTime = time.time()
    if myMode == 'encrypt':
        translated = transpositionEncrypt.encryptMessage(myKey, content)
    elif myMode == 'decrypt':
```

```
        translated = transpositionDecrypt.decryptMessage(myKey, content)
    totalTime = round(time.time() - startTime, 2)
    print('%sion time: %s seconds' % (myMode.title(), totalTime))

    # Write out the translated message to the output file.
    outputFileObj = open(outputFilename, 'w')
    outputFileObj.write(translated)
    outputFileObj.close()

    print('Done %sing %s (%s characters).' % (myMode, inputFilename, len(content)))
    print('%sed file is %s.' % (myMode.title(), outputFilename))


# If transpositionCipherFile.py is run (instead of imported as a module)
# call the main() function.
if __name__ == '__main__':
    main()
```

In the directory that *frankenstein.txt* and *transpositionFileCipher.py* files are in, there will be a new file named *frankenstein.encrypted.txt* that contains the content of *frankenstein.txt* in encrypted form. If you double-click the file to open it, it should look something like this:

```
PtFiyedleo  a arnvmt eneeGLchongnes Mmuyedlsu0#uiSHTGA r sy,n t ys
s nuaoGeL
sc7s,
(the rest has been cut out for brevity)
```

To decrypt, make the following changes to the source code (written in bold) and run the transposition cipher program again:

transpositionFileCipher.py

```
    inputFilename = 'frankenstein.encrypted.txt'
    # BE CAREFUL! If a file with the outputFilename name already exists,
    # this program will overwrite that file.
    outputFilename = 'frankenstein.decrypted.txt'
    myKey = 10
    myMode = 'decrypt' # set to 'encrypt' or 'decrypt'
```

This time when you run the program a new file will appear in the folder named *frankenstein.decrypted.txt* that is identical to the original *frankenstein.txt* file.

Sample Run of the Transposition File Cipher Program

When you run the above program, it produces this output:

```
Encrypting...
Encryption time: 1.21 seconds
Done encrypting frankenstein.txt (441034 characters).
Encrypted file is frankenstein.encrypted.txt.
```

A new *frankenstein.encrypted.txt* file will have been created in the same directory as *transpositionFileCipher.py*. If you open this file with IDLE's file editor, you will see the encrypted contents of *frankenstein.py*. You can now email this encrypted file to someone for them to decrypt.

Reading From Files

Up until now, any input we want to give our programs would have to be typed in by the user. Python programs can open and read files directly off of the hard drive. There are three steps to reading the contents of a file: opening the file, reading into a variable, and then closing the file.

The `open()` Function and File Objects

The `open()` function's first parameter is a string for the name of the file to open. If the file is in the same directory as the Python program then you can just type in the name, such as `'thetimemachine.txt'`. You can always specify the **absolute path** of the file, which includes the directory that it is in. For example, `'c:\\Python32\\frankenstein.txt'` (on Windows) and `'/usr/foobar/frankenstein.txt'` (on OS X and Linux) are absolute filenames. (Remember that the \ backslash must be escaped with another backslash before it.)

The `open()` function returns a value of the "file object" data type. This value has several methods for reading from, writing to, and closing the file.

The `read()` File Object Method

The `read()` method will return a string containing all the text in the file. For example, say the file *spam.txt* contained the text "Hello world!". (You can create this file yourself using IDLE's file editor. Just save the file with a .txt extension.) Run the following from the interactive shell (this codes assumes you are running Windows and the *spam.txt* file is in the *c:* directory):

```
>>> fo = open('c:\\spam.txt', 'r')
>>> content = fo.read()
>>> print(content)
Hello world!
```

```
>>>
```

If your text file has multiple lines, the string returned by `read()` will have `\n` newline characters in it at the end of each line. When you try to print a string with newline characters, the string will print across several lines:

```
>>> print('Hello\nworld!')
Hello
world!
>>>
```

If you get an error message that says "`IOError: [Errno 2] No such file or directory`" then double check that you typed the filename (and if it is an absolute path, the directory name) correctly. Also make sure that the file actually is where you think it is.

The `close()` File Object Method

After you have read the file's contents into a variable, you can tell Python that you are done with the file by calling the `close()` method on the file object.

```
>>> fo.close()
>>>
```

Python will automatically close any open files when the program terminates. But when you want to re-read the contents of a file, you must close the file object and then call the `open()` function on the file again.

Here's the code in our transposition cipher program that reads the file whose filename is stored in the `inputFilename` variable:

transpositionFileCipher.py

```
    # Read in the message from the input file
    fileObj = open(inputFilename)
    content = fileObj.read()
    fileObj.close()
```

Writing To Files

We read the original file and now will write the encrypted (or decrypted) form to a different file. The file object returned by `open()` has a `write()` function, although you can only use this function if you open the file in "write" mode instead of "read" mode. You do this by passing the string value `'w'` as the second parameter. For example:

```
>>> fo = open('filename.txt', 'w')
>>>
```

Along with "read" and "write", there is also an "append" mode. The "append" is like "write" mode, except any strings written to the file will be appended to the end of any content that is already in the file. "Append" mode will not overwrite the file if it already exists. To open a file in append mode, pass the string `'a'` as the second argument to `open()`.

(Just in case you were curious, you could pass the string `'r'` to `open()` to open the file in read mode. But since passing no second argument at all also opens the file in read mode, there's no reason to pass `'r'`.)

The `write()` File Object Method

You can write text to a file by calling the file object's `write()` method. The file object must have been opened in write mode, otherwise, you will get a "`io.UnsupportedOperation: not readable`" error message. (And if you try to call `read()` on a file object that was opened in write mode, you will get a "`io.UnsupportedOperation: not readable`" error message.)

The `write()` method takes one argument: a string of text that is to be written to the file. Lines 43 to 45 open a file in write mode, write to the file, and then close the file object.

transpositionFileCipher.py

```
42.     # Write out the translated message to the output file.
43.     outputFileObj = open(outputFilename, 'w')
44.     outputFileObj.write(translated)
45.     outputFileObj.close()
```

Now that we have the basics of reading and writing files, let's look at the source code to the transposition file cipher program.

How the Program Works

transpositionFileCipher.py

```
# Transposition Cipher Encrypt/Decrypt File
# http://inventwithpython.com/hacking (BSD Licensed)

import time, os, sys, transpositionEncrypt, transpositionDecrypt

def main():
    inputFilename = 'frankenstein.txt'
    # BE CAREFUL! If a file with the outputFilename name already exists,
    # this program will overwrite that file.
```

```
10.     outputFilename = 'frankenstein.encrypted.txt'
11.     myKey = 10
12.     myMode = 'encrypt' # set to 'encrypt' or 'decrypt'
```

The first part of the program should look familiar. Line 4 is an `import` statement for our *transpositionEncrypt.py* and *transpositionDecrypt.py* programs. It also imports the Python's `time`, `os`, and `sys` modules.

The `main()` function will be called after the `def` statements have been executed to define all the functions in the program. The `inputFilename` variable holds a string of the file to read, and the encrypted (or decrypted) text is written to the file with the name in `outputFilename`.

The transposition cipher uses an integer for a key, stored in `myKey`. If `'encrypt'` is stored in `myMode`, the program will encrypt the contents of the `inputFilename` file. If `'decrypt'` is stored in `myMode`, the contents of `inputFilename` will be decrypted.

The `os.path.exists()` Function

Reading files is always harmless, but we need to be careful when writing files. If we call the `open()` function in write mode with a filename that already exists, that file will first be deleted to make way for the new file. This means we could accidentally erase an important file if we pass the important file's name to the `open()` function. Using the `os.path.exists()` function, we can check if a file with a certain filename already exists.

The `os.path.exists()` file has a single string parameter for the filename, and returns `True` if this file already exists and `False` if it doesn't. The `os.path.exists()` function exists inside the `path` module, which itself exists inside the `os` module. But if we import the `os` module, the `path` module will be imported too.

Try typing the following into the interactive shell:

```
>>> import os
>>> os.path.exists('abcdef')
False
>>> os.path.exists('C:\\Windows\\System32\\calc.exe')
True
>>>
```

(Of course, you will only get the above results if you are running Python on Windows. The *calc.exe* file does not exist on OS X or Linux.)

transpositionFileCipher.py
```
    # If the input file does not exist, then the program terminates early.
    if not os.path.exists(inputFilename):
        print('The file %s does not exist. Quitting...' % (inputFilename))
        sys.exit()
```

We use the `os.path.exists()` function to check that the filename in `inputFilename` actually exists. Otherwise, we have no file to encrypt or decrypt. In that case, we display a message to the user and then quit the program.

The `startswith()` and `endswith()` String Methods

transpositionFileCipher.py
```
19.     # If the output file already exists, give the user a chance to quit.
20.     if os.path.exists(outputFilename):
21.         print('This will overwrite the file %s. (C)ontinue or (Q)uit?' % (outputFilename))
22.         response = input('> ')
23.         if not response.lower().startswith('c'):
24.             sys.exit()
```

If the file the program will write to already exists, the user is asked to type in "C" if they want to continue running the program or "Q" to quit the program.

The string in the response variable will have `lower()` called on it, and the returned string from `lower()` will have the string method `startswith()` called on it. The `startswith()` method will return `True` if its string argument can be found at the beginning of the string. Try typing the following into the interactive shell:

```
>>> 'hello'.startswith('h')
True
>>> 'hello world!'.startswith('hello wo')
True
>>> 'hello'.startswith('H')
False
>>> spam = 'Albert'
>>> spam.startswith('Al')
True
>>>
```

On line 23, if the user did not type in `'c'`, `'continue'`, `'C'`, or another string that begins with C, then `sys.exit()` will be called to end the program. Technically, the user doesn't have to enter "Q" to quit; any string that does not begin with "C" will cause the sys.exit() function to be called to quit the program.

There is also an `endswith()` string method that can be used to check if a string value ends with another certain string value. Try typing the following into the interactive shell:

```
>>> 'Hello world!'.endswith('world!')
True
>>> 'Hello world!'.endswith('world')
False
>>>
```

The `title()` String Method

Just like the `lower()` and `upper()` string methods will return a string in lowercase or uppercase, the `title()` string method returns a string in "title case". Title case is where every word is uppercase for the first character and lowercase for the rest of the characters. Try typing the following into the interactive shell:

```
>>> 'hello'.title()
'Hello'
>>> 'HELLO'.title()
'Hello'
>>> 'hElLo'.title()
'Hello'
>>> 'hello world! HOW ARE YOU?'.title()
'Hello World! How Are You?'
>>> 'extra! extra! man bites shark!'.title()
'Extra! Extra! Man Bites Shark!'
>>>
```

transpositionFileCipher.py

```
26.     # Read in the message from the input file
27.     fileObj = open(inputFilename)
28.     content = fileObj.read()
29.     fileObj.close()
30.
31.     print('%sing...' % (myMode.title()))
```

Lines 27 to 29 open the file with the name stored in `inputFilename` and read in its contents into the `content` variable. On line 31, we display a message telling the user that the encryption or decryption has begun. Since `myMode` should either contain the string `'encrypt'` or `'decrypt'`, calling the `title()` string method will either display `'Encrypting...'` or `'Decrypting...'`.

The `time` Module and `time.time()` Function

All computers have a clock that keeps track of the current date and time. Your Python programs can access this clock by calling the `time.time()` function. (This is a function named `time()` that is in a module named `time`.)

The `time.time()` function will return a float value of the number of seconds since January 1st, 1970. This moment is called the **Unix Epoch**. Try typing the following into the interactive shell:

```
>>> import time
>>> time.time()
1349411356.892
>>> time.time()
1349411359.326
>>>
```

The float value shows that the `time.time()` function can be precise down to a **millisecond** (that is, 1/1,000 of a second). Of course, the numbers that `time.time()` displays for you will depend on the moment in time that you call this function. It might not be clear that 1349411356.892 is Thursday, October 4th, 2012 around 9:30 pm. However, the `time.time()` function is useful for comparing the number of seconds between calls to `time.time()`. We can use this function to determine how long our program has been running.

transpositionFileCipher.py

```
33.     # Measure how long the encryption/decryption takes.
34.     startTime = time.time()
35.     if myMode == 'encrypt':
36.         translated = transpositionEncrypt.encryptMessage(myKey, content)
37.     elif myMode == 'decrypt':
38.         translated = transpositionDecrypt.decryptMessage(myKey, content)
39.     totalTime = round(time.time() - startTime, 2)
40.     print('%sion time: %s seconds' % (myMode.title(), totalTime))
```

We want to measure how long the encryption or decryption process takes for the contents of the file. Lines 35 to 38 call the `encryptMessage()` or `decryptMessage()` (depending on whether `'encrypt'` or `'decrypt'` is stored in the `myMode` variable). Before this code however, we will call `time.time()` and store the current time in a variable named `startTime`.

On line 39 after the encryption or decryption function calls have returned, we will call `time.time()` again and subtract `startTime` from it. This will give us the number of seconds between the two calls to `time.time()`.

For example, if you subtract the floating point values returned when I called `time.time()` before in the interactive shell, you would get the amount of time in between those calls while I was typing:

```
>>> 1349411359.326 - 1349411356.892
2.434000015258789
>>>
```

(The difference Python calculated between the two floating point values is not precise due to rounding errors, which cause very slight inaccuracies when doing math with floats. For our programs, it will not matter. But you can read more about rounding errors at http://invpy.com/rounding.)

The `time.time() - startTime` expression evaluates to a value that is passed to the `round()` function which rounds to the nearest two decimal points. This value is stored in `totalTime`. On line 40, the amount of time is displayed to the user by calling `print()`.

Back to the Code

transpositionFileCipher.py

```
42.     # Write out the translated message to the output file.
43.     outputFileObj = open(outputFilename, 'w')
44.     outputFileObj.write(translated)
45.     outputFileObj.close()
```

The encrypted (or decrypted) file contents are now stored in the `translated` variable. But this string will be forgotten when the program terminates, so we want to write the string out to a file to store it on the hard drive. The code on lines 43 to 45 do this by opening a new file (passing `'w'` to `open()` to open the file in write mode) and then calling the `write()` file object method.

transpositionFileCipher.py

```
    print('Done %sing %s (%s characters).' % (myMode, inputFilename, len(content)))
    print('%sed file is %s.' % (myMode.title(), outputFilename))


# If transpositionCipherFile.py is run (instead of imported as a module)
# call the main() function.
if __name__ == '__main__':
    main()
```

Afterwards, we print some more messages to the user telling them that the process is done and what the name of the written file is. Line 48 is the last line of the `main()` function.

Lines 53 and 54 (which get executed after the `def` statement on line 6 is executed) will call the `main()` function if this program is being run instead of being imported. (This is explained in Chapter 8's "The Special `__name__` Variable" section.)

Practice Exercises, Chapter 11, Set A

Practice exercises can be found at http://invpy.com/hackingpractice11A.

Summary

Congratulations! There wasn't much to this new program aside from the `open()`, `write()`, `read()`, and `close()` functions, but this lets us encrypt text files on our hard drive that are megabytes or gigabytes in size. It doesn't take much new code because all of the implementation for the cipher has already been written. We can extend our programs (such as adding file reading and writing capabilities) by importing their functions for use in new programs. This greatly increases our ability to use computers to encrypt information.

There are too many possible keys to simply brute-force and examine the output of a message encrypted with the transposition cipher. But if we can write a program that recognizes English (as opposed to strings of gibberish), we can have the computer examine the output of thousands of decryption attempts and determine which key can successfully decrypt a message to English.

CHAPTER 12

DETECTING ENGLISH PROGRAMMATICALLY

Topics Covered In This Chapter:

- Dictionaries
- The `split()` Method
- The `None` Value
- "Divide by Zero" Errors
- The `float()`, `int()`, and `str()` Functions and Python 2 Division
- The `append()` List Method
- Default Arguments
- Calculating Percentage

> The gaffer says something longer and more complicated. After a while, Waterhouse (now wearing his cryptoanalyst hat, searching for meaning midst apparent randomness, his neural circuits exploiting the redundancies in the signal) realizes that the man is speaking heavily accented English.
>
> "Cryptonomicon" by Neal Stephenson

A message encrypted with the transposition cipher can have thousands of possible keys. Your computer can still easily brute-force this many keys, but you would then have to look through thousands of decryptions to find the one correct plaintext. This is a big problem for the brute-force method of cracking the transposition cipher.

When the computer decrypts a message with the wrong key, the resulting plaintext is garbage text. We need to program the computer to be able to recognize if the plaintext is garbage text or English text. That way, if the computer decrypts with the wrong key, it knows to go on and try the next possible key. And when the computer tries a key that decrypts to English text, it can stop and bring that key to the attention of the cryptanalyst. Now the cryptanalyst won't have to look through thousands of incorrect decryptions.

How Can a Computer Understand English?

It can't. At least, not in the way that human beings like you or I understand English. Computers don't really understand math, chess, or lethal military androids either, any more than a clock understands lunchtime. Computers just execute instructions one after another. But these instructions can mimic very complicated behaviors that solve math problems, win at chess, or hunt down the future leaders of the human resistance.

Ideally, what we need is a Python function (let's call it `isEnglish()`) that has a string passed to it and then returns `True` if the string is English text and `False` if it's random gibberish. Let's take a look at some English text and some garbage text and try to see what patterns the two have:

```
Robots are your friends. Except for RX-686. She will try to eat you.

ai-pey  e. xrx ne augur iirl6 Rtiyt fhubE6d hrSei t8..ow eo.telyoosEs  t
```

One thing we can notice is that the English text is made up of words that you could find in a dictionary, but the garbage text is made up of words that you won't. Splitting up the string into individual words is easy. There is already a Python string method named `split()` that will do this for us (this method will be explained later). The `split()` method just sees when each word begins or ends by looking for the space characters. Once we have the individual words, we can test to see if each word is a word in the dictionary with code like this:

```
if word == 'aardvark' or word == 'abacus' or word == 'abandon' or word ==
'abandoned' or word == 'abbreviate' or word == 'abbreviation' or word ==
'abdomen' or …
```

We *can* write code like that, but we probably shouldn't. The computer won't mind running through all this code, but you wouldn't want to type it all out. Besides, somebody else has already typed out a text file full of nearly all English words. These text files are called **dictionary files**. So we just need to write a function that checks if the words in the string exist somewhere in that file.

Remember, a *dictionary file* is a text file that contains a large list of English words. A *dictionary value* is a Python value that has key-value pairs.

Not every word will exist in our "dictionary file". Maybe the dictionary file is incomplete and doesn't have the word, say, "aardvark". There are also perfectly good decryptions that might have non-English words in them, such as "RX-686" in our above English sentence. (Or maybe the plaintext is in a different language besides English. But we'll just assume it is in English for now.)

And garbage text might just happen to have an English word or two in it by coincidence. For example, it turns out the word "augur" means a person who tries to predict the future by studying the way birds are flying. Seriously.

So our function will not be foolproof. But if most of the words in the string argument are English words, it is a good bet to say that the string is English text. It is a very low probability that a ciphertext will decrypt to English if decrypted with the wrong key.

The dictionary text file will have one word per line in uppercase. It will look like this:

```
AARHUS
AARON
ABABA
ABACK
ABAFT
ABANDON
ABANDONED
ABANDONING
ABANDONMENT
ABANDONS
```

…and so on. You can download this entire file (which has over 45,000 words) from http://invpy.com/dictionary.txt.

Our `isEnglish()` function will have to split up a decrypted string into words, check if each word is in a file full of thousands of English words, and if a certain amount of the words are English words, then we will say that the text is in English. And if the text is in English, then there's a good bet that we have decrypted the ciphertext with the correct key.

And that is how the computer can understand if a string is English or if it is gibberish.

Practice Exercises, Chapter 12, Section A

Practice exercises can be found at http://invpy.com/hackingpractice12A.

The Detect English Module

The *detectEnglish.py* program that we write in this chapter isn't a program that runs by itself. Instead, it will be imported by our encryption programs so that they can call the `detectEnglish.isEnglish()` function. This is why we don't give *detectEnglish.py* a `main()` function. The other functions in the program are all provided for `isEnglish()` to call.

Source Code for the Detect English Module

Open a new file editor window by clicking on **File ► New Window**. Type in the following code into the file editor, and then save it as *detectEnglish.py*. Press **F5** to run the program.

Source code for detectEnglish.py

```
# Detect English module
# http://inventwithpython.com/hacking (BSD Licensed)

# To use, type this code:
#   import detectEnglish
#   detectEnglish.isEnglish(someString) # returns True or False
# (There must be a "dictionary.txt" file in this directory with all English
# words in it, one word per line. You can download this from
# http://invpy.com/dictionary.txt)
UPPERLETTERS = 'ABCDEFGHIJKLMNOPQRSTUVWXYZ'
LETTERS_AND_SPACE = UPPERLETTERS + UPPERLETTERS.lower() + ' \t\n'

def loadDictionary():
    dictionaryFile = open('dictionary.txt')
    englishWords = {}
    for word in dictionaryFile.read().split('\n'):
        englishWords[word] = None
    dictionaryFile.close()
    return englishWords

ENGLISH_WORDS = loadDictionary()


def getEnglishCount(message):
    message = message.upper()
    message = removeNonLetters(message)
    possibleWords = message.split()
```

```

    if possibleWords == []:
        return 0.0 # no words at all, so return 0.0

    matches = 0
    for word in possibleWords:
        if word in ENGLISH_WORDS:
            matches += 1
    return float(matches) / len(possibleWords)


def removeNonLetters(message):
    lettersOnly = []
    for symbol in message:
        if symbol in LETTERS_AND_SPACE:
            lettersOnly.append(symbol)
    return ''.join(lettersOnly)


def isEnglish(message, wordPercentage=20, letterPercentage=85):
    # By default, 20% of the words must exist in the dictionary file, and
    # 85% of all the characters in the message must be letters or spaces
    # (not punctuation or numbers).
    wordsMatch = getEnglishCount(message) * 100 >= wordPercentage
    numLetters = len(removeNonLetters(message))
    messageLettersPercentage = float(numLetters) / len(message) * 100
    lettersMatch = messageLettersPercentage >= letterPercentage
    return wordsMatch and lettersMatch
```

How the Program Works

detectEnglish.py

```
# Detect English module
# http://inventwithpython.com/hacking (BSD Licensed)

# To use, type this code:
#   import detectEnglish
#   detectEnglish.isEnglish(someString) # returns True or False
# (There must be a "dictionary.txt" file in this directory with all English
# words in it, one word per line. You can download this from
# http://invpy.com/dictionary.txt)
```

These comments at the top of the file give instructions to programmers on how to use this module. They give the important reminder that if there is no file named *dictionary.txt* in the same directory as *detectEnglish.py* then this module will not work. If the user doesn't have this file, the comments tell them they can download it from http://invpy.com/dictionary.txt.

detectEnglish.py
```
10. UPPERLETTERS = 'ABCDEFGHIJKLMNOPQRSTUVWXYZ'
11. LETTERS_AND_SPACE = UPPERLETTERS + UPPERLETTERS.lower() + ' \t\n'
```

Lines 10 and 11 set up a few variables that are constants, which is why they have uppercase names. `UPPERLETTERS` is a variable containing the 26 uppercase letters, and `LETTERS_AND_SPACE` contain these letters (and the lowercase letters returned from `UPPERLETTERS.lower()`) but also the space character, the tab character, and the newline character. The tab and newline characters are represented with escape characters `\t` and `\n`.

detectEnglish.py
```
def loadDictionary():
    dictionaryFile = open('dictionary.txt')
```

The dictionary file sits on the user's hard drive, but we need to load the text in this file as a string value so our Python code can use it. First, we get a file object by calling `open()` and passing the string of the filename `'dictionary.txt'`. Before we continue with the `loadDictionary()` code, let's learn about the dictionary data type.

Dictionaries and the Dictionary Data Type

The **dictionary** data type has values which can contain multiple other values, just like lists do. In list values, you use an integer index value to retrieve items in the list, like `spam[42]`. For each item in the dictionary value, there is a key used to retrieve it. (Values stored inside lists and dictionaries are also sometimes called items.) The key can be an integer or a string value, like `spam['hello']` or `spam[42]`. Dictionaries let us organize our program's data with even more flexibility than lists.

Instead of typing square brackets like list values, dictionary values (or simply, dictionaries) use curly braces. Try typing the following into the interactive shell:

```
>>> emptyList = []
>>> emptyDictionary = {}
>>>
```

A dictionary's values are typed out as key-value pairs, which are separated by colons. Multiple key-value pairs are separated by commas. To retrieve values from a dictionary, just use square brackets with the key in between them (just like indexing with lists). Try typing the following into the interactive shell:

```
>>> spam = {'key1':'This is a value', 'key2':42}
>>> spam['key1']
'This is a value'
>>> spam['key2']
42
>>>
```

It is important to know that, just as with lists, variables do not store dictionary values themselves, but references to dictionaries. The example code below has two variables with references to the same dictionary:

```
>>> spam = {'hello': 42}
>>> eggs = spam
>>> eggs['hello'] = 99
>>> eggs
{'hello': 99}
>>> spam
{'hello': 99}
>>>
```

Adding or Changing Items in a Dictionary

You can add or change values in a dictionary with indexes as well. Try typing the following into the interactive shell:

```
>>> spam = {42:'hello'}
>>> print(spam[42])
hello
>>> spam[42] = 'goodbye'
>>> print(spam[42])
goodbye
>>>
```

And just like lists can contain other lists, dictionaries can also contain other dictionaries (or lists). Try typing the following into the interactive shell:

```
>>> foo = {'fizz': {'name': 'Al', 'age': 144}, 'moo':['a', 'brown', 'cow']}
>>> foo['fizz']
{'age': 144, 'name': 'Al'}
>>> foo['fizz']['name']
'Al'
>>> foo['moo']
['a', 'brown', 'cow']
>>> foo['moo'][1]
```

```
'brown'
>>>
```

Practice Exercises, Chapter 12, Set B

Practice exercises can be found at http://invpy.com/hackingpractice12B.

Using the `len()` Function with Dictionaries

The `len()` function can tell you how many items are in a list or how many characters are in a string, but it can also tell you how many items are in a dictionary as well. Try typing the following into the interactive shell:

```
>>> spam = {}
>>> len(spam)
0
>>> spam['name'] = 'Al'
>>> spam['pet'] = 'Zophie the cat'
>>> spam['age'] = 89
>>> len(spam)
3
>>>
```

Using the `in` Operator with Dictionaries

The `in` operator can also be used to see if a certain key value exists in a dictionary. It is important to remember that the `in` operator checks if a key exists in the dictionary, not a value. Try typing the following into the interactive shell:

```
>>> eggs = {'foo': 'milk', 'bar': 'bread'}
>>> 'foo' in eggs
True
>>> 'blah blah blah' in eggs
False
>>> 'milk' in eggs
False
>>> 'bar' in eggs
True
>>> 'bread' in eggs
False
>>>
```

The `not in` operator works with dictionary values as well.

Using `for` Loops with Dictionaries

You can also iterate over the keys in a dictionary with `for` loops, just like you can iterate over the items in a list. Try typing the following into the interactive shell:

```
>>> spam = {'name':'Al', 'age':99}
>>> for k in spam:
...   print(k)
...   print(spam[k])
...   print('==========')
...
age
99
==========
name
Al
==========
>>>
```

Practice Exercises, Chapter 12, Set C

Practice exercises can be found at http://invpy.com/hackingpractice12C.

The Difference Between Dictionaries and Lists

Dictionaries are like lists in many ways, but there are a few important differences:

1. Dictionary items are not in any order. There is no "first" or "last" item in a dictionary like there is in a list.
2. Dictionaries do not have concatenation with the + operator. If you want to add a new item, you can just use indexing with a new key. For example, `foo['a new key'] = 'a string'`
3. Lists only have integer index values that range from `0` to the length of the list minus one. But dictionaries can have any key. If you have a dictionary stored in a variable `spam`, then you can store a value in `spam[3]` without needing values for `spam[0]`, `spam[1]`, or `spam[2]` first.

Finding Items is Faster with Dictionaries Than Lists

detectEnglish.py

```
    englishWords = {}
```

In the `loadDictionary()` function, we will store all the words in the "dictionary file" (as in, a file that has all the words in an English dictionary book) in a dictionary value (as in, the Python data type.) The similar names are unfortunate, but they are two completely different things.

We could have also used a list to store the string values of each word from the dictionary file. The reason we use a dictionary is because the `in` operator works faster on dictionaries than lists. Imagine that we had the following list and dictionary values:

```
>>> listVal = ['spam', 'eggs', 'bacon']
>>> dictionaryVal = {'spam':0, 'eggs':0, 'bacon':0}
```

Python can evaluate the expression `'bacon' in dictionaryVal` a little bit faster than `'bacon' in listVal`. The reason is technical and you don't need to know it for the purposes of this book (but you can read more about it at http://invpy.com/listvsdict). This faster speed doesn't make that much of a difference for lists and dictionaries with only a few items in them like in the above example. But our `detectEnglish` module will have tens of thousands of items, and the expression `word in ENGLISH_WORDS` will be evaluated many times when the `isEnglish()` function is called. The speed difference really adds up for the `detectEnglish` module.

The `split()` Method

The `split()` string method returns a list of several strings. The "split" between each string occurs wherever a space is. For an example of how the `split()` string method works, try typing this into the shell:

```
>>> 'My very energetic mother    just served us Nutella.'.split()
['My', 'very', 'energetic', 'mother', 'just', 'served', 'us', 'Nutella.']
>>>
```

The result is a list of eight strings, one string for each of the words in the original string. The spaces are dropped from the items in the list (even if there is more than one space). You can pass an optional argument to the `split()` method to tell it to split on a different string other than just a space. Try typing the following into the interactive shell:

```
>>> 'helloXXXworldXXXhowXXXareXXyou?'.split('XXX')
['hello', 'world', 'how', 'areXXyou?']
>>>
```

detectEnglish.py
```
16.     for word in dictionaryFile.read().split('\n'):
```

Line 16 is a `for` loop that will set the `word` variable to each value in the list `dictionaryFile.read().split('\n')`. Let's break this expression down. `dictionaryFile` is the variable that stores the file object of the opened file. The `dictionaryFile.read()` method call will read the entire file and return it as a very large string value. On this string, we will call the `split()` method and split on newline characters. This `split()` call will return a list value made up of each word in the dictionary file (because the dictionary file has one word per line.)

This is why the expression `dictionaryFile.read().split('\n')` will evaluate to a list of string values. Since the dictionary text file has one word on each line, the strings in the list that `split()` returns will each have one word.

The `None` Value

`None` is a special value that you can assign to a variable. The **None value** represents the lack of a value. `None` is the only value of the data type NoneType. (Just like how the Boolean data type has only two values, the NoneType data type has only one value, `None`.) It can be very useful to use the `None` value when you need a value that means "does not exist". The `None` value is always written without quotes and with a capital "N" and lowercase "one".

For example, say you had a variable named `quizAnswer` which holds the user's answer to some True-False pop quiz question. You could set `quizAnswer` to `None` if the user skipped the question and did not answer it. Using `None` would be better because if you set it to `True` or `False` before assigning the value of the user's answer, it may look like the user gave an answer for the question even though they didn't.

Calls to functions that do not return anything (that is, they exit by reaching the end of the function and not from a `return` statement) will evaluate to `None`.

detectEnglish.py
```
17.         englishWords[word] = None
```

In our program, we only use a dictionary for the `englishWords` variable so that the `in` operator can find keys in it. We don't care what is stored for each key, so we will just use the `None` value. The `for` loop that starts on line 16 will iterate over each word in the dictionary file, and line 17 will use that word as a key in `englishWords` with `None` stored for that key.

Back to the Code

detectEnglish.py

```
18.     dictionaryFile.close()
19.     return englishWords
```

After the `for` loop finishes, the `englishWords` dictionary will have tens of thousands of keys in it. At this point, we close the file object since we are done reading from it and then return `englishWords`.

detectEnglish.py

```
21. ENGLISH_WORDS = loadDictionary()
```

Line 21 calls `loadDictionary()` and stores the dictionary value it returns in a variable named `ENGLISH_WORDS`. We want to call `loadDictionary()` before the rest of the code in the `detectEnglish` module, but Python has to execute the `def` statement for `loadDictionary()` before we can call the function. This is why the assignment for `ENGLISH_WORDS` comes after the `loadDictionary()` function's code.

detectEnglish.py

```
24. def getEnglishCount(message):
25.     message = message.upper()
26.     message = removeNonLetters(message)
27.     possibleWords = message.split()
```

The `getEnglishCount()` function will take one string argument and return a float value indicating the amount of recognized English words in it. The value `0.0` will mean none of the words in `message` are English words and `1.0` will mean all of the words in `message` are English words, but most likely `getEnglishCount()` will return something in between `0.0` and `1.0`. The `isEnglish()` function will use this return value as part of whether it returns `True` or `False`.

First we must create a list of individual word strings from the string in `message`. Line 25 will convert it to uppercase letters. Then line 26 will remove the non-letter characters from the string, such as numbers and punctuation, by calling `removeNonLetters()`. (We will see how this function works later.) Finally, the `split()` method on line 27 will split up the string into individual words that are stored in a variable named `possibleWords`.

So if the string `'Hello there. How are you?'` was passed when `getEnglishCount()` was called, the value stored in `possibleWords` after lines 25 to 27 execute would be `['HELLO', 'THERE', 'HOW', 'ARE', 'YOU']`.

detectEnglish.py

```
29.     if possibleWords == []:
30.         return 0.0 # no words at all, so return 0.0
```

If the string in `message` was something like `'12345'`, all of these non-letter characters would have been taken out of the string returned from `removeNonLetters()`. The call to `removeNonLetters()` would return the blank string, and when `split()` is called on the blank string, it will return an empty list.

Line 29 does a special check for this case, and returns `0.0`. This is done to avoid a "divide-by-zero" error (which is explained later on).

detectEnglish.py

```
32.     matches = 0
33.     for word in possibleWords:
34.         if word in ENGLISH_WORDS:
35.             matches += 1
```

The float value that is returned from `getEnglishCount()` ranges between `0.0` and `1.0`. To produce this number, we will divide the number of the words in `possibleWords` that are recognized as English by the total number of words in `possibleWords`.

The first part of this is to count the number of recognized English words in `possibleWords`, which is done on lines 32 to 35. The `matches` variable starts off as `0`. The `for` loop on line 33 will loop over each of the words in `possibleWords`, and checks if the word exists in the `ENGLISH_WORDS` dictionary. If it does, the value in `matches` is incremented on line 35.

Once the `for` loop has completed, the number of English words is stored in the `matches` variable. Note that technically this is only the number of words that are recognized as English because they existed in our dictionary text file. As far as the program is concerned, if the word exists in *dictionary.txt*, then it is a real English word. And if it doesn't exist in the dictionary file, it is not an English word. We are relying on the dictionary file to be accurate and complete in order for the `detectEnglish` module to work correctly.

"Divide by Zero" Errors

detectEnglish.py

```
36.     return float(matches) / len(possibleWords)
```

Returning a float value between `0.0` and `1.0` is a simple matter of dividing the number of recognized words by the total number of words.

However, whenever we divide numbers using the / operator in Python, we should be careful not to cause a "divide-by-zero" error. In mathematics, dividing by zero has no meaning. If we try to get Python to do it, it will result in an error. Try typing the following into the interactive shell:

```
>>> 42 / 0
Traceback (most recent call last):
  File "<pyshell#0>", line 1, in <module>
    42 / 0
ZeroDivisionError: int division or modulo by zero
>>>
```

But a divide by zero can't possibly happen on line 36. The only way it could is if `len(possibleWords)` evaluated to `0`. And the only way that would be possible is if `possibleWords` were the empty list. However, our code on lines 29 and 30 specifically checks for this case and returns `0.0`. So if `possibleWords` had been set to the empty list, the program execution would have never gotten past line 30 and line 36 would not cause a "divide-by-zero" error.

The `float()`, `int()`, and `str()` Functions and Integer Division

detectEnglish.py

```
36.     return float(matches) / len(possibleWords)
```

The value stored in `matches` is an integer. However, we pass this integer to the `float()` function which returns a float version of that number. Try typing the following into the interactive shell:

```
>>> float(42)
42.0
>>>
```

The `int()` function returns an integer version of its argument, and the `str()` function returns a string. Try typing the following into the interactive shell:

```
>>> float(42)
42.0
>>> int(42.0)
42
>>> int(42.7)
42
>>> int("42")
```

```
42
>>> str(42)
'42'
>>> str(42.7)
'42.7'
>>>
```

The `float()`, `int()`, and `str()` functions are helpful if you need a value's equivalent in a different data type. But you might be wondering why we pass `matches` to `float()` on line 36 in the first place.

The reason is to make our `detectEnglish` module work with Python 2. Python 2 will do integer division when both values in the division operation are integers. This means that the result will be rounded down. So using Python 2, `22 / 7` will evaluate to `3`. However, if one of the values is a float, Python 2 will do regular division: `22.0 / 7` will evaluate to `3.142857142857143`. This is why line 36 calls `float()`. This is called making the code **backwards compatible** with previous versions.

Python 3 always does regular division no matter if the values are floats or ints.

Practice Exercises, Chapter 12, Set D

Practice exercises can be found at http://invpy.com/hackingpractice12D.

Back to the Code

detectEnglish.py

```
39. def removeNonLetters(message):
40.     lettersOnly = []
41.     for symbol in message:
```

The previously explained `getEnglishCount()` function calls the `removeNonLetters()` function to return a string that is the passed argument, except with all the numbers and punctuation characters removed.

The code in `removeNonLetters()` starts with a blank list and loops over each character in the `message` argument. If the character exists in the `LETTERS_AND_SPACE` string, then it is added to the end of the list. If the character is a number or punctuation mark, then it won't exist in the `LETTERS_AND_SPACE` string and won't be added to the list.

The append() List Method

detectEnglish.py

```
42.         if symbol in LETTERS_AND_SPACE:
43.             lettersOnly.append(symbol)
```

Line 42 checks if `symbol` (which is set to a single character on each iteration of line 41's `for` loop) exists in the `LETTERS_AND_SPACE` string. If it does, then it is added to the end of the `lettersOnly` list with the `append()` list method.

If you want to add a single value to the end of a list, you could put the value in its own list and then use list concatenation to add it. Try typing the following into the interactive shell, where the value `42` is added to the end of the list stored in `spam`:

```
>>> spam = [2, 3, 5, 7, 9, 11]
>>> spam
[2, 3, 5, 7, 9, 11]
>>> spam = spam + [42]
>>> spam
[2, 3, 5, 7, 9, 11, 42]
>>>
```

When we add a value to the end of a list, we say we are **appending** the value to the list. This is done with lists so frequently in Python that there is an `append()` list method which takes a single argument to append to the end of the list. Try typing the following into the shell:

```
>>> eggs = []
>>> eggs.append('hovercraft')
>>> eggs
['hovercraft']
>>> eggs.append('eels')
>>> eggs
['hovercraft', 'eels']
>>> eggs.append(42)
>>> eggs
['hovercraft', 'eels', 42]
>>>
```

For technical reasons, using the `append()` method is faster than putting a value in a list and adding it with the + operator. The `append()` method modifies the list in-place to include the new value. You should always prefer the `append()` method for adding values to the end of a list.

detectEnglish.py
```
    return ''.join(lettersOnly)
```

After line 41's `for` loop is done, only the letter and space characters are in the `lettersOnly` list. To make a single string value from this list of strings, we call the `join()` string method on a blank string. This will join the strings in `lettersOnly` together with a blank string (that is, nothing) between them. This string value is then returned as `removeNonLetters()`'s return value.

Default Arguments

detectEnglish.py
```
47. def isEnglish(message, wordPercentage=20, letterPercentage=85):
48.     # By default, 20% of the words must exist in the dictionary file, and
49.     # 85% of all the characters in the message must be letters or spaces
50.     # (not punctuation or numbers).
```

The `isEnglish()` function will accept a string argument and return a Boolean value that indicates whether or not it is English text. But when you look at line 47, you can see it has three parameters. The second and third parameters (`wordPercentage` and `letterPercentage`) have equal signs and values next to them. These are called **default arguments**. Parameters that have default arguments are optional. If the function call does not pass an argument for these parameters, the default argument is used by default.

If `isEnglish()` is called with only one argument, the default arguments are used for the `wordPercentage` (the integer `20`) and `letterPercentage` (the integer `85`) parameters. Table 12-1 shows function calls to `isEnglish()`, and what they are equivalent to:

Table 12-1. Function calls with and without default arguments.

Function Call	Equivalent To
`isEnglish('Hello')`	`isEnglish('Hello', 20, 85)`
`isEnglish('Hello', 50)`	`isEnglish('Hello', 50, 85)`
`isEnglish('Hello', 50, 60)`	`isEnglish('Hello', 50, 60)`
`isEnglish('Hello',` `letterPercentage=60)`	`isEnglish('Hello', 20, 60)`

When `isEnglish()` is called with no second and third argument, the function will require that 20% of the words in `message` are English words that exist in the dictionary text file and 85% of the characters in `message` are letters. These percentages work for detecting English in most cases. But sometimes a program calling `isEnglish()` will want looser or more restrictive thresholds. If so, a program can just pass arguments for `wordPercentage` and `letterPercentage` instead of using the default arguments.

Calculating Percentage

A percentage is a number between 0 and 100 that shows how much of something there is proportional to the total number of those things. In the string value `'Hello cat MOOSE fsdkl ewpin'` there are five "words" but only three of them are English words. **To calculate the percentage of English words, you divide the number of English words by the total number of words and multiply by 100.** The percentage of English words in `'Hello cat MOOSE fsdkl ewpin'` is `3 / 5 * 100`, which is `60`.

Table 12-2 shows some percentage calculations:

Table 12-2. Some percentage calculations.

Number of English Words	Total Number of Words	English Words / Total	* 100	=	Percentage
3	5	0.6	* 100	=	60
6	10	0.6	*100	=	60
300	500	0.6	* 100	=	60
32	87	0.3678	* 100	=	36.78
87	87	1.0	* 100	=	100
0	10	0	* 100	=	0

The percentage will always be between 0% (meaning none of the words) and 100% (meaning all of the words). Our `isEnglish()` function will consider a string to be English if at least 20% of the words are English words that exist in the dictionary file and 85% of the characters in the string are letters (or spaces).

detectEnglish.py

```
51.     wordsMatch = getEnglishCount(message) * 100 >= wordPercentage
```

Line 51 calculates the percentage of recognized English words in `message` by passing `message` to `getEnglishCount()`, which does the division for us and returns a float between `0.0` and `1.0`. To get a percentage from this float, we just have to multiply it by `100`. If this number is greater than or equal to the `wordPercentage` parameter, then `True` is stored in `wordsMatch`. (Remember, the >= comparison operator evaluates expressions to a Boolean value.) Otherwise, `False` is stored in `wordsMatch`.

detectEnglish.py
```
52.     numLetters = len(removeNonLetters(message))
53.     messageLettersPercentage = float(numLetters) / len(message) * 100
54.     lettersMatch = messageLettersPercentage >= letterPercentage
```

Lines 52 to 54 calculate the percentage of letter characters in the `message` string. To determine the percentage of letter (and space) characters in `message`, our code must divide the number of letter characters by the total number of characters in `message`. Line 52 calls `removeNonLetters(message)`. This call will return a string that has the number and punctuation characters removed from the string. Passing this string to `len()` will return the number of letter and space characters that were in `message`. This integer is stored in the `numLetters` variable.

Line 53 determines the percentage of letters getting a float version of the integer in `numLetters` and dividing this by `len(message)`. The return value of `len(message)` will be the total number of characters in `message`. (The call to `float()` was made so that if the programmer who imports our `detectEnglish` module is running Python 2, the division done on line 53 will always be regular division instead of integer division.)

Line 54 checks if the percentage in `messageLettersPercentage` is greater than or equal to the `letterPercentage` parameter. This expression evaluates to a Boolean value that is stored in `lettersMatch`.

detectEnglish.py
```
55.     return wordsMatch and lettersMatch
```

We want `isEnglish()` to return `True` only if both the `wordsMatch` and `lettersMatch` variables contain `True`, so we put them in an expression with the `and` operator. If both the `wordsMatch` and `lettersMatch` variables are `True`, then `isEnglish()` will declare that the message argument is English and return `True`. Otherwise, `isEnglish()` will return `False`.

Practice Exercises, Chapter 12, Set E

Practice exercises can be found at http://invpy.com/hackingpractice12E.

Summary

The dictionary data type is useful because like a list it can contain multiple values. However unlike the list, we can index values in it with string values instead of only integers. Most of the the things we can do with lists we can also do with dictionaries, such as pass it to `len()` or use the in and not in operators on it. In fact, using the in operator on a very large dictionary value executes much faster than using in on a very large list.

The NoneType data type is also a new data type introduced in this chapter. It only has one value: None. This value is very useful for representing a lack of a value.

We can convert values to other data types by using the int(), float(), and str() functions. This chapter brings up "divide-by-zero" errors, which we need to add code to check for and avoid. The split() string method can convert a single string value into a list value of many strings. The split() string method is sort of the reverse of the join() list method. The append() list method adds a value to the end of the list.

When we define functions, we can give some of the parameters "default arguments". If no argument is passed for these parameters when the function is called, the default argument value is used instead. This can be a useful shortcut in our programs.

The transposition cipher is an improvement over the Caesar cipher because it can have hundreds or thousands of possible keys for messages instead of just 26 different keys. A computer has no problem decrypting a message with thousands of different keys, but to hack this cipher, we need to write code that can determine if a string value is valid English or not.

Since this code will probably be useful in our other hacking programs, we will put it in its own module so it can be imported by any program that wants to call its isEnglish() function. All of the work we've done in this chapter is so that any program can do the following:

```
>>> import detectEnglish
>>> detectEnglish.isEnglish('Is this sentence English text?')
True
>>>
```

Now armed with code that can detect English, let's move on to the next chapter and hack the transposition cipher!

CHAPTER 13

HACKING THE TRANSPOSITION CIPHER

Topics Covered In This Chapter:

- Multi-line Strings with Triple Quotes
- The `strip()` String Method

To hack the transposition cipher, we will use a brute-force approach. Of the thousands of keys, the correct key is most likely that only one that will result in readable English. We developed English-detection code in the last chapter so the program can realize when it has found the correct key.

Source Code of the Transposition Cipher Hacker Program

Open a new file editor window by clicking on **File ► New Window**. Type in the following code into the file editor, and then save it as *transpositionHacker.py*. Press **F5** to run the program. Note that first you will need to download the *pyperclip.py* module and place this file in the same directory as the *transpositionHacker.py* file. You can download this file from http://invpy.com/pyperclip.py.

Source code for transpositionHacker.py

```
# Transposition Cipher Hacker
# http://inventwithpython.com/hacking (BSD Licensed)

import pyperclip, detectEnglish, transpositionDecrypt

```

```
def main():
    # You might want to copy & paste this text from the source code at
    # http://invpy.com/transpositionHacker.py
    myMessage = """Cb b rssti aieih rooaopbrtnsceee er es no npfgcwu  plri
ch nitaalr eiuengiteehb(e1  hilincegeoamn fubehgtarndcstudmd nM eu eacBoltaetee
oinebcdkyremdteghn.aa2r81a condari fmps" tad   l t oisn sit u1rnd stara nvhn fs
edbh ee,n  e necrg6  8nmisv l nc muiftegiitm tutmg cm shSs9fcie ebintcaets h  a
ihda cctrhe ele 1O7 aaoem waoaatdahretnhechaopnooeapece9etfncdbgsoeb uuteitgna.
rteoh add e,D7c1Etnpneehtn beete" evecoal lsfmcrl iu1cifgo ai. sl1rchdnheev sh
meBd ies e9t)nh,htcnoecplrrh ,ide hmtlme. pheaLem,toeinfgn t e9yce da' eN eMp a
ffn Fc1o ge eohg dere.eec s nfap yox hla yon. lnrnsreaBoa t,e eitsw il ulpbdofg
BRe bwlmprraio po  droB wtinue r Pieno nc ayieeto'lulcih sfnc  ownaSserbereiaSm
-eaiah, nnrttgcC  maciiritvledastinideI  nn rms iehn tsigaBmuoetcetias rn"""

    hackedMessage = hackTransposition(myMessage)

    if hackedMessage == None:
        print('Failed to hack encryption.')
    else:
        print('Copying hacked message to clipboard:')
        print(hackedMessage)
        pyperclip.copy(hackedMessage)


def hackTransposition(message):
    print('Hacking...')

    # Python programs can be stopped at any time by pressing Ctrl-C (on
    # Windows) or Ctrl-D (on Mac and Linux)
    print('(Press Ctrl-C or Ctrl-D to quit at any time.)')

    # brute-force by looping through every possible key
    for key in range(1, len(message)):
        print('Trying key #%s...' % (key))

        decryptedText = transpositionDecrypt.decryptMessage(key, message)

        if detectEnglish.isEnglish(decryptedText):
            # Check with user to see if the decrypted key has been found.
            print()
            print('Possible encryption hack:')
            print('Key %s: %s' % (key, decryptedText[:100]))
            print()
            print('Enter D for done, or just press Enter to continue
hacking:')
            response = input('> ')
```

```

            if response.strip().upper().startswith('D'):
                return decryptedText

    return None

if __name__ == '__main__':
    main()
```

Sample Run of the Transposition Breaker Program

When you run this program, the output will look this:

```
Hacking...
(Press Ctrl-C or Ctrl-D to quit at any time.)
Trying key #1...
Trying key #2...
Trying key #3...
Trying key #4...
Trying key #5...
Trying key #6...
Trying key #7...
Trying key #8...
Trying key #9...
Trying key #10...

Possible encryption hack:
Key 10: Charles Babbage, FRS (26 December 1791 - 18 October 1871) was an
English mathematician, philosopher,

Enter D for done, or just press Enter to continue hacking:
> D
Copying hacked message to clipboard:
Charles Babbage, FRS (26 December 1791 - 18 October 1871) was an English
mathematician, philosopher, inventor and mechanical engineer who originated the
concept of a programmable computer. Considered a "father of the computer",
Babbage is credited with inventing the first mechanical computer that
eventually led to more complex designs. Parts of his uncompleted mechanisms are
on display in the London Science Museum. In 1991, a perfectly functioning
difference engine was constructed from Babbage's original plans. Built to
tolerances achievable in the 19th century, the success of the finished engine
indicated that Babbage's machine would have worked. Nine years later, the
Science Museum completed the printer Babbage had designed for the difference
engine.
```

When the hacker program has found a likely correct decryption, it will pause and wait for the user to press "D" and then Enter. If the decryption is a false positive, the user can just press Enter and the program will continue to try other keys.

Run the program again and skip the correct decryption by just pressing Enter. The program assumes that it was not a correct decryption and continues brute-forcing through the other possible keys. Eventually the program runs through all the possible keys and then gives up, telling the user that it was unable to hack the ciphertext:

```
Trying key #757...
Trying key #758...
Trying key #759...
Trying key #760...
Trying key #761...
Failed to hack encryption.
```

How the Program Works

transpositionHacker.py

```
1. # Transposition Cipher Hacker
2. # http://inventwithpython.com/hacking (BSD Licensed)
3.
4. import pyperclip, detectEnglish, transpositionDecrypt
```

The transposition hacker program is under 50 lines of code because much of it exists in other programs. Several modules are imported on line 4.

Multi-line Strings with Triple Quotes

transpositionHacker.py

```
def main():
    # You might want to copy & paste this text from the source code at
    # http://invpy.com/transpositionHacker.py
    myMessage = """Cb b rssti aieih rooaopbrtnsceee er es no npfgcwu  plri
ch nitaalr eiuengiteehb(e1  hilincegeoamn fubehgtarndcstudmd nM eu eacBoltaetee
oinebcdkyremdteghn.aa2r81a condari fmps" tad   l t oisn sit u1rnd stara nvhn fs
edbh ee,n  e necrg6  8nmisv l nc muiftegiitm tutmg cm shSs9fcie ebintcaets h  a
ihda cctrhe ele 1O7 aaoem waoaatdahretnhechaopnooeapece9etfncdbgsoeb uuteitgna.
rteoh add e,D7c1Etnpneehtn beete" evecoal lsfmcrl iu1cifgo ai. sl1rchdnheev sh
meBd ies e9t)nh,htcnoecplrrh ,ide hmtlme. pheaLem,toeinfgn t e9yce da' eN eMp a
ffn Fc1o ge eohg dere.eec s nfap yox hla yon. lnrnsreaBoa t,e eitsw il ulpbdofg
BRe bwlmprraio po  droB wtinue r Pieno nc ayieeto'lulcih sfnc  ownaSserbereiaSm
-eaiah, nnrttgcC  maciiritvledastinideI  nn rms iehn tsigaBmuoetcetias rn"""
```

The ciphertext to be hacked is stored in the `myMessage` variable. Line 9 has a string value that begins and ends with triple quotes. These strings do not have to have literal single and double quotes escaped inside of them. Triple quote strings are also called multi-line strings, because they can also contain actual newlines within them. Try typing the following into the interactive shell:

```
>>> spam = """Dear Alice,
Why did you dress up my hamster in doll clothing?
I look at Mr. Fuzz and think, "I know this was Alice's doing."
Sincerely,
Bob"""
>>> print(spam)
Dear Alice,
Why did you dress up my hamster in doll clothing?
I look at Mr. Fuzz and think, "I know this was Alice's doing."
Sincerely,
Bob
>>>
```

Notice that this string value can span over multiple lines. Everything after the opening triple quotes will be interpreted as part of the string until it reaches triple quotes ending it. Multi-line strings can either use three double quote characters or three single quote characters.

Multi-line strings are useful for putting very large strings into the source code for a program, which is why it is used on line 9 to store the ciphertext to be broken.

Back to the Code

transpositionHacker.py

```
11.     hackedMessage = hackTransposition(myMessage)
```

The ciphertext hacking code exists inside the `hackTransposition()` function. This function takes one string argument: the encrypted ciphertext message to be broken. If the function can hack the ciphertext, it returns a string of the decrypted text. Otherwise, it returns the `None` value. This value is stored in the `hackedMessage` variable.

transpositionHacker.py

```
13.     if hackedMessage == None:
14.         print('Failed to hack encryption.')
```

If `None` was stored in `hackedMessage`, the program prints that it was unable to break the encryption on the message.

transpositionHacker.py

```
15.     else:
16.         print('Copying hacked message to clipboard:')
17.         print(hackedMessage)
18.         pyperclip.copy(hackedMessage)
```

Otherwise, the text of the decrypted message is printed to the screen on line 17 and also copied to the clipboard on line 18.

transpositionHacker.py

```
21. def hackTransposition(message):
22.     print('Hacking...')
23.
24.     # Python programs can be stopped at any time by pressing Ctrl-C (on
25.     # Windows) or Ctrl-D (on Mac and Linux)
26.     print('(Press Ctrl-C or Ctrl-D to quit at any time.)')
```

Because there are many keys the program can go through, the program displays a message to the user telling her that the hacking has started. The `print()` call on line 26 also tells her that she can press Ctrl-C (on Windows) or Ctrl-D (on OS X and Linux) to exit the program at any point. (Pressing these keys will always exit a running Python program.)

transpositionHacker.py

```
28.     # brute-force by looping through every possible key
29.     for key in range(1, len(message)):
30.         print('Trying key #%s...' % (key))
```

The range of possible keys for the transposition cipher is the integers between 1 and the length of the message. The `for` loop on line 29 will run the hacking part of the function with each of these keys.

To provide feedback to the user, the key that is being tested is printed to the string on line 30, using string interpolation to place the integer in `key` inside the `'Trying key #%s...' % (key)` string.

transpositionHacker.py

```
32.         decryptedText = transpositionDecrypt.decryptMessage(key, message)
```

Using the `decryptMessage()` function in the *transpositionDecrypt.py* program that we've already written, line 32 gets the decrypted output from the current key being tested and stores it in the `decryptedText` variable.

transpositionHacker.py

```
34.         if detectEnglish.isEnglish(decryptedText):
35.             # Check with user to see if the decrypted key has been found.
36.             print()
37.             print('Possible encryption hack:')
38.             print('Key %s: %s' % (key, decryptedText[:100]))
39.             print()
40.             print('Enter D for done, or just press Enter to continue
hacking:')
41.             response = input('> ')
```

The decrypted output in `decryptedText` will most likely only be English if the correct key was used (otherwise, it will appear to be random garbage). The string in `decryptedText` is passed to the `detectEnglish.isEnglish()` function we wrote in the last chapter.

But just because `detectEnglish.isEnglish()` returns `True` (making the program execution enter the block following the `if` statement on line 34) doesn't mean the program has found the correct key. It could be a "false positive". To be sure, line 38 prints out the first 100 characters of the `decryptedText` string (by using the slice `decryptedText[:100]`) on the screen for the user to look at.

The program pauses when line 41 executes, waiting for the user to type something in either D on nothing before pressing Enter. This input is stored as a string in `response`.

The `strip()` String Method

```
The strip() string method returns a version of the string that has any
whitespace at the beginning and end of the string stripped out. Try typing in
the following into the interactive shell:
>>> '       Hello'.strip()
'Hello'
>>> 'Hello       '.strip()
'Hello'
>>> '      Hello World      '.strip()
'Hello World'
>>> 'Hello        x'.strip()
'Hello        x'
>>>
```

The `strip()` method can also have a string argument passed to it that tells the method which characters should be removed from the start and end of the string instead of removing whitespace. The **whitespace characters** are the space character, the tab character, and the newline character. Try typing the following into the interactive shell:

```
>>> 'Helloxxxxxx'.strip('x')
'Hello'
>>> 'aaaaaHELLOaa'.strip('a')
'HELLO'
>>> 'ababaHELLOab'.strip('ab')
'HELLO'
>>> 'abccabcbacbXYZabcXYZacccab'.strip('abc')
'XYZabcXYZ'
>>>
```

transpositionHacker.py

```
43.             if response.strip().upper().startswith('D'):
44.                 return decryptedText
```

The expression on line 43 used for the `if` statement's condition lets the user have some flexibility with what has to be typed in. If the condition were `response == 'D'`, then the user would have to type in exactly "D" and nothing else in order to end the program.

If the user typed in `'d'` or `'     D'` or `'Done'` then the condition would be `False` and the program would continue. To avoid this, the string in `response` has any whitespace removed from the start or end with the call to `strip()`. Then the string that `response.strip()` evaluates to has the `upper()` method called on it. If the user typed in either "d" or "D", the string returned from `upper()` will be `'D'`. Little things like this make our programs easier for the user to use.

If the user has indicated that the decrypted string is correct, the decrypted text is returned from `hackTransposition()` on line 44.

transpositionHacker.py

```
46.     return None
```

Line 46 is the first line after the `for` loop that began on line 29. If the program execution reaches this point, it's because the `return` statement on line 44 was never reached. That would only happen if the correctly decrypted text was never found for any of the keys that were tried.

In that case, line 46 returns the `None` value to indicate that the hacking has failed.

transpositionHacker.py

```
48. if __name__ == '__main__':
49.     main()
```

Lines 48 and 49 call the `main()` function if this program was run by itself, rather than imported by another program that wants to use its `hackTransposition()` function.

Practice Exercises, Chapter 13, Set A

Practice exercises can be found at http://invpy.com/hackingpractice13A.

Summary

This chapter was short like the "Breaking the Caesar Cipher with the Brute-Force Technique" chapter because (also like that chapter) most of the code was already written in other programs. Our hacking program can import functions from these other programs by importing them as modules.

The `strip()` string method is useful for removing whitespace (or other) characters from the beginning or end of a string. If we use triple quotes, then a string value can span across multiple lines in our source code.

The *detectEnglish.py* program removes a lot of the work of inspecting the decrypted output to see if it's English. This allows the brute-force technique to be applied to a cipher that can have thousands of keys.

Our programs are becoming more sophisticated. Before we learn the next cipher, we should learn how to use Python's debugger tool to help us find bugs in our programs.

CHAPTER 14

MODULAR ARITHMETIC WITH THE MULTIPLICATIVE AND AFFINE CIPHERS

Topics Covered In This Chapter:

- Modular Arithmetic
- "Mod" is "Remainder Of"(Sort Of)
- GCD: Greatest Common Divisor (aka Greatest Common Factor)
- Multiple Assignment Trick
- Euclid's Algorithm for Finding the GCD of Two Numbers
- "Relatively Prime"
- The Multiplicative Cipher
- Finding Modular Inverses
- The `cryptomath` Module

"People have been defending their own privacy for centuries with whispers, darkness, envelopes, closed doors, secret handshakes, and couriers. The technologies of the past did not allow for strong privacy, but electronic technologies do."

Eric Hughes, "A Cypherpunk's Manifesto", 1993

The multiplicative and affine ciphers are similar to the Caesar cipher, except instead of adding a key to a symbol's index in a string, these ciphers use multiplication. But before we learn how to encrypt and decrypt with these ciphers, we're going to need to learn a little math. This knowledge is also needed for the last cipher in this book, the RSA cipher.

Oh No Math!

Don't let it scare you that you need to learn some math. The principles here are easy to learn from pictures, and we'll see that they are directly useful in cryptography.

Math Oh Yeah!

That's more like it.

Modular Arithmetic (aka Clock Arithmetic)

This is a clock in which I've replaced the 12 with a 0. (I'm a programmer. I think it's weird that the day begins at 12 AM instead of 0 AM.) Ignore the hour, minute, and second hands. We just need to pay attention to the numbers.

Figure 14-1. A clock with a zero o'clock.

3 O'Clock + 5 Hours = 8 O'Clock

If the current time is 3 o'clock, what time will it be in 5 hours? This is easy enough to figure out. 3 + 5 = 8. It will be 8 o'clock. Think of the hour hand on the clock in Figure 14-1 starting at 3, and then moving 5 hours clockwise. It will end up at 8. This is one way we can double-check our math.

10 O'Clock + 5 Hours = 3 O'Clock

If the current time is 10 o'clock, what time will it be in 5 hours? If you add 10 + 5, you get 15. But 15 o'clock doesn't make sense for clocks like the one to the right. It only goes up to 12. So to find out what time it will be, we subtract 15 – 12 = 3. The answer is it will be 3 o'clock. (Whether or not it is 3 AM or 3PM depends on if the current time is 10 AM or 10 PM. But it doesn't matter for modular arithmetic.)

If you think of the hour hand as starting at 10 and then moving forward 5 hours, it will land on 3. So double-checking our math by moving the hour hand clockwise shows us that we are correct.

10 O'Clock + 200 Hours = 6 O'Clock

If the current time is 10 o'clock, what time will it be in 200 hours? 200 + 10 = 210, and 210 is larger than 12. So we subtract 210 – 12 = 198. But 198 is still larger than 12, so we subtract 12 again. 198 – 12 = 186. If we keep subtracting 12 until the difference is less than 12, we end up with 6. If the current time is 10 o'clock, the time 200 hours later will be 6 o'clock.

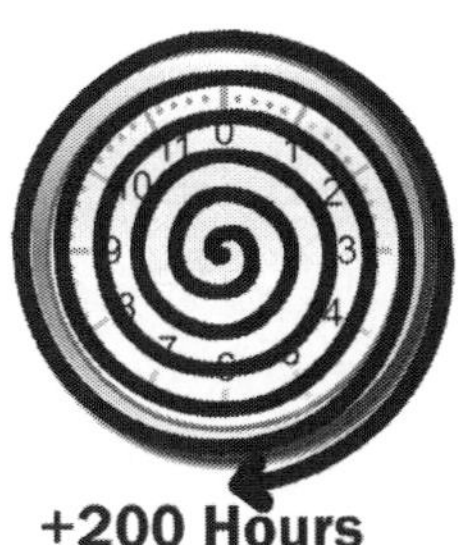

If we wanted to double check our 10 o'clock + 200 hours math, we would keep moving the hour hand around and around the clock face. When we've moved the hour hand the 200th time, it will end up landing on 6.

The % Mod Operator

This sort of "wrap-around" arithmetic is called **modular arithmetic**. We say "fifteen mod twelve" is equal to 3. (Just like how "15 o'clock" mod twelve would be "3 o'clock.) In Python, the mod operator is the `%` percent sign. Try typing the following into the interactive shell:

```
>>> 15 % 12
3
>>> 210 % 12
6
>>> 10 % 10
0
>>> 20 % 10
0
>>>
```

"Mod" is "Division Remainder"(Sort Of)

You can think of the mod operator as a "division remainder" operator. 21 ÷ 5 = 4 remainder 1. And 21 % 5 = 1. This works pretty well for positive numbers, but not for negative numbers. -21 ÷ 5 = -4 remainder -1. But the result of a mod operation will never be negative. Instead, think of that -1 remainder as being the same as 5 – 1, which comes to 4. This is exactly what -21 % 5 evaluates to:

```
>>> -21 % 5
4
>>>
```

But for the purposes of cryptography in this book, we'll only be modding positive numbers.

Practice Exercises, Chapter 14, Set A

Practice exercises can be found at http://invpy.com/hackingpractice14A.

GCD: Greatest Common Divisor (aka Greatest Common Factor)

Factors are the numbers that can be multiplied to produce a particular number. Look at this simple multiplication:

$$4 \times 6 = 24$$

In the above math problem, we say 4 and 6 are factors of 24. (Another name for factor is **divisor**.) The number 24 also has some other factors:

$$8 \times 3 = 24$$

$$12 \times 2 = 24$$

$$24 \times 1 = 24$$

From the above three math problems, we can see that 8 and 3 are also factors of 24, as are 12 and 2, and 24 and 1. So we can say the factors of 24 are: 1, 2, 3, 4, 6, 8, 12, and 24.

Let's look at the factors of 30:

$$1 \times 30 = 30$$

$$2 \times 15 = 30$$

$$3 \times 10 = 30$$

$$5 \times 6 = 30$$

So the factors of 30 are 1, 2, 3, 5, 6, 10, 15, and 30. (Notice that any number will always have 1 and itself as factors.) If you look at the list of factors for 24 and 30, you can see that the factors that they have in common are 1, 2, 3, and 6. The greatest number of these is 6, so we call 6 the greatest common factor (or, more commonly, the greatest common divisor) of 24 and 30.

Visualize Factors and GCD with Cuisenaire Rods

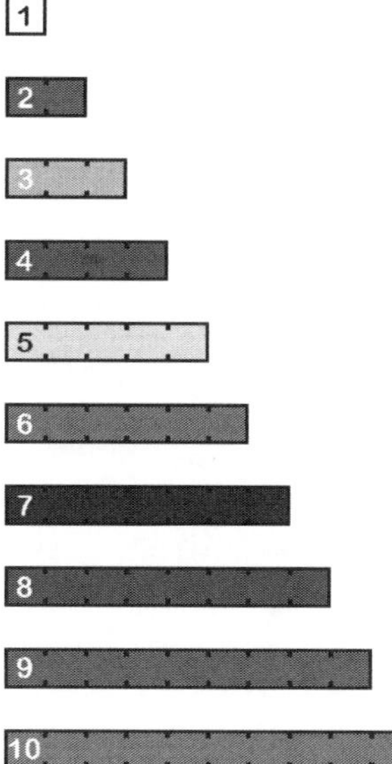

Figure 14-2. Each Cuisenaire rod has a different color for each integer length.

Above are some rectangular blocks with a width of 1 unit, 2 units, 3 units, and so on. The block's length can be used to represent a number. You can count the number of squares in each block to determine the length and number. These blocks (sometimes called Cuisenaire rods) can be used to visualize math operations, like 3 + 2 = 5 or 5 × 3 = 15:

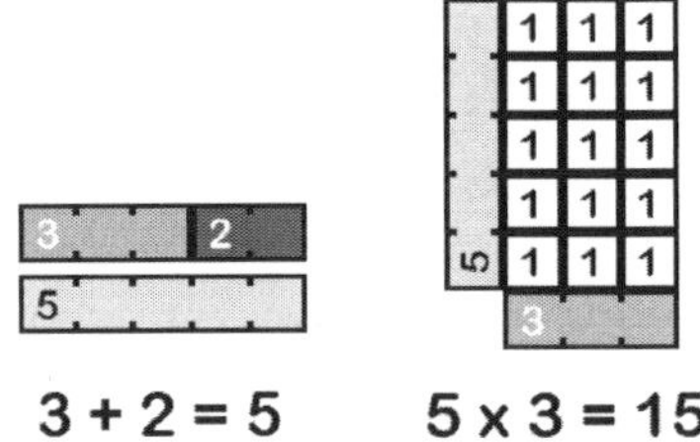

Figure 14-3. Using Cuisenaire rods to demonstrate addition and multiplication.

If we represent the number 30 as a block that is 30 units long, a number is a factor of 30 if the number's blocks can evenly fit with the 30-block. You can see that 3 and 10 are factors of 30:

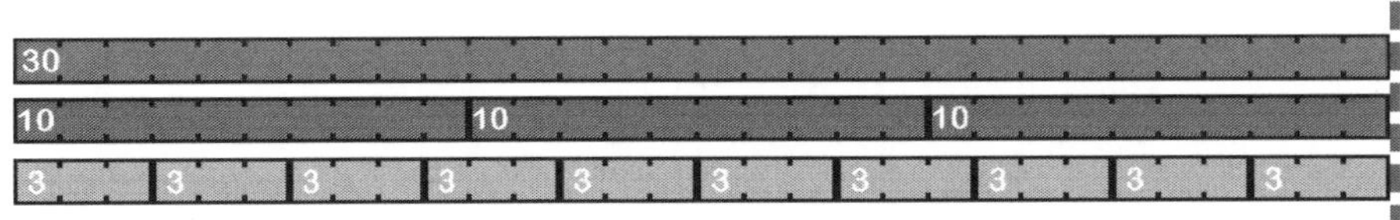

Figure 14-4. Cuisenaire rods demonstrating factors.

But 4 and 7 are not factors of 30, because the 4-blocks and 7-blocks won't evenly fit into the 30-block:

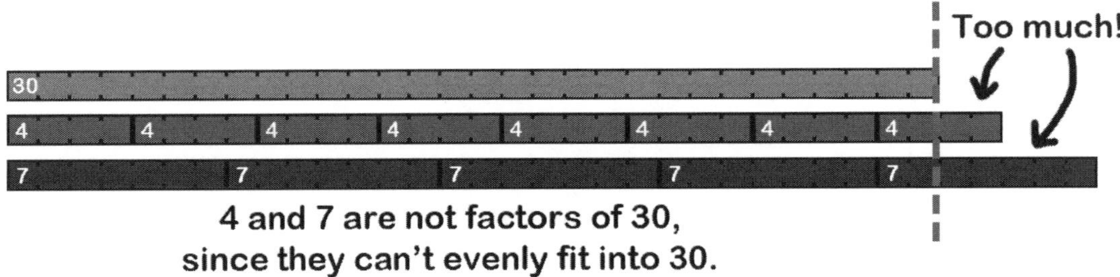

Figure 14-5. Cuisenaire rods demonstrating numbers that are not factors of 30.

The Greatest Common Divisor of two blocks (that is, two numbers represented by those blocks) is the **longest** block that can evenly fit **both** blocks.

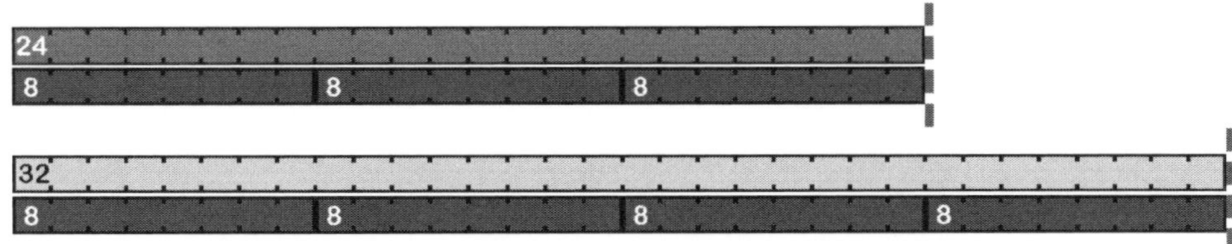

Figure 14-6. Cuisenaire rods demonstrating Greatest Common Divisor.

More information about Cuisenaire rods can be found at http://invpy.com/cuisenaire.

Practice Exercises, Chapter 14, Set B

Practice exercises can be found at http://invpy.com/hackingpractice14B.

Multiple Assignment

Our GCD function will use Python's multiple assignment trick. The multiple assignment trick lets you assign more than one variable with a single assignment statement. Try typing the following into the interactive shell:

```
>>> spam, eggs = 42, 'Hello'
>>> spam
42
>>> eggs
'Hello'
>>> a, b, c, d = ['Alice', 'Bob', 'Carol', 'David']
>>> a
'Alice'
>>> b
'Bob'
>>> c
'Carol'
>>> d
'David'
>>>
```

The variable names on the left side of the = operator and the values on the right side of the = operator are separated by a comma. You can also assign each of the values in a list to its own variable, if the number of items in the list is the same as the number of variables on the left side of the = operator.

Be sure to have the same number of variables as you have values, otherwise Python will raise an error that says the call needs more or has too many values:

```
>>> a, b, c = 1, 2
Traceback (most recent call last):
  File "<pyshell#8>", line 1, in <module>
    a, b, c = 1, 2
ValueError: need more than 2 values to unpack

>>> a, b, c = 1, 2, 3, 4, 5, 6
Traceback (most recent call last):
  File "<pyshell#9>", line 1, in <module>
    a, b, c = 1, 2, 3, 4, 5, 6
ValueError: too many values to unpack
>>>
```

Swapping Values with the Multiple Assignment Trick

One of the main uses of the multiple assignment trick is to swap the values in two variables. Try typing the following into the interactive shell:

```
>>> spam = 'hello'
>>> eggs = 'goodbye'
>>> spam, eggs = eggs, spam
>>> spam
'goodbye'
>>> eggs
'hello'
```

We will use this swapping trick in our implementation of Euclid's algorithm.

Euclid's Algorithm for Finding the GCD of Two Numbers

Figuring out the GCD of two numbers will be important for doing the multiplicative and affine ciphers. It seems simple enough: just look at the numbers and write down any factors you can think of, then compare the lists and find the largest number that is in both of them.

But to program a computer to do it, we'll need to be more precise. We need an algorithm (that is, a specific series of steps we execute) to find the GCD of two numbers.

A mathematician who lived 2,000 years ago named Euclid came up with an algorithm for finding the greatest common divisor of two numbers. Here's a statue of Euclid at Oxford University:

Figure 14-7. Euclid may or may not have looked like this.

Of course since no likeness or description of Euclid exists in any historical document, no one knows what he actually looked like at all. (Artists and sculptors just make it up.) This statue could also be called, "Statue of Some Guy with a Beard".

Euclid's GCD algorithm is short. Here's a function that implements his algorithm as Python code, which returns the GCD of integers `a` and `b`:

```
def gcd(a, b):
    while a != 0:
        a, b = b % a, a
    return b
```

If you call this function from the interactive shell and pass it `24` and `30` for the `a` and `b` parameters, the function will return `6`. You could have done this yourself with pencil and paper. But since you've programmed a computer to do this, it can easily handle very large numbers:

```
>>> gcd(24, 30)
6
>>> gcd(409119243, 87780243)
6837
>>>
```

How Euclid's algorithm works is beyond the scope of this book, but you can rely on this function to return the GCD of the two integers you pass it.

"Relatively Prime"

Relatively prime numbers are used for the multiplicative and affine ciphers. We say that two numbers are relatively prime if their greatest common divisor is 1. That is, the numbers `a` and `b` are relatively prime to each other if `gcd(a, b) == 1`.

Practice Exercises, Chapter 14, Set C

Practice exercises can be found at http://invpy.com/hackingpractice14C.

The Multiplicative Cipher

In the Caesar cipher, encrypting and decrypting symbols involved converting them to numbers, adding or subtracting the key, and then converting the new number back to a symbol.

What if instead of adding the key to do the encryption, we use multiplication? There would be a "wrap-around" issue, but the mod operator would solve that. For example, let's use the symbol set of just uppercase letters and the key 7. Here's a list of the letters and their numbers:

0	1	2	3	4	5	6	7	8	9	10	11	12
A	B	C	D	E	F	G	H	I	J	K	L	M

13	14	15	16	17	18	19	20	21	22	23	24	25
N	O	P	Q	R	S	T	U	V	W	X	Y	Z

To find what the symbol F encrypts to with key 7, multiply its number (5) by 7 and mod by 26 (to handle the "wrap-around" with our 26-symbol set). Then use that number's symbol. (5 × 7) mod 26 = 9, and 9 is the number for the symbol J. So F encrypts to J in the multiplicative cipher with key 7. Do the same with all of the letters:

Table 14-1. Encrypting each letter with the multiplicative cipher with key 7.

Plaintext Symbol	Number	Encryption with Key 7	Ciphertext Symbol
A	0	(0 * 7) % 26 = 0	A
B	1	(1 * 7) % 26 = 7	H
C	2	(2 * 7) % 26 = 14	O
D	3	(3 * 7) % 26 = 21	V
E	4	(4 * 7) % 26 = 2	C
F	5	(5 * 7) % 26 = 9	J
G	6	(6 * 7) % 26 = 16	Q
H	7	(7 * 7) % 26 = 23	X
I	8	(8 * 7) % 26 = 4	E
J	9	(9 * 7) % 26 = 11	L
K	10	(10 * 7) % 26 = 18	S
L	11	(11 * 7) % 26 = 25	Y
M	12	(12 * 7) % 26 = 6	G
N	13	(13 * 7) % 26 = 13	N
O	14	(14 * 7) % 26 = 20	U
P	15	(15 * 7) % 26 = 1	B
Q	16	(16 * 7) % 26 = 8	I
R	17	(17 * 7) % 26 = 15	P
S	18	(18 * 7) % 26 = 22	W
T	19	(19 * 7) % 26 = 3	D
U	20	(20 * 7) % 26 = 10	K
V	21	(21 * 7) % 26 = 17	R
W	22	(22 * 7) % 26 = 24	Y
X	23	(23 * 7) % 26 = 5	F
Y	24	(24 * 7) % 26 = 12	M
Z	25	(25 * 7) % 26 = 19	T

You will end up with this mapping for the key 7: to encrypt you replace the top letter with the letter under it, and vice versa to decrypt:

It wouldn't take long for an attacker to brute-force through the first 7 keys. But the good thing about the multiplicative cipher is that it can work with very large keys, like 8,953,851 (which has the letters of the alphabet map to the letters AXUROLIFCZWTQNKHEBYVSPMJGD). It would take quite some time for a computer to brute-force through nearly nine million keys.

Practice Exercises, Chapter 14, Set D

Practice exercises can be found at http://invpy.com/hackingpractice14D.

Multiplicative Cipher + Caesar Cipher = The Affine Cipher

One downside to the multiplicative cipher is that the letter A always maps to the letter A. This is because A's number is 0, and 0 multiplied by anything will always be 0. We can fix this by adding a second key that performs a Caesar cipher encryption after the multiplicative cipher's multiplication and modding is done.

This is called the affine cipher. The affine cipher has two keys. "Key A" is the integer that the letter's number is multiplied by. After modding this number by 26, "Key B" is the integer that is added to the number. This sum is also modded by 26, just like in the original Caesar cipher.

This means that the affine cipher has 26 times as many possible keys as the multiplicative cipher. It also ensures that the letter A does not always encrypt to the letter A.

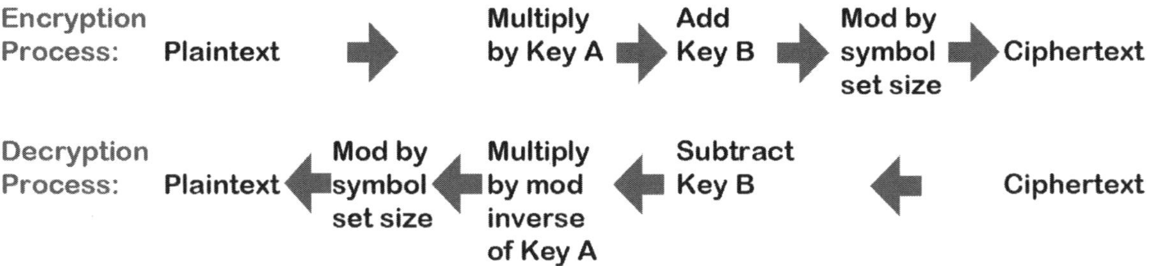

Figure 14-8. The encryption and decryption are mirrors of each other.

The First Affine Key Problem

There are two problems with the multiplicative cipher's key and affine cipher's Key A. You cannot just use any number for Key A. For example, if you chose the key 8, here is the mapping you would end up with:

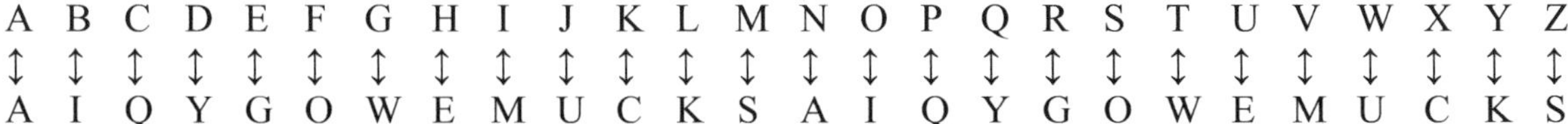

This mapping doesn't work at all! Both the letters C and P encrypt to Q. When we encounter a Q in the ciphertext, how do we know which it decrypts to?! The same problem exists for encrypting A and N, F and S, and many others.

So some keys will work in the affine cipher while others will not. The secret to determining which key numbers will work is this:

In the affine cipher, the Key A number and the size of the symbol set must be relatively prime to each other. That is, gcd(key, size of symbol set) == 1.

We can use the `gcd()` function we wrote earlier to test this. The key 7 works as an affine cipher key because `gcd(7, 26)` returns 1. The larger key 8,953,851 will also work because `gcd(8953851, 26)` also returns `1`. However, the key 8 did not work because `gcd(8, 26)` is `2`. If the GCD of the key and the symbol set size is not 1, then they are not relatively prime and the key won't work.

The math we learned earlier sure is coming in handy now. We need to know how mod works because it is part of the GCD and affine cipher algorithms. And we need to know how GCD works because that will tell us if a pair of numbers is relatively prime. And we need to know if a pair of numbers is relatively prime or not in order to choose valid keys for the affine cipher.

The second problem with affine cipher's key is discussed in the next chapter.

Decrypting with the Affine Cipher

In the Caesar cipher, we used addition to encrypt and subtraction to decrypt. In the affine cipher, we use multiplication to encrypt. You might think that we need to divide to decrypt with the affine cipher. But if you try this yourself, you'll quickly see that it doesn't work. To decrypt with the affine cipher, we need to multiply by the key's modular inverse.

A **modular inverse** (which we will call `i`) of two numbers (which we will call `a` and `m`) is such that `(a * i) % m == 1`. For example, let's find the modular inverse of "5 mod 7". There is some number `i` where `(5 * i) % 7` will equal "1". We will have to brute-force this calculation:

- 1 isn't the modular inverse of 5 mod 7, because (5 * 1) % 7 = 5.
- 2 isn't the modular inverse of 5 mod 7, because (5 * 2) % 7 = 3.
- 3 is the modular inverse of 5 mod 7, because (5 * 3) % 7 = 1.

The encryption key and decryption keys for the affine cipher are two different numbers. The encryption key can be anything we choose as long as it is relatively prime to 26 (which is the size of our symbol set). If we have chosen the key 7 for encrypting with the affine cipher, the decryption key will be the modular inverse of 7 mod 26:

- 1 is not the modular inverse of 7 mod 26, because (7 * 1) % 26 = 7.
- 2 is not the modular inverse of 7 mod 26, because (7 * 2) % 26 = 14.

- 3 is not the modular inverse of 7 mod 26, because (7 * 3) % 26 = 21.
- 4 is not the modular inverse of 7 mod 26, because (7 * 4) % 26 = 2.
- 5 is not the modular inverse of 7 mod 26, because (7 * 5) % 26 = 9.
- 6 is not the modular inverse of 7 mod 26, because (7 * 6) % 26 = 16.
- 7 is not the modular inverse of 7 mod 26, because (7 * 7) % 26 = 23.
- 8 is not the modular inverse of 7 mod 26, because (7 * 8) % 26 = 4.
- 9 is not the modular inverse of 7 mod 26, because (7 * 9) % 26 = 11.
- 10 is not the modular inverse of 7 mod 26, because (7 * 10) % 26 = 18.
- 11 is not the modular inverse of 7 mod 26, because (7 * 11) % 26 = 25.
- 12 is not the modular inverse of 7 mod 26, because (7 * 12) % 26 = 6.
- 13 is not the modular inverse of 7 mod 26, because (7 * 13) % 26 = 13.
- 14 is not the modular inverse of 7 mod 26, because (7 * 14) % 26 = 20.
- 15 **is** the modular inverse of 7 mod 26, because (7 * 15) % 26 = 1.

So the affine cipher decryption key is 15. To decrypt a ciphertext letter, we take that letter's number and multiply it by 15, and then mod 26. This will be the number of the original plaintext's letter.

Finding Modular Inverses

In order to calculate the modular inverse to get the decryption key, we could take a brute-force approach and start testing the integer 1, and then 2, and then 3, and so on like we did above. But this will be very time-consuming for large keys like 8,953,851.

There is an algorithm for finding the modular inverse just like there was for finding the Greatest Common Divisor. Euclid's Extended Algorithm can be used to find the modular inverse of a number:

```
def findModInverse(a, m):
    if gcd(a, m) != 1:
        return None # no mod inverse exists if a & m aren't relatively prime
    u1, u2, u3 = 1, 0, a
    v1, v2, v3 = 0, 1, m
    while v3 != 0:
        q = u3 // v3 # // is the integer division operator
        v1, v2, v3, u1, u2, u3 = (u1 - q * v1), (u2 - q * v2), (u3 - q * v3),
v1, v2, v3
    return u1 % m
```

You don't have to understand how Euclid's Extended Algorithm works in order to make use of it. We're just going to have our programs call this function. If you'd like to learn more about how it works, you can read http://invpy.com/euclid.

The // Integer Division Operator

You may have noticed the `//` operator used in the `findModInverse()` function above. This is the integer division operator. It divides two numbers and rounds down. Try typing the following into the interactive shell:

```
>>> 41 // 7
5
>>> 41 / 7
5.857142857142857
>>> 10 // 5
2
>>> 10 / 5
2.0
>>>
```

Notice that an expression with the `//` integer division operator always evaluates to an int, not a float.

Source Code of the `cryptomath` Module

The `gcd()` and `findModInverse()` functions will be used by more than one of our cipher programs later in this book, so we should put this code into a separate module. In the file editor, type in the following code and save it as *cryptomath.py*:

Source code for cryptomath.py

```
# Cryptomath Module
# http://inventwithpython.com/hacking (BSD Licensed)

def gcd(a, b):
    # Return the GCD of a and b using Euclid's Algorithm
    while a != 0:
        a, b = b % a, a
    return b


def findModInverse(a, m):
    # Returns the modular inverse of a % m, which is
    # the number x such that a*x % m = 1

```

```
    if gcd(a, m) != 1:
        return None # no mod inverse if a & m aren't relatively prime

    # Calculate using the Extended Euclidean Algorithm:
    u1, u2, u3 = 1, 0, a
    v1, v2, v3 = 0, 1, m
    while v3 != 0:
        q = u3 // v3 # // is the integer division operator
        v1, v2, v3, u1, u2, u3 = (u1 - q * v1), (u2 - q * v2), (u3 - q * v3), v1, v2, v3
    return u1 % m
```

The GCD algorithm is described earlier in this chapter. The `findModInverse()` function implements an algorithm called Euclid's Extended Algorithm. How these functions work is beyond the scope of this book, but you don't have to know how the code works in order to make use of it.

From the interactive shell, you can try out these functions after importing the module. Try typing the following into the interactive shell:

```
>>> import cryptomath
>>> cryptomath.gcd(24, 32)
8
>>> cryptomath.gcd(37, 41)
1
>>> cryptomath.findModInverse(7, 26)
15
>>> cryptomath.findModInverse(8953851, 26)
17
>>>
```

Practice Exercises, Chapter 14, Set E

Practice exercises can be found at http://invpy.com/hackingpractice14E.

Summary

Since the multiplicative cipher is the same thing as the affine cipher except using Key B of `0`, we won't have a separate program for the multiplicative cipher. And since it is just a less secure version of the affine cipher, you shouldn't use it anyway. The source code to our affine cipher program will be presented in the next chapter.

The math presented in this chapter isn't so hard to understand. Modding with the `%` operator finds the "remainder" between two numbers. The Greatest Common Divisor function returns the largest number that can divide two numbers. If the GCD of two numbers is 1, we say that those numbers are "relatively prime" to each other. The most useful algorithm to find the GCD of two numbers is Euclid's Algorithm.

The affine cipher is sort of like the Caesar cipher, except it uses multiplication instead of addition to encrypt letters. Not all numbers will work as keys though. The key number and the size of the symbol set must be relatively prime towards each other.

To decrypt with the affine cipher we also use multiplication. To decrypt, the modular inverse of the key is the number that is multiplied. The modular inverse of "a mod m" is a number `i` such that `(a * i) % m == 1`. To write a function that finds the modular inverse of a number, we use Euclid's Extended Algorithm.

Once we understand these math concepts, we can write a program for the affine cipher in the next chapter.

Chapter 15

The Affine Cipher

> Topics Covered In This Chapter:
> - The Affine Cipher
> - Generating random keys
> - How many different keys can the affine cipher have?

"I should be able to whisper something in your ear, even if your ear is 1000 miles away, and the government disagrees with that."

Philip Zimmermann, creator of Pretty Good Privacy (PGP), the most widely used email encryption software in the world.

This chapter's programs implement the multiplicative and affine ciphers. The multiplicative cipher is like the Caesar cipher from Chapter 6, except it uses multiplication instead of addition. The affine cipher is the multiplicative cipher, which is then encrypted by the Caesar cipher on top of that. The affine cipher needs two keys: one for the multiplicative cipher multiplication and the other for the Caesar cipher addition.

For the affine cipher program, we will use a single integer for the key. We will use some simple math to split this key into the two keys, which we will call Key A and Key B.

Source Code of the Affine Cipher Program

How the affine cipher works was covered in the last chapter. Here is the source code for a Python program that implements the affine cipher. Open a new file editor window by clicking on **File ► New Window**. Type in the following code into the file editor, and then save it as *affineCipher.py*. Press **F5** to run the program. Note that first you will need to download the *pyperclip.py* module and place this file in the same directory as the *affineCipher.py* file. You can download this file from http://invpy.com/pyperclip.py.

Source code for affineCipher.py

```
# Affine Cipher
# http://inventwithpython.com/hacking (BSD Licensed)

import sys, pyperclip, cryptomath, random
SYMBOLS = """ !"#$%&'()*+,-./0123456789:;<=>?@ABCDEFGHIJKLMNOPQRSTUVWXYZ[\]^_`abcdefghijklmnopqrstuvwxyz{|}~""" # note the space at the front


def main():
    myMessage = """"A computer would deserve to be called intelligent if it could deceive a human into believing that it was human." -Alan Turing"""
    myKey = 2023
    myMode = 'encrypt' # set to 'encrypt' or 'decrypt'

    if myMode == 'encrypt':
        translated = encryptMessage(myKey, myMessage)
    elif myMode == 'decrypt':
        translated = decryptMessage(myKey, myMessage)
    print('Key: %s' % (myKey))
    print('%sed text:' % (myMode.title()))
    print(translated)
    pyperclip.copy(translated)
    print('Full %sed text copied to clipboard.' % (myMode))


def getKeyParts(key):
    keyA = key // len(SYMBOLS)
    keyB = key % len(SYMBOLS)
    return (keyA, keyB)


def checkKeys(keyA, keyB, mode):
    if keyA == 1 and mode == 'encrypt':
        sys.exit('The affine cipher becomes incredibly weak when key A is set to 1. Choose a different key.')
```

```
    if keyB == 0 and mode == 'encrypt':
        sys.exit('The affine cipher becomes incredibly weak when key B is set to 0. Choose a different key.')
    if keyA < 0 or keyB < 0 or keyB > len(SYMBOLS) - 1:
        sys.exit('Key A must be greater than 0 and Key B must be between 0 and %s.' % (len(SYMBOLS) - 1))
    if cryptomath.gcd(keyA, len(SYMBOLS)) != 1:
        sys.exit('Key A (%s) and the symbol set size (%s) are not relatively prime. Choose a different key.' % (keyA, len(SYMBOLS)))


def encryptMessage(key, message):
    keyA, keyB = getKeyParts(key)
    checkKeys(keyA, keyB, 'encrypt')
    ciphertext = ''
    for symbol in message:
        if symbol in SYMBOLS:
            # encrypt this symbol
            symIndex = SYMBOLS.find(symbol)
            ciphertext += SYMBOLS[(symIndex * keyA + keyB) % len(SYMBOLS)]
        else:
            ciphertext += symbol # just append this symbol unencrypted
    return ciphertext


def decryptMessage(key, message):
    keyA, keyB = getKeyParts(key)
    checkKeys(keyA, keyB, 'decrypt')
    plaintext = ''
    modInverseOfKeyA = cryptomath.findModInverse(keyA, len(SYMBOLS))

    for symbol in message:
        if symbol in SYMBOLS:
            # decrypt this symbol
            symIndex = SYMBOLS.find(symbol)
            plaintext += SYMBOLS[(symIndex - keyB) * modInverseOfKeyA % len(SYMBOLS)]
        else:
            plaintext += symbol # just append this symbol undecrypted
    return plaintext


def getRandomKey():
    while True:
        keyA = random.randint(2, len(SYMBOLS))
        keyB = random.randint(2, len(SYMBOLS))
```

```
        if cryptomath.gcd(keyA, len(SYMBOLS)) != 1:
            return keyA * len(SYMBOLS) + keyB


# If affineCipher.py is run (instead of imported as a module) call
# the main() function.
if __name__ == '__main__':
    main()
```

Sample Run of the Affine Cipher Program

When you press **F5** from the file editor to run this program, the output will look like this:

```
Key: 2023
Encrypted text:
fX<*h>}(rTH<Rh()?<?T]TH=T<rh<tT<*_))T?<ISrT))I~TSr<Ii<Ir<*h()?<?T*TI=T<_<4(>_S<
ISrh<tT)IT=IS~<r4_r<Ir<R_]<4(>_SEf<0X)_S<
k(HIS~
Full encrypted text copied to clipboard.
```

The message “"A computer would deserve to be called intelligent if it could deceive a human into believing that it was human." -Alan Turing” gets encrypted with the key 2023 into the above ciphertext.

To decrypt, paste this text as the new value to be stored in `myMessage` and change `myMode` to the string `'decrypt'`.

Practice Exercises, Chapter 15, Set A

Practice exercises can be found at http://invpy.com/hackingpractice15A.

How the Program Works

affineCipher.py

```
 1. # Affine Cipher
 2. # http://inventwithpython.com/hacking (BSD Licensed)
 3.
 4. import sys, pyperclip, cryptomath, random
 5. SYMBOLS = """ !"#$%&'()*+,-./0123456789:;<=>?@ABCDEFGHIJKLMNOPQRSTUVWXYZ[\]
^_`abcdefghijklmnopqrstuvwxyz{|}~""" # note the space at the front
```

Lines 1 and 2 are the usual comments describing what the program is. There is also an `import` statement for the modules used in this program.

- The `sys` module is imported for the `exit()` function.
- The `pyperclip` module is imported for the `copy()` clipboard function.
- The `cryptomath` module that we created in the last chapter is imported for the `gcd()` and `findModInverse()` function.

In our program, the string stored in the `SYMBOLS` variable is the symbol set. The symbol set is the list of all characters that can be encrypted. Any characters in the message to be encrypted that don't appear in `SYMBOLS` will be added to the ciphertext unencrypted.

affineCipher.py
```
 8. def main():
 9.     myMessage = """"A computer would deserve to be called intelligent if it
could deceive a human into believing that it was human." -Alan Turing"""
10.     myKey = 2023
11.     myMode = 'encrypt' # set to 'encrypt' or 'decrypt'
```

The `main()` function is almost exactly the same as the one from the transposition cipher programs. The message, key, and mode are stored in variables on lines 9, 10, and 11.

affineCipher.py
```
13.     if myMode == 'encrypt':
14.         translated = encryptMessage(myKey, myMessage)
15.     elif myMode == 'decrypt':
16.         translated = decryptMessage(myKey, myMessage)
```

If `myMode` is set to `'encrypt'`, then line 14 will be executed and the return value of `encryptMessage()` is stored in `translated`. Or else, if `myMode` is set to `'decrypt'`, then `decryptMessage()` is called on line 16 and the return value is stored in `translated`.

Either way, after the execution has passed line 16, the `translated` variable will have the encrypted or decrypted version of the message in `myMessage`.

affineCipher.py
```
17.     print('Key: %s' % (myKey))
18.     print('%sed text:' % (myMode.title()))
19.     print(translated)
20.     pyperclip.copy(translated)
21.     print('Full %sed text copied to clipboard.' % (myMode))
```

The string in `translated` (which is the encrypted or decrypted version of the string in `myMessage`) is displayed on the screen on line 19 and copied to the clipboard on line 20.

Splitting One Key into Two Keys

affineCipher.py

```
24. def getKeyParts(key):
25.     keyA = key // len(SYMBOLS)
26.     keyB = key % len(SYMBOLS)
27.     return (keyA, keyB)
```

The affine cipher is like the Caesar cipher, except that it uses multiplication and addition (with two integer keys, which we called Key A and Key B) instead of just addition (with one key). It's easier to remember just one number, so we will use a mathematical trick to convert between two keys and one key.

The `getKeyParts()` function splits a single integer key into two integers for Key A and Key B. The single key (which is in the parameter key) is divided by the size of the symbol set, and Key A is the quotient and Key B is the remainder. The quotient part (without any remainder) can be calculated using the `//` integer division operator, which is what line 25 does. The remainder part (without the quotient) can be calculated using the `%` mod operator, which is what line 26 does.

It is assumed that the symbol set, as well as the size of the symbol set, is publicly known along with the rest of the source code.

For example, with `2023` as the `key` parameter and a `SYMBOLS` string of 95 characters, Key A would be `2023 // 95` or `21` and Key B would be `2023 % 95` or `28`.

To combine Key A and Key B back into the single key, multiply Key A by the size of the symbol set and add Key B: `(21 * 95) + 28` evaluates to `2023`.

The Tuple Data Type

affineCipher.py

```
27.     return (keyA, keyB)
```

A tuple value is similar to a list: it is a value that can store other values, which can be accessed with indexes or slices. However, the values in a tuple cannot be modified. There is no `append()` method for tuple values. A tuple is written using parentheses instead of square brackets. The value returned on line 27 is a tuple.

For technical reasons beyond the scope of this book, the Python interpreter can execute code faster if it uses tuples compared to code that uses lists.

Input Validation on the Keys

affineCipher.py

```
30. def checkKeys(keyA, keyB, mode):
31.     if keyA == 1 and mode == 'encrypt':
32.         sys.exit('The affine cipher becomes incredibly weak when key A is set to 1. Choose a different key.')
33.     if keyB == 0 and mode == 'encrypt':
34.         sys.exit('The affine cipher becomes incredibly weak when key B is set to 0. Choose a different key.')
```

Encrypting with the affine cipher involves a character's index in `SYMBOLS` being multiplied by Key A and added to Key B. But if `keyA` is `1`, the encrypted text will be very weak because multiplying the index by `1` does not change it. Similarly, if `keyB` is `0`, the encrypted text will be weak because adding the index to `0` does not change it. And if both `keyA` was `1` and `keyB` was `0`, the "encrypted" message would be the exact same as the original message. It wouldn't be encrypted at all!

The `if` statements on line 31 and 33 check for these "weak key" conditions, and exit the program with a message telling the user what was wrong. Notice on lines 32 and 34, a string is being passed to the `sys.exit()` call. The `sys.exit()` function has an optional parameter of a string that will be printed to the screen before terminating the program. This can be used to display an error message on the screen before the program quits.

Of course, these checks only apply to prevent you from encrypting with weak keys. If `mode` is set to `'decrypt'`, then the checks on lines 31 and 33 don't apply.

affineCipher.py

```
35.     if keyA < 0 or keyB < 0 or keyB > len(SYMBOLS) - 1:
36.         sys.exit('Key A must be greater than 0 and Key B must be between 0 and %s.' % (len(SYMBOLS) - 1))
```

The condition on line 35 checks if `keyA` is a negative number (that is, it is greater than `0`) *or* if `keyB` is greater than `0` *or* less than the size of the symbol set minus one. (The reason the Key B check has this range is described later in the "How Many Keys Does the Affine Cipher Have?" section.) If any of these things are `True`, the keys are invalid and the program exits.

affineCipher.py

```
37.     if cryptomath.gcd(keyA, len(SYMBOLS)) != 1:
38.         sys.exit('Key A (%s) and the symbol set size (%s) are not relatively prime. Choose a different key.' % (keyA, len(SYMBOLS)))
```

Finally, Key A must be relatively prime with the symbol set size. This means that the greatest common divisor of keyA and len(SYMBOLS) must be equal to 1. Line 37's if statement checks for this and exits the program if they are not relatively prime.

If all of the conditions in the checkKeys() function were False, there is nothing wrong with the key and the program will not exit. Line 38 is the last line in the function, so the program execution next returns to the line that originally called checkKeys().

The Affine Cipher Encryption Function

affineCipher.py

```
41. def encryptMessage(key, message):
42.     keyA, keyB = getKeyParts(key)
43.     checkKeys(keyA, keyB, 'encrypt')
```

First we get the integer values for Key A and Key B from the getKeyParts() function. These values are checked if they are valid keys or not by passing them to the checkKeys() function. If the checkKeys() function does not cause the program to exit, then the rest of the code in the encryptMessage() function after line 43 can assume that the keys are valid.

affineCipher.py

```
44.     ciphertext = ''
45.     for symbol in message:
```

The ciphertext variable will eventually hold the encrypted string, but starts off as a blank string. The for loop that begins on line 45 will iterate through each of the characters in message, and then add the encrypted character to ciphertext. By the time the for loop is done looping, the ciphertext variable will have the complete string of the encrypted message.

affineCipher.py

```
46.         if symbol in SYMBOLS:
47.             # encrypt this symbol
48.             symIndex = SYMBOLS.find(symbol)
49.             ciphertext += SYMBOLS[(symIndex * keyA + keyB) % len(SYMBOLS)]
50.         else:
51.             ciphertext += symbol # just append this symbol unencrypted
```

On each iteration of the loop, the symbol variable is assigned the single character from message. If this character exists in SYMBOLS (that is, our symbol set), then the index in SYMBOLS is found and assigned to symIndex. The value in symIndex is the "number" version of the character.

To encrypt it, we need to calculate the index of the encrypted letter. We multiply this `symIndex` by `keyA` and add `keyB`, and mod the number by the size of the symbol set (that is, the expression `len(SYMBOLS)`). We mod by `len(SYMBOLS)` because the affine cipher has a similar "wrap-around" issue that the Caesar cipher had. Modding by `len(SYMBOLS)` handles the "wrap-around" by ensuring the calculated index is always between `0` up to (but not including) `len(SYMBOLS)`. The number that we calculate will be the index in `SYMBOLS` of the encrypted character, which is concatenated to the end of the string in `ciphertext`.

Everything that happens in the above paragraph was done on line 49.

If `symbol` was not in our symbol set, then `symbol` is concatenated to the end of the `ciphertext` string on line 51.

affineCipher.py

```
    return ciphertext
```

Once we have iterated through each character in the message string, the `ciphertext` variable should contain the full encrypted string. This string is returned from `encryptMessage()`.

The Affine Cipher Decryption Function

affineCipher.py

```
55. def decryptMessage(key, message):
56.     keyA, keyB = getKeyParts(key)
57.     checkKeys(keyA, keyB, 'decrypt')
58.     plaintext = ''
59.     modInverseOfKeyA = cryptomath.findModInverse(keyA, len(SYMBOLS))
```

The `decryptMessage()` function is almost the same as the `encryptMessage()`. Lines 56 to 58 are equivalent to lines 44 to 46.

However, instead of multiplying by Key A, the decryption process needs to multiply by the modular inverse of Key A. The mod inverse can be calculated by calling `cryptomath.findModInverse()`. This function was explained in the previous chapter.

affineCipher.py

```
    for symbol in message:
        if symbol in SYMBOLS:
            # decrypt this symbol
            symIndex = SYMBOLS.find(symbol)
            plaintext += SYMBOLS[(symIndex - keyB) * modInverseOfKeyA % len(SYMBOLS)]
        else:
```

```
67.             plaintext += symbol # just append this symbol undecrypted
68.     return plaintext
```

Lines 61 to 68 are almost identical to the `encryptMessage()` function's lines 45 to 52. The only difference is on line 65. In the `encryptMessage()` function, the symbol index was multiplied by Key A and then had Key B added to it. In `decryptMessage()`'s line 65, the symbol index first has Key B subtracted from it, and then is multiplied by the modular inverse. Then this number is modded by the size of the symbol set, `len(SYMBOLS)`. This is how the decryption process undoes the encryption.

Generating Random Keys

It can be difficult to come up with a valid key for the affine cipher, so we will create a `getRandomKey()` function that generates a random (but valid) key for the user to use. To use this, the user simply has to change line 10 to store the return value of `getRandomKey()` in the `myKey` variable:

affineCipher.py

```
10.     myKey = getRandomKey()
```

Now the key that is used to encrypt is randomly selected for us. It will be printed to the screen when line 17 is executed.

affineCipher.py

```
71. def getRandomKey():
72.     while True:
73.         keyA = random.randint(2, len(SYMBOLS))
74.         keyB = random.randint(2, len(SYMBOLS))
```

The code in `getRandomKey()` enters a `while` loop on line 72 where the condition is `True`. This is called an **infinite loop**, because the loop's condition is never `False`. If your program gets stuck in an infinite loop, you can terminate it by pressing Ctrl-C or Ctrl-D.

The code on lines 73 and 74 determine random numbers between 2 and the size of the symbol set for `keyA` and for `keyB`. This way there is no chance that Key A or Key B are equal to the invalid values `0` or `1`.

affineCipher.py

```
75.         if cryptomath.gcd(keyA, len(SYMBOLS)) != 1:
76.             return keyA * len(SYMBOLS) + keyB
```

The `if` statement on line 75 checks to make sure that `keyA` is relatively prime with the size of the symbol set by calling the `gcd()` function in the `cryptomath` module. If it is, then these two keys are combined into a single key by multiplying `keyA` by the symbol set size and adding `keyB`. (This is the opposite of what the `getKeyParts()` function does.) This value is returned from the `getRandomKey()` function.

If the condition on line 75 was `False`, then the code loops back to the start of the `while` loop on line 73 and picks random numbers for `keyA` and `keyB` again. The infinite loop ensures that the program keeps looping again and again until it finds random numbers that are valid keys.

affineCipher.py

```
79. # If affineCipher.py is run (instead of imported as a module) call
80. # the main() function.
81. if __name__ == '__main__':
82.     main()
```

Lines 81 and 82 call the `main()` function if this program was run by itself, rather than imported by another program.

The Second Affine Key Problem: How Many Keys Can the Affine Cipher Have?

Key B of the affine cipher is limited to the size of the symbol set (in the case of *affineCipher.py*, `len(SYMBOLS)` is `95`). But it seems like Key A could be as large as we want it to be (as long as it is relatively prime to the symbol set size). Therefore the affine cipher should have an infinite number of keys and therefore cannot be brute-forced.

As it turns out, no. Remember how large keys in the Caesar cipher ended up being the same as smaller keys due to the "wrap-around" effect. With a symbol set size of 26, the key `27` in the Caesar cipher would produce the same encrypted text as the key `1`. The affine cipher also "wraps around".

Since the Key B part of the affine cipher is the same as the Caesar cipher, we know it is limited from 1 to the size of the symbol set. But to find out if the affine cipher's Key A is also limited, we can write a small program to encrypt a message with several different integers for Key A and see what the ciphertext looks like.

Open a new file editor window and type the following source code. Save this file as *affineKeyTest.py*, and then press **F5** to run it.

Source code for affineKeyTest.py

```
1. # This program proves that the keyspace of the affine cipher is limited
2. # to len(SYMBOLS) ^ 2.
3.
4. import affineCipher, cryptomath
5.
6. message = 'Make things as simple as possible, but not simpler.'
7. for keyA in range(2, 100):
8.     key = keyA * len(affineCipher.SYMBOLS) + 1
9.
10.     if cryptomath.gcd(keyA, len(affineCipher.SYMBOLS)) == 1:
11.         print(keyA, affineCipher.encryptMessage(key, message))
```

This is a fairly simple program. It imports the `affineCipher` module for its `encryptMessage()` function and the `cryptomath` module for its `gcd()` function. We will always encrypt the string stored in the `message` variable. The `for` loop will range between `2` (since `0` and `1` are not allowed as valid Key A integers) and `100`.

On each iteration of the loop, we calculate the key from the current `keyA` value and always use `1` for Key B (this is why 1 is added on line 8). Remember that it is not valid to use a Key A that is not relatively prime with the symbol set size. So if the greatest common divisor of the key and the symbol set size is not equal to `1`, the `if` statement on line 10 will skip the call to `encryptMessage()` on line 11.

Basically, this program will print out the same message encrypted with several different integers for Key A. The output of this program will look like this:

```
2 {DXL!jRT^Ph!Dh!hT\bZL!Dh!b`hhTFZL9!Flj!^`j!hT\bZLf=
3 I&D2!_;>M8\!&\!\>JSG2!&\!SP\\>)G2E!)b_!MP_!\>JSG2YK
4 vg0w!T$(< P!gP!P(8D4w!gP!D@PP(k4wQ!kXT!<@T!P(8D4wLY
6 q+gC!>U[yO8!+8!8[s&mC!+8!& 88[1mCi!1D>!y >!8[s&mC2u

...skipped for brevity...

92 X{]o!BfcTiE!{E!EcWNZo!{E!NQEEcxZo\!x?B!TQB!EcWNZoHV
93 &]IU!7OMCQ9!]9!9ME?GU!]9!?A99M[GUh![57!CA7!9ME?GU;d
94 S?5;!,8729-!?-!-7304;!?-!01--7>4;t!>+,!21,!-7304;.r
96 Nblf!uijoht!bt!tjnqmf!bt!qpttjcmf-!cvu!opu!tjnqmfs/
97 {DXL!jRT^Ph!Dh!hT\bZL!Dh!b`hhTFZL9!Flj!^`j!hT\bZLf=
98 I&D2!_;>M8\!&\!\>JSG2!&\!SP\\>)G2E!)b_!MP_!\>JSG2YK
99 vg0w!T$(< P!gP!P(8D4w!gP!D@PP(k4wQ!kXT!<@T!P(8D4wLY
```

Look carefully at the output. You'll notice that the ciphertext for Key A of 2 is the exact same as the ciphertext for Key A of 97! In fact, the ciphertext from keys 3 and 98 are the same, as are the ciphertext from keys 4 and 99!

Notice that 97 - 95 is 2. This is why a Key A of 97 does the same thing as a Key A of 2: the encrypted output repeats itself (that is, "wraps around") every 95 keys. The affine cipher has the same "wrap-around" for the Key A as it does for Key B! It seems like it is limited to the symbol set size.

95 possible Key A keys multiplied by 95 possible Key B keys means there are 9,025 possible combinations. If you subtract the integers that can't be used for Key A (because they are not relatively prime with 95), this number drops to 7,125 possible keys.

Summary

7,125 is about the same number of keys that's possible with most transposition cipher messages, and we've already learned how to program a computer to hack that number of keys with brute-force. This means that we'll have to toss the affine cipher onto the heap of weak ciphers that are easily hacked.

The affine cipher isn't any more secure than the previous ciphers we've looked at. The transposition cipher can have more possible keys, but the number of possible keys is limited to the size of the message. For a message with only 20 characters, the transposition cipher can only have at most 18 keys (the keys 2 to 19). The affine cipher can be used to encrypt short messages with more security than the Caesar cipher provided, since its number of possible keys is based on the symbol set.

But we did learn some new mathematical concepts that we will use later on. The concepts of modular arithmetic, greatest common divisor, and modular inverses will help us in the RSA cipher at the end of this book.

But enough about how the affine cipher is weak in theory. Let's write a brute-force program that can actually break affine cipher encrypted messages!

HACKING THE AFFINE CIPHER

> Topics Covered In This Chapter:
> - The `**` Exponent Operator
> - The `continue` Statement

We know that the affine cipher is limited to only a few thousand keys. This means it is trivial to perform a brute-force attack against it. Open a new File Editor and type in the following code. Save the file as *affineHacker.py*.

Source Code of the Affine Cipher Hacker Program

Open a new file editor window by clicking on **File ► New Window**. Type in the following code into the file editor, and then save it as *affineHacker.py*. Press **F5** to run the program. Note that first you will need to download the *pyperclip.py* module and place this file in the same directory as the *affineHacker.py* file. You can download this file from http://invpy.com/pyperclip.py.

Typing the string for the `myMessage` variable might be tricky, but you can copy and paste it from http://invpy.com/affineHacker.py to save time.

Source Code for affineHacker.py

```
# Affine Cipher Hacker
# http://inventwithpython.com/hacking (BSD Licensed)

import pyperclip, affineCipher, detectEnglish, cryptomath

SILENT_MODE = False

```

```
def main():
    # You might want to copy & paste this text from the source code at
    # http://invpy.com/affineHacker.py
    myMessage = """U&'<3dJ^Gjx'-3^MS'Sj0jxuj'G3'%j'<mMMjS'g{GjMMg9j{G'g"'gG '<3^MS'Sj<jguj'm'P^dm{'g{G3'%jMgjug{9'GPmG'gG'-m0'P^dm{LU'5&Mm{'_^xg{9"""

    hackedMessage = hackAffine(myMessage)

    if hackedMessage != None:
        # The plaintext is displayed on the screen. For the convenience of
        # the user, we copy the text of the code to the clipboard.
        print('Copying hacked message to clipboard:')
        print(hackedMessage)
        pyperclip.copy(hackedMessage)
    else:
        print('Failed to hack encryption.')


def hackAffine(message):
    print('Hacking...')

    # Python programs can be stopped at any time by pressing Ctrl-C (on
    # Windows) or Ctrl-D (on Mac and Linux)
    print('(Press Ctrl-C or Ctrl-D to quit at any time.)')

    # brute-force by looping through every possible key
    for key in range(len(affineCipher.SYMBOLS) ** 2):
        keyA = affineCipher.getKeyParts(key)[0]
        if cryptomath.gcd(keyA, len(affineCipher.SYMBOLS)) != 1:
            continue

        decryptedText = affineCipher.decryptMessage(key, message)
        if not SILENT_MODE:
            print('Tried Key %s... (%s)' % (key, decryptedText[:40]))

        if detectEnglish.isEnglish(decryptedText):
            # Check with the user if the decrypted key has been found.
            print()
            print('Possible encryption hack:')
            print('Key: %s' % (key))
            print('Decrypted message: ' + decryptedText[:200])
            print()
            print('Enter D for done, or just press Enter to continue hacking:')
            response = input('> ')

```

```
                if response.strip().upper().startswith('D'):
                    return decryptedText
    return None


# If affineHacker.py is run (instead of imported as a module) call
# the main() function.
if __name__ == '__main__':
    main()
```

Sample Run of the Affine Cipher Hacker Program

When you press **F5** from the file editor to run this program, the output will look like this:

```
Hacking...
(Press Ctrl-C or Ctrl-D to quit at any time.)
Tried Key 95... (U&'<3dJ^Gjx'-3^MS'SjOjxuj'G3'%j'<mMMjS'g)
Tried Key 96... (T%&;2cI]Fiw&,2]LR&Ri/iwti&F2&$i&;lLLiR&f)
Tried Key 97... (S$%:1bH\Ehv%+1\KQ%Qh.hvsh%E1%#h%:kKKhQ%e)

...skipped for brevity...

Tried Key 2190... (?^=!-+.32#0=5-3*"="#1#04#=2-= #=!~**#"=')
Tried Key 2191... (` ^BNLOTSDQ^VNTKC^CDRDQUD^SN^AD^B@KKDC^H)
Tried Key 2192... ("A computer would deserve to be called i)

Possible encryption hack:
Key: 2192
Decrypted message: "A computer would deserve to be called intelligent if it
could deceive a human into believing that it was human." -Alan Turing

Enter D for done, or just press Enter to continue hacking:
> d
Copying hacked message to clipboard:
"A computer would deserve to be called intelligent if it could deceive a human
into believing that it was human." -Alan Turing
```

How the Program Works

```
affineHacker.py
# Affine Cipher Hacker
# http://inventwithpython.com/hacking (BSD Licensed)

import pyperclip, affineCipher, detectEnglish, cryptomath

```

```
 6. SILENT_MODE = False
```

Our affine cipher hacking program fits in 60 lines of code because we've already written much of the code it uses.

When you run the hacker program, you can see that this program produces a lot of output as it works its way through all the possible decryptions. However, printing out this input does slow down the program. If you change line 6 to set the `SILENT_MODE` variable to `True`, the program will be silenced and not print out all these messages. This will speed up the program immensely.

But showing all that text while your hacking program runs makes it look cool. (And if you want your programs to look cool by printing out text slowly one character at a time for a "typewriter" effect, check out the *typewriter.py* module at http://invpy.com/typewriter.py.)

affineHacker.py

```
 8. def main():
 9.     # You might want to copy & paste this text from the source code at
10.     # http://invpy.com/affineHacker.py
11.     myMessage = """U&'<3dJ^Gjx'-3^MS'Sj0jxuj'G3'%j'<mMMjS'g{GjMMg9j{G'g"'gG'<3^MS'Sj<jguj'm'P^dm{'g{G3'%jMgjug{9'GPmG'gG'-m0'P^dm{LU'5&Mm{'_^xg{9"""
12.
13.     hackedMessage = hackAffine(myMessage)
14.
15.     if hackedMessage != None:
16.         # The plaintext is displayed on the screen. For the convenience of
17.         # the user, we copy the text of the code to the clipboard.
18.         print('Copying hacked message to clipboard:')
19.         print(hackedMessage)
20.         pyperclip.copy(hackedMessage)
21.     else:
22.         print('Failed to hack encryption.')
```

The ciphertext to be hacked is stored as a string in `myMessage`, and this string is passed to the `hackAffine()` function (described next). The return value from this call is either a string of the original message (if the ciphertext was hacked) or the `None` value (if the hacking failed).

The code on lines 15 to 22 will check if `hackedMessage` was set to `None` or not. If `hackedMessage` is not equal to `None`, then the message will be printed to the screen on line 19 and copied to the clipboard on line 20. Otherwise, the program will simply print that it was unable to hack the message.

The Affine Cipher Hacking Function

affineHacker.py

```
def hackAffine(message):
    print('Hacking...')

    # Python programs can be stopped at any time by pressing Ctrl-C (on
    # Windows) or Ctrl-D (on Mac and Linux)
    print('(Press Ctrl-C or Ctrl-D to quit at any time.)')
```

The `hackAffine()` function has the code that does the decryption. This can take a while, so if the user wants to exit the program early, she can press Ctrl-C (on Windows) or Ctrl-D (on OS X and Linux).

The ** Exponent Operator

There is another math operator besides the basic `+`, `-`, `*`, `/`, and `//` operators. The `**` operator is Python's **exponent operator**. This does "to the power of" math on two numbers. For example, "two to the power of five" would be `2 ** 5` in Python code. This is equivalent to two multiplied by itself five times: `2 * 2 * 2 * 2 * 2`. Both the expressions `2 ** 5` and `2 * 2 * 2 * 2 * 2` evaluate to the integer `32`.

Try typing the following into the interactive shell:

```
>>> 2 ** 6
64
>>> 4**2
16
>>> 2**4
16
>>> 123**10
792594609605189126649
>>>
```

affineHacker.py

```
    # brute-force by looping through every possible key
    for key in range(len(affineCipher.SYMBOLS) ** 2):
        keyA = affineCipher.getKeyParts(key)[0]
```

The range of integers for the keys used to brute-force the ciphertext will range from `0` to the size of the symbol set to the second power. The expression:

```
len(affineCipher.SYMBOLS) ** 2
```

...is the same as:

```
len(affineCipher.SYMBOLS) * len(affineCipher.SYMBOLS)
```

We multiply this because there are at most `len(affineCipher.SYMBOLS)` possible integers for Key A and `len(affineCipher.SYMBOLS)` possible integers for Key B. To get the entire range of possible keys, we multiply these values together.

Line 34 calls the `getKeyParts()` function that we made in *affineCipher.py* to get the Key A part of the key we are testing. Remember that the return value of this function call is a tuple of two integers (one for Key A and one for Key B). Since `hackAffine()` only needs Key A, the `[0]` after the function call works on the return value to evaluate to just the first integer in the returned tuple.

That is, `affineCipher.getKeyParts(key)[0]` will evaluate to (for example), the tuple `(42, 22)[0]`, which will then evaluate to `42`. This is how we can get just the Key A part of the return value. The Key B part (that is, the second value in the returned tuple) is just ignored because we don't need Key B to calculate if Key A is valid.

The `continue` Statement

The `continue` statement is simply the `continue` keyword by itself. A `continue` statement is found inside the block of a `while` or `for` loop. When a `continue` statement is executed, the program execution immediately jumps to the start of the loop for the next iteration.

This is exactly the same thing that happens when the program execution reaches the end of the loop's block. But a `continue` statement makes the program execution jump back to the start of the loop early.

Try typing the following into the interactive shell:

```
>>> for i in range(3):
...   print(i)
...   print('Hello!')
...
0
Hello!
1
Hello!
2
Hello!
>>>
```

This is pretty obvious. The `for` loop will loop through the `range` object, and the value in `i` becomes each integer between `0` and `4`. Also on each iteration, the `print('Hello!')` function call will display "Hello!" on the screen.

Try typing in this code, which adds a `continue` statement before the `print('Hello!')` line:

```
>>> for i in range(3):
...     print(i)
...     continue
...     print('Hello!')
...
0
1
2
>>>
```

Notice that "Hello!" never appears, because the `continue` statement causes the program execution to jump back to the start of the `for` loop for the next iteration. So the execution never reaches the `print('Hello!')` line.

A `continue` statement is often put inside an `if` statement's block so that execution will continue at the beginning of the loop based on some condition.

affineHacker.py

```
35.         if cryptomath.gcd(keyA, len(affineCipher.SYMBOLS)) != 1:
36.             continue
```

With the Key A integer stored in the variable `keyA`, line 35 uses the `gcd()` function in our `cryptomath` module to determine if Key A is not relatively prime with the symbol set size. Remember, two numbers are relatively prime if their GCD (greatest common divisor) is one.

If Key A and the symbol set size are not relatively prime, then the condition on line 35 is `True` and the `continue` statement on line 36 is executed. This will cause the program execution to jump back to the start of the loop for the next iteration. This way, the program will skip line 38's call to `decryptMessage()` if the key is invalid, and continue to the next key.

affineHacker.py

```
38.         decryptedText = affineCipher.decryptMessage(key, message)
39.         if not SILENT_MODE:
40.             print('Tried Key %s... (%s)' % (key, decryptedText[:40]))
```

The message is then decrypted with the key by calling `decryptMessage()`. If `SILENT_MODE` is `False` the "Tried Key" message will be printed on the screen. If `SILENT_MODE` was set to `True`, the `print()` call on line 40 will be skipped.

affineHacker.py

```
42.         if detectEnglish.isEnglish(decryptedText):
43.             # Check with the user if the decrypted key has been found.
44.             print()
45.             print('Possible encryption hack:')
46.             print('Key: %s' % (key))
47.             print('Decrypted message: ' + decryptedText[:200])
48.             print()
```

Next, we use the `isEnglish()` function from our `detectEnglish` module to check if the decrypted message is recognized as English. If the wrong decryption key was used, then the decrypted message will look like random characters and `isEnglish()` will return `False`.

But if the decrypted message is recognized as readable English (by the `isEnglish()` function anyway), then we will display this to the user.

affineHacker.py

```
49.             print('Enter D for done, or just press Enter to continue hacking:')
50.             response = input('> ')
51.
52.             if response.strip().upper().startswith('D'):
53.                 return decryptedText
```

The program might not have found the correct key, but rather a key that produces gibberish that the `isEnglish()` function mistakenly thinks is English. To prevent false positives, the decrypted text is printed on the screen for the user to read. If the user decides that this is the correct decryption, she can type in D and press Enter. Otherwise, she can just press Enter (which returns a blank string from the `input()` call) and the `hackAffine()` function will continue trying more keys.

affineHacker.py

```
54.     return None
```

From the indentation of line 54, you can see that this is line is executed after the `for` loop on line 33 has completed. If this loop has finished, then it has gone through every possible decryption key without finding the correct key. (If the program had found the correct key, then the execution would have previously returned from the function on line 53.)

But at this point, the `hackAffine()` function returns the `None` value to signal that it was unsuccessful at hacking the ciphertext.

affineHacker.py

```
# If affineHacker.py is run (instead of imported as a module) call
# the main() function.
if __name__ == '__main__':
    main()
```

Just like the other programs, we want the *affineHacker.py* file to be run on its own or be imported as a module. If *affineHacker.py* is run as a program, then the special `__name__` variable will be set to the string `'__main__'` (instead of `'affineHacker'`). In this case, we want to call the `main()` function.

Practice Exercises, Chapter 16, Set A

Practice exercises can be found at http://invpy.com/hackingpractice16A.

Summary

This chapter was fairly short because it hasn't introduced any new hacking techniques. As long as the number of possible keys is less than a million or so, it won't take long for our computers to brute-force through every possible key and use `isEnglish()` to check if it has found the right key.

And a lot of the code we use for the affine cipher hacker has already been written in *affineCipher.py*, *detectEnglish.py*, *cryptomath.py*, and *pyperclip.py*. The `main()` function trick is really helpful in making the code in our programs reusable.

The `**` exponent operator can be used to raise a number to the power of another number. The `continue` statement sends the program execution back to the beginning of the loop (instead of waiting until the execution reaches the end of the block).

In the next chapter, we will learn a new cipher that cannot be brute-forced by our computers. The number of possible keys is more than a trillion trillion! A single laptop couldn't possible go through a fraction of those keys in our life time. This makes it immune to brute-forcing. Let's learn about the simple substitution cipher.

Chapter 17

The Simple Substitution Cipher

Topics Covered In This Chapter:

- The Set data type and `set()` function
- The `sort()` list method
- Getting rid of duplicate characters from a string
- The `isupper()` and `islower()` string methods
- Wrapper functions

> "In my role as Wikileaks editor, I've been involved in fighting off many legal attacks. To do that, and keep our sources safe, we have had to spread assets, encrypt everything, and move telecommunications and people around the world to activate protective laws in different national jurisdictions."
>
> Julian Assange, editor-in-chief of Wikileaks

The transposition and affine ciphers have thousands of possible keys, but a computer can still brute-force through all of them easily. We'll need a cipher that has so many possible keys, no computer can possibly brute-force through them all.

The simple substitution cipher is effectively invulnerable to a brute-force attack. Even if your computer could try out a trillion keys every second, it would still take twelve million years for it to try out every key.

The Simple Substitution Cipher with Paper and Pencil

To implement the simple substitution cipher, choose a random letter to encrypt each letter of the alphabet. Use each letter once and only once. The key will end up being a string of 26 letters of the alphabet in random order. There are 403,291,461,126,605,635,584,000,000 possible orderings for keys. (To see how this number was calculated, see http://invpy.com/factorial).

Let's do the simple substitution cipher with paper and pencil first. For example, let's encrypt the message, "Attack at dawn." with the key VJZBGNFEPLITMXDWKQUCRYAHSO. First write out the letters of the alphabet and then write the key underneath it.

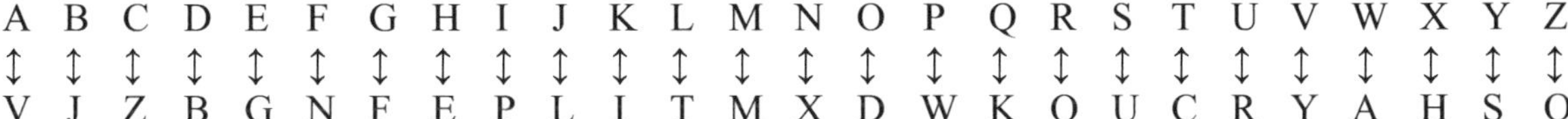

To encrypt a message, find the letter from the plaintext in the top row and substitute it with the letter in the bottom row. A encrypts to V, and T encrypts to C, C encrypts to Z, and so on. So the message "Attack at dawn." encrypts to "Vccvzi vc bvax."

To decrypt, find the letter from the ciphertext in the bottom row and replace it with the letter from the top row. V decrypts to A, C decrypts to T, Z decrypts to C, and so on.

This is very similar to how the Caesar cipher works with the St. Cyr slide, except the bottom row is scrambled instead of in alphabetical order and just shifted over. The advantage of the simple substitution cipher is that there are far more possible keys. The disadvantage is that the key is 26 characters long and harder to memorize. If you write down the key, make sure that this key is never read by anyone else!

Practice Exercises, Chapter 17, Set A

Practice exercises can be found at http://invpy.com/hackingpractice17A.

Source Code of the Simple Substitution Cipher

Open a new file editor window by clicking on **File ► New Window**. Type in the following code into the file editor, and then save it as *simpleSubCipher.py*. Press **F5** to run the program. Note that first you will need to download the *pyperclip.py* module and place this file in the same directory as the *simpleSubCipher.py* file. You can download this file from http://invpy.com/pyperclip.py.

Source code for simpleSubCipher.py

```
# Simple Substitution Cipher
# http://inventwithpython.com/hacking (BSD Licensed)

import pyperclip, sys, random


LETTERS = 'ABCDEFGHIJKLMNOPQRSTUVWXYZ'

def main():
    myMessage = 'If a man is offered a fact which goes against his
instincts, he will scrutinize it closely, and unless the evidence is
overwhelming, he will refuse to believe it. If, on the other hand, he is
offered something which affords a reason for acting in accordance to his
instincts, he will accept it even on the slightest evidence. The origin of
myths is explained in this way. -Bertrand Russell'
    myKey = 'LFWOAYUISVKMNXPBDCRJTQEGHZ'
    myMode = 'encrypt' # set to 'encrypt' or 'decrypt'

    checkValidKey(myKey)

    if myMode == 'encrypt':
        translated = encryptMessage(myKey, myMessage)
    elif myMode == 'decrypt':
        translated = decryptMessage(myKey, myMessage)
    print('Using key %s' % (myKey))
    print('The %sed message is:' % (myMode))
    print(translated)
    pyperclip.copy(translated)
    print()
    print('This message has been copied to the clipboard.')


def checkValidKey(key):
    keyList = list(key)
    lettersList = list(LETTERS)
    keyList.sort()
    lettersList.sort()
```

```
    if keyList != lettersList:
        sys.exit('There is an error in the key or symbol set.')


def encryptMessage(key, message):
    return translateMessage(key, message, 'encrypt')


def decryptMessage(key, message):
    return translateMessage(key, message, 'decrypt')


def translateMessage(key, message, mode):
    translated = ''
    charsA = LETTERS
    charsB = key
    if mode == 'decrypt':
        # For decrypting, we can use the same code as encrypting. We
        # just need to swap where the key and LETTERS strings are used.
        charsA, charsB = charsB, charsA

    # loop through each symbol in the message
    for symbol in message:
        if symbol.upper() in charsA:
            # encrypt/decrypt the symbol
            symIndex = charsA.find(symbol.upper())
            if symbol.isupper():
                translated += charsB[symIndex].upper()
            else:
                translated += charsB[symIndex].lower()
        else:
            # symbol is not in LETTERS, just add it
            translated += symbol

    return translated


def getRandomKey():
    key = list(LETTERS)
    random.shuffle(key)
    return ''.join(key)


if __name__ == '__main__':
    main()
```

Sample Run of the Simple Substitution Cipher Program

When you run this program, the output will look like this:

```
Using key LFWOAYUISVKMNXPBDCRJTQEGHZ
The encrypted message is:
Sy l nlx sr pyyacao l ylwj eiswi upar lulsxrj isr sxrjsxwjr, ia esmm rwctjsxsza
sj wmpramh, lxo txmarr jia aqsoaxwa sr pqaceiamnsxu, ia esmm caytra jp famsaqa
sj. Sy, px jia pjiac ilxo, ia sr pyyacao rpnajisxu eiswi lyypcor l calrpx ypc
lwjsxu sx lwwpcolxwa jp isr sxrjsxwjr, ia esmm lwwabj sj aqax px jia rmsuijarj
aqsoaxwa. Jia pcsusx py nhjir sr agbmlsxao sx jisr elh. -Facjclxo Ctrramm

This message has been copied to the clipboard.
```

Notice that if the letter in the plaintext was lowercase, it will be lowercase in the ciphertext. If the letter was uppercase in the plaintext, it will be uppercase in the ciphertext. The simple substitution cipher does not encrypt spaces or punctuation marks. (Although the end of this chapter explains how to modify the program to encrypt those characters too.)

To decrypt this ciphertext, paste it as the value for the `myMessage` variable on line 10 and change `myMode` to the string `'decrypt'`. Then run the program again. The output will look like this:

```
Using key LFWOAYUISVKMNXPBDCRJTQEGHZ
The decrypted message is:
If a man is offered a fact which goes against his instincts, he will scrutinize
it closely, and unless the evidence is overwhelming, he will refuse to believe
it. If, on the other hand, he is offered something which affords a reason for
acting in accordance to his instincts, he will accept it even on the slightest
evidence. The origin of myths is explained in this way. -Bertrand Russell

This message has been copied to the clipboard.
```

How the Program Works

simpleSubCipher.py

```
1. # Simple Substitution Cipher
2. # http://inventwithpython.com/hacking (BSD Licensed)
3.
4. import pyperclip, sys, random
5.
6.
7. LETTERS = 'ABCDEFGHIJKLMNOPQRSTUVWXYZ'
```

The first few lines are comments describing the program. Then the `pyperclip`, `sys`, and `random` modules are imported. Finally, the `LETTERS` constant variable is set to a string of all the uppercase letters. The `LETTERS` string will be our symbol set for the simple substitution cipher program.

The Program's `main()` Function

simpleSubCipher.py

```
 9. def main():
10.     myMessage = 'If a man is offered a fact which goes against his instincts, he will scrutinize it closely, and unless the evidence is overwhelming, he will refuse to believe it. If, on the other hand, he is offered something which affords a reason for acting in accordance to his instincts, he will accept it even on the slightest evidence. The origin of myths is explained in this way. -Bertrand Russell'
11.     myKey = 'LFWOAYUISVKMNXPBDCRJTQEGHZ'
12.     myMode = 'encrypt' # set to 'encrypt' or 'decrypt'
```

The `main()` function is similar to the `main()` function of cipher programs in the previous chapters. It contains the variables that store the `message`, `key`, and `mode` that will be used for the program.

simpleSubCipher.py

```
14.     checkValidKey(myKey)
```

The keys for simple substitution ciphers are easy to get wrong. For example, the key might not have every letter of the alphabet. Or the key may have the same letter twice. The `checkValidKey()` function (which is explained later) makes sure the key is usable by the encryption and decryption functions, and will exit the program with an error message if they are not.

simpleSubCipher.py

```
16.     if myMode == 'encrypt':
17.         translated = encryptMessage(myKey, myMessage)
18.     elif myMode == 'decrypt':
19.         translated = decryptMessage(myKey, myMessage)
```

If the program execution returns from `checkValidKey()` instead of terminating, we can assume the key is valid. Lines 16 through 19 check whether the `myMode` variable is set to `'encrypt'` or `'decrypt'` and calls either `encryptMessage()` or `decryptMessage()`. The return value of `encryptMessage()` and `decryptMessage()` (which is explained later) will be a string of the encrypted (or decrypted) message. This string will be stored in the `translated` variable.

simpleSubCipher.py

```
20.     print('Using key %s' % (myKey))
21.     print('The %sed message is:' % (myMode))
22.     print(translated)
23.     pyperclip.copy(translated)
24.     print()
25.     print('This message has been copied to the clipboard.')
```

The key that was used is printed to the screen on line 20. The encrypted (or decrypted) message is printed on the screen and also copied to the clipboard. Line 25 is the last line of code in the `main()` function, so the program execution returns after line 25. Since the `main()` call is done at the last line of the program, the program will then exit.

The `sort()` List Method

simpleSubCipher.py

```
28. def checkValidKey(key):
29.     keyList = list(key)
30.     lettersList = list(LETTERS)
31.     keyList.sort()
32.     lettersList.sort()
```

A simple substitution key string value is only valid if it has each of the characters in the symbol set with no duplicate or missing letters. We can check if a string value is a valid key by sorting it and the symbol set into alphabetical order and checking if they are equal. (Although `LETTERS` is already in alphabetical order, we still need to sort it since it could be expanded to contain other characters.)

On line 29 the string in `key` is passed to `list()`. The list value returned is stored in a variable named `keyList`. On line 30, the `LETTERS` constant variable (which, remember, is the string `'ABCDEFGHIJKLMNOPQRSTUVWXYZ'`) is passed to `list()` which returns the list `['A', 'B', 'C', 'D', 'E', 'F', 'G', 'H', 'I', 'J', 'K', 'L', 'M', 'N', 'O', 'P', 'Q', 'R', 'S', 'T', 'U', 'V', 'W', 'X', 'Y', 'Z']`.

The `sort()` list method will rearrange the order of items in the list into alphabetical order. The lists in `keyList` and `lettersList` are then sorted in alphabetical order by calling the `sort()` list method on them. Note that just like the `append()` list method, the `sort()` list method modifies the list in place and does not have a return value. You want your code to look like this:

```
keyList.sort()
```

...and **not** look like this:

```
keyList = keyList.sort()
```

```
simpleSubCipher.py
33.     if keyList != lettersList:
34.         sys.exit('There is an error in the key or symbol set.')
```

Once sorted, the `keyList` and `lettersList` values *should* be the same, since `keyList` was just the characters in `LETTERS` with the order scrambled. If `keyList` and `lettersList` are equal, we also know that `keyList` (and, therefore, the `key` parameter) does not have any duplicates in it, since `LETTERS` does not have any duplicates in it.

However, if the condition on line 33 is `True`, then the value in `myKey` was set to an invalid value and the program will exit by calling `sys.exit()`.

Wrapper Functions

```
simpleSubCipher.py
def encryptMessage(key, message):
    return translateMessage(key, message, 'encrypt')


def decryptMessage(key, message):
    return translateMessage(key, message, 'decrypt')


def translateMessage(key, message, mode):
```

The code for encrypting and the code for decrypting are almost exactly the same. It's always a good idea to put code into a function and call it twice rather than type out the code twice. First, this saves you some typing. But second, if there's ever a bug in the duplicate code, you only have to fix the bug in one place instead of multiple places. It is (usually) much more reasonable to replace duplicate code with a single function that has the code.

Wrapper functions simply wrap the code of another function, and return the value the wrapped function returns. Often the wrapper function might make a slight change to the arguments or return value of wrapped function (otherwise you would just call the wrapped function directly.) In this case, `encryptMessage()` and `decryptMessage()` (the wrapper functions) calls `translateMessage()` (the wrapped function) and returns the value `translateMessage()` returns.

On line 45 notice that `translateMessage()` has the parameters `key` and `message`, but also a third parameter named `mode`. When it calls `translateMessage()`, the call in `encryptMessage()` function passes `'encrypt'` for the `mode` parameter, and the call in `decryptMessage()` function passes `'decrypt'`. This is how the `translateMessage()` function knows whether it should encrypt or decrypt the message it is passed.

With these wrapper functions, someone who imports the *simpleSubCipher.py* program can call functions named `encryptMessage()` and `decryptMessage()` like they do with all the other cipher programs in this book. They might create a program that encrypts with various ciphers, like below:

```
import affineCipher, simpleSubCipher, transpositionCipher
...some other code here...
ciphertext1 =        affineCipher.encryptMessage(encKey1, 'Hello!')
ciphertext2 = transpositionCipher.encryptMessage(encKey2, 'Hello!')
ciphertext3 =     simpleSubCipher.encryptMessage(encKey3, 'Hello!')
```

The wrapper functions give the simple substitution cipher program function names that are consistent with the other cipher programs. Consistent names are very helpful, because it makes it easier for someone familiar with one of the cipher programs in this book to already be familiar with the other cipher programs. (You can even see that the first parameter was always made the key and the second parameter is always the message.) This is the reason we have these wrapper functions, because making the programmer call the `translateMessage()` function would be inconsistent with the other programs.

The Program's `translateMessage()` Function

simpleSubCipher.py

```
45. def translateMessage(key, message, mode):
46.     translated = ''
47.     charsA = LETTERS
48.     charsB = key
49.     if mode == 'decrypt':
50.         # For decrypting, we can use the same code as encrypting. We
51.         # just need to swap where the key and LETTERS strings are used.
52.         charsA, charsB = charsB, charsA
```

The `translateMessage()` function does the encryption (or decryption, if the `mode` parameter is set to the string `'decrypt'`). The encryption process is very simple: for each letter in the `message` parameter, we look up its index in `LETTERS` and replace it with the letter at that same index in the `key` parameter. To decrypt we do the opposite: we look up the index in `key` and replace it with the letter at the same index in the `LETTERS`.

The table below shows why using the same index will encrypt or decrypt the letter. The top row shows the characters in `charsA` (which is set to `LETTERS` on line 47), the middle row shows the characters in `charsB` (which is set to `key` on line 48), and the bottom row are the integer indexes (for our own reference in this example).

A	B	C	D	E	F	G	H	I	J	K	L	M
↕	↕	↕	↕	↕	↕	↕	↕	↕	↕	↕	↕	↕
V	J	Z	B	G	N	F	E	P	L	I	T	M
0	1	2	3	4	5	6	7	8	9	10	11	12

N	O	P	Q	R	S	T	U	V	W	X	Y	Z
↕	↕	↕	↕	↕	↕	↕	↕	↕	↕	↕	↕	↕
X	D	W	K	Q	U	C	R	Y	A	H	S	O
13	14	15	16	17	18	19	20	21	22	23	24	25

The code in `translateMessage()` will *always* look up the message character's index in `charsA` and replace it with the character at that index in `charsB`.

So to encrypt, we can just leave `charsA` and `charsB` as they are. This will replace the character in `LETTERS` with the character in `key`, because `charsA` is set to `LETTERS` and `charsB` is set to `key`.

When decrypting, the values in `charsA` and `charsB` (that is, `LETTERS` and `key`) are swapped on line 52, so the table would look like this:

V	J	Z	B	G	N	F	E	P	L	I	T	M
↕	↕	↕	↕	↕	↕	↕	↕	↕	↕	↕	↕	↕
A	B	C	D	E	F	G	H	I	J	K	L	M
0	1	2	3	4	5	6	7	8	9	10	11	12

X	D	W	K	Q	U	C	R	Y	A	H	S	O
↕	↕	↕	↕	↕	↕	↕	↕	↕	↕	↕	↕	↕
N	O	P	Q	R	S	T	U	V	W	X	Y	Z
13	14	15	16	17	18	19	20	21	22	23	24	25

Remember, our code in `translateMessage()` *always* replaces the character in `charsA` (the top row) with the character at that same index in `charsB` (the middle row). So when lines 47 and

48 will swap the values in charsA and charsB, the code in translateMessage() will be doing the decryption process instead of the encryption process.

simpleSubCipher.py

```
54.     # loop through each symbol in the message
55.     for symbol in message:
56.         if symbol.upper() in charsA:
57.             # encrypt/decrypt the symbol
58.             symIndex = charsA.find(symbol.upper())
```

The for loop on line 55 will set the symbol variable to a character in the message string on each iteration through the loop. If the uppercase form of this symbol exists in charsA (remember that both the key and LETTERS only have uppercase characters in them), then we will find the index of the uppercase form of symbol in charsA. This index will be stored in a variable named symIndex.

We already know that the find() method will never return -1 (remember, a -1 from the find() method means the argument could not be found the string) because the if statement on line 56 guarantees that symbol.upper() will exist in charsA. Otherwise line 58 wouldn't have been executed in the first place.

The isupper() and islower() String Methods

The isupper() string method returns True if:

1. The string has at least one uppercase letter.
2. The string does not have any lowercase letters in it.

The islower() string method returns True if:

1. The string has at least one lowercase letter.
2. The string does not have any uppercase letters in it.

Non-letter characters in the string do not affect whether these methods return True or False. Try typing the following into the interactive shell:

```
>>> 'HELLO'.isupper()
True
>>> 'HELLO WORLD 123'.isupper()
True
>>> 'hELLO'.isupper()
False
>>> 'hELLO'.islower()
False
```

```
>>> 'hello'.islower()
True
>>> '123'.isupper()
False
>>> ''.islower()
False
>>>
```

simpleSubCipher.py

```
59.             if symbol.isupper():
60.                 translated += charsB[symIndex].upper()
61.             else:
62.                 translated += charsB[symIndex].lower()
```

If `symbol` is an uppercase letter, than we want to concatenate the uppercase version of the character at `charsB[symIndex]` to `translated`. Otherwise we will concatenate the lowercase version of the character at `charsB[symIndex]` to `translated`.

If `symbol` was a number or punctuation mark like `'5'` or `'?'`, then the condition on line 59 would be `False` (since those strings don't have at least one uppercase letter in them) and line 62 would have been executed. In this case, line 62's `lower()` method call would have no effect on the string since it has no letters in it. Try typing the following into the interactive shell:

```
>>> '5'.lower()
'5'
>>> '?'.lower()
'?'
>>>
```

So line 62 in the `else` block takes care of translating any lowercase characters **and** non-letter characters.

simpleSubCipher.py

```
63.         else:
64.             # symbol is not in LETTERS, just add it
65.             translated += symbol
```

By looking at the indentation, you can tell that the `else` statement on line 63 is paired with the `if` statement on line 56. The code in the block that follows (that is, line 65) is executed if `symbol` is not in `LETTERS`. This means that we cannot encrypt (or decrypt) the character in `symbol`, so we will just concatenate it to the end of `translated` as is.

simpleSubCipher.py

```
67.     return translated
```

At the end of the `translateMessage()` function we return the value in the `translated` variable, which will contain the encrypted or decrypted message.

Practice Exercises, Chapter 17, Set B

Practice exercises can be found at http://invpy.com/hackingpractice17B.

Generating a Random Key

simpleSubCipher.py

```
70. def getRandomKey():
71.     key = list(LETTERS)
72.     random.shuffle(key)
73.     return ''.join(key)
```

Typing up a string that contains each letter of the alphabet once and only once can be difficult. To aid the user, the `getRandomKey()` function will return a valid key to use. Lines 71 to 73 do this by randomly scrambling the characters in the `LETTERS` constant. See the "Randomly Scrambling a String" section in Chapter 10 for an explanation of how to scramble a string using `list()`, `random.shuffle()`, and `join()`.

To use the `getRandomKey()` function, line 11 can be changed to this:

```
11.     myKey = getRandomKey()
```

Remember that our cipher program will print out the key being used on line 20. This is how the user can find out what key the `getRandomKey()` function returned.

simpleSubCipher.py

```
76. if __name__ == '__main__':
77.     main()
```

Lines 76 and 77 are at the bottom of the program, and call `main()` if *simpleSubCipher.py* is being run as a program instead of imported as a module by another program.

Encrypting Spaces and Punctuation

The simple substitution cipher in this chapter only encrypts the letters in the plaintext. This artificial limitation is here because the hacking program in the next chapter only works if the letters alone have been substituted.

If you want the simple substitution program to encrypt more than just the letter characters, make the following changes:

```
simpleSubCipher.py
7. LETTERS = r""" !"#$%&'()*+,-./0123456789:;<=>?@ABCDEFGHIJKLMNOPQRSTUVWXY
Z[\]^_`abcdefghijklmnopqrstuvwxyz{|}~"""
```

Line 7's value stored in the `LETTERS` constant is changed to a string of all the characters Using a triple-quotes raw string so you do not have to escape the quotes and \ slash character makes typing this easier.

The key used must also have all of these characters, so line 11 changes to something like this:

```
simpleSubCipher.py
11.     myKey = r"""/{9@6hUf:q?_)^eTi|W1,NLD7xk(-
SF>IzOE=d;Bu#c]w~'VvHKmpJ+}s8y& XtP43.b[OA!*\Q<M%$ZgG52YloaRCn"`rj"""
```

The code that differentiates between upper and lowercase letters on lines 58 to 62 can be replaced with these two lines:

```
simpleSubCipher.py
58.             symIndex = charsA.find(symbol.upper())
59.             if symbol.isupper():
60.                 translated += charsB[symIndex].upper()
61.             else:
62.                 translated += charsB[symIndex].lower()

58.             symIndex = charsA.find(symbol)
59.             translated += charsB[symIndex]
```

Now when you run the simple substitution cipher program, the ciphertext looks much more like random gibberish:

```
Using key /{9@6hUf:q?_)^eTi|W1,NLD7xk(-SF>IzOE=d;Bu#c]w~'VvHKmpJ+}s8y&
XtP43.b[OA!*\Q<M%$ZgG52YloaRCn"`rj
The encrypted message is:
#A/3/%3$/\2/ZAA050[/3/A3bY/a*\b*/!Z02/3!3\$2Y/*\2/\$2Y\$bY2)/*0/a\MM/2b5lY\$\n0
/\Y/bMZ20MC)/3$[/1$M022/Y*0/Oo\[0$b0/\2/Zo05a*0M%\$!)/*0/a\MM/50Al20/YZ/.0M\Oo0
/\Ye/#A)/Z$/Y*0/ZY*05/*3$[)/*0/\2/ZAA050[/2Z%0Y*\$!/a*\b*/3AAZ5[2/3/5032Z$/AZ5/
3bY\$!/\$/3bbZ5[3$b0/YZ/*\2/\$2Y\$bY2)/*0/a\MM/3bb0gY/\Y/0o0$/Z$/Y*0/2M\!*Y02Y/
Oo\[0$b0e/p*0/Z5\!\$/ZA/%CY*2/\2/0RgM3\$0[/\$/Y*\2/a3Ce/^005Y53$[/Kl220MM

This message has been copied to the clipboard.
```

Practice Exercises, Chapter 17, Set C

Practice exercises can be found at http://invpy.com/hackingpractice17C.

Summary

In this chapter, we have learned about the new "set" data type. In many of our programs, lists are much easier to use than sets, but sets are a simple way to get rid of duplicate values from lists or strings.

The `isupper()` and `islower()` string methods can tell us if a string value is made up of only uppercase or lowercase letters. And the `sort()` list method is very useful at putting the items in a list in order.

The simple substitution cipher has far too many possible keys to brute-force through. This makes it impervious to the techniques that our previous cipher hacking programs have used. We are going to have to make smarter programs in order to break this code.

In the next chapter, we will learn how to hack the simple substitution cipher. Instead of brute-forcing through all the keys, we will use a much more intelligent and sophisticated algorithm.

CHAPTER 18

HACKING THE SIMPLE SUBSTITUTION CIPHER

Topics Covered In This Chapter:

- Word patterns, candidates, potential decryption letters, and cipherletter mappings.
- The `pprint.pprint()` and `pprint.pformat()` functions
- Building strings using the list-append-join process
- Regular expressions
- The `sub()` regex method

"Cypherpunks deplore regulations on cryptography, for encryption is fundamentally a private act. The act of encryption, in fact, removes information from the public realm. Even laws against cryptography reach only so far as a nation's border and the arm of its violence."

Eric Hughes, "A Cypherpunk's Manifesto", 1993
http://invpy.com/cypherpunk

Computing Word Patterns

There are too many possible keys to brute-force a simple substitution cipher-encrypted message. We need to employ a more intelligent attack if we want to crack a substitution ciphertext. Let's examine one possible word from an example ciphertext:

```
HGHHU
```

Think about what we can learn from this one word of ciphertext (which we will call a **cipherword** in this book). We can tell that whatever the original plaintext word is, it must:

1. Be five letters long.
2. Have the first, third, and fourth letters be the same.
3. Have exactly three different letters in the word, where the first, second, and fifth letters in the word are all different from each other.

What words in the English language fit this pattern? "Puppy" is one word that fits this pattern. It is five letters long (P, U, P, P, Y) using three different letters (P, U, Y) in that same pattern (P for the first, third, and fourth letter and U for the second letter and Y for the fifth letter). "Mommy", "Bobby", "lulls", "nanny", and "lilly" fit the pattern too. ("Lilly" is a name, not to be confused with "Lily" the flower. But since "Lilly" can appear in an Engish message it is a possible word that fits the pattern.) If we had a lot of time on our hands, we could go through an entire dictionary and find all the words that fit this pattern. Even better, we could have a computer go through a dictionary file for us.

In this book a **word pattern** will be a set of numbers with periods in between the numbers that tells us the pattern of letters for a word, in either ciphertext or plaintext.

Creating word patterns for cipherwords is easy: the first letter gets the number 0 and the first occurrence of each different letter after that gets the next number. For example:

- The word pattern for "cat" is 0.1.2.
- The word pattern for "catty" is 0.1.2.2.3.
- The word pattern for "roofer" is 0.1.1.2.3.0.
- The word pattern for "blimp" is 0.1.2.3.4.
- The word pattern for "classification" is 0.1.2.3.3.4.5.4.0.2.6.4.7.8.

A plaintext word and its cipherword will always have the same word pattern, no matter which simple substitution key was used to do the encryption.

Getting a List of Candidates for a Cipherword

To take a guess at what HGHHU could decrypt to, we can go through the dictionary file and find all of the words that also have a word pattern of 0.1.0.0.2. In this book, we will call these plaintext words (that have the same word pattern as the cipherword) the **candidates** for that cipherword:

Ciphertext word:	H G H H U
Word pattern:	0.1.0.0.2
Candidates:	p u p p y
	m o m m y
	b o b b y
	l u l l s
	n a n n y
	l i l l y

So if we look at the letters in the cipherword (which will be called **cipherletters** in this book), we can guess which letters they may decrypt to (we will call these letters the cipherletter's **potential decryption letters** in this book):

Cipherletters:	H	G	U
Potential decryption letters:	p	u	y
	m	o	y
	b	o	y
	l	u	s
	n	a	y
	l	i	y

From this table we can create a **cipherletter mapping**:

- The cipher letter H has the potential decryption letters P, M, B, L, and N
- The cipher letter G has the potential decryption letters U, O, A, and I
- The cipher letter U has the potential decryption letters Y and S
- All of the other cipher letters besides H, G, and U will have no potential decryption letters.

When we represent a cipherletter mapping in Python code, we will use a dictionary value:

```
{'A': [], 'B': [], 'C': [], 'D': [], 'E': [], 'F': [], 'G': ['U', 'O', 'A',
'I'], 'H': ['P', 'B', 'L', 'N'], 'I': [], 'J': [], 'K': [], 'L': [], 'M': [],
'N': [], 'O': [], 'P': [], 'Q': [], 'R': [], 'S': [], 'T': [], 'U': ['Y', 'S'],
'V': [], 'W': [], 'X': [], 'Y': [], 'Z': []}
```

In our program, a cipherletter mapping dictionary will have 26 keys, one for each letter. The mapping above has potential decryption letters for `'H'`, `'G'`, and `'U'` above. The other keys have no potential decryption letters, which is why they have empty lists for values.

If we reduce the number of potential decryption letters for a cipherletter to just one letter, then we have solved what that cipherletter decrypts to. Even if we do not solve all 26 cipherletters, we might be able to hack most of the ciphertext's cipherletters.

But first we must find the pattern for every word in the dictionary file and sort them in a list so it will be easy to get a list of all the candidates for a given cipherword's word pattern. We can use the same dictionary file from Chapter 12, which you can download from http://invpy.com/dictionary.txt.

(Note that the terms "word pattern", "candidate", and "cipherletter mapping" are terms I came up with to describe things in this particular hacking program. These are not general cryptography terms.)

Practice Exercises, Chapter 18, Set A

Practice exercises can be found at http://invpy.com/hackingpractice18A.

Source Code of the Word Pattern Module

Since the word patterns for words never change, we can just calculate the word pattern for every word in a dictionary file once and store them in another file. Our *makeWordPatterns.py* program creates a file named *wordPatterns.py* that will contain a dictionary value with the word pattern for every word in the dictionary file. Our hacking program can then just import `wordPatterns` to look up the candidates for a certain word pattern.

Source code for makeWordPatterns.py

```
# Makes the wordPatterns.py File
# http://inventwithpython.com/hacking (BSD Licensed)

# Creates wordPatterns.py based on the words in our dictionary
# text file, dictionary.txt. (Download this file from
# http://invpy.com/dictionary.txt)

import pprint
```

```


def getWordPattern(word):
    # Returns a string of the pattern form of the given word.
    # e.g. '0.1.2.3.4.1.2.3.5.6' for 'DUSTBUSTER'
    word = word.upper()
    nextNum = 0
    letterNums = {}
    wordPattern = []

    for letter in word:
        if letter not in letterNums:
            letterNums[letter] = str(nextNum)
            nextNum += 1
        wordPattern.append(letterNums[letter])
    return '.'.join(wordPattern)


def main():
    allPatterns = {}

    fo = open('dictionary.txt')
    wordList = fo.read().split('\n')
    fo.close()

    for word in wordList:
        # Get the pattern for each string in wordList.
        pattern = getWordPattern(word)

        if pattern not in allPatterns:
            allPatterns[pattern] = [word]
        else:
            allPatterns[pattern].append(word)

    # This is code that writes code. The wordPatterns.py file contains
    # one very, very large assignment statement.
    fo = open('wordPatterns.py', 'w')
    fo.write('allPatterns = ')
    fo.write(pprint.pformat(allPatterns))
    fo.close()


if __name__ == '__main__':
    main()
```

Sample Run of the Word Pattern Module

Running this program doesn't print anything out to the screen. Instead it silently creates a file named *wordPatterns.py* in the same folder as *makeWordPatterns.py*. Open this file in IDLE's file editor, and you will see it looks like this:

```
allPatterns = {'0.0.1': ['EEL'],
 '0.0.1.2': ['EELS', 'OOZE'],
 '0.0.1.2.0': ['EERIE'],
 '0.0.1.2.3': ['AARON', 'LLOYD', 'OOZED'],
...the rest has been cut for brevity...
```

The *makeWordPatterns.py* program creates *wordPatterns.py*. Our Python program creates a Python program! The entire *wordPatterns.py* program is just one (very big) assignment statement for a variable named `allPatterns`. Even though this assignment statement stretches over many lines in the file, it is considered one "line of code" because Python knows that if a line ends with a comma but it is currently in the middle of a dictionary value, it ignores the indentation of the next line and just considers it part of the previous line. (This is a rare exception for Python's significant indentation rules.)

The `allPatterns` variable contains a dictionary value where the keys are all the word patterns made from the English words in the dictionary file. The keys' values are lists of strings of English words with that pattern. When *wordPatterns.py* is imported as a module, our program will be able to look up all the English words for any given word pattern.

After running the *makeWordPatterns.py* program to create the *wordPatterns.py* file, try typing the following into the interactive shell:

```
>>> import wordPatterns
>>> wordPatterns.allPatterns['0.1.2.1.1.3.4']
['BAZAARS', 'BESEECH', 'REDEEMS', 'STUTTER']
>>>
>>> wordPatterns.allPatterns['0.1.2.2.3.2.4.1.5.5']
['CANNONBALL']
>>>
>>> wordPatterns.allPatterns['0.1.0.1.0.1']
Traceback (most recent call last):
  File "<stdin>", line 1, in <module>
KeyError: '0.1.0.1.0.1'
>>>
>>> '0.1.0.1.0.1' in wordPatterns.allPatterns
False
>>>
```

The pattern `'0.1.0.1.0.1'` does not exist in the dictionary. This is why the expression `wordPatterns.allPatterns['0.1.0.1.0.1']` causes an error (because there is no `'0.1.0.1.0.1'` key in `allPatterns`) and why `'0.1.0.1.0.1'` in `wordPatterns.allPatterns` evaluates to `False`.

How the Program Works

makeWordPatterns.py

```
# Makes the wordPatterns.py File
# http://inventwithpython.com/hacking (BSD Licensed)

# Creates wordPatterns.py based on the words in our dictionary
# text file, dictionary.txt. (Download this file from
# http://invpy.com/dictionary.txt)
```

The top part of this file has the usual comments describing what the program is.

The `pprint.pprint()` and `pprint.pformat()` Functions

makeWordPatterns.py

```
import pprint
```

The `pprint` module has functions for **pretty printing** values, which is useful for printing dictionary and list values on the screen. The `print()` function simply prints these values going left to right:

```
>>> print(someListOfListsVar))
[['ant'], ['baboon', 'badger', 'bat', 'bear', 'beaver'], ['camel', 'cat',
'clam', 'cobra', 'cougar', 'coyote', 'crow'], ['deer', 'dog', 'donkey',
'duck'], ['eagle'], ['ferret', 'fox', 'frog'], ['goat']]
```

The `pprint` module has a function named `pprint()`. The value passed to `pprint.pprint()` will be "pretty printed" to the screen so that it is easier to read:

```
>>> import pprint
>>> pprint.pprint(someListOfListsVar))
[['ant'],
 ['baboon', 'badger', 'bat', 'bear', 'beaver'],
 ['camel', 'cat', 'clam', 'cobra', 'cougar', 'coyote', 'crow'],
 ['deer', 'dog', 'donkey', 'duck'],
 ['eagle'],
 ['ferret', 'fox', 'frog'],
 ['goat']]
```

However, if you want to have this "prettified" text as a string value **instead** of displaying it on the screen, you can use the `pprint.pformat()` function, which returns the prettified string:

```
>>> import pprint
>>> prettifiedString = pprint.pformat(someListOfListsVar)
>>> print(prettifiedString)
[['ant'],
 ['baboon', 'badger', 'bat', 'bear', 'beaver'],
 ['camel', 'cat', 'clam', 'cobra', 'cougar', 'coyote', 'crow'],
 ['deer', 'dog', 'donkey', 'duck'],
 ['eagle'],
 ['ferret', 'fox', 'frog'],
 ['goat']]
>>>
```

When we write the value of `allPatterns` to the *wordPatterns.py* file, we will use the `pprint` module to prevent it from being printed crammed together all on one line.

Building Strings in Python with Lists

Almost all of our programs have done some form of "building a string" code. That is, a variable will start as a blank string and then new characters are added with string concatenation. (We've done this in many previous cipher programs with the `translated` variable.) This is usually done with the + operator to do string concatenation, as in the following short program:

```
# The slow way to build a string using string concatenation.
building = ''
for c in 'Hello world!':
    building += c
print(building)
```

The above program loops through each character in the string `'Hello world!'` and concatenates it to the end of the string stored in `building`. At the end of the loop, `building` holds the complete string.

This seems like a straightforward way to do this. However, it is very inefficient for Python to concatenate strings. The reasons are technical and beyond the scope of this book, but **it is much faster to start with a blank list instead of a blank string, and then use the `append()` list method instead of string concatenation**. After you are done building the list of strings, you can convert the list of strings to a single string value with the `join()` method. The following short program does exactly the same thing as the previous example, but faster:

```
# The fast way to build a string using a list, append(), and join().
building = []
for c in 'Hello world!':
    building.append(c)
building = ''.join(building)
print(building)
```

Using this approach for building up strings in your code will result in much faster programs. We will be using this list-append-join process to build strings in the remaining programs of this book.

Calculating the Word Pattern

makeWordPatterns.py

```
11. def getWordPattern(word):
12.     # Returns a string of the pattern form of the given word.
13.     # e.g. '0.1.2.3.4.1.2.3.5.6' for 'DUSTBUSTER'
14.     word = word.upper()
15.     nextNum = 0
16.     letterNums = {}
17.     wordPattern = []
```

The `getWordPattern()` function takes one string argument and returns a string of that word's pattern. For example, if `getWordPattern()` were passed the string `'Buffoon'` as an argument then `getWordPattern()` would return the string `'0.1.2.2.3.3.4'`.

First, in order to make sure all the letters have the same case, line 14 changes the `word` parameter to an uppercase version of itself. We then need three variables:

- `nextNum` stores the next number used when a new letter is found.
- `letterNums` stores a dictionary with keys of single-letter strings of single letters, and values of the integer number for that letter. As we find new letters in the word, the letter and its number are stored in `letterNums`.
- `wordPattern` will be the string that is returned from this function. But we will be building this string one character at a time, so we will use the list-append-join process to do this. This is why `wordPattern` starts as a blank list instead of a blank string.

makeWordPatterns.py

```
    for letter in word:
        if letter not in letterNums:
            letterNums[letter] = str(nextNum)
            nextNum += 1
```

Line 19's `for` loop will loop through each character in the `word` parameter, assigning each character to a variable named `letter`.

Line 20 checks if `letter` has not been seen before by checking that `letter` does not exist as a key in the `letterNums` dictionary. (On the first iteration of the loop, the condition on line 20 will always be `True` because `letterNums` will be a blank dictionary that doesn't have anything in it.)

If we have not seen this letter before, line 21 adds this letter as the key and the string form of `nextNum` as the key's value to the `letterNums` dictionary. For the next new letter we find we want to use the next integer after the one currently in `nextNum` anymore, so line 22 increments the integer in `nextNum` by `1`.

makeWordPatterns.py

```
23.         wordPattern.append(letterNums[letter])
```

On line 23, `letterNums[letter]` evaluates to the integer used for the letter in the `letter` variable, so this is appended to the end of `wordPattern`. The `letterNums` dictionary is guaranteed to have `letter` for a key, because if it hadn't, then lines 20 to 22 would have handled adding it to `letterNums` before line 23.

makeWordPatterns.py

```
24.     return '.'.join(wordPattern)
```

After the `for` loop on line 19 is finished looping, the `wordPattern` list will contain all the strings of the complete word pattern. Our word patterns have periods separating the integers, so that we could tell the difference between "1.12" and "11.2". To put these periods in between each of the strings in the `wordPattern` list, line 24 calls the `join()` method on the string `'.'`. This will evaluate to a string such as `'0.1.2.2.3.3.4'`. The completely-built string that `join()` returns will be the return value of `getWordPattern()`.

The Word Pattern Program's `main()` Function

makeWordPatterns.py

```
27. def main():
28.     allPatterns = {}
```

The value stored in `allPatterns` is what we will write to the *wordPatterns.py* file. It is a dictionary whose keys are strings of word patterns (such as `'0.1.2.3.0.4.5'` or `'0.1.1.2'`) and the keys' values are a list of strings of English words that match that pattern. For example, here's one of the key-value pairs that will end up in `allPatterns`:

```
'0.1.0.2.3.1.4': ['DEDUCER', 'DEDUCES', 'GIGABIT', 'RARITAN']
```

But at the beginning of the `main()` function on line 28, the `allPatterns` variable will start off as a blank dictionary value.

makeWordPatterns.py

```
30.     fo = open('dictionary.txt')
31.     wordList = fo.read().split('\n')
32.     fo.close()
```

Lines 30 to 32 read in the contents of the dictionary file into `wordList`. Chapter 11 covered these file-related functions in more detail. Line 30 opens the *dictionary.txt* file in "reading" mode and returns a file object. Line 31 calls the file object's `read()` method which returns a string of all text from this file. The rest of line 31 splits it up whenever there is a `\n` newline character, and returns a list of strings: one string per line in the file. This list value returned from `split()` is stored in the `wordList` variable. At this point we are done reading the file, so line 34 calls the file object's `close()` method.

The `wordList` variable will contain a list of tens of thousands of strings. Since the *dictionary.txt* file has one English word per line of text, each string in the `wordList` variable will be one English word.

makeWordPatterns.py

```
34.     for word in wordList:
35.         # Get the pattern for each string in wordList.
36.         pattern = getWordPattern(word)
```

The `for` loop on line 34 will iterate over each string in the `wordList` list and store it in the `word` variable. The `word` variable is passed to the `getWordPattern()` function, which returns a word pattern string for the string in `word`. The word pattern string is stored in a variable named `pattern`.

makeWordPatterns.py

```
38.         if pattern not in allPatterns:
39.             allPatterns[pattern] = [word]
40.         else:
41.             allPatterns[pattern].append(word)
```

There must be a value for the `pattern` key first before we can append `word` to `allPatterns[pattern]`, otherwise this would cause an error. So, first line 38 will check if the pattern is not already in `allPatterns`. If `pattern` is not a key in `allPatterns` yet, line 39 creates a list with `word` in it to store in `allPatterns[pattern]`.

If the pattern already is in `allPatterns`, we do not have to create the list. Line 41 will just append the word to the list value that is already there.

By the time the `for` loop that started on line 34 finishes, the `allPatterns` dictionary will contain the word pattern of each English word that was in `wordList` as its keys. Each of these keys has a value that is a list of the words that produce the word pattern. With our data organized this way, given a word pattern we can easily look up all the English words that produce that particular pattern.

makeWordPatterns.py

```
43.     # This is code that writes code. The wordPatterns.py file contains
44.     # one very, very large assignment statement.
45.     fo = open('wordPatterns.py', 'w')
46.     fo.write('allPatterns = ')
47.     fo.write(pprint.pformat(allPatterns))
48.     fo.close()
```

Now that we have this very large dictionary in `allPatterns`, we want to save it to a file on the hard drive. The last part of the `main()` function will create a file called *wordPatterns.py* which will just have one huge assignment statement in it.

Line 45 creates a new file by passing the `'wordPatterns.py'` string for the filename and `'w'` to indicate that this file will be opened in "write" mode. If there is already a file with the name `'wordPatterns.py'`, opening it in write mode will cause the file to be deleted to make way for the new file we are creating.

Line 46 starts the file off with `'allPatterns = '`, which is the first part of the assignment statement. Line 47 finishes it by writing a prettified version of `allPatterns` to the file. Line 48 closes the file since we are done writing to it.

makeWordPatterns.py

```
51. if __name__ == '__main__':
52.     main()
```

Lines 51 and 52 call the `main()` function if this program was run by itself (to create the *wordPattern.py* file) rather than imported by another program that wants to use its `getWordPattern()` function.

Hacking the Simple Substitution Cipher

The hacking program uses the abstract concepts of "word patterns" and "cipherletter mappings". But don't worry, in our Python program "word patterns" are represented by string values and "cipherletter mappings" are represented with dictionary values. The previous sections explained what word patterns are and how to generate them from a string. Cipherletter mappings are used in the hacking program to keep track of the possible letters that each of the 26 cipherletters could decrypt to. Go ahead and type in the source code for the *simpleSubHacker.py* program.

Source Code of the Simple Substitution Hacking Program

Source code for simpleSubHacker.py

```
# Simple Substitution Cipher Hacker
# http://inventwithpython.com/hacking (BSD Licensed)

import os, re, copy, pprint, pyperclip, simpleSubCipher, makeWordPatterns

if not os.path.exists('wordPatterns.py'):
    makeWordPatterns.main() # create the wordPatterns.py file
import wordPatterns

LETTERS = 'ABCDEFGHIJKLMNOPQRSTUVWXYZ'
nonLettersOrSpacePattern = re.compile('[^A-Z\s]')

def main():
    message = 'Sy l nlx sr pyyacao l ylwj eiswi upar lulsxrj isr sxrjsxwjr, ia esmm rwctjsxsza sj wmpramh, lxo txmarr jia aqsoaxwa sr pqaceiamnsxu, ia esmm caytra jp famsaqa sj. Sy, px jia pjiac ilxo, ia sr pyyacao rpnajisxu eiswi lyypcor l calrpx ypc lwjsxu sx lwwpcolxwa jp isr sxrjsxwjr, ia esmm lwwabj sj aqax px jia rmsuijarj aqsoaxwa. Jia pcsusx py nhjir sr agbmlsxao sx jisr elh. -Facjclxo Ctrramm'

    # Determine the possible valid ciphertext translations.
    print('Hacking...')
    letterMapping = hackSimpleSub(message)

    # Display the results to the user.
    print('Mapping:')
    pprint.pprint(letterMapping)
    print()
    print('Original ciphertext:')
    print(message)
    print()
    print('Copying hacked message to clipboard:')
    hackedMessage = decryptWithCipherletterMapping(message, letterMapping)
    pyperclip.copy(hackedMessage)
    print(hackedMessage)


def getBlankCipherletterMapping():
    # Returns a dictionary value that is a blank cipherletter mapping.
```

```
    return {'A': [], 'B': [], 'C': [], 'D': [], 'E': [], 'F': [], 'G': [], 'H': [], 'I': [], 'J': [], 'K': [], 'L': [], 'M': [], 'N': [], 'O': [], 'P': [], 'Q': [], 'R': [], 'S': [], 'T': [], 'U': [], 'V': [], 'W': [], 'X': [], 'Y': [], 'Z': []}


def addLettersToMapping(letterMapping, cipherword, candidate):
    # The letterMapping parameter is a "cipherletter mapping" dictionary
    # value that the return value of this function starts as a copy of.
    # The cipherword parameter is a string value of the ciphertext word.
    # The candidate parameter is a possible English word that the
    # cipherword could decrypt to.

    # This function adds the letters of the candidate as potential
    # decryption letters for the cipherletters in the cipherletter
    # mapping.

    letterMapping = copy.deepcopy(letterMapping)
    for i in range(len(cipherword)):
        if candidate[i] not in letterMapping[cipherword[i]]:
            letterMapping[cipherword[i]].append(candidate[i])
    return letterMapping


def intersectMappings(mapA, mapB):
    # To intersect two maps, create a blank map, and then add only the
    # potential decryption letters if they exist in BOTH maps.
    intersectedMapping = getBlankCipherletterMapping()
    for letter in LETTERS:

        # An empty list means "any letter is possible". In this case just
        # copy the other map entirely.
        if mapA[letter] == []:
            intersectedMapping[letter] = copy.deepcopy(mapB[letter])
        elif mapB[letter] == []:
            intersectedMapping[letter] = copy.deepcopy(mapA[letter])
        else:
            # If a letter in mapA[letter] exists in mapB[letter], add
            # that letter to intersectedMapping[letter].
            for mappedLetter in mapA[letter]:
                if mappedLetter in mapB[letter]:
                    intersectedMapping[letter].append(mappedLetter)

    return intersectedMapping


```

```
def removeSolvedLettersFromMapping(letterMapping):
    # Cipher letters in the mapping that map to only one letter are
    # "solved" and can be removed from the other letters.
    # For example, if 'A' maps to potential letters ['M', 'N'], and 'B'
    # maps to ['N'], then we know that 'B' must map to 'N', so we can
    # remove 'N' from the list of what 'A' could map to. So 'A' then maps
    # to ['M']. Note that now that 'A' maps to only one letter, we can
    # remove 'M' from the list of letters for every other
    # letter. (This is why there is a loop that keeps reducing the map.)
    letterMapping = copy.deepcopy(letterMapping)
    loopAgain = True
    while loopAgain:
        # First assume that we will not loop again:
        loopAgain = False

        # solvedLetters will be a list of uppercase letters that have one
        # and only one possible mapping in letterMapping
        solvedLetters = []
        for cipherletter in LETTERS:
            if len(letterMapping[cipherletter]) == 1:
                solvedLetters.append(letterMapping[cipherletter][0])

        # If a letter is solved, than it cannot possibly be a potential
        # decryption letter for a different ciphertext letter, so we
        # should remove it from those other lists.
        for cipherletter in LETTERS:
            for s in solvedLetters:
                if len(letterMapping[cipherletter]) != 1 and s in letterMapping[cipherletter]:
                    letterMapping[cipherletter].remove(s)
                    if len(letterMapping[cipherletter]) == 1:
                        # A new letter is now solved, so loop again.
                        loopAgain = True
    return letterMapping


def hackSimpleSub(message):
    intersectedMap = getBlankCipherletterMapping()
    cipherwordList = nonLettersOrSpacePattern.sub('', message.upper()).split()
    for cipherword in cipherwordList:
        # Get a new cipherletter mapping for each ciphertext word.
        newMap = getBlankCipherletterMapping()

        wordPattern = makeWordPatterns.getWordPattern(cipherword)
        if wordPattern not in wordPatterns.allPatterns:
```

```
            continue # This word was not in our dictionary, so continue.

        # Add the letters of each candidate to the mapping.
        for candidate in wordPatterns.allPatterns[wordPattern]:
            newMap = addLettersToMapping(newMap, cipherword, candidate)

        # Intersect the new mapping with the existing intersected mapping.
        intersectedMap = intersectMappings(intersectedMap, newMap)

    # Remove any solved letters from the other lists.
    return removeSolvedLettersFromMapping(intersectedMap)


def decryptWithCipherletterMapping(ciphertext, letterMapping):
    # Return a string of the ciphertext decrypted with the letter mapping,
    # with any ambiguous decrypted letters replaced with an _ underscore.

    # First create a simple sub key from the letterMapping mapping.
    key = ['x'] * len(LETTERS)
    for cipherletter in LETTERS:
        if len(letterMapping[cipherletter]) == 1:
            # If there's only one letter, add it to the key.
            keyIndex = LETTERS.find(letterMapping[cipherletter][0])
            key[keyIndex] = cipherletter
        else:
            ciphertext = ciphertext.replace(cipherletter.lower(), '_')
            ciphertext = ciphertext.replace(cipherletter.upper(), '_')
    key = ''.join(key)

    # With the key we've created, decrypt the ciphertext.
    return simpleSubCipher.decryptMessage(key, ciphertext)


if __name__ == '__main__':
    main()
```

Hacking the Simple Substitution Cipher (in Theory)

Hacking the simple substitution cipher is pretty easy. The five steps are:

1. Find the word pattern for each cipherword in the ciphertext.
2. Find the list of English word candidates that each cipherword could decrypt to.
3. Create one cipherletter mapping for each cipherword using the cipherword's list of candidates. (A cipherletter mapping is just a dictionary value.)
4. Intersect each of the cipherletter mappings into a single intersected cipherletter mapping.

5. Remove any solved letters from the intersected cipherletter mapping.

The more cipher words that are in the ciphertext, the more cipherletter mappings we have that can be intersected. The more cipherletter mappings we intersect together, the fewer the number of potential decryption letters there will be for each cipher letter. This means that **the longer the ciphertext message, the more likely we are to hack and decrypt it**.

Explore the Hacking Functions with the Interactive Shell

We've already described the steps used to hack a simple substitution encrypted message by using word patterns. Before we learn how the code in these functions works, let's use the interactive shell to call them and see what values they return depending on what arguments we pass them.

Here is the example we will hack: OLQIHXIRCKGNZ PLQRZKBZB MPBKSSIPLC

The `getBlankCipherletterMapping()` function returns a cipherletter mapping. **A cipherletter mapping is just a dictionary with 26 keys of uppercase single-letter strings and values of lists of single-letter uppercase strings like 'A' or 'Q'.** We will store this blank cipherletter mapping in a variable named `letterMapping1`. Try typing the following into the interactive shell:

```
>>> letterMapping1 = simpleSubHacker.getBlankCipherletterMapping()
>>> letterMapping1
{'A': [], 'C': [], 'B': [], 'E': [], 'D': [], 'G': [], 'F': [], 'I': [], 'H':
[], 'K': [], 'J': [], 'M': [], 'L': [], 'O': [], 'N': [], 'Q': [], 'P': [],
'S': [], 'R': [], 'U': [], 'T': [], 'W': [], 'V': [], 'Y': [], 'X': [], 'Z':
[]}
>>>
```

Let's start hacking the first cipherword, OLQIHXIRCKGNZ. First we will need to get the word pattern for this cipherword by calling the `makeWordPattern` module's `getWordPattern()` function. Try typing the following into the interactive shell:

```
>>> import makeWordPatterns
>>> wordPat = makeWordPatterns.getWordPattern('OLQIHXIRCKGNZ')
>>> wordPat
0.1.2.3.4.5.3.6.7.8.9.10.11
>>>
```

To figure out which English words in the dictionary have the word pattern 0.1.2.3.4.5.3.6.7.8.9.10.11 (that is, to figure out the candidates for the cipherword OLQIHXIRCKGNZ) we will import the `wordPatterns` module and look up this pattern. Try typing the following into the interactive shell:

```
>>> import wordPatterns
>>> candidates = wordPatterns.allPatterns['0.1.2.3.4.5.3.6.7.8.9.10.11']
>>> candidates
['UNCOMFORTABLE', 'UNCOMFORTABLY']
>>>
```

There are two English words that OLQIHXIRCKGNZ could decrypt to (that is, only two English words that have the same word pattern that OLQIHXIRCKGNZ does): UNCOMFORTABLE and UNCOMFORTABLY. (It's also possible that the cipherword decrypts to a word that does not exist in our dictionary, but we will just have to assume that's not the case.) We need to create a cipherletter mapping that has the cipherletters in OLQIHXIRCKGNZ map to letters in UNCOMFORTABLE and UNCOMFORTABLY as potential decryption letters. That is, O maps to U, L maps to N, Q maps to C, and so on. Z will map to two different letters: E and Y.

We can do this with the `addLettersToMapping()` function. We will need to pass it our (currently blank) cipherletter mapping in `letterMapping1`, the string `'OLQIHXIRCKGNZ'`, and the string `'UNCOMFORTABLE'` (which is the first string in the `candidates` list). Try typing the following into the interactive shell:

```
>>> letterMapping1 = simpleSubHacker.addLettersToMapping(letterMapping1,
'OLQIHXIRCKGNZ', candidates[0])
>>> letterMapping1
{'A': [], 'C': ['T'], 'B': [], 'E': [], 'D': [], 'G': ['B'], 'F': [], 'I':
['O'], 'H': ['M'], 'K': ['A'], 'J': [], 'M': [], 'L': ['N'], 'O': ['U'], 'N':
['L'], 'Q': ['C'], 'P': [], 'S': [], 'R': ['R'], 'U': [], 'T': [], 'W': [],
'V': [], 'Y': [], 'X': ['F'], 'Z': ['E']}
>>>
```

From the `letterMapping1` value, you can see that the letters in OLQIHXIRCKGNZ map to the letters in UNCOMFORTABLE: `'O'` maps to `['U']`, `'L'` maps to `['N']`, `'Q'` maps to `['C']`, and so on.

But since the letters in OLQIHXIRCKGNZ could also possibly decrypt to UNCOMFORTABLY, we also need to add UNCOMFORTABLY to the cipherletter mapping. Try typing the following into the interactive shell:

```
>>> letterMapping1 = simpleSubHacker.addLettersToMapping(letterMapping1,
'OLQIHXIRCKGNZ', candidates[1])
>>> letterMapping1
{'A': [], 'C': ['T'], 'B': [], 'E': [], 'D': [], 'G': ['B'], 'F': [], 'I':
['O'], 'H': ['M'], 'K': ['A'], 'J': [], 'M': [], 'L': ['N'], 'O': ['U'], 'N':
['L'], 'Q': ['C'], 'P': [], 'S': [], 'R': ['R'], 'U': [], 'T': [], 'W': [],
'V': [], 'Y': [], 'X': ['F'], 'Z': ['E', 'Y']}
```

```
>>>
```

You'll notice that not much has changed in `letterMapping1`. The cipherletter mapping in `letterMapping1` now has `'Z'` map to both `'E'` and `'Y'`. That's because the candidates for OLQIHXIRCKGNZ (that is, UNCOMFORTABLE and UNCOMFORTABLY) are very similar to each other and `addLettersToMapping()` only adds the letter to the list if the letter is not already there. This is why `'O'` maps to `['U']` instead of `['U', 'U']`.

We now have a cipherletter mapping for the first of the three cipherwords. We need to get a new mapping for the second cipherword, PLQRZKBZB. Call `getBlankCipherletterMapping()` and store the returned dictionary value in a variable named `letterMapping2`. Get the word pattern for PLQRZKBZB and use it to look up all the candidates in `wordPatterns.allPatterns`. This is done by typing the following into the interactive shell:

```
>>> letterMapping2 = simpleSubHacker.getBlankCipherletterMapping()
>>> wordPat = makeWordPatterns.getWordPattern('PLQRZKBZB')
>>> candidates = wordPatterns.allPatterns[wordPat]
>>> candidates
['CONVERSES', 'INCREASES', 'PORTENDED', 'UNIVERSES']
>>>
```

Instead of typing out four calls to `addLettersToMapping()` for each of these four candidate words, we can write a `for` loop that will go through the list in `candidates` and call `addLettersToMapping()` each time.

```
>>> for candidate in candidates:
...    letterMapping2 = simpleSubHacker.addLettersToMapping(letterMapping2,
'PLQRZKBZB', candidate)
...
>>> letterMapping2
{'A': [], 'C': [], 'B': ['S', 'D'], 'E': [], 'D': [], 'G': [], 'F': [], 'I':
[], 'H': [], 'K': ['R', 'A', 'N'], 'J': [], 'M': [], 'L': ['O', 'N'], 'O': [],
'N': [], 'Q': ['N', 'C', 'R', 'I'], 'P': ['C', 'I', 'P', 'U'], 'S': [], 'R':
['V', 'R', 'T'], 'U': [], 'T': [], 'W': [], 'V': [], 'Y': [], 'X': [], 'Z':
['E']}
>>>
```

This finishes the cipherletter mapping for our second cipherword. Now we need to get the intersection of the cipherletter mappings in `letterMapping1` and `letterMapping2` by passing them to `intersectMappings()`. Try typing the following into the interactive shell:

```
>>> intersectedMapping = simpleSubHacker.intersectMappings(letterMapping1,
letterMapping2)
>>> intersectedMapping
{'A': [], 'C': ['T'], 'B': ['S', 'D'], 'E': [], 'D': [], 'G': ['B'], 'F': [],
'I': ['O'], 'H': ['M'], 'K': ['A'], 'J': [], 'M': [], 'L': ['N'], 'O': ['U'],
'N': ['L'], 'Q': ['C'], 'P': ['C', 'I', 'P', 'U'], 'S': [], 'R': ['R'], 'U':
[], 'T': [], 'W': [], 'V': [], 'Y': [], 'X': ['F'], 'Z': ['E']}
>>>
```

The intersected mapping is just a cipherletter mapping. The list of potential decryption letters for any cipherletter in the intersected mapping will only be the potential decryption letters that were in the cipherletter's list in **both** `letterMapping1` and `letterMapping2`.

For example, this is why `intersectedMapping`'s list for the `'Z'` key is just `['E']`: because `letterMapping1` had `['E', 'Y']` but `letterMapping2` had `['E']`. The intersection of `['E', 'Y']` and `['E']` is just the potential decryption letters that exist in **both** mappings: `['E']`

There is an exception. If one of the mapping's lists was *blank*, then *all* of the potential decryption letters in the *other* mapping are put into the intersected mapping. This is because in our program a blank map represents any possible letter can be used since nothing is known about the mapping.

Then we do all these steps for the third cipherword, MPBKSSIPLC. Try typing the following into the interactive shell:

```
>>> letterMapping3 = simpleSubHacker.getBlankCipherletterMapping()
>>> wordPat = makeWordPatterns.getWordPattern('MPBKSSIPLC')
>>> candidates = wordPatterns.allPatterns[wordPat]
>>> candidates
['ADMITTEDLY', 'DISAPPOINT']
>>> for i in range(len(candidates)):
...     letterMapping3 = simpleSubHacker.addLettersToMapping(letterMapping3,
'MPBKSSIPLC', candidates[i])
...
>>> letterMapping3
{'A': [], 'C': ['Y', 'T'], 'B': ['M', 'S'], 'E': [], 'D': [], 'G': [], 'F': [],
'I': ['E', 'O'], 'H': [], 'K': ['I', 'A'], 'J': [], 'M': ['A', 'D'], 'L': ['L',
'N'], 'O': [], 'N': [], 'Q': [], 'P': ['D', 'I'], 'S': ['T', 'P'], 'R': [],
'U': [], 'T': [], 'W': [], 'V': [], 'Y': [], 'X': [], 'Z': []}
```

We intersect `letterMapping3` with `intersectedMapping`. This also ends up indirectly intersecting `letterMapping3` with `letterMapping1` and `letterMapping2`, since intersectedMapping is currently the intersection of letterMapping1 and letterMapping2. Try typing the following into the interactive shell:

```
>>> intersectedMapping = simpleSubHacker.intersectMappings(intersectedMapping,
letterMapping3)
>>> intersectedMapping
{'A': [], 'C': ['T'], 'B': ['S'], 'E': [], 'D': [], 'G': ['B'], 'F': [], 'I':
['O'], 'H': ['M'], 'K': ['A'], 'J': [], 'M': ['A', 'D'], 'L': ['N'], 'O':
['U'], 'N': ['L'], 'Q': ['C'], 'P': ['I'], 'S': ['T', 'P'], 'R': ['R'], 'U':
[], 'T': [], 'W': [], 'V': [], 'Y': [], 'X': ['F'], 'Z': ['E']}
>>>
```

We can now pass the intersected cipherletter mapping to decryptWithCipherletterMapping() to decrypt the ciphertext. Try typing the following into the interactive shell:

```
>>> simpleSubHacker.decryptWithCipherletterMapping('OLQIHXIRCKGNZ PLQRZKBZB
MPBKSSIPLC', intersectedMapping)
UNCOMFORTABLE INCREASES _ISA__OINT
>>>
```

The intersected mapping is not yet complete. Notice how the intersected mapping has a solution for the cipherletter K, because the key 'K''s value to a list with just one string in it: ['A']. Because we know that the K cipherletters will decrypt to A, no other cipherletter can possibly decrypt to A.

In the intersected mapping, the cipherletter M maps to ['A', 'D']. This means that judging from the candidates for the cipherwords in our encrypted message, the cipherletter M could decrypt to A or D.

But since we know K decrypts to A, we can remove A from the list of potential decryption letters for cipherletter M. This shortens the list down to just ['D']. Because this new list only has one string in it, we've also solved the cipherletter M!

The removeSolvedLettersFromMapping() function takes a cipherletter mapping and removes these solved potential decryption letters from the other cipherletters' lists. Try typing the following into the interactive shell:

```
>>> letterMapping = removeSolvedLettersFromMapping(letterMapping)
>>> intersectedMapping
{'A': [], 'C': ['T'], 'B': ['S'], 'E': [], 'D': [], 'G': ['B'], 'F': [], 'I':
['O'], 'H': ['M'], 'K': ['A'], 'J': [], 'M
```

```
': ['D'], 'L': ['N'], 'O': ['U'], 'N': ['L'], 'Q': ['C'], 'P': ['I'], 'S':
['P'], 'R': ['R'], 'U': [], 'T': [], 'W': [],
 'V': [], 'Y': [], 'X': ['F'], 'Z': ['E']}
>>>
```

Now when we pass the intersected mapping to `decryptWithCipherletterMapping()`, it gives us the full solution. Try typing the following into the interactive shell:

```
>>> simpleSubHacker.decryptWithCipherletterMapping('OLQIHXIRCKGNZ PLQRZKBZB
MPBKSSIPLC', intersectedMapping)
UNCOMFORTABLE INCREASES DISAPPOINT
>>>
```

The ciphertext OLQIHXIRCKGNZ PLQRZKBZB MPBKSSIPLC decrypts to the message, “Uncomfortable increases disappoint”.

This is a rather short ciphertext to hack. Normally the encrypted messages we hack will be much longer. (Messages as short as our example usually cannot be hacked with our word pattern method.) We’ll have to create a cipherletter mapping for each cipherword in these longer messages and then intersect them all together, which is exactly what the `hackSimpleSub()` function does.

Now that we know the basic steps and what each function does, let’s learn how the code in these functions work.

How the Program Works

simpleSubHacker.py

```
# Simple Substitution Cipher Hacker
# http://inventwithpython.com/hacking (BSD Licensed)
```

The comments at the top of the source code explain what the program is.

Import All the Things

simpleSubHacker.py

```
import os, re, copy, pprint, pyperclip, simpleSubCipher, makeWordPatterns
```

Our simple substitution hacking program imports eight different modules, more than any other program so far. By reusing the code in these modules, our hacking program becomes much shorter and easier to write.

The `re` module is a module we haven't seen before. This is the regular expression module which lets our code do sophisticated string manipulation. Regular expressions are explained in the next section.

simpleSubHacker.py

```
6. if not os.path.exists('wordPatterns.py'):
7.     makeWordPatterns.main() # create the wordPatterns.py file
8. import wordPatterns
```

The simple substitution cipher also needs the `wordPatterns` module. The .py file for this module is created when the `makeWordPatterns.py` program is run. But *makeWordPatterns.py* might not have been run before our hacking program has. In this case, our hacking program checks if this file exists on line 6 and if it doesn't, the `makeWordPatterns.main()` function is called.

Remember, the `main()` function is the function that is run in our programs when they are run as programs (rather than just imported with an `import` statement.) When we imported the `makeWordPatterns` module on line 4, the `main()` function in *makeWordPatterns.py* was not run. Since `main()` is the function that creates the *wordPatterns.py* file, we will call `makeWordPatterns.main()` if *wordPatterns.py* does not yet exist.

Either way, by the time the program execution reaches line 8, the `wordPatterns` module will exist and can be imported.

A Brief Intro to Regular Expressions and the sub() Regex Method

simpleSubHacker.py

```
LETTERS = 'ABCDEFGHIJKLMNOPQRSTUVWXYZ'
nonLettersOrSpacePattern = re.compile('[^A-Z\s]')
```

The simple substitution hacking program will have a `LETTERS` global variable like many of our previous cipher programs.

The `re.compile()` function is new. This function compiles (that is, creates) a new regular expression pattern object, or "regex object" or "pattern object" for short. Regular expressions are strings that define a specific pattern that matches certain strings. Regular expressions can do many special things with strings that are beyond the scope of this book, but you can learn about them at http://invpy.com/regex.

The string `'[^A-Za-z\s]'` is a regular expression that matches any character that is not a letter from A to Z or a "whitespace" character (e.g. a space, tab, or newline character). The pattern object has a `sub()` method (short for "substitute") that works very similar to the `replace()` string method. The first argument to `sub()` is the string that replaces any instances of the pattern in the second string argument. Try typing the following into the interactive shell:

```
>>> pat = re.compile('[^A-Z\s]')
>>> pat.sub('abc', 'ALL! NON!LETTERS? AND123 NONSPACES. REPLACED')
'ALLabc NONabcLETTERSabc ANDabcabcabc NONSPACESabc REPLACED'
>>> pat.sub('', 'ALL! NON!LETTERS? AND123 NONSPACES. REPLACED')
'ALL NONLETTERS AND NONSPACES REPLACED'
>>>
```

There are many sophisticated string manipulations you can perform if you learn more about regular expressions, but we will only use them in this book to remove characters from a string that are not uppercase letters or spaces.

The Hacking Program's `main()` Function

simpleSubHacker.py

```
def main():
    message = 'Sy l nlx sr pyyacao l ylwj eiswi upar lulsxrj isr sxrjsxwjr, ia esmm rwctjsxsza sj wmpramh, lxo txmarr jia aqsoaxwa sr pqaceiamnsxu, ia esmm caytra jp famsaqa sj. Sy, px jia pjiac ilxo, ia sr pyyacao rpnajisxu eiswi lyypcor l calrpx ypc lwjsxu sx lwwpcolxwa jp isr sxrjsxwjr, ia esmm lwwabj sj aqax px jia rmsuijarj aqsoaxwa. Jia pcsusx py nhjir sr agbmlsxao sx jisr elh. -Facjclxo Ctrramm'

    # Determine the possible valid ciphertext translations.
    print('Hacking...')
    letterMapping = hackSimpleSub(message)
```

Like all our previous hacking programs, the `main()` function will store the ciphertext to be hacked in a variable named `message`. We will pass this variable to the `hackSimpleSub()` function. However, unlike our previous hacking programs, the hacking function will not return a string of the decrypted message (or `None` if it was unable to decrypt it).

Instead, `hackSimpleSub()` will return a cipherletter mapping (specifically, an intersected cipherletter mapping that had the solved letters removed, like the kind we made in our interactive shell exercise). This returned cipherletter mapping will be passed to `decryptWithCipherletterMapping()` to decrypt the ciphertext in `message`.

Partially Hacking the Cipher

simpleSubHacker.py

```
    # Display the results to the user.
    print('Mapping:')
```

```
    pprint.pprint(letterMapping)
    print()
```

Since the cipherletter mapping stored in `letterMapping` is a dictionary, we can use the `pprint.pprint()` "pretty print" function to display it on the screen. It will look something like this:

```
{'A': ['E'],
 'B': ['B', 'W', 'P'],
 'C': ['R'],
 'D': [],
 'E': ['K', 'W'],
 'F': ['B', 'P'],
 'G': ['B', 'Q', 'X', 'Y', 'P', 'W'],
 'H': ['B', 'K', 'P', 'W', 'X', 'Y'],
 'I': ['H'],
 'J': ['T'],
 'K': [],
 'L': ['A'],
 'M': ['L'],
 'N': ['M'],
 'O': ['D'],
 'P': ['O'],
 'Q': ['V'],
 'R': ['S'],
 'S': ['I'],
 'T': ['U'],
 'U': ['G'],
 'V': [],
 'W': ['C'],
 'X': ['N'],
 'Y': ['F'],
 'Z': ['Z']}
```

In the above example, the cipherletters A, C, I, J, L, M, N, O, P, Q, R, S, T, U, X, Y, and Z all have one and only one potential decryption letter. These cipher letters have been solved. The `decryptWithCipherletterMapping()` function, explained later, will print underscores for any cipherletters that have not been solved (that is, B, D, E, F, G, H, K, and V.)

simpleSubHacker.py

```
    print('Original ciphertext:')
    print(message)
    print()
```

First the original encrypted message is displayed on the screen so the programmer can compare it to the decryption.

simpleSubHacker.py
```
27.     print('Copying hacked message to clipboard:')
28.     hackedMessage = decryptWithCipherletterMapping(message, letterMapping)
29.     pyperclip.copy(hackedMessage)
30.     print(hackedMessage)
```

Next the decrypted message is returned from the `decryptWithCipherletterMapping()` function on line 28. This hacked message is copied to the clipboard on line 29 and printed to the screen on line 30.

Next, let's look at all the functions that are called by `main()`.

Blank Cipherletter Mappings

simpleSubHacker.py
```
def getBlankCipherletterMapping():
    # Returns a dictionary value that is a blank cipherletter mapping.
    return {'A': [], 'B': [], 'C': [], 'D': [], 'E': [], 'F': [], 'G': [], 'H': [], 'I': [], 'J': [], 'K': [], 'L': [], 'M': [], 'N': [], 'O': [], 'P': [], 'Q': [], 'R': [], 'S': [], 'T': [], 'U': [], 'V': [], 'W': [], 'X': [], 'Y': [], 'Z': []}
```

Our program will need a cipherletter mapping for each cipherword in the ciphertext, so we will create the `getBlankCipherletterMapping()` function which can return a new, blank mapping when called.

Adding Letters to a Cipherletter Mapping

simpleSubHacker.py
```
def addLettersToMapping(letterMapping, cipherword, candidate):
```

The `addLettersToMapping()` function attempts to make sure that every letter in the candidate can be mapped to a letter in the cipherword. It checks over each letter in `candidate` and adds its corresponding letter in `cipherword` to `letterMapping` if it wasn't already there.

For example, if `'PUPPY'` is our candidate word for the `'HGHHU'` cipherword, the `addLettersToMapping()` function will change `letterMapping` so that the key `'H'` has `'P'` added to its list of potential decryption letters. Then the function will change the key `'G'` so that its list has `'U'` appended to it.

If the letter is already in the list of potential decryption letters, the `addLettersToMapping()` will not add a letter to the list. We can skip adding `'P'` to the `'H'` key the next two times since it's already been done. Finally, the function will change the key `'U'` so that it has `'Y'` in its list of potential decryption letters.

The code in this function assumes that `len(cipherword)` is the same as `len(candidate)`.

simpleSubHacker.py
```
49.     letterMapping = copy.deepcopy(letterMapping)
```

To avoid changing the original dictionary value passed for the `letterMapping` parameter, line 49 will copy the dictionary in `letterMapping` and make this copy the new value in `letterMapping`. (We have to do this because `letterMapping` was passed a copy of a dictionary reference value, instead of a copy of the dictionary value. See the "List Reference" section in Chapter 10 for an explanation of references.)

simpleSubHacker.py
```
50.     for i in range(len(cipherword)):
```

Line 50 will iterate over each index in the string in `cipherword`. We need the index (which is stored in the variable `i`) because the potential decryption letter to be added will be `candidate[i]` for the cipherletter `cipherword[i]`.

simpleSubHacker.py
```
51.         if candidate[i] not in letterMapping[cipherword[i]]:
52.             letterMapping[cipherword[i]].append(candidate[i])
```

The `if` statement on line 51 checks that the potential decryption letter is not already in the list of potential decryption letters for the cipherletter. This prevents the list of potential decryption letters in the cipherletter mapping from having duplicate letters in it. For example, we never want the list to be a value like `['U', 'U']`.

Line 52 adds the new potential decryption letter (that is, `candidate[i]`) to the list of potential decryption letters in the cipherletter mapping (that is, `letterMapping[cipherword[i]]`).

simpleSubHacker.py
```
53.     return letterMapping
```

After looping through all the indexes in `cipherword`, the additions to the cipherletter mapping are complete and the dictionary in `letterMapping` is returned.

Intersecting Two Letter Mappings

simpleSubHacker.py

```
56. def intersectMappings(mapA, mapB):
57.     # To intersect two maps, create a blank map, and then add only the
58.     # potential decryption letters if they exist in BOTH maps.
59.     intersectedMapping = getBlankCipherletterMapping()
60.     for letter in LETTERS:
```

The `intersectMappings()` function will return a new cipherletter mapping that is an intersection of the two cipherletter mappings passed for the `mapA` and `mapB` parameters. Line 59 creates a new cipherletter mapping by calling `getBlankCipherletterMapping()` and storing the returned value in the `intersectedMapping` variable.

The `for` loop will loop through each of the uppercase letters in the `LETTERS` constant variable, and the `letter` variable can be used for the keys of the `mapA` and `mapB` dictionaries.

simpleSubHacker.py

```
62.         # An empty list means "any letter is possible". In this case just
63.         # copy the other map entirely.
64.         if mapA[letter] == []:
65.             intersectedMapping[letter] = copy.deepcopy(mapB[letter])
66.         elif mapB[letter] == []:
67.             intersectedMapping[letter] = copy.deepcopy(mapA[letter])
```

If the list of potential decryption letters for a cipherletter in a cipherletter mapping is blank, this means that this cipherletter could potentially decrypt to *any* letter. In this case, the intersected cipherletter mapping will just be a copy of the *other* mapping's list of potential decryption letters.

That is, if `mapA`'s list of potential decryption letters is blank, then set the intersected mapping's list to be a copy of `mapB`'s list. Or if `mapB`'s list is blank, then set the intersected mapping's list to be a copy of `mapA`'s list.

(If both mappings' lists were blank, then line 65 will simply copy `mapB`'s blank list to the intersected mapping. This is the behavior we want: if both lists are blank then the intersected mapping will have a blank list.)

simpleSubHacker.py

```
68.         else:
69.             # If a letter in mapA[letter] exists in mapB[letter], add
70.             # that letter to intersectedMapping[letter].
71.             for mappedLetter in mapA[letter]:
72.                 if mappedLetter in mapB[letter]:
```

```
73.                     intersectedMapping[letter].append(mappedLetter)
```

The `else` block handles the case where neither `mapA` nor `mapB` are blank. In this case, line 71 loops through the uppercase letter strings in the list at `mapA[letter]`. Line 72 checks if this uppercase letter in `mapA[letter]` also exists in the list of uppercase letter strings in `mapB[letter]`. If it does, then line 73 will add this common letter to the list of potential decryption letters at `intersectedMapping[letter]`.

simpleSubHacker.py

```
75.     return intersectedMapping
```

Once the `for` loop that started on line 60 has finished, the cipherletter mapping in `intersectedMapping` will only have the potential decryption letters that exist in the lists of potential decryption letters of both `mapA` and `mapB`. This completely intersected cipherletter mapping is returned on line 75.

Removing Solved Letters from the Letter Mapping

simpleSubHacker.py

```
def removeSolvedLettersFromMapping(letterMapping):
    # Cipher letters in the mapping that map to only one letter are
    # "solved" and can be removed from the other letters.
    # For example, if 'A' maps to potential letters ['M', 'N'], and 'B'
    # maps to ['N'], then we know that 'B' must map to 'N', so we can
    # remove 'N' from the list of what 'A' could map to. So 'A' then maps
    # to ['M']. Note that now that 'A' maps to only one letter, we can
    # remove 'M' from the list of potential letters for every other
    # key. (This is why there is a loop that keeps reducing the map.)
    letterMapping = copy.deepcopy(letterMapping)
    loopAgain = True
```

The `removeSolvedLettersFromMapping()` function searches for any cipherletters in the `letterMapping` parameter which have one and only one potential decryption letter. These cipherletters are considered solved: the cipherletter must decrypt to that one potential decryption letter. This means that any other cipherletters that have this solved letter can have that letter removed from their lists of potential decryption letters.

This could cause a chain reaction, because when the one potential decryption letter is removed from other lists of potential decryption letters, it could result in a new solved cipherletter. In that case, the program will loop and perform the solved letter removal over the whole cipherletter mapping again.

The cipherletter mapping in letterMapping is copied on line 87 so that changes made to it in the function do not affect the dictionary value outside the function. Line 88 creates `loopAgain`, which is a variable that holds a Boolean value that tells us if the code found a new solved letter and needs to loop again. In that case the `loopAgain` variable is set to `True` on line 88 so that the program execution will enter the `while` loop on line 89.

simpleSubHacker.py
```
89.     while loopAgain:
90.         # First assume that we will not loop again:
91.         loopAgain = False
```

At the very beginning of the loop, line 91 will set `loopAgain` to `False`. The code assumes that this will be the last iteration through line 89's `while` loop. The `loopAgain` variable is only set to `True` if we find a new solved cipherletter during this iteration.

simpleSubHacker.py
```
93.         # solvedLetters will be a list of uppercase letters that have one
94.         # and only one possible mapping in letterMapping
95.         solvedLetters = []
96.         for cipherletter in LETTERS:
97.             if len(letterMapping[cipherletter]) == 1:
98.                 solvedLetters.append(letterMapping[cipherletter][0])
```

The next part of the code creates a list of cipherletters that have exactly one potential decryption letter. We will put these cipherletter strings in a list that is in `solvedLetters`. The `solvedLetters` variable starts off as a blank list on line 95.

The `for` loop on line 96 goes through all 26 possible cipherletters and looks at the cipherletter mapping's list of potential decryption letters for that cipherletter. (That is, the list is at `letterMapping[cipherletter]`.)

If the length of this list is `1` (which is checked on line 97), then we know that there is only one letter that the cipherletter could decrypt to and the cipherletter is solved. We will add the letter (the potential decryption letter, not the cipherletter) to the `solvedLetters` list on line 98. The solved letter will always be at `letterMapping[cipherletter][0]` because `letterMapping[cipherletter]` is a list of potential decryption letters that only has one string value in it at index `0` of the list.

simpleSubHacker.py
```
        # If a letter is solved, than it cannot possibly be a potential
        # decryption letter for a different ciphertext letter, so we
        # should remove it from those other lists.
```

```
103.         for cipherletter in LETTERS:
104.             for s in solvedLetters:
105.                 if len(letterMapping[cipherletter]) != 1 and s in
letterMapping[cipherletter]:
106.                     letterMapping[cipherletter].remove(s)
```

After the previous `for` loop that started on line 96 has finished, the `solvedLetters` variable will be a list of all the letters that are solved decryptions of a cipherletter. The `for` loop on line 103 loops through all 26 possible cipherletters and looks at the cipherletter mapping's list of potential decryption letters.

For each cipherletter that is examined, the letters in `solvedLetters` are looped through on line 104 to check if each of them exist in the list of potential decryption letters for `letterMapping[cipherletter]`. Line 105 checks if a list of potential decryption letters is not solved (that is, if `len(letterMapping[cipherletter]) != 1`) **and** the solved letter exists in the list of potential decryption letters. If this condition is `True`, then the solved letter in `s` is removed from the list of potential decryption letters on line 106.

simpleSubHacker.py

```
107.                 if len(letterMapping[cipherletter]) == 1:
108.                     # A new letter is now solved, so loop again.
109.                     loopAgain = True
```

If by chance this removal caused the list of potential decryption letters to now only have one letter in it, then the `loopAgain` variable is set to `True` on line 109 so that the code will check for this new solved letter in the cipherletter mapping on the next iteration.

simpleSubHacker.py

```
    return letterMapping
```

After the code in line 89's `while` loop has gone through a full iteration without `loopAgain` being set to `True`, the program execution goes past the loop and returns the cipherletter mapping stored in `letterMapping`.

Hacking the Simple Substitution Cipher

simpleSubHacker.py

```
def hackSimpleSub(message):
    intersectedMap = getBlankCipherletterMapping()
```

Now that we've created the `getBlankCipherletterMapping()`, `addLettersToMapping()`, `intersectMappings()`, and `removeSolvedLettersFromMapping()` functions that can manipulate the cipherletter mappings we pass them, we can use them all together to hack a simple substitution message.

Remember the steps from our interactive shell exercise for hacking a simple substitution cipher message: for each cipherword, get all the candidates based on the cipherword's word pattern, then add these candidates to a cipherletter mapping. Then take the cipherletter mapping for each cipherword and intersect them together.

The `intersectedMap` variable will hold the intersected cipherletter mapping of each cipherword's cipherletter mapping. At the beginning of the `hackSimpleSub()` function, it will start as a blank cipherletter mapping.

simpleSubHacker.py

```
115.     cipherwordList = nonLettersOrSpacePattern.sub('',
message.upper()).split()
```

The `sub()` regex method will substitute (that is, replace) any occurrences of the string pattern in the second argument (`message.upper()`) with the first argument (a blank string). Regular expressions and the `sub()` method were explained earlier in this chapter.

On line 115, the regex object in `nonLettersOrSpacePattern` matches any string that is not a letter or whitespace character. The `sub()` method will return a string that is the `message` variable with all non-letter and non-space characters replaced by a blank string. This effectively returns a string that has all punctuation and number characters removed from `message`.

This string then has the `upper()` method called on it to return an uppercase version of the string, and that string has the `split()` method called on it to return the individual words in the string in a list. To see what each part of line 115 does, type the following into the interactive shell:

```
>>> import re
>>> nonLettersOrSpacePattern = re.compile('[^A-Z\s]')
>>> message = 'Hello, this is my 1st test message.'
>>> message = nonLettersOrSpacePattern.sub('', message.upper())
>>> message
'HELLO THIS IS MY ST TEST MESSAGE'
>>> cipherwordList = message.split()
>>> cipherwordList
['HELLO', 'THIS', 'IS', 'MY', 'ST', 'TEST', 'MESSAGE']
```

After line 115 executes, the `cipherwordList` variable will contain a list of uppercase strings of the individual words that were previously in `message`.

simpleSubHacker.py

```
116.     for cipherword in cipherwordList:
117.         # Get a new cipherletter mapping for each ciphertext word.
118.         newMap = getBlankCipherletterMapping()
```

The `for` loop on line 116 will assign each string in the `message` list to the `cipherword` variable. Inside this loop we will get the cipherword's candidates, add the candidates to a cipherletter mapping, and then intersect this mapping with `intersectedMap`.

First, line 118 will get a new, blank cipherletter mapping from `getBlankCipherletterMapping()` and store it in the `newMap` variable.

simpleSubHacker.py

```
120.         wordPattern = makeWordPatterns.getWordPattern(cipherword)
121.         if wordPattern not in wordPatterns.allPatterns:
122.             continue # This word was not in our dictionary, so continue.
```

To find the candidates for the current cipherword, we call `getWordPattern()` in the `makeWordPatterns` module on line 120. If the word pattern of the cipherword does not exist in the keys of the `wordPatterns.allPatterns` dictionary, then whatever the cipherword decrypts to does not exist in our dictionary file. In that case the `continue` statement on line 122 will skip back to line 116, to the next cipherword in the list.

simpleSubHacker.py

```
124.         # Add the letters of each candidate to the mapping.
125.         for candidate in wordPatterns.allPatterns[wordPattern]:
126.             newMap = addLettersToMapping(newMap, cipherword, candidate)
```

On line 125, we know the word pattern exists in `wordPatterns.allPatterns`. The values in the `allPatterns` dictionary are lists of strings of the English words with the pattern in `wordPattern`. Since it is a list, we can use a `for` loop to iterate over this list. The variable `candidate` will be set to each of these English word strings on each iteration of the loop.

The only line inside line 125's `for` loop is the call to `addLettersToMapping()` on line 126. We will use this to update the cipherletter mapping in `newMap` with the letters in each of the candidates.

simpleSubHacker.py

```
128.         # Intersect the new mapping with the existing intersected mapping.
129.         intersectedMap = intersectMappings(intersectedMap, newMap)
```

Once all of the letters in the candidates are added to the cipherletter mapping in `newMap`, line 129 will intersect `newMap` with `intersectedMap`, and make the return value the new value of `intersectedMap`.

At this point the program execution jumps back to the beginning of the `for` loop on line 116 to run the code on the next cipherword in the `cipherwordList` list.

simpleSubHacker.py

```
    # Remove any solved letters from the other lists.
    return removeSolvedLettersFromMapping(intersectedMap)
```

Once we have the final intersected cipherletter mapping, we can remove any solved letters from it by passing it to `removeSolvedLettersFromMapping()`. The cipherletter mapping that is returned from the function will be the return value for `hackSimpleSubstitution()`.

Creating a Key from a Letter Mapping

simpleSubHacker.py

```
135. def decryptWithCipherletterMapping(ciphertext, letterMapping):
136.     # Return a string of the ciphertext decrypted with the letter mapping,
137.     # with any ambiguous decrypted letters replaced with an _ underscore.
138.
139.     # First create a simple sub key from the letterMapping mapping.
140.     key = ['x'] * len(LETTERS)
```

Since the `simpleSubstitutionCipher.decryptMessage()` function only decrypts with keys instead of letter mappings, we need the `decryptWithCipherletterMapping()` function to convert a letter mapping into a string key.

The simple substitution keys are strings of 26 characters. The character at index `0` in the key string is the substitution for A, the character at index `1` is the substitution for B, and so on.

Since the letter mapping might only have solutions for some of the letters, we will start out with a key of `['x', 'x', 'x', 'x', 'x', 'x', 'x', 'x', 'x', 'x', 'x', 'x', 'x', 'x', 'x', 'x', 'x', 'x', 'x', 'x', 'x', 'x', 'x', 'x', 'x', 'x']`. This list is created on line 140 by using list replication to replicate the list `['x']` 26 times. Since `LETTERS` is a string of the letters of the alphabet, `len(LETTERS)` evaluates to `26`. When the multiplication operator is used on a list and integer, it does list replication.

We don't have to use `'x'`, we can use any lowercase letter. The reason we need to use a lowercase letter is because it acts as a "placeholder" for the simple substitution key. The way *simpleSubCipher.py* works, since `LETTERS` only contains uppercase letters, any lowercase letters in the key will not be used to decrypt a message.

The 26-item list in `key` will be joined together into a 26-character string at the end of the `decryptWithCipherletterMapping()` function.

simpleSubHacker.py
```
141.     for cipherletter in LETTERS:
142.         if len(letterMapping[cipherletter]) == 1:
143.             # If there's only one letter, add it to the key.
144.             keyIndex = LETTERS.find(letterMapping[cipherletter][0])
145.             key[keyIndex] = cipherletter
```

The `for` loop on line 141 will let us go through each of the letters in `LETTERS` for the `cipherletter` variable, and if the cipherletter is solved (that is, `letterMapping[cipherletter]` has only one letter in it) then we can replace an `'x'` in the key with the letter.

So on line 144 `letterMapping[cipherletter][0]` is the decryption letter, and `keyIndex` is the index of the decryption letter in `LETTERS` (which is returned from the `find()` call). This index in the key list is set to the decryption letter on line 145.

simpleSubHacker.py
```
146.         else:
147.             ciphertext = ciphertext.replace(cipherletter.lower(), '_')
148.             ciphertext = ciphertext.replace(cipherletter.upper(), '_')
```

Or else, if the cipherletter does not have a solution, then we want to replace everywhere that cipherletter appears in the ciphertext with an underscore so the user can tell which characters were unsolved. Line 147 handles replacing the lowercase form of `cipherletter` with an underscore and line 148 handles replacing the uppercase form of `cipherletter` with an underscore.

simpleSubHacker.py
```
149.     key = ''.join(key)
150.
151.     # With the key we've created, decrypt the ciphertext.
152.     return simpleSubCipher.decryptMessage(key, ciphertext)
```

When we have finally replaced all the parts in the list in `key` with the solved letters, we convert the list of strings into a single string with the `join()` method to create a simple substitution key. This string is passed to the `decryptMessage()` function in our *simpleSubCipher.py* program.

The decrypted message string returned from `decryptMessage()` is then returned from `decryptWithCipherletterMapping()` on line 152.

simpleSubHacker.py

```
155. if __name__ == '__main__':
156.     main()
```

That completes all the functions our hacking program needs. Lines 155 and 156 just call the `main()` function to run the program if *simpleSubHacker.py* is being run directly, instead of being imported as a module by another Python program.

Couldn't We Just Encrypt the Spaces Too?

Yes. Our hacking approach only works if the spaces were not encrypted. You can modify the simple substitution cipher from the previous chapter to encrypt spaces, numbers, and punctuation characters as well as letters, and it would make your encrypted messages harder (but not impossible) to hack. However, since the spaces will probably be the most common symbol in the ciphertext, you can write a program to replace it back to spaces, and then hack the ciphertext as normal. So encrypting the space characters would not offer much more protection.

Summary

Whew! This hacking program was fairly complicated. The cipherletter mapping is the main tool for modeling the possible letters that each ciphertext letter can decrypt to. By adding letters (based on the candidates for each cipherword) to the mapping, and then intersecting mappings and removing solved letters from other lists of potential decryption letters, we can narrow down the number of possible keys. Instead of trying all 403,291,461,126,605,635,584,000,000 possible keys we can use some sophisticated Python code to figure out exactly what most (if not all) of the original simple substitution key was.

The main strength of the simple substitution cipher is the large number of possible keys. But the downfall is that it is easy enough to compare the cipherwords to words in a dictionary file to slowly figure out which cipherletters decrypt to which letters. The next chapter's cipher is much more powerful. For several hundred years, it was considered impossible to break. It is a "polyalphabetic" substitution cipher called the Vigenère cipher.

CHAPTER 19

THE VIGENÈRE CIPHER

Topics Covered In This Chapter:

- Subkeys

"I believed then, and continue to believe now, that the benefits to our security and freedom of widely available cryptography far, far outweigh the inevitable damage that comes from its use by criminals and terrorists... I believed, and continue to believe, that the arguments against widely available cryptography, while certainly advanced by people of good will, did not hold up against the cold light of reason and were inconsistent with the most basic American values."

Matt Blaze, AT&T Labs, September 2001

Le Chiffre Indéchiffrable

The Vigenère cipher is a stronger cipher than the ones we've seen before. There are too many possible keys to brute-force, even with English detection. It cannot be broken with the word pattern attack that worked on the simple substitution cipher. It was possibly first described in 1553 by Italian cryptographer Giovan Battista Bellaso (though it has been reinvented many times, including by Blaise de Vigenère). It is thought to have remained unbroken until Charles Babbage, considered to be the father of computers, broke it in the 19th century. It was called "le chiffre indéchiffrable", French for "the indecipherable cipher".

Figure 19-1. Blaise de Vigenère
April 5, 1523 - 1596

Figure 19-2. Charles Babbage
December 26, 1791 - October 18, 1871

Multiple "Keys" in the Vigenère Key

The Vigenère cipher is similar to the Caesar cipher, except with multiple keys. Because it uses more than one set of substitutions, it is also called a **polyalphabetic substitution cipher**. Remember that the Caesar cipher had a key from 0 to 25. For the Vigenère cipher, instead of using a numeric key, we will use a letter key. The letter A will be used for key 0. The letter B will be used for key 1, and so on up to Z for the key 25.

0	1	2	3	4	5	6	7	8	9	10	11	12
A	B	C	D	E	F	G	H	I	J	K	L	M

13	14	15	16	17	18	19	20	21	22	23	24	25
N	O	P	Q	R	S	T	U	V	W	X	Y	Z

The key in a Vigenère cipher is a series of letters, such as a single English word. **This single word key will be split into multiple subkeys.** If we use a Vigenère key of "PIZZA", then the first subkey is P, the second subkey is I, the third and fourth subkeys are both Z and the fifth subkey is A. We will use the first subkey to encrypt the first letter of the plaintext, and the second subkey to encrypt the second letter, and so on. When we get to the sixth letter of the plaintext, we will go back to using the *first* subkey.

The Vigenère cipher is the same as using multiple Caesar ciphers in the same message.

Figure 19-3. Multiple Caesar ciphers combine to make the Vigenère cipher

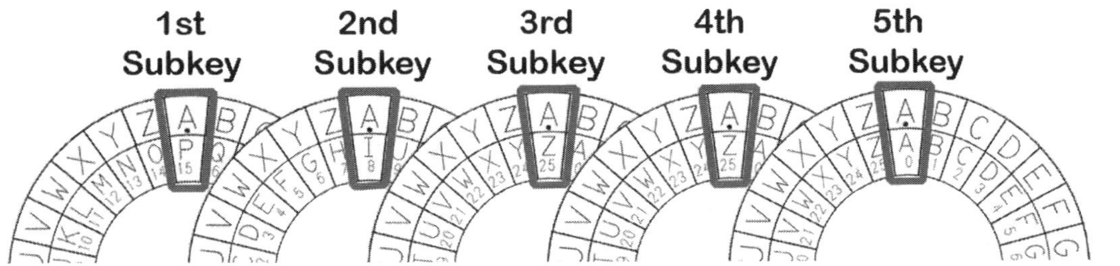

The following shows which subkey will encrypt which letters in the message, "Common sense is not so common." with the Vigenère key, "PIZZA".

```
COMMONSENSEISNOTSOCOMMON
PIZZAPIZZAPIZZAPIZZAPIZZ
```

To encrypt the first C with the subkey P, encrypt it with the Caesar cipher using numeric key 15 (15 is the number for the letter P) which creates the ciphertext R, and so on. Do this for each of the letters of the plaintext. The following table shows this process:

Table 19-1. Numbers of the letters before and after encryption.

Plaintext Letter	Subkey		Ciphertext Letter
C (2)	P (15)	→	R (17)
O (14)	I (8)	→	W (22)
M (12)	Z (25)	→	L (11)
M (12)	Z (25)	→	L (11)
O (14)	A (0)	→	O (14)
N (13)	P (15)	→	C (2)
S (18)	I (8)	→	A (0)
E (4)	Z (25)	→	D (3)
N (13)	Z (25)	→	M (12)
S (18)	A (0)	→	S (18)
E (4)	P (15)	→	T (19)
I (8)	I (8)	→	Q (16)
S (18)	Z (25)	→	R (17)
N (13)	Z (25)	→	M (12)
O (14)	A (0)	→	O (14)
T (19)	P (15)	→	I (8)
S (18)	I (8)	→	A (0)
O (14)	Z (25)	→	N (13)
C (2)	Z (25)	→	B (1)
O (14)	A (0)	→	O (14)
M (12)	P (15)	→	B (1)
M (12)	I (8)	→	U (20)
O (14)	Z (25)	→	N (13)
N (13)	Z (25)	→	M (12)

So using the Vigenère cipher with the key "PIZZA" (which is made up of the subkeys 15, 8, 25, 25, 0) the plaintext "Common sense is not so common." becomes the ciphertext "Rwlloc admst qr moi an bobunm."

The more letters in the Vigenère key, the stronger the encrypted message will be against a brute-force attack. The choice of "PIZZA" is a poor one for a Vigenère key, because it only has five letters. A key with only five letters has 11,881,376 possible combinations. (26 ^ 5 = 26 × 26 × 26 × 26 × 26 = 11,881,376) Eleven million keys is far too many for a human to try out, but a computer could try them all in a few hours. It would first try to decrypt the message with the key "AAAAA" and check if the resulting decryption was in English. Then it could try "AAAAB", then "AAAAC", until it got to "PIZZA".

The good news is that for every additional letter the key has, the number of possible keys multiplies by 26. Once there are quadrillions of possible keys, it would take a computer years to break. Table 19-2 shows how many possible keys there are for each length:

Table 19-2. Number of possible keys based on Vigenère key length.

Key Length	Equation	Possible Keys
1	26	= 26
2	26 × 26	= 676
3	676 × 26	= 17,576
4	17,576 × 26	= 456,976
5	456,976 × 26	= 11,881,376
6	11,881,376 × 26	= 308,915,776
7	308,915,776 × 26	= 8,031,810,176
8	8,031,810,176 × 26	= 208,827,064,576
9	208,827,064,576 × 26	= 5,429,503,678,976
10	5,429,503,678,976 × 26	= 141,167,095,653,376
11	141,167,095,653,376 × 26	= 3,670,344,486,987,776
12	3,670,344,486,987,776 × 26	= 95,428,956,661,682,176
13	95,428,956,661,682,176 × 26	= 2,481,152,873,203,736,576
14	2,481,152,873,203,736,576 × 26	= 64,509,974,703,297,150,976

Once we get to keys that are twelve or more letters long, then it becomes impossible for most consumer laptops to crack in a reasonable amount of time.

A Vigenère key does not have to be a word like "PIZZA". It can be any combination of letters, such as "DURIWKNMFICK". In fact, it is much better not to use a word that can be found in the dictionary. The word "RADIOLOGISTS" is a 12-letter key that is easier to remember than "DURIWKNMFICK" even though they have the same number of letters. But a cryptanalyst might anticipate that the cryptographer is being lazy by using an English word for the Vigenère key. There are 95,428,956,661,682,176 possible 12-letter keys, but there are only about 1,800 12-letter words in our dictionary file. If you are using a 12-letter English word, it would be easier to brute-force that ciphertext than it would be to brute-force the ciphertext from a 3-letter random key.

Of course, the cryptographer is helped by the fact that the cryptanalyst does not know how many letters long the Vigenère key is. But the cryptanalyst could try all 1-letter keys, then all 2-letter keys, and so on.

Source Code of Vigenère Cipher Program

Open a new file editor window by clicking on **File ► New Window**. Type in the following code into the file editor, and then save it as *vigenereCipher.py*. Press **F5** to run the program. Note that first you will need to download the *pyperclip.py* module and place this file in the same directory as the *vigenereCipher.py* file. You can download this file from http://invpy.com/pyperclip.py.

Source code for vigenereCipher.py

```
# Vigenere Cipher (Polyalphabetic Substitution Cipher)
# http://inventwithpython.com/hacking (BSD Licensed)

import pyperclip

LETTERS = 'ABCDEFGHIJKLMNOPQRSTUVWXYZ'

def main():
    # This text can be copy/pasted from http://invpy.com/vigenereCipher.py
    myMessage = """Alan Mathison Turing was a British mathematician,
logician, cryptanalyst, and computer scientist. He was highly influential in
the development of computer science, providing a formalisation of the concepts
of "algorithm" and "computation" with the Turing machine. Turing is widely
considered to be the father of computer science and artificial intelligence.
During World War II, Turing worked for the Government Code and Cypher School
(GCCS) at Bletchley Park, Britain's codebreaking centre. For a time he was head
of Hut 8, the section responsible for German naval cryptanalysis. He devised a
number of techniques for breaking German ciphers, including the method of the
bombe, an electromechanical machine that could find settings for the Enigma
machine. After the war he worked at the National Physical Laboratory, where he
created one of the first designs for a stored-program computer, the ACE. In
1948 Turing joined Max Newman's Computing Laboratory at Manchester University,
where he assisted in the development of the Manchester computers and became
interested in mathematical biology. He wrote a paper on the chemical basis of
morphogenesis, and predicted oscillating chemical reactions such as the
Belousov-Zhabotinsky reaction, which were first observed in the 1960s. Turing's
homosexuality resulted in a criminal prosecution in 1952, when homosexual acts
were still illegal in the United Kingdom. He accepted treatment with female
hormones (chemical castration) as an alternative to prison. Turing died in
1954, just over two weeks before his 42nd birthday, from cyanide poisoning. An
inquest determined that his death was suicide; his mother and some others
believed his death was accidental. On 10 September 2009, following an Internet
campaign, British Prime Minister Gordon Brown made an official public apology
on behalf of the British government for "the appalling way he was treated." As
of May 2012 a private member's bill was before the House of Lords which would
grant Turing a statutory pardon if enacted."""
    myKey = 'ASIMOV'
    myMode = 'encrypt' # set to 'encrypt' or 'decrypt'

    if myMode == 'encrypt':
        translated = encryptMessage(myKey, myMessage)
    elif myMode == 'decrypt':
```

```
        translated = decryptMessage(myKey, myMessage)

    print('%sed message:' % (myMode.title()))
    print(translated)
    pyperclip.copy(translated)
    print()
    print('The message has been copied to the clipboard.')


def encryptMessage(key, message):
    return translateMessage(key, message, 'encrypt')


def decryptMessage(key, message):
    return translateMessage(key, message, 'decrypt')


def translateMessage(key, message, mode):
    translated = [] # stores the encrypted/decrypted message string

    keyIndex = 0
    key = key.upper()

    for symbol in message: # loop through each character in message
        num = LETTERS.find(symbol.upper())
        if num != -1: # -1 means symbol.upper() was not found in LETTERS
            if mode == 'encrypt':
                num += LETTERS.find(key[keyIndex]) # add if encrypting
            elif mode == 'decrypt':
                num -= LETTERS.find(key[keyIndex]) # subtract if decrypting

            num %= len(LETTERS) # handle the potential wrap-around

            # add the encrypted/decrypted symbol to the end of translated.
            if symbol.isupper():
                translated.append(LETTERS[num])
            elif symbol.islower():
                translated.append(LETTERS[num].lower())

            keyIndex += 1 # move to the next letter in the key
            if keyIndex == len(key):
                keyIndex = 0
        else:
            # The symbol was not in LETTERS, so add it to translated as is.
            translated.append(symbol)

```

```
    return ''.join(translated)


# If vigenereCipher.py is run (instead of imported as a module) call
# the main() function.
if __name__ == '__main__':
    main()
```

Sample Run of the Vigenère Cipher Program

```
Encrypted message:
Adiz Avtzqeci Tmzubb wsa m Pmilqev halpqavtakuoi, lgouqdaf, kdmktsvmztsl, izr
xoexghzr kkusitaaf. Vz wsa twbhdg ubalmmzhdad qz hce vmhsgohuqbo ox kaakulmd
gxiwvos, krgdurdny i rcmmstugvtawz ca tzm ocicwxfg jf "stscmilpy" oid

...skipped for brevity...

uiydviyv, Nfdtaat Dmiem Ywiikbqf Bojlab Wrgez avdw iz cafakuog pmjxwx ahwxcby
gv nscadn at ohw Jdwoikp scqejvysit xwd "hce sxboglavs kvy zm ion tjmmhzd." Sa
at Haq 2012 i bfdvsbq azmtmd'g widt ion bwnafz tzm Tcpsw wr Zjrva ivdcz eaigd
yzmbo Tmzubb a kbmhptgzk dvrvwz wa efiohzd.

The message has been copied to the clipboard.
```

How the Program Works

vigenereCipher.py

```
# Vigenere Cipher (Polyalphabetic Substitution Cipher)
# http://inventwithpython.com/hacking (BSD Licensed)

import pyperclip

LETTERS = 'ABCDEFGHIJKLMNOPQRSTUVWXYZ'
```

The beginning of the program has the usual comments to describe the program, an `import` statement for the `pyperclip` module, and creates a variable called `LETTERS` with a string of every uppercase letter.

vigenereCipher.py

```
def main():
    # This text can be copy/pasted from http://invpy.com/vigenereCipher.py
    myMessage = """Alan Mathison Turing was a British mathematician,

    ...skipped for brevity...
```

```
grant Turing a statutory pardon if enacted."""
11.     myKey = 'ASIMOV'
12.     myMode = 'encrypt' # set to 'encrypt' or 'decrypt'
13.
14.     if myMode == 'encrypt':
15.         translated = encryptMessage(myKey, myMessage)
16.     elif myMode == 'decrypt':
17.         translated = decryptMessage(myKey, myMessage)
18.
19.     print('%sed message:' % (myMode.title()))
20.     print(translated)
21.     pyperclip.copy(translated)
22.     print()
23.     print('The message has been copied to the clipboard.')
```

The `main()` function for the Vigenère cipher is exactly like the other `main()` functions in this book: there are variables for `message`, `key`, and `mode`. The user sets these variables on lines 10, 11, and 12 before running the program. The encrypted or decrypted message (depending on what `myMode` is set to) is stored in a variable named `translated` so that it can be printed to the screen (on line 20) and copied to the clipboard (on line 21).

The code that does the actual encryption and decryption is in `translateMessage()`, which is explained later.

vigenereCipher.py

```
def encryptMessage(key, message):
    return translateMessage(key, message, 'encrypt')


def decryptMessage(key, message):
    return translateMessage(key, message, 'decrypt')
```

Since the encryption and decryption use much of the same code as the other, we put them both in `translateMessage()`. The `encryptMessage()` and `decryptMessage()` functions are wrapper functions for `translateMessage()`. (Wrapper functions were covered in Chapter 17.)

vigenereCipher.py

```
def translateMessage(key, message, mode):
    translated = [] # stores the encrypted/decrypted message string

    keyIndex = 0
```

```
38.     key = key.upper()
```

In the `translateMessage()` function, we will slowly build the encrypted (or decrypted) string one character at a time. The list in `translated` will store these characters so that they can be joined together once the string building is done. (The reason we use a list instead of just appending the characters to a string is explained in the "Building Strings in Python with Lists" section in Chapter 18.)

Remember, the Vigenère cipher is just the Caesar cipher except that a different key is used depending on the position of the letter in the message. The `keyIndex` variable keeps track of which subkey to use. The `keyIndex` variable starts off as `0`, because the letter used to encrypt or decrypt the first character of the message will be the one at `key[0]`.

Our code assumes that the key has only uppercase letters. To make sure the key is valid, line 38 sets the key to be the uppercase version of it.

vigenereCipher.py

```
40.     for symbol in message: # loop through each character in message
41.         num = LETTERS.find(symbol.upper())
42.         if num != -1: # -1 means symbol.upper() was not found in LETTERS
43.             if mode == 'encrypt':
44.                 num += LETTERS.find(key[keyIndex]) # add if encrypting
45.             elif mode == 'decrypt':
46.                 num -= LETTERS.find(key[keyIndex]) # subtract if decrypting
```

The rest of the code in `translateMessage()` is similar to the Caesar cipher code. The `for` loop on line 40 sets the characters in `message` to the variable `symbol` on each iteration of the loop. On line 41 we find the index of the uppercase version of this symbol in `LETTERS`. (This is how we translate a letter into a number).

If `num` was not set to `-1` on line 41, then the uppercase version of `symbol` was found in `LETTERS` (meaning that `symbol` is a letter). The `keyIndex` variable keeps track of which subkey to use, and the subkey itself will always be what `key[keyIndex]` evaluates to.

Of course, this is just a single letter string. We need to find this letter's index in the `LETTERS` to convert the subkey into an integer. This integer is then added (if encrypting) to the symbol's number on line 44 or subtracted (if decrypting) to the symbol's number on line 46.

vigenereCipher.py

```
48.             num %= len(LETTERS) # handle the potential wrap-around
```

In the Caesar cipher code, we checked if the new value of num was less than 0 (in which case, we added len(LETTERS) to it) or if the new value of num was len(LETTERS) or greater (in which case, we subtracted len(LETTERS) from it). This handles the "wrap-around" cases.

However, there is a simpler way that handles both of these cases. If we mod the integer stored in num by len(LETTERS), then this will do the exact same thing except in a single line of code.

For example, if num was -8 we would want to add 26 (that is, len(LETTERS)) to it to get 18. Or if num was 31 we would want to subtract 26 to get 5. However -8 % 26 evaluates to 18 and 31 % 26 evaluates to 5. The modular arithmetic on line 48 handles both "wrap-around" cases for us.

vigenereCipher.py

```
50.             # add the encrypted/decrypted symbol to the end of translated.
51.             if symbol.isupper():
52.                 translated.append(LETTERS[num])
53.             elif symbol.islower():
54.                 translated.append(LETTERS[num].lower())
```

The encrypted (or decrypted) character exists at LETTERS[num]. However, we want the encrypted (or decrypted) character's case to match symbol's original case. So if symbol is an uppercase letter, the condition on line 51 will be True and line 52 will append the character at LETTERS[num] to translated. (Remember, all the characters in the LETTERS string are already uppercase.)

However, if symbol is a lowercase letter, than the condition on line 53 will be True instead and line 54 will append the lowercase form of LETTERS[num] to translated instead. This is how we can get the encrypted (or decrypted) message to match the casing of the original message.

vigenereCipher.py

```
56.             keyIndex += 1 # move to the next letter in the key
57.             if keyIndex == len(key):
58.                 keyIndex = 0
```

Now that we have translated the symbol, we want to make sure that on the next iteration of the for loop we use the next subkey. Line 56 increments keyIndex by one. This way when the next iteration uses key[keyIndex] to get the subkey, it will be the index to the next subkey.

However, if we were on the last subkey in the key, then keyIndex would be equal to the length of key. Line 57 checks for this condition, and resets keyIndex back to 0 on line 58. That way key[keyIndex] will point back to the first subkey.

vigenereCipher.py
```
59.         else:
60.             # The symbol was not in LETTERS, so add it to translated as is.
61.             translated.append(symbol)
```

From the indentation you can tell that the `else` statement on line 59 is paired with the `if` statement on line 42. The code on line 61 executes if the symbol was not found in the `LETTERS` string. This happens if `symbol` is a number or punctuation mark such as `'5'` or `'?'`. In this case, line 61 will just append the symbol untranslated.

vigenereCipher.py
```
63.     return ''.join(translated)
```

Now that we are done building the string in `translated`, we call the `join()` method on the blank string to join together all the strings in `translated` (with a blank in between them).

vigenereCipher.py
```
66. # If vigenereCipher.py is run (instead of imported as a module) call
67. # the main() function.
68. if __name__ == '__main__':
69.     main()
```

Lines 68 and 69 call the `main()` function if this program was run by itself, rather than imported by another program that wants to use its `encryptMessage()` and `decryptMessage()` functions.

Summary

We are close to the end of the book, but notice how the Vigenère cipher isn't that much more complicated than the second cipher program in this book, the Caesar cipher. With just a few changes, we can create a cipher that has exponentially many more possible keys than can be brute-forced.

The Vigenère cipher is not vulnerable to the dictionary word pattern attack that our Simple Substitution hacker program uses. The "indecipherable cipher" kept secret messages secret for hundreds of years. The attack on the Vigenère cipher was not widely known until the early 20th century. But of course, this cipher too eventually fell. In the next couple of chapters, we will learn new "frequency analysis" techniques to hack the Vigenère cipher.

Chapter 20

Frequency Analysis

Topics Covered In This Chapter:

- Letter Frequency and ETAOIN
- The `sort()` Method's `key` and `reverse` Keyword Arguments
- Passing Functions as Values Instead of Calling Functions
- Converting Dictionaries to Lists with the `keys()`, `values()`, `items()` Dictionary Methods

> The ineffable talent for finding patterns in chaos cannot do its thing unless he immerses himself in the chaos first. If they do contain patterns, he does not see them just now, in any rational way. But there may be some subrational part of his mind that can go to work, now that the letters have passed before his eyes and through his pencil, and that may suddenly present him with a gift-wrapped clue--or even a full solution--a few weeks from now while he is shaving or antenna-twiddling.
>
> "Cryptonomicon" by Neal Stephenson

A coin has 2 sides, and when you flip a coin, about half the time it will come up heads and half of the time it comes up tails. The **frequency** (that is, how often) that the coin flip ends up heads is the same as the frequency that it ends up tails: about one-half or 50%.

There are 26 letters in the English alphabet, but they don't each appear an equal amount of the time in English text. Some letters are used more often than others. For example, if you look at the letters in this book you will find that the letters E, T, A and O occur very frequently in English words. But the letters J, X, Q, and Z are rarely found in English text. We can use this fact to help crack Vigenère-encrypted messages. This technique is called frequency analysis.

Here are the frequencies of the 26 letters in average English text. This graph is compiled by grabbing English text from books, newspapers, and other sources to count often each letter appears:

Figure 20-1. Letter frequency of normal English.

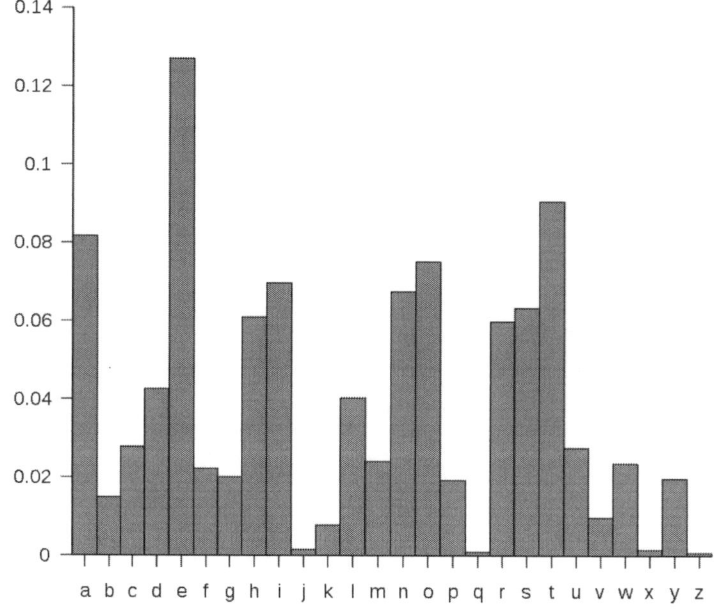

If we sort these in order of greatest frequency to least, we find that E is the most frequent letter, followed by T, followed by A, and so on:

Figure 20-2. Letter frequency of normal English, sorted.

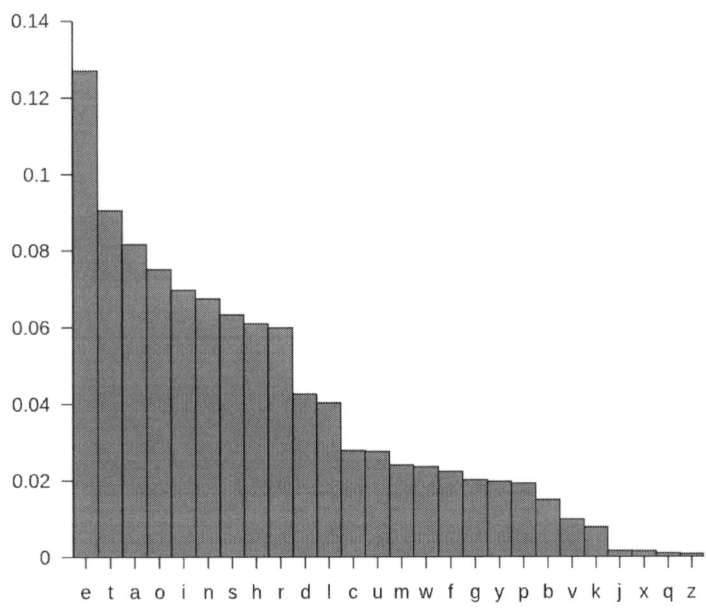

The word "ETAOIN" is a handy way to remember the six most frequent letters. The full list of letters ordered by frequency is "ETAOINSHRDLCUMWFGYPBVKJXQZ".

Think about the transposition cipher: Messages encrypted with the transposition cipher contain all the original letters of the original English plaintext, except in a different order. But the frequency of each letter in the ciphertext remains the same: E, T, and A should occur much more often than Q and Z. Because they are the same letters, the frequencies of these letters in the ciphertext are the same as the plaintext.

The Caesar and simple substitution ciphers have their letters replaced, but you can still count the frequency of the letters. The letters may be different but the frequencies are the same. There should be letters that occur the most often in the ciphertext. These letters are good candidates for being cipherletters for the E, T, or A letters. The letters in the ciphertext that occur least are more likely to be X, Q, and Z.

This counting of letters and how frequently they appear in both plaintexts and ciphertexts is called **frequency analysis**.

Since the Vigenère cipher is essentially multiple Caesar cipher keys used in the same message, we can use frequency analysis to hack each subkey one at a time based on the letter frequency of the attempted decryptions. We can't use English word detection, since any word in the ciphertext will have been encrypted with multiple subkeys. But we don't need full words, we can analyze the letter frequency of each subkey's decrypted text. (This will be explained more in the next chapter.)

Matching Letter Frequencies

By "matching the letter frequency of regular English" we could try several different algorithms. The one used in our hacking program will simply order the letters from most frequent to least frequent. We will calculate what we will call in this book a **frequency match score** for this ordering of frequencies. To calculate the frequency match score for a string, the score starts at 0 and each time one of the letters E, T, A, O, I, N appears among the six most frequent letters of the string, we add a point to the score. And each time one of the letters V, K, J, X, Q, or Z appears among the six least frequent letters of the string, we add a point to the score. The frequency match score for a string will be an integer from 0 (meaning the letter frequency of the string is completely unlike regular English's letter frequency) to 12 (meaning it is identical to regular English's letter frequency).

An Example of Calculating Frequency Match Score

For example, look at this ciphertext which was encrypted with a simple substitution cipher:

```
"Sy l nlx sr pyyacao l ylwj eiswi upar lulsxrj isr sxrjsxwjr, ia esmm
rwctjsxsza sj wmpramh, lxo txmarr jia aqsoaxwa sr pqaceiamnsxu, ia esmm caytra
jp famsaqa sj. Sy, px jia pjiac ilxo, ia sr pyyacao rpnajisxu eiswi lyypcor l
calrpx ypc lwjsxu sx lwwpcolxwa jp isr sxrjsxwjr, ia esmm lwwabj sj aqax px jia
rmsuijarj aqsoaxwa. Jia pcsusx py nhjir sr agbmlsxao sx jisr elh. -Facjclxo
Ctrramm"
```

If we count the frequency of each letter and then arrange them by order of its frequency, we end up with this ordering: ASRXJILPWMCYOUEQNTHBFZGKVD. That is, A is the most frequent letter, S is the 2nd most frequent letter, and so on down to the letter D, which appears the least frequently.

The six most frequent letters in this ordering are A, S, R, X, J, and I. Only two of these letters (A and I) appear in the ETAOIN set of letters. The six least frequent letters in the ordering are F, Z, G, K, V, and D. Only three of these letters (Z, K, and V) appear in the VKJXQZ set of letters. So the frequency ordering ASRXJILPWMCYOUEQNTHBFZGKVD (which comes from the above ciphertext) has a frequency match score of 5.

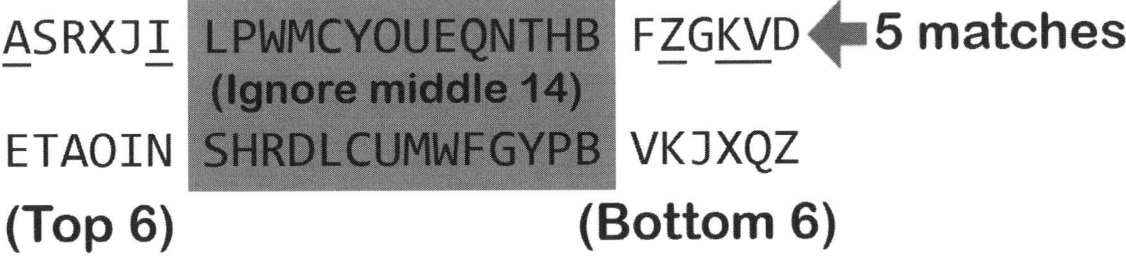

Figure 20-3. How the frequency match score of ASRXJILPWMCYOUEQNTHBFZGKVD is calculated.

The above ciphertext was encrypted with a simple substitution cipher, which is why the frequency match score isn't very high. The letter frequencies of simple substitution ciphertext won't match regular English's letter frequencies.

Another Example of Calculating Frequency Match Score

For another example, look at this ciphertext which was encrypted with a transposition cipher:

```
"I rc ascwuiluhnviwuetnh,osgaa ice tipeeeee slnatsfietgi tittynecenisl. e fo f
fnc isltn sn o a yrs sd onisli ,l erglei trhfmwfrogotn,l  stcofiit.aea
wesn,lnc ee w,l eIh eeehoer ros  iol er snh nl oahsts  ilasvih  tvfeh rtira id
thatnie.im ei-dlmf i  thszonsisehroe, aiehcdsanahiec  gv gyedsB affcahiecesd d
lee   onsdihsoc nin cethiTitx  eRneahgin r e teom fbiotd  n
ntacscwevhtdhnhpiwru"
```

The ordering of most to least frequent letters in the above ciphertext is: EISNTHAOCLRFDGWVMUYBPZXQJK. (That is, E is the most frequent letter, I the 2nd most frequent letter, and so on.)

Of the top and bottom six letters in this ordering, the four letters E, I, N, and T appear in ETAOIN and the five letters Z, X, Q, J, and K appear in VKJXQZ. This gives the ordering a frequency match score of 9.

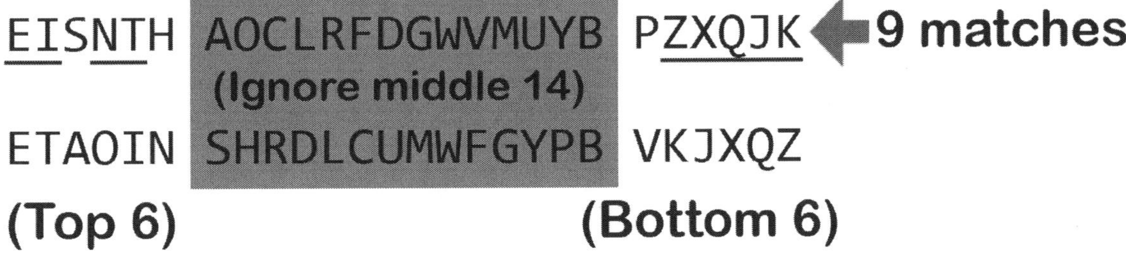

Figure 20-4. How the frequency match score of EISNTHAOCLRFDGWVMUYBPZXQJK is calculated.

The above ciphertext was encrypted with a transposition cipher, so it has all the same letters as the original English plaintext (their order has just been switched around.) This is why the frequency ordering has a much higher frequency match score.

Hacking Each Subkey

When hacking the Vigenère cipher, we try to decrypt the letters for the first subkey with each of the 26 possible letters and find out which decrypted ciphertext produces a letter frequency that closest matches that of regular English. This is a good indication that we have found the correct subkey.

We can do this same thing for the second, third, fourth, and fifth subkey as well. Since we are only doing 26 decryptions for each subkey individually, our computer only has to perform 26 + 26 + 26 + 26 + 26, or 156, decryptions. This is much easier than trying to do 11,881,376 decryptions!

So, hacking the Vigenère cipher sounds simple in theory. Just try all 26 possible subkeys for each subkey in the key, and see which one produces decrypted text that has a letter frequency that closest matches the letter frequency of English.

It turns out that there are a few more steps than this, though, but we can cover them when we write the hacking program in the next chapter. For this chapter, we will write a module with several helpful functions that perform frequency analysis. This module will have these functions:

- `getLetterCount()` – This function will take a string parameter and return a dictionary that has the count of how often each letter appears in the string.
- `getFrequencyOrder()` – This function will take a string parameter and return a string of the 26 letters ordered from those that appear most frequently to least frequently in the string parameter.
- `englishFreqMatchScore()` – This function will take a string parameter and return an integer from 0 to 12 of the string's letter frequency match score.

The Code for Matching Letter Frequencies

Type in the following code into the file editor, and then save it as *freqAnalysis.py*. Press **F5** to run the program.

Source code for freqAnalysis.py

```
# Frequency Finder
# http://inventwithpython.com/hacking (BSD Licensed)
```

```

# frequency taken from http://en.wikipedia.org/wiki/Letter_frequency
englishLetterFreq = {'E': 12.70, 'T': 9.06, 'A': 8.17, 'O': 7.51, 'I': 6.97, 'N': 6.75, 'S': 6.33, 'H': 6.09, 'R': 5.99, 'D': 4.25, 'L': 4.03, 'C': 2.78, 'U': 2.76, 'M': 2.41, 'W': 2.36, 'F': 2.23, 'G': 2.02, 'Y': 1.97, 'P': 1.93, 'B': 1.29, 'V': 0.98, 'K': 0.77, 'J': 0.15, 'X': 0.15, 'Q': 0.10, 'Z': 0.07}
ETAOIN = 'ETAOINSHRDLCUMWFGYPBVKJXQZ'
LETTERS = 'ABCDEFGHIJKLMNOPQRSTUVWXYZ'



def getLetterCount(message):
    # Returns a dictionary with keys of single letters and values of the
    # count of how many times they appear in the message parameter.
    letterCount = {'A': 0, 'B': 0, 'C': 0, 'D': 0, 'E': 0, 'F': 0, 'G': 0, 'H': 0, 'I': 0, 'J': 0, 'K': 0, 'L': 0, 'M': 0, 'N': 0, 'O': 0, 'P': 0, 'Q': 0, 'R': 0, 'S': 0, 'T': 0, 'U': 0, 'V': 0, 'W': 0, 'X': 0, 'Y': 0, 'Z': 0}

    for letter in message.upper():
        if letter in LETTERS:
            letterCount[letter] += 1

    return letterCount


def getItemAtIndexZero(x):
    return x[0]


def getFrequencyOrder(message):
    # Returns a string of the alphabet letters arranged in order of most
    # frequently occurring in the message parameter.

    # first, get a dictionary of each letter and its frequency count
    letterToFreq = getLetterCount(message)

    # second, make a dictionary of each frequency count to each letter(s)
    # with that frequency
    freqToLetter = {}
    for letter in LETTERS:
        if letterToFreq[letter] not in freqToLetter:
            freqToLetter[letterToFreq[letter]] = [letter]
        else:
            freqToLetter[letterToFreq[letter]].append(letter)

```

```
    # third, put each list of letters in reverse "ETAOIN" order, and then
    # convert it to a string
    for freq in freqToLetter:
        freqToLetter[freq].sort(key=ETAOIN.find, reverse=True)
        freqToLetter[freq] = ''.join(freqToLetter[freq])

    # fourth, convert the freqToLetter dictionary to a list of tuple
    # pairs (key, value), then sort them
    freqPairs = list(freqToLetter.items())
    freqPairs.sort(key=getItemAtIndexZero, reverse=True)

    # fifth, now that the letters are ordered by frequency, extract all
    # the letters for the final string
    freqOrder = []
    for freqPair in freqPairs:
        freqOrder.append(freqPair[1])

    return ''.join(freqOrder)


def englishFreqMatchScore(message):
    # Return the number of matches that the string in the message
    # parameter has when its letter frequency is compared to English
    # letter frequency. A "match" is how many of its six most frequent
    # and six least frequent letters is among the six most frequent and
    # six least frequent letters for English.
    freqOrder = getFrequencyOrder(message)

    matchScore = 0
    # Find how many matches for the six most common letters there are.
    for commonLetter in ETAOIN[:6]:
        if commonLetter in freqOrder[:6]:
            matchScore += 1
    # Find how many matches for the six least common letters there are.
    for uncommonLetter in ETAOIN[-6:]:
        if uncommonLetter in freqOrder[-6:]:
            matchScore += 1

    return matchScore
```

How the Program Works

freqAnalysis.py

```
# Frequency Finder
# http://inventwithpython.com/hacking (BSD Licensed)

```

```
# frequency taken from http://en.wikipedia.org/wiki/Letter_frequency
englishLetterFreq = {'E': 12.70, 'T': 9.06, 'A': 8.17, 'O': 7.51, 'I': 6.97, 'N': 6.75, 'S': 6.33, 'H': 6.09, 'R': 5.99, 'D': 4.25, 'L': 4.03, 'C': 2.78, 'U': 2.76, 'M': 2.41, 'W': 2.36, 'F': 2.23, 'G': 2.02, 'Y': 1.97, 'P': 1.93, 'B': 1.29, 'V': 0.98, 'K': 0.77, 'J': 0.15, 'X': 0.15, 'Q': 0.10, 'Z': 0.07}
```

The `englishLetterFreq` dictionary will contain strings of the letters of the alphabet as keys and a float for their percentage frequency as the value. (These values come from the Wikipedia article for letter frequency: https://en.wikipedia.org/wiki/Letter_frequency) The `englishLetterFreq` value isn't actually used by our program. It is simply here for your future reference in case you write a program that needs it.

The Most Common Letters, "ETAOIN"

freqAnalysis.py

```
8. ETAOIN = 'ETAOINSHRDLCUMWFGYPBVKJXQZ'
```

We will create a variable named `ETAOIN` on line 8 which will have the 26 letters of the alphabet in order of most frequent to least frequent. The word ETAOIN is a handy way to remember the six most common letters in English. Of course, this ordering isn't always going to be perfect. You could easily find a book that has a set of letter frequencies where Z is used more often than Q, for example. *Gadsby* by Ernest Vicent Wright is a novel that never uses the letter E, which gives it a very odd set of letter frequencies. But in most cases, the "ETAOIN order" will be accurate.

freqAnalysis.py

```
9. LETTERS = 'ABCDEFGHIJKLMNOPQRSTUVWXYZ'
```

Our module will also need a string of all the uppercase letters of the alphabet for a few different functions, so we set the `LETTERS` constant variable on line 9.

The Program's `getLettersCount()` Function

freqAnalysis.py

```
def getLetterCount(message):
    # Returns a dictionary with keys of single letters and values of the
    # count of how many times they appear in the message parameter.
    letterCount = {'A': 0, 'B': 0, 'C': 0, 'D': 0, 'E': 0, 'F': 0, 'G': 0, 'H': 0, 'I': 0, 'J': 0, 'K': 0, 'L': 0, 'M': 0, 'N': 0, 'O': 0, 'P': 0, 'Q': 0, 'R': 0, 'S': 0, 'T': 0, 'U': 0, 'V': 0, 'W': 0, 'X': 0, 'Y': 0, 'Z': 0}
```

The getLetterCount() function returns a dictionary value where the keys are single uppercase letter strings, and the values are an integer showing how many times that letter occurs in the message parameter. For example, a certain string value for the message parameter with 135 A's, 30 B's, and so on will cause getLetterCount() to return {'A': 135, 'B': 30, 'C': 74, 'D': 58, 'E': 196, 'F': 37, 'G': 39, 'H': 87, 'I': 139, 'J': 2, 'K': 8, 'L': 62, 'M': 58, 'N': 122, 'O': 113, 'P': 36, 'Q': 2, 'R': 106, 'S': 89, 'T': 140, 'U': 37, 'V': 14, 'W': 30, 'X': 3, 'Y': 21, 'Z': 1}

Line 16 starts the letterCount variable with a dictionary that has all keys with a value of 0.

freqAnalysis.py

```
18.     for letter in message.upper():
19.         if letter in LETTERS:
20.             letterCount[letter] += 1
```

The for loop on line 18 iterates through each character in the uppercase version of message. On line 19, if the character exists in the LETTERS string, we know it is an uppercase letter. In that case line 20 will increment the value at letterCount[letter].

freqAnalysis.py

```
    return letterCount
```

After the for loop on line 18 finishes, the letterCount dictionary will have a count of how often each letter appeared in message. This dictionary is returned from getLetterCount().

The Program's getItemAtIndexZero() Function

freqAnalysis.py

```
def getItemAtIndexZero(x):
    return x[0]
```

The getItemAtIndexZero() function is very simple: it is passed a tuple and returns the items at index 1. This function will be passed as the key keyword argument for the sort() method. (The reason for this will be explained later.)

The Program's getFrequencyOrder() Function

freqAnalysis.py

```
def getFrequencyOrder(message):
    # Returns a string of the alphabet letters arranged in order of most
    # frequently occurring in the message parameter.
```

```
32.
33.     # first, get a dictionary of each letter and its frequency count
34.     letterToFreq = getLetterCount(message)
```

The `getFrequencyOrder()` function will return a string with the 26 uppercase letters of the alphabet arranged in order of how frequently they appear in the `message` parameter. If `message` is readable English instead of random gibberish, this string will most likely be similar (if not identical to) the string in the `ETAOIN` constant.

For example, if the "Alan Mathison Turing was a British mathematician…" text from Chapter 19's *vigenereCipher.py* program was passed as a string to `getFrequencyOrder()`, the function would return the string `'ETIANORSHCLMDGFUPBWYVKXQJZ'` because E is the most common letter in that paragraph, followed by T, then I, then A, and so on.

This function is somewhat complicated, but it breaks down to five simple steps.

The first step of `getFrequencyOrder()`, line 34 gets a dictionary value of the letter frequency count from `getLetterCount()` for the string in the `message` parameter. (The `getLetterCount()` function was described previously.)

If the "Alan Mathison Turing…" text was passed as a string value for the `message` parameter, then line 34 would assign `letterToFreq` the dictionary value, `{'A': 135, 'C': 74, 'B': 30, 'E': 196, 'D': 58, 'G': 39, 'F': 37, 'I': 139, 'H': 87, 'K': 8, 'J': 2, 'M': 58, 'L': 62, 'O': 113, 'N': 122, 'Q': 2, 'P': 36, 'S': 89, 'R': 106, 'U': 37, 'T': 140, 'W': 30, 'V': 14, 'Y': 21, 'X': 3, 'Z': 1}`.

freqAnalysis.py

```
36.     # second, make a dictionary of each frequency count to each letter(s)
37.     # with that frequency
38.     freqToLetter = {}
39.     for letter in LETTERS:
40.         if letterToFreq[letter] not in freqToLetter:
41.             freqToLetter[letterToFreq[letter]] = [letter]
42.         else:
43.             freqToLetter[letterToFreq[letter]].append(letter)
```

For the second step of `getFrequencyOrder()`, while the `letterToFreq` dictionary has keys of each of the 26 letters and values of their frequency count, what we need is a dictionary value that maps the opposite: a dictionary where the keys are the frequency count and values are a list of letters that appear that many times. While the `letterToFreq` dictionary maps letter keys to frequency values, the `freqToLetter` dictionary will map frequency keys to list of letter values.

Line 38 creates a blank dictionary. Line 44 loops over all the letters in `LETTERS`. The `if` statement on line 40 checks if the letter's frequency (that is, `letterToFreq[letter]`) already exists as a key in `freqToLetter`. If not, then line 41 adds this key with a list of the letter as the value. Or else, line 43 appends the letter to the end of the list that is already at `letterToFreq[letter]`.

If we continue to use our "Alan Mathison Turing…" example value of `letterToFreq` then `freqToLetter` would end up looking like this: `{1: ['Z'], 2: ['J', 'Q'], 3: ['X'], 135: ['A'], 8: ['K'], 139: ['I'], 140: ['T'], 14: ['V'], 21: ['Y'], 30: ['B', 'W'], 36: ['P'], 37: ['F', 'U'], 39: ['G'], 58: ['D', 'M'], 62: ['L'], 196: ['E'], 74: ['C'], 87: ['H'], 89: ['S'], 106: ['R'], 113: ['O'], 122: ['N']}`

The `sort()` Method's `key` and `reverse` Keyword Arguments

freqAnalysis.py

```
    # third, put each list of letters in reverse "ETAOIN" order, and then
    # convert it to a string
    for freq in freqToLetter:
        freqToLetter[freq].sort(key=ETAOIN.find, reverse=True)
        freqToLetter[freq] = ''.join(freqToLetter[freq])
```

The third step of `getFrequencyOrder()` to is sort the letter strings in each list in `freqToLetter` in reverse ETAOIN order (as opposed to alphabetical order).

Remember that `freqToLetter[freq]` will evaluate to a *list* of letters that have a frequency count of `freq`. A list is used because it's possible that two or more letters have the exact same frequency count, in which case this list will have two-or-more-letters strings in it.

When multiple letters are tied for frequency, we want these tied letters to be sorted in the reverse order that they appear in the `ETAOIN` string. We need this so that we have a consistent way of breaking ties. Otherwise messages with the same letter frequencies might produce different return values from `getFrequencyOrder()`!

For example, if E appears 15 times, D and W appear 8 times each, and H appears 4 times, we would want them to be sorted as `'EWDH'` and not `'EDWH'`. This is because while E is the most frequent, D and W have the same frequency count but W comes after D in the `ETAOIN` string.

Python's `sort()` function can do this sorting for us if we pass it a function or method for its `key` keyword argument. Normally the `sort()` function simply sorts the list it is called on into alphabetical (or numeric) order. However, we can change this by passing the `find()` method of the `ETAOIN` string as the `key` keyword argument. This will sort the items in the `freqToLetter[freq]` list by the integer returned from the `ETAOIN.find()` method, that is, the order that they appear in the `ETAOIN` string.

Normally the `sort()` method sorts the values in a list in **ascending order** (that is, lowest to highest or the letter A first and letter Z last). If we pass `True` for the `sort()` method's `reverse` keyword argument, it will sort the items in **descending order** instead. The reason we want to sort the letters in reverse ETAOIN order is so that ties result in lower match scores in the `englishFreqMatchScore()` function rather than higher match scores. (This function is explained later.)

If we continue using our "Alan Mathison Turing…" example value for `freqToLetter`, then after the loop finishes the value stored in `freqToLetter` would be: `{1: 'Z', 2: 'QJ', 3: 'X', 135: 'A', 8: 'K', 139: 'I', 140: 'T', 14: 'V', 21: 'Y', 30: 'BW', 36: 'P', 37: 'FU', 39: 'G', 58: 'MD', 62: 'L', 196: 'E', 74: 'C', 87: 'H', 89: 'S', 106: 'R', 113: 'O', 122: 'N'}`

Notice that the strings for the `30`, `37`, and `58` keys are all sorted in reverse ETAOIN order.

Passing Functions as Values

```
freqAnalysis.py
48.         freqToLetter[freq].sort(key=ETAOIN.find, reverse=True)
```

If you look on line 47, you'll notice that we are not calling the `find()` method but instead using the find method itself as a value that is passed to the `sort()` method call. In Python, functions themselves are values just like any other values. For example, try typing this into the interactive shell:

```
>>> def foo():
...   print('Hello!')
...
>>> bar = foo
>>> bar()
Hello!
```

In the above code, we define a function named `foo()` that prints out the string `'Hello!'`. But this is basically defining a function and then storing it in a variable named `foo`. Then we copy the function in `foo` to the variable `bar`. This means we can call `bar()` just like we can call `foo()`! Note that in this assignment statement we do **not** have parentheses after `foo`. If we did, we would be *calling* the function `foo()` and setting `bar` to its return value. Just like `spam[42]` has the `[42]` index operating on `spam`, the parentheses means, "Call the value in `foo` as a function."

You can also pass functions as values just like any other value. Try typing the following into the interactive shell:

```
>>> def doMath(func):
...   return func(10, 5)
...
>>> def adding(a, b):
...   return a + b
...
>>> def subtracting(a, b):
...   return a - b
...
>>> doMath(adding)
15
>>> doMath(subtracting)
5
>>>
```

When the function in `adding` is passed to the `doMath()` call, the `func(10, 5)` line is calling `adding()` and passing `10` and `5` to it. So the call `func(10, 5)` is effectively the same as the call `adding(10, 5)`. This is why `doMath(adding)` returns `15`.

When `subtracting` is passed to the `doMath()` call, `func(10, 5)` is the same as `subtracting(10, 5)`. This is why `doMath(subtracting)` returns `5`.

Passing a function or method to a function or method call is how the `sort()` method lets you implement different sorting behavior. The function or method that is passed to `sort()` should accept a single parameter and returns a value that is used to alphabetically sort the item.

To put it another way: normally `sort()` sorts the values in a list by the alphabetical order of the list values.. But if we pass a function (or method) for the `key` keyword argument, then the values in the list are sorted *by the alphabetical or numeric order of the return value of the function* when the value in the list is passed to that function.

You can think of a normal `sort()` call such as this:

```
someListVariable.sort()
```

…as being equivalent to this:

```
def func(x):
    return x   # sorting based on the value itself
someListVariable.sort(key=func)
```

So when the `sort()` method call is passed `ETAOIN.find`, instead of sorting the strings like `'A'`, `'B'`, and `'C'` by the alphabetical order the `sort()` method sorts them by the numeric order of the integers returned from `ETAOIN.find('A')`, `ETAOIN.find('B')`, and `ETAOIN.find('C')`: that is, `2`, `19`, and `11` respectively. So the `'A'`, `'B'`, and `'C'` strings get sorted as `'A'`, `'C'`, and then `'B'` (the order they appear in `ETAOIN`).

Converting Dictionaries to Lists with the keys(), values(), items() Dictionary Methods

If you want to get a list value of all the keys in a dictionary, the `keys()` method will return a dict_keys object that can be passed to `list()` to get a list of all the keys. There is a similar dictionary method named `values()` that returns a dict_values object. Try typing the following into the interactive shell:

```
>>> spam = {'cats': 10, 'dogs': 3, 'mice': 3}
>>> spam.keys()
dict_keys(['mice', 'cats', 'dogs'])
>>> list(spam.keys())
['mice', 'cats', 'dogs']
>>> list(spam.values())
[3, 10, 3]
>>>
```

Remember, dictionaries do not have any ordering associated with the key-value pairs they contain. When getting a list of the keys or values, they will be in a random order in the list. If you want to get the keys and values together, the `items()` dictionary method returns a dict_items object that can be passed to `list()`. The `list()` function will then return a list of tuples where the tuples contain a key and value pair of values. Try typing the following into the interactive shell:

```
>>> spam = {'cats': 10, 'dogs': 3, 'mice': 3}
>>> list(spam.items())
[('mice', 3), ('cats', 10), ('dogs', 3)]
```

We will be using the `items()` method in our `getFrequencyOrder()` function, but you should know about the `keys()` and `values()` methods too. Remember, in order to use the return values from these methods as lists, they must be passed to the `list()` function. The `list()` function then returns a list version of the dict_keys, dict_values, or dict_items object.

Sorting the Items from a Dictionary

freqAnalysis.py

```
51.     # fourth, convert the freqToLetter dictionary to a list of tuple
52.     # pairs (key, value), then sort them
53.     freqPairs = list(freqToLetter.items())
```

The fourth step of `getFrequencyOrder()` is to sort the strings from the `freqToLetter` dictionary by the frequency count. Remember that the `freqToLetter` dictionary has integer frequency counts for the keys and lists of single-letter strings for the values. But since dictionaries do not have an ordering for the key-value pairs in them, we will call the `items()` method and `list()` function to create a list of tuples of the dictionary's key-value pairs. This list of tuples (stored in a variable named `freqPairs` on line 53) is what we will sort.

freqAnalysis.py

```
54.     freqPairs.sort(key=getItemAtIndexZero, reverse=True)
```

The `sort()` method call is passed the `getItemAtIndexZero` function value itself. This means the items in the `freqPairs` will be sorted by the numeric order of the value at index `0` of the tuple value, which is the frequency count integer. Line 54 also passes `True` for the `reverse` keyword argument so that the tuples are reverse ordered from largest frequency count to smallest.

If we continue using the previous "Alan Mathison Turing…" example, the value of `freqPairs` will be `[(196, 'E'), (140, 'T'), (139, 'I'), (135, 'A'), (122, 'N'), (113, 'O'), (106, 'R'), (89, 'S'), (87, 'H'), (74, 'C'), (62, 'L'), (58, 'MD'), (39, 'G'), (37, 'FU'), (36, 'P'), (30, 'BW'), (21, 'Y'), (14, 'V'), (8, 'K'), (3, 'X'), (2, 'QJ'), (1, 'Z')]`

freqAnalysis.py

```
56.     # fifth, now that the letters are ordered by frequency, extract all
57.     # the letters for the final string
58.     freqOrder = []
59.     for freqPair in freqPairs:
60.         freqOrder.append(freqPair[1])
```

The fifth step is to create a list of all the strings from the sorted list in `freqPairs`. The variable `freqOrder` will start as a blank list on line 58, and the string at index `1` of the tuple in `freqPairs` will be appended to the end of `freqOrder`.

If we continue with the "Alan Mathison Turing was a British mathematician..." example from before, after this loop has finished, `freqOrder` will contain the value `['E', 'T', 'I', 'A', 'N', 'O', 'R', 'S', 'H', 'C', 'L', 'MD', 'G', 'FU', 'P', 'BW', 'Y', 'V', 'K', 'X', 'QJ', 'Z']` freqAnalysis.py

```
62.     return ''.join(freqOrder)
```

Line 62 creates a string from the list of strings in `freqOrder` by joining them together with the `join()` method. If we continue using the previous example, `getFrequencyOrder()` will return the string `'ETIANORSHCLMDGFUPBWYVKXQJZ'`. According to this ordering, E is the most frequent letter in the "Alan Mathison Turing…" example string, T is the second most frequent letter, I is the third most frequent, and so on.

The Program's `englishFreqMatchScore()` Function

freqAnalysis.py

```
def englishFreqMatchScore(message):
    # Return the number of matches that the string in the message
    # parameter has when its letter frequency is compared to English
    # letter frequency. A "match" is how many of its six most frequent
    # and six least frequent letters is among the six most frequent and
    # six least frequent letters for English.
    freqOrder = getFrequencyOrder(message)
```

The `englishFreqMatchScore()` function takes a string for `message`, and then returns an integer between `0` and `12` to show `message`'s frequency match score with readable English's letter frequency. The higher the integer, the more that the frequency of the letters in `message` matches the frequency of normal English text.

The first step in calculating the match score is to get the letter frequency ordering of `message` by calling the `getFrequencyOrder()` function.

freqAnalysis.py

```
73.     matchScore = 0
74.     # Find how many matches for the six most common letters there are.
75.     for commonLetter in ETAOIN[:6]:
76.         if commonLetter in freqOrder[:6]:
77.             matchScore += 1
```

The `matchScore` variable starts off at `0` on line 73. The `for` loop on line 75 goes through each of the first 6 letters of the `ETAOIN` string. Remember that the `[:6]` slice is the same thing as `[0:6]`. If one of these E, T, A, O, I, or N letters is in the first six letters in the `freqOrder` string, then line 76's condition is `True` and line 77 will increment `matchScore`.

freqAnalysis.py

```
    # Find how many matches for the six least common letters there are.
    for uncommonLetter in ETAOIN[-6:]:
```

```
80.         if uncommonLetter in freqOrder[-6:]:
81.             matchScore += 1
```

Lines 79 to 81 are much like lines 75 to 77, except the *last* six letters in `ETAOIN` (V, K, J, X, Q, and Z) are checked to see if they are in the *last* six letters in the `freqOrder` string. If they are, then `matchScore` is incremented.

```
                                                          freqAnalysis.py
83.     return matchScore
```

The integer in `matchScore` is returned on line 83.

The 14 letters in the middle of the frequency ordering are ignored with our frequency match score calculation. This approach to comparing letter frequencies is pretty simple, but it works well enough for our hacking program in the next chapter.

Summary

The `sort()` function is useful for sorting the values in a list. Normally `sort()` will sort them in alphabetical or numerical order. But the `reverse` and `key` keyword arguments can be used to sort them in different orders. This chapter also explains how functions themselves can be passed as values in function calls.

Let's use the frequency analysis module to hack the Vigenère cipher, a cipher that perplexed cryptanalysts for hundreds of years!

CHAPTER 21

HACKING THE VIGENÈRE CIPHER

Topics Covered In This Chapter:
- The `extend()` list method
- The `itertools.product()` function

Alan says, "When we want to sink a convey, we send out an observation plane first. It is ostensibly an observation plane. Of course, to observe is not its real duty—We already know exactly where the convoy is. Its real duty is to be observed—That is, to fly close enough to the convoy that it will be noticed by the lookouts on the ships. The ships will then send out a radio message to the effect that they have been sighted by an Allied observation plane. Then, when we come round and sink them, the Germans will not find it suspicious—At least, not quite so monstrously suspicious that we knew exactly where to go."

...

Alan says, "Unless we continue to do stunningly idiotic things like sinking convoys in the fog, they will never receive any clear and unmistakable indications that we have broken Enigma."

"Cryptonomicon" by Neal Stephenson

There are two different methods to hack the Vigenère cipher. The first is a brute-force attack that tries every word in the dictionary file as the Vigenère key. This method will only work if an English word like "RAVEN" or "DESK" was used for the key instead of a random key like "VUWFE" or "PNFJ". The second is a more sophisticated method that works even if a random key was used. The earliest record of its use was by the mathematician Charles Babbage in the 19th century.

The Dictionary Attack

If the Vigenère key is an English word it is very easy to memorize. **But never use an English word for the encryption key. This makes your ciphertext vulnerable to a dictionary attack.**

A dictionary attack is a brute-force technique where a hacker attempts to decrypt the ciphertext using the words from a dictionary file as the keys. The *dictionary.txt* dictionary file available on this book's website (at http://invpy.com/dictionary.txt) has about 45,000 English words. It takes less than 5 minutes for my computer to run through all of these decryptions for a message the size of a long paragraph.

Source Code for a Vigenère Dictionary Attack Program

Open a new file editor window by clicking on **File ► New Window**. Type in the following code into the file editor, and then save it as *vigenereDictionaryHacker.py*. Press **F5** to run the program. Note that first you will need to download the *pyperclip.py* module and place this file in the same directory as the *vigenereDictionaryHacker.py* file. You can download this file from http://invpy.com/pyperclip.py.

Source code for vigenereDictionaryHacker.py

```
# Vigenere Cipher Dictionary Hacker
# http://inventwithpython.com/hacking (BSD Licensed)

import detectEnglish, vigenereCipher, pyperclip

def main():
    ciphertext = """Tzx isnz eccjxkg nfq lol mys bbqq I lxcz."""
    hackedMessage = hackVigenere(ciphertext)

    if hackedMessage != None:
        print('Copying hacked message to clipboard:')
        print(hackedMessage)
        pyperclip.copy(hackedMessage)
    else:
        print('Failed to hack encryption.')

```

```

def hackVigenere(ciphertext):
    fo = open('dictionary.txt')
    words = fo.readlines()
    fo.close()

    for word in words:
        word = word.strip() # remove the newline at the end
        decryptedText = vigenereCipher.decryptMessage(word, ciphertext)
        if detectEnglish.isEnglish(decryptedText, wordPercentage=40):
            # Check with user to see if the decrypted key has been found.
            print()
            print('Possible encryption break:')
            print('Key ' + str(word) + ': ' + decryptedText[:100])
            print()
            print('Enter D for done, or just press Enter to continue breaking:')
            response = input('> ')

            if response.upper().startswith('D'):
                return decryptedText

if __name__ == '__main__':
    main()
```

Sample Run of the Vigenère Dictionary Hacker Program

When you run this program the output will look like this:

```
Possible encryption break:
Key ASTROLOGY: The recl yecrets crk not the qnks I tell.

Enter D for done, or just press Enter to continue breaking:
>

Possible encryption break:
Key ASTRONOMY: The real secrets are not the ones I tell.

Enter D for done, or just press Enter to continue breaking:
> d
Copying hacked message to clipboard:
The real secrets are not the ones I tell.
```

The first keyword it suggests (“ASTROLOGY”) doesn’t quite work, so the user presses Enter to let the hacking program continue until it gets the correct decryption key (“ASTRONOMY”).

The `readlines()` File Object Method

```
words = fo.readlines()
```

File objects returned from `open()` have a `readlines()` method. Unlike the `read()` method which returns the full contents of the file as a single string, the `readlines()` method will return a list of strings, where each string is a single line from the file. Note that each of the strings in the list will end with a `\n` newline character (except for possibly the very last string, since the file might not have ended with a newline).

The source code for this program isn't anything we haven't seen in previous hacking programs in this book, aside from the new `readlines()` method. The `hackVigenere()` function reads in the contents of the dictionary file, uses each word in that file to decrypt the ciphertext, and if the decrypted text looks like readable English it will prompt the user to quit or continue.

As such, we won't do a line-by-line explanation for this program, and instead continue on with a program that can hack the Vigenère cipher even when the key was not a word that can be found in the dictionary.

The Babbage Attack & Kasiski Examination

Charles Babbage is known to have broken the Vigenère cipher, but he never published his results. Later studies revealed he used a method that was later published by early 20th-century mathematician Friedrich Kasiski.

"Kasiski Examination" is a process used to determine how long the Vigenère key used to encrypt a ciphertext was. After this is determined, frequency analysis can be used to break each of the subkeys.

Kasiski Examination, Step 1 – Find Repeat Sequences' Spacings

The first part of Kasiski Examination is to find every repeated set of letters at least three letters long in the ciphertext. These are significant, because they could indicate that they were the same letters of plaintext encrypted with the same subkeys of the key. For example, if the ciphertext is "Ppqca xqvekg ybnkmazu ybngbal jon i tszm jyim. Vrag voht vrau c tksg. Ddwuo xitlazu vavv raz c vkb qp iwpou." and we remove the non-letters, the ciphertext looks like this:

```
PPQCAXQVEKGYBNKMAZUYBNGBALJONITSZMJYIMVRAGVOHTVRAUCTKSGDDWUOXITLA
ZUVAVVRAZCVKBQPIWPOU
```

You can see that the sequences VRA, AZU, and YBN repeat in this ciphertext:

PPQCAXQVEKGYBNKMAZUYBNGBALJONITSZMJYIM**VRA**GVOHT**VRA**UCTKSGDDWUOXITLA ZUVAV**VRA**ZCVKBQPIWPOU

PPQCAXQVEKGYBNKM**AZU**YBNGBALJONITSZMJYIMVRAGVOHTVRAUCTKSGDDWUOXITL**A** **ZU**VAVVRAZCVKBQPIWPOU

PPQCAXQVEKG**YBN**KMAZU**YBN**GBALJONITSZMJYIMVRAGVOHTVRAUCTKSGDDWUOXITLA ZUVAVVRAZCVKBQPIWPOU

After finding the repeated sequences, get a count of the spacing between the sequences. If we count the number of letters between the start of each of these sequences, we find that:

- Between the first and second VRA sequences there are 8 letters.
- Between the second and third VRA sequences there are 24 letters.
- Between the first and third VRA sequences there are 32 letters.
- Between the first and second AZU there are 48 letters.
- Between the first and second YBN there are 8 letters.

Kasiski Examination, Step 2 – Get Factors of Spacings

So the spacings are 8, 8, 24, 32, and 48. Let's find the factors of each of these numbers (not including one):

- The factors of 8 are 2, 4, and 8.
- The factors of 24 are 2, 4, 6, 8, 12, and 24.
- The factors of 32 are 2, 4, 8, and 16.
- The factors of 48 are 2, 4, 6, 8, 12, 24, and 48.

So the spacings of 8, 8, 24, 32, and 48 expand to this list of factors: 2, 2, 2, 2, 4, 4, 4, 4, 6, 6, 8, 8, 8, 8, 12, 12, 16, 24, 24, and 48. If we do a count of these factors, we get this:

Table 21-1. Factor count from our "Ppqca xqvekg..." example.

Factor	Count
2	Appears 4 times.
4	Appears 4 times.
6	Appears 2 times.
8	Appears 4 times.
12	Appears 2 times.
16	Appears 1 time.
24	Appears 2 times.
48	Appears 1 time.

The factors that have the highest count are the most likely lengths of the Vigenère key. In our example above, these are 2, 4, and 8. The Vigenère key is probably 2, 4, or 8 letters long.

Get Every Nth Letters from a String

For this example, we will guess that the key length is 4. Next we will want to split up the ciphertext into every 4th letter. This means we want the following underlined letters as a separate string:

Every 4th letter starting with the first letter:
PPQC**A**XQV**E**KGY**B**NKM**A**ZUY**B**NGB**A**LJO**N**ITS**Z**MJY**I**MVR**A**GVO**H**TVR**A**UCT**K**SGD**D**WUO**X**ITL**A**ZUV**A**VVR**A**ZCV**K**BQP**I**WPO**U**

Every 4th letter starting with the second letter:
P**P**QCA**X**QVE**K**GYB**N**KMA**Z**UYB**N**GBA**L**JON**I**TSZ**M**JYI**M**VRA**G**VOH**T**VRA**U**CTK**S**GDD**W**UOX**I**TLA**Z**UVA**V**VRA**Z**CVK**B**QPI**W**POU

Every 4th letter starting with the third letter:
PP**Q**CAX**Q**VEK**G**YBN**K**MAZ**U**YBN**G**BAL**J**ONI**T**SZM**J**YIM**V**RAG**V**OHT**V**RAU**C**TKS**G**DDW**U**OXI**T**LAZ**U**VAV**V**RAZ**C**VKB**Q**PIW**P**OU

Every 4th letter starting with the fourth lettter:
PPQ**C**AXQ**V**EKG**Y**BNK**M**AZU**Y**BNG**B**ALJ**O**NIT**S**ZMJ**Y**IMV**R**AGV**O**HTV**R**AUC**T**KSG**D**DWU**O**XIT**L**AZU**V**AVV**R**AZC**V**KBQ**P**IWP**O**U

When combined, they become these four strings:

Every 4th letter starting with the first letter:	PAEBABANZIAHAKDXAAAKIU
Every 4th letter starting with the second letter:	PXKNZNLIMMGTUSWIZVZBW
Every 4th letter starting with the third letter:	QQGKUGJTJVVVCGUTUVCQP
Every 4th letter starting with the fourth letter:	CVYMYBOSYRORTDOLVRVPO

If our guess from Kasiski Examination was correct and the decryption key was in fact 4 characters long, then the first subkey of the key would have been used to encrypt the characters in the first string above, the second subkey of the key would have been used to encrypt the characters in the second string above, and so on.

Frequency Analysis

Remember, the Vigenère cipher is the same as the Caesar cipher, except it uses multiple subkeys. Kasiski Examination tells us how many subkeys were used for the ciphertext, now we just have to hack each subkey one at a time. Let's try to hack the first of these four ciphertext strings: `PAEBABANZIAHAKDXAAAKIU`

We will decrypt this string 26 times, once for each of the 26 possible subkeys, and then see what English frequency match score the decrypted text has. In the table below, the first column is the subkey used to decrypt the `PAEBABANZIAHAKDXAAAKIU` string. The second column is the returned decrypted text value from `vigenereCipher.decryptMessage(subkey,`

'PAEBABANZIAHAKDXAAAKIU') where subkey is the subkey from the first column. The third column is the returned value from freqAnalysis.englishFreqMatchScore(decryptedText) where decryptedText is the value from the second column.

Table 21-2. English frequency match score for each decryption.

Subkey	Text When PAEB... is Decrypted with the Subkey	English Frequency Match Score
'A'	'PAEBABANZIAHAKDXAAAKIU'	2
'B'	'OZDAZAZMYHZGZJCWZZZJHT'	1
'C'	'NYCZYZYLXGYFYIBVYYYIGS'	1
'D'	'MXBYXYXKWFXEXHAUXXXHFR'	0
'E'	'LWAXWXWJVEWDWGZTWWWGEQ'	1
'F'	'KVZWVWVIUDVCVFYSVVVFDP'	0
'G'	'JUYVUVUHTCUBUEXRUUUECO'	1
'H'	'ITXUTUTGSBTATDWQTTTDBN'	1
'I'	'HSWTSTSFRASZSCVPSSSCAM'	2
'J'	'GRVSRSREQZRYRBUORRRBZL'	0
'K'	'FQURQRQDPYQXQATNQQQAYK'	1
'L'	'EPTQPQPCOXPWPZSMPPPZXJ'	0
'M'	'DOSPOPOBNWOVOYRLOOOYWI'	1
'N'	'CNRONONAMVNUNXQKNNNXVH'	2
'O'	'BMQNMNMZLUMTMWPJMMMWUG'	1
'P'	'ALPMLMLYKTLSLVOILLLVTF'	1
'Q'	'ZKOLKLKXJSKRKUNHKKKUSE'	0
'R'	'YJNKJKJWIRJQJTMGJJJTRD'	1
'S'	'XIMJIJIVHQIPISLFIIISQC'	1
'T'	'WHLIHIHUGPHOHRKEHHHRPB'	1
'U'	'VGKHGHGTFOGNGQJDGGGQOA'	1
'V'	'UFJGFGFSENFMFPICFFFPNZ'	1
'W'	'TEIFEFERDMELEOHBEEEOMY'	2
'X'	'SDHEDEDQCLDKDNGADDDNLX'	2
'Y'	'RCGDCDCPBKCJCMFZCCCMKW'	0
'Z'	'QBFCBCBOAJBIBLEYBBBLJV'	0

The subkeys that produce decryptions with the closest frequency match to English are the ones that are most likely to be the real subkey. In the above decryptions (for the 1st of the four ciphertext strings), `'A'`, `'I'`, `'N'`, `'W'`, and `'X'` are the subkeys that have the highest frequency matches with English. Note that these scores are low in general because there isn't enough ciphertext to give us a large sample of text, but it still ends up working well.

We need to repeat this 26-decryptions-and-frequency-match for the other three strings to find out their most likely subkeys. After this frequency analysis, we find:

The most likely subkeys for the first string are:	A, I, N, W, and X
The most likely subkeys for the second string are:	I and Z
The most likely subkey for the third string is:	C
The most likely subkeys for the fourth string are:	K, N, R, V, and Y

Brute-Force through the Possible Keys

Next we will brute-force the key by trying out every combination of subkey. Because there are 5 possible subkeys for the first subkey, 2 for the second subkey, 1 for the third subkey, and 5 for the fourth subkey, the number of combinations is 5 × 2 × 1 × 5 or 50 possible keys to brute-force through. This is much better than the 26 × 26 × 26 × 26 or 456,976 possible keys we would have to brute-force through if we had not narrowed the list of possible subkeys. This difference becomes even greater if the Vigenère key had been longer!

AICK	IICK	NICK	WICK	XICK
AICN	IICN	NICN	WICN	XICN
AICR	IICR	NICR	WICR	XICR
AICV	IICV	NICV	WICV	XICV
AICY	IICY	NICY	WICY	XICY
AZCK	IZCK	NZCK	WZCK	XZCK
AZCN	IZCN	NZCN	WZCN	XZCN
AZCR	IZCR	NZCR	WZCR	XZCR
AZCV	IZCV	NZCV	WZCV	XZCV
AZCY	IZCY	NZCY	WZCY	XZCY

Now it's just a matter of going through all 50 of these decryption keys for the full ciphertext and seeing which one produces a readable English plaintext. If you do this, you'll find that the key to the "Ppqca xqvekg…" ciphertext is "WICK".

Source Code for the Vigenère Hacking Program

Open a new file editor window by clicking on **File ► New Window**. Type in the following code into the file editor, and then save it as *vigenereHacker.py*. Press **F5** to run the program. Note that first you will need to download the *pyperclip.py* module and place this file in the same directory as the *vigenereHacker.py* file. You can download this file from http://invpy.com/pyperclip.py.

The ciphertext in this program may be difficult to copy from the book, but you can copy & paste it from http://invpy.com/vigenereHacking.py. You can see if there are any differences between the text in your program to the text of the program in this book by using the online diff tool at http://invpy.com/hackingdiff.

Source code for vigenereHacker.py

```
# Vigenere Cipher Hacker
# http://inventwithpython.com/hacking (BSD Licensed)

import itertools, re
import vigenereCipher, pyperclip, freqAnalysis, detectEnglish

LETTERS = 'ABCDEFGHIJKLMNOPQRSTUVWXYZ'
SILENT_MODE = False # if set to True, program doesn't print attempts
NUM_MOST_FREQ_LETTERS = 4 # attempts this many letters per subkey
MAX_KEY_LENGTH = 16 # will not attempt keys longer than this
NONLETTERS_PATTERN = re.compile('[^A-Z]')


def main():
    # Instead of typing this ciphertext out, you can copy & paste it
    # from http://invpy.com/vigenereHacker.py
    ciphertext = """Adiz Avtzqeci Tmzubb wsa m Pmilqev halpqavtakuoi,
lgouqdaf, kdmktsvmztsl, izr xoexghzr kkusitaaf. Vz wsa twbhdg ubalmmzhdad qz
hce vmhsgohuqbo ox kaakulmd gxiwvos, krgdurdny i rcmmstugvtawz ca tzm ocicwxfg
jf "stscmilpy" oid "uwydptsbuci" wabt hce Lcdwig eiovdnw. Bgfdny qe kddwtk
qjnkqpsmev ba pz tzm roohwz at xoexghzr kkusicw izr vrlqrwxist uboedtuuznum.
Pimifo Icmlv Emf DI, Lcdwig owdyzd xwd hce Ywhsmnemzh Xovm mby Cqxtsm Supacg
(GUKE) oo Bdmfqclwg Bomk, Tzuhvif'a ocyetzqofifo ositjm. Rcm a lqys ce oie vzav
wr Vpt 8, lpq gzclqab mekxabnittq tjr Ymdavn fihog cjgbhvnstkgds. Zm psqikmp o
iuejqf jf lmoviiicqg aoj jdsvkavs Uzreiz qdpzmdg, dnutgrdny bts helpar jf lpq
pjmtm, mb zlwkffjmwktoiiuix avczqzs ohsb ocplv nuby swbfwigk naf ohw Mzwbms
umqcifm. Mtoej bts raj pq kjrcmp oo tzm Zooigvmz Khqauqvl Dincmalwdm, rhwzq vz
cjmmhzd gvq ca tzm rwmsl lqgdgfa rcm a kbafzd-hzaumae kaakulmd, hce SKQ. Wi
1948 Tmzubb jgqzsy Msf Zsrmsv'e Qjmhcfwig Dincmalwdm vt Eizqcekbqf Pnadqfnilg,
ivzrw pq onsaafsy if bts yenmxckmwvf ca tzm Yoiczmehzr uwydptwze oid tmoohe
avfsmekbqr dn eifvzmsbuqvl tqazjgq. Pq kmolm m dvpwz ab ohw ktshiuix pvsaa at
hojxtcbefmewn, afl bfzdakfsy okkuzgalqzu xhwuuqvl jmmqoigve gpcz ie hce
```

```
Tmxcpsgd-Lvvbgbubnkq zqoxtawz, kciup isme xqdgo otaqfqev qz hce 1960k. Bgfdny'a
tchokmjivlabk fzsmtfsy if i ofdmavmz krgaqqptawz wi 1952, wzmz vjmgaqlpad iohn
wwzq goidt uzgeyix wi tzm Gbdtwl Wwigvwy. Vz aukqdoev bdsvtemzh rilp rshadm
tcmmgvqg (xhwuuqvl uiehmalqab) vs sv mzoejvmhdvw ba dmikwz. Hpravs rdev qz
1954, xpsl whsm tow iszkk jqtjrw pug 42id tqdhcdsg, rfjm ugmbddw xawnofqzu. Vn
avcizsl lqhzreqzsy tzif vds vmmhc wsa eidcalq; vds ewfvzr svp gjmw wfvzrk
jqzdenmp vds vmmhc wsa mqxivmzhvl. Gv 10 Esktwunsm 2009, fgtxcrifo mb Dnlmdbzt
uiydviyv, Nfdtaat Dmiem Ywiikbqf Bojlab Wrgez avdw iz cafakuog pmjxwx ahwxcby
gv nscadn at ohw Jdwoikp scqejvysit xwd "hce sxboglavs kvy zm ion tjmmhzd." Sa
at Haq 2012 i bfdvsbq azmtmd'g widt ion bwnafz tzm Tcpsw wr Zjrva ivdcz eaigd
yzmbo Tmzubb a kbmhptgzk dvrvwz wa efiohzd."""
    hackedMessage = hackVigenere(ciphertext)

    if hackedMessage != None:
        print('Copying hacked message to clipboard:')
        print(hackedMessage)
        pyperclip.copy(hackedMessage)
    else:
        print('Failed to hack encryption.')


def findRepeatSequencesSpacings(message):
    # Goes through the message and finds any 3 to 5 letter sequences
    # that are repeated. Returns a dict with the keys of the sequence and
    # values of a list of spacings (num of letters between the repeats).

    # Use a regular expression to remove non-letters from the message.
    message = NONLETTERS_PATTERN.sub('', message.upper())

    # Compile a list of seqLen-letter sequences found in the message.
    seqSpacings = {} # keys are sequences, values are list of int spacings
    for seqLen in range(3, 6):
        for seqStart in range(len(message) - seqLen):
            # Determine what the sequence is, and store it in seq
            seq = message[seqStart:seqStart + seqLen]

            # Look for this sequence in the rest of the message
            for i in range(seqStart + seqLen, len(message) - seqLen):
                if message[i:i + seqLen] == seq:
                    # Found a repeated sequence.
                    if seq not in seqSpacings:
                        seqSpacings[seq] = [] # initialize blank list

                    # Append the spacing distance between the repeated
                    # sequence and the original sequence.
                    seqSpacings[seq].append(i - seqStart)
    return seqSpacings
```

```
def getUsefulFactors(num):
    # Returns a list of useful factors of num. By "useful" we mean factors
    # less than MAX_KEY_LENGTH + 1. For example, getUsefulFactors(144)
    # returns [2, 72, 3, 48, 4, 36, 6, 24, 8, 18, 9, 16, 12]

    if num < 2:
        return [] # numbers less than 2 have no useful factors

    factors = [] # the list of factors found

    # When finding factors, you only need to check the integers up to
    # MAX_KEY_LENGTH.
    for i in range(2, MAX_KEY_LENGTH + 1): # don't test 1
        if num % i == 0:
            factors.append(i)
            factors.append(int(num / i))
    if 1 in factors:
        factors.remove(1)
    return list(set(factors))


def getItemAtIndexOne(x):
    return x[1]


def getMostCommonFactors(seqFactors):
    # First, get a count of how many times a factor occurs in seqFactors.
    factorCounts = {} # key is a factor, value is how often if occurs

    # seqFactors keys are sequences, values are lists of factors of the
    # spacings. seqFactors has a value like: {'GFD': [2, 3, 4, 6, 9, 12,
    # 18, 23, 36, 46, 69, 92, 138, 207], 'ALW': [2, 3, 4, 6, ...], ...}
    for seq in seqFactors:
        factorList = seqFactors[seq]
        for factor in factorList:
            if factor not in factorCounts:
                factorCounts[factor] = 0
            factorCounts[factor] += 1

    # Second, put the factor and its count into a tuple, and make a list
    # of these tuples so we can sort them.
    factorsByCount = []
    for factor in factorCounts:
        # exclude factors larger than MAX_KEY_LENGTH
```

```
        if factor <= MAX_KEY_LENGTH:
            # factorsByCount is a list of tuples: (factor, factorCount)
            # factorsByCount has a value like: [(3, 497), (2, 487), ...]
            factorsByCount.append( (factor, factorCounts[factor]) )

    # Sort the list by the factor count.
    factorsByCount.sort(key=getItemAtIndexOne, reverse=True)

    return factorsByCount


def kasiskiExamination(ciphertext):
    # Find out the sequences of 3 to 5 letters that occur multiple times
    # in the ciphertext. repeatedSeqSpacings has a value like:
    # {'EXG': [192], 'NAF': [339, 972, 633], ... }
    repeatedSeqSpacings = findRepeatSequencesSpacings(ciphertext)

    # See getMostCommonFactors() for a description of seqFactors.
    seqFactors = {}
    for seq in repeatedSeqSpacings:
        seqFactors[seq] = []
        for spacing in repeatedSeqSpacings[seq]:
            seqFactors[seq].extend(getUsefulFactors(spacing))

    # See getMostCommonFactors() for a description of factorsByCount.
    factorsByCount = getMostCommonFactors(seqFactors)

    # Now we extract the factor counts from factorsByCount and
    # put them in allLikelyKeyLengths so that they are easier to
    # use later.
    allLikelyKeyLengths = []
    for twoIntTuple in factorsByCount:
        allLikelyKeyLengths.append(twoIntTuple[0])

    return allLikelyKeyLengths


def getNthSubkeysLetters(n, keyLength, message):
    # Returns every Nth letter for each keyLength set of letters in text.
    # E.g. getNthSubkeysLetters(1, 3, 'ABCABCABC') returns 'AAA'
    #      getNthSubkeysLetters(2, 3, 'ABCABCABC') returns 'BBB'
    #      getNthSubkeysLetters(3, 3, 'ABCABCABC') returns 'CCC'
    #      getNthSubkeysLetters(1, 5, 'ABCDEFGHI') returns 'AF'

    # Use a regular expression to remove non-letters from the message.
    message = NONLETTERS_PATTERN.sub('', message)
```

```

    i = n - 1
    letters = []
    while i < len(message):
        letters.append(message[i])
        i += keyLength
    return ''.join(letters)


def attemptHackWithKeyLength(ciphertext, mostLikelyKeyLength):
    # Determine the most likely letters for each letter in the key.
    ciphertextUp = ciphertext.upper()
    # allFreqScores is a list of mostLikelyKeyLength number of lists.
    # These inner lists are the freqScores lists.
    allFreqScores = []
    for nth in range(1, mostLikelyKeyLength + 1):
        nthLetters = getNthSubkeysLetters(nth, mostLikelyKeyLength, ciphertextUp)

        # freqScores is a list of tuples like:
        # [(<letter>, <Eng. Freq. match score>), ... ]
        # List is sorted by match score. Higher score means better match.
        # See the englishFreqMatchScore() comments in freqAnalysis.py.
        freqScores = []
        for possibleKey in LETTERS:
            decryptedText = vigenereCipher.decryptMessage(possibleKey, nthLetters)
            keyAndFreqMatchTuple = (possibleKey, freqAnalysis.englishFreqMatchScore(decryptedText))
            freqScores.append(keyAndFreqMatchTuple)
        # Sort by match score
        freqScores.sort(key=getItemAtIndexOne, reverse=True)

        allFreqScores.append(freqScores[:NUM_MOST_FREQ_LETTERS])

    if not SILENT_MODE:
        for i in range(len(allFreqScores)):
            # use i + 1 so the first letter is not called the "0th" letter
            print('Possible letters for letter %s of the key: ' % (i + 1), end='')
            for freqScore in allFreqScores[i]:
                print('%s ' % freqScore[0], end='')
            print() # print a newline

    # Try every combination of the most likely letters for each position
    # in the key.
```

```
    for indexes in itertools.product(range(NUM_MOST_FREQ_LETTERS), repeat=mostLikelyKeyLength):
        # Create a possible key from the letters in allFreqScores
        possibleKey = ''
        for i in range(mostLikelyKeyLength):
            possibleKey += allFreqScores[i][indexes[i]][0]

        if not SILENT_MODE:
            print('Attempting with key: %s' % (possibleKey))

        decryptedText = vigenereCipher.decryptMessage(possibleKey, ciphertextUp)

        if detectEnglish.isEnglish(decryptedText):
            # Set the hacked ciphertext to the original casing.
            origCase = []
            for i in range(len(ciphertext)):
                if ciphertext[i].isupper():
                    origCase.append(decryptedText[i].upper())
                else:
                    origCase.append(decryptedText[i].lower())
            decryptedText = ''.join(origCase)

            # Check with user to see if the key has been found.
            print('Possible encryption hack with key %s:' % (possibleKey))
            print(decryptedText[:200]) # only show first 200 characters
            print()
            print('Enter D for done, or just press Enter to continue hacking:')
            response = input('> ')

            if response.strip().upper().startswith('D'):
                return decryptedText

    # No English-looking decryption found, so return None.
    return None


def hackVigenere(ciphertext):
    # First, we need to do Kasiski Examination to figure out what the
    # length of the ciphertext's encryption key is.
    allLikelyKeyLengths = kasiskiExamination(ciphertext)
    if not SILENT_MODE:
        keyLengthStr = ''
        for keyLength in allLikelyKeyLengths:
            keyLengthStr += '%s ' % (keyLength)
```

```
        print('Kasiski Examination results say the most likely key lengths are: ' + keyLengthStr + '\n')

    for keyLength in allLikelyKeyLengths:
        if not SILENT_MODE:
            print('Attempting hack with key length %s (%s possible keys)...' % (keyLength, NUM_MOST_FREQ_LETTERS ** keyLength))
        hackedMessage = attemptHackWithKeyLength(ciphertext, keyLength)
        if hackedMessage != None:
            break

    # If none of the key lengths we found using Kasiski Examination
    # worked, start brute-forcing through key lengths.
    if hackedMessage == None:
        if not SILENT_MODE:
            print('Unable to hack message with likely key length(s). Brute-forcing key length...')
        for keyLength in range(1, MAX_KEY_LENGTH + 1):
            # don't re-check key lengths already tried from Kasiski
            if keyLength not in allLikelyKeyLengths:
                if not SILENT_MODE:
                    print('Attempting hack with key length %s (%s possible keys)...' % (keyLength, NUM_MOST_FREQ_LETTERS ** keyLength))
                hackedMessage = attemptHackWithKeyLength(ciphertext, keyLength)
                if hackedMessage != None:
                    break
    return hackedMessage


# If vigenereHacker.py is run (instead of imported as a module) call
# the main() function.
if __name__ == '__main__':
    main()
```

Sample Run of the Vigenère Hacking Program

When you run the *vigenereHacker.py* program, the output will look like this:

```
Kasiski Examination results say the most likely key lengths are: 3 2 6 4 12

Attempting hack with key length 3 (27 possible keys)...
Possible letters for letter 1 of the key: A L M
Possible letters for letter 2 of the key: S N O
Possible letters for letter 3 of the key: V I Z
Attempting with key: ASV
```

```
Attempting with key: ASI
Attempting with key: ASZ
Attempting with key: ANV
Attempting with key: ANI
Attempting with key: ANZ
Attempting with key: AOV
Attempting with key: AOI
Attempting with key: AOZ
Attempting with key: LSV
Attempting with key: LSI
Attempting with key: LSZ
Attempting with key: LNV
Attempting with key: LNI
Attempting with key: LNZ
Attempting with key: LOV
Attempting with key: LOI
Attempting with key: LOZ
Attempting with key: MSV
Attempting with key: MSI
Attempting with key: MSZ
Attempting with key: MNV
Attempting with key: MNI
Attempting with key: MNZ
Attempting with key: MOV
Attempting with key: MOI
Attempting with key: MOZ
Attempting hack with key length 2 (9 possible keys)...
Possible letters for letter 1 of the key: O A E
Possible letters for letter 2 of the key: M S I
Attempting with key: OM
Attempting with key: OS
Attempting with key: OI
Attempting with key: AM
Attempting with key: AS
Attempting with key: AI
Attempting with key: EM
Attempting with key: ES
Attempting with key: EI
Attempting hack with key length 6 (729 possible keys)...
Possible letters for letter 1 of the key: A E O
Possible letters for letter 2 of the key: S D G
Possible letters for letter 3 of the key: I V X
Possible letters for letter 4 of the key: M Z Q
Possible letters for letter 5 of the key: O B Z
Possible letters for letter 6 of the key: V I K
Attempting with key: ASIMOV
```

```
Possible encryption hack with key ASIMOV:
ALAN MATHISON TURING WAS A BRITISH MATHEMATICIAN, LOGICIAN, CRYPTANALYST, AND
COMPUTER SCIENTIST. HE WAS HIGHLY INFLUENTIAL IN THE DEVELOPMENT OF COMPUTER
SCIENCE, PROVIDING A FORMALISATION OF THE CON

Enter D for done, or just press Enter to continue hacking:
> d
Copying hacked message to clipboard:
Alan Mathison Turing was a British mathematician, logician, cryptanalyst, and
computer scientist. He was highly influential in the development of computer

    ...skipped for brevity...

his death was accidental. On 10 September 2009, following an Internet campaign,
British Prime Minister Gordon Brown made an official public apology on behalf
of the British government for "the appalling way he was treated." As of May
2012 a private member's bill was before the House of Lords which would grant
Turing a statutory pardon if enacted.
```

How the Program Works

vigenereHacker.py

```
# Vigenere Cipher Hacker
# http://inventwithpython.com/hacking (BSD Licensed)

import itertools, re
import vigenereCipher, pyperclip, freqAnalysis, detectEnglish

LETTERS = 'ABCDEFGHIJKLMNOPQRSTUVWXYZ'
SILENT_MODE = False # if set to True, program doesn't print attempts
NUM_MOST_FREQ_LETTERS = 4 # attempts this many letters per subkey
MAX_KEY_LENGTH = 16 # will not attempt keys longer than this
NONLETTERS_PATTERN = re.compile('[^A-Z]')
```

The hacking program imports many different modules, including a new module named `itertools`. The constants will be explained as they are used in the program.

vigenereHacker.py

```
def main():
    # Instead of typing this ciphertext out, you can copy & paste it
    # from http://invpy.com/vigenereHacker.py
    ciphertext = """Adiz Avtzqeci Tmzubb wsa m Pmilqev halpqavtakuoi,
lgouqdaf, kdmktsvmztsl, izr xoexghzr kkusitaaf. Vz wsa twbhdg ubalmmzhdad qz

        ...skipped for brevity...
```

```
at Haq 2012 i bfdvsbq azmtmd'g widt ion bwnafz tzm Tcpsw wr Zjrva ivdcz eaigd yzmbo Tmzubb a kbmhptgzk dvrvwz wa efiohzd."""
    hackedMessage = hackVigenere(ciphertext)

    if hackedMessage != None:
        print('Copying hacked message to clipboard:')
        print(hackedMessage)
        pyperclip.copy(hackedMessage)
    else:
        print('Failed to hack encryption.')
```

The `main()` function of the hacking program is similar to the `main()` functions of previous hacking functions. The ciphertext is passed to the `hackVigenere()` cipher, which either returns the decrypted string (if the hack was successful) or the `None` value (if the hack failed). If successful, the hacked message is printed to the screen and copied to the clipboard.

Finding Repeated Sequences

vigenereHacker.py

```
28. def findRepeatSequencesSpacings(message):
29.     # Goes through the message and finds any 3 to 5 letter sequences
30.     # that are repeated. Returns a dict with the keys of the sequence and
31.     # values of a list of spacings (num of letters between the repeats).
32.
33.     # Use a regular expression to remove non-letters from the message.
34.     message = NONLETTERS_PATTERN.sub('', message.upper())
35.
36.     # Compile a list of seqLen-letter sequences found in the message.
37.     seqSpacings = {} # keys are sequences, values are list of int spacings
38.     for seqLen in range(3, 6):
```

The `findRepeatSequencesSpacings()` locates all the repeated sequences of letters in the `message` string and counts the spacings (that is, the number of letters) between the sequences. First, line 34 converts the message to uppercase and removes any non-letter characters from `message` using the `sub()` regular expression method.

The `seqSpacings` dictionary will have keys of the sequence strings and values of a list with the integer number of letters between all the occurrences of that sequence in the key. The previous "PPQCAXQV…" example string from earlier in the "Kasiski Examination, Step 1" section, if passed as `message`, would cause `findRepeatSequenceSpacings()` to return `{'VRA': [8, 24, 32], 'AZU': [48], 'YBN': [8]}`.

The code inside line 38's `for` loop will find the repeated sequences in `message` and calculate the spacings. On the first iteration, it will find sequences that are exactly 3 letters long. On the next iteration it will find sequences exactly 4 letters long, and then 5 letters long. (You can change what sequence lengths the code searches for by modifying the `range(3, 6)` call on line 38, but finding repeated sequences of length 3, 4 and 5 seems to work for most ciphertexts.)

vigenereHacker.py

```
39.         for seqStart in range(len(message) - seqLen):
40.             # Determine what the sequence is, and store it in seq
41.             seq = message[seqStart:seqStart + seqLen]
```

The `for` loop on line 39 makes sure that we iterate over every possible substring of length `seqLen` in the `message` string. Line 41 sets the `seq` variable with the sequence we are looking for. For example, if `seqLen` is `3` and message is `'PPQCAXQ'`, we would want to search for the following sequences (notice the indexes at the top of the `'PPQCAXQ'` string):

Table 21-3. Values of `seq` from `message` depending on the value in `seqStart`.

Indexes:	0123456	
On 1st iteration, `seqStart` is `0`:	`'PPQCAXQ'`	(PPQ starts at index `0`.)
On 2nd iteration, `seqStart` is `1`:	`'PPQCAXQ'`	(PQC starts at index `1`.)
On 3rd iteration, `seqStart` is `2`:	`'PPQCAXQ'`	(QCA starts at index `2`.)
On 4th iteration, `seqStart` is `3`:	`'PPQCAXQ'`	(CAX starts at index `3`.)
On 5th iteration, `seqStart` is `4`:	`'PPQCAXQ'`	(AXQ starts at index `4`, which is what `len(message) - seqLen` evaluates to and is the last index.)

vigenereHacker.py

```
43.             # Look for this sequence in the rest of the message
44.             for i in range(seqStart + seqLen, len(message) - seqLen):
45.                 if message[i:i + seqLen] == seq:
```

The `for` loop on line 44 is inside line 39's `for` loop and sets `i` to be the indexes of every possible sequence of length `seqLen` in `message`. These indexes start at `seqStart + seqLen` (that is, after the sequence currently in `seq`) and go up to `len(message) - seqLen` (which is the last index where a sequence of length `seqLen` can be found).

The expression `message[i:i + seqLen]` will evaluate to the substring of `message` that gets checked for being a repeat of `seq` on line 45. If it is, then we need to calculate the spacing and add it to the `seqSpacings` dictionary. This is done on lines 46 to 52.

vigenereHacker.py
```
46.                     # Found a repeated sequence.
47.                     if seq not in seqSpacings:
48.                         seqSpacings[seq] = [] # initialize blank list
49.
50.                     # Append the spacing distance between the repeated
51.                     # sequence and the original sequence.
52.                     seqSpacings[seq].append(i - seqStart)
```

The spacing between the sequence we've found at `message[i:i + seqLen]` and the original sequence at `message[seqStart:seqStart+seqLen]` is simply `i - seqStart`. Notice that `i` and `seqStart` are the beginning indexes before the colons. So the integer that `i - seqStart` evaluates to is the spacing between the two sequences, which is appended to the list stored at `seqSpacings[seq]`.

(Lines 47 and 48 guarantee there is a list at this key by checking beforehand if `seq` exists as a key in `seqSpacings`. If it does not, then `seqSpacings[seq]` is set as a key with a blank list as its value.)

vigenereHacker.py
```
53.     return seqSpacings
```

By the time all these `for` loops have finished, the `seqSpacings` dictionary will contain every repeated sequence of length 3, 4, and 5 and their spacings. This dictionary is returned from `findRepeatSequencesSpacings()` on line 53.

Calculating Factors

vigenereHacker.py
```
56. def getUsefulFactors(num):
57.     # Returns a list of useful factors of num. By "useful" we mean factors
58.     # less than MAX_KEY_LENGTH + 1. For example, getUsefulFactors(144)
59.     # returns [2, 72, 3, 48, 4, 36, 6, 24, 8, 18, 9, 16, 12]
60.
61.     if num < 2:
62.         return [] # numbers less than 2 have no useful factors
63.
64.     factors = [] # the list of factors found
```

The only useful factors for the hacking program's Kasiski Examination code are of length `MAX_KEY_LENGTH` and under, not including `1`. The `getUsefulFactors()` takes a `num` parameter and returns a list of "useful" factors. The function does not necessarily return all the factors of `num` in this list.

Line 61 checks for the special case where `num` is less than `2`. In this case, line 62 returns the empty list because these numbers have no useful factors.

vigenereHacker.py

```
66.     # When finding factors, you only need to check the integers up to
67.     # MAX_KEY_LENGTH.
68.     for i in range(2, MAX_KEY_LENGTH + 1): # don't test 1
69.         if num % i == 0:
70.             factors.append(i)
71.             factors.append(int(num / i))
```

The `for` loop on line 68 loops through the integers `2` up to `MAX_KEY_LENGTH` (including the value in `MAX_KEY_LENGTH` itself, since the second argument to `range()` is `MAX_KEY_LENGTH + 1`).

If `num % i` is equal to `0`, then we know that `i` evenly divides (that is, has `0` remainder) `num` and is a factor of `num`. In this case, line 70 appends `i` to the list of factors in the `factors` variable. Line 71 also appends `num / i` (after converting it from a float to an int, since the `/` operator always evaluates to a float value).

vigenereHacker.py

```
72.     if 1 in factors:
73.         factors.remove(1)
```

The value `1` is not a useful factor, so we remove it from the `factors` list. (If the Vigenère key had a length of 1, the Vigenère cipher would be no different from the Caesar cipher!)

Removing Duplicates with the set() Function

vigenereHacker.py

```
74.     return list(set(factors))
```

The `factors` list might contain duplicates. For example, if `getUsefulFactors()` was passed `9` for the `num` parameter, then `9 % 3 == 0` would be `True` and both `i` and `int(num / i)` (both of which evaluate to `3`) would have been appended to `factors`. But we don't want duplicate numbers to appear in our `factors` list.

Line 74 passes the list value in `factors` to `set()` which returns a set form of the list. The set data type is similar to the list data type, except a set value can only contain unique values. You can pass a list value to the `set()` function and it will return a set value form of the list. This set value will not have any duplicate values in it. If you pass this set value to `list()`, it will return a list value version of the set. This is how line 74 removes duplicate values from the factors list. Try typing the following into the interactive shell:

```
>>> set([1, 2, 3, 3, 4])
set([1, 2, 3, 4])
>>> spam = list(set([2, 2, 2, 'cats', 2, 2]))
>>> spam
[2, 'cats']
>>>
```

This `list(set(factors))` code is an easy way to remove duplicate factors from the `factors` list. The final list value is then returned from the function.

vigenereHacker.py

```
77. def getItemAtIndexOne(x):
78.     return x[1]
```

The `getItemAtIndexOne()` is almost identical to `getItemAtIndexZero()` from the *freqAnalysis.py* program in the previous chapter. This function is passed to `sort()` to sort based on the item at index `1` of the items being sorted. (See the "The Program's `getItemAtIndexZero()` Function" section in Chapter 20.)

vigenereHacker.py

```
81. def getMostCommonFactors(seqFactors):
82.     # First, get a count of how many times a factor occurs in seqFactors.
83.     factorCounts = {} # key is a factor, value is how often if occurs
84.
85.     # seqFactors keys are sequences, values are lists of factors of the
86.     # spacings. seqFactors has a value like: {'GFD': [2, 3, 4, 6, 9, 12,
87.     # 18, 23, 36, 46, 69, 92, 138, 207], 'ALW': [2, 3, 4, 6, ...], ...}
```

Remember, we need to know the most common factor of the sequence spacings as a part of the Kasiski Examination because the most common factor is most likely going to be the length of the Vigenère key.

The `seqFactors` parameter is a dictionary value created in the `kasiskiExamination()` function, which is explained later. This dictionary has strings of sequences for keys and a list of integer factors for the value of each key. (These are factors of the spacing integers found by `findRepeatSequencesSpacings()`.) For example, `seqFactors` could contain a dictionary value like `{'VRA': [8, 2, 4, 2, 3, 4, 6, 8, 12, 16, 8, 2, 4], 'AZU': [2, 3, 4, 6, 8, 12, 16, 24], 'YBN': [8, 2, 4]}`.

The `getMostCommonFactors()` function will find the most common factors in `seqFactors` and return a list of two-integer tuples. The first integer in the tuple will be the factor and the second integer will be how many times it was in `seqFactors`.

For example, `getMostCommonFactors()` may return a list value such as `[(3, 556), (2, 541), (6, 529), (4, 331), (12, 325), (8, 171), (9, 156), (16, 105), (5, 98), (11, 86), (10, 84), (15, 84), (7, 83), (14, 68), (13, 52)]`. This means that in the `seqFactors` dictionary passed to `getMostCommonFactors()`, the factor 3 showed up 556 times, the factor 2 showed up 541 times, the factor 5 showed up 529 times, and so on. Note that 3 is the most frequent factor in the list and appears first in the list. 13 is the least frequent factor and is last in the list.

vigenereHacker.py

```
 88.     for seq in seqFactors:
 89.         factorList = seqFactors[seq]
 90.         for factor in factorList:
 91.             if factor not in factorCounts:
 92.                 factorCounts[factor] = 0
 93.             factorCounts[factor] += 1
```

For the first step of `getMostCommonFactors()` the `for` loop on line 88 loops over every sequence in `seqFactors`, storing it in a variable named `seq` on each iteration. The list of factors in `seqFactors` for `seq` is stored in a variable named `factorList` on line 89.

The factors in this list are looped over with a `for` loop on line 90. If a factor does not exist as a key in `factorCounts`, it is added on line 92 with a value of `0`. On line 93, `factorCounts[factor]` (that is, the factor's value in `factorCounts`) is incremented.

vigenereHacker.py

```
 95.     # Second, put the factor and its count into a tuple, and make a list
 96.     # of these tuples so we can sort them.
 97.     factorsByCount = []
 98.     for factor in factorCounts:
 99.         # exclude factors larger than MAX_KEY_LENGTH
100.         if factor <= MAX_KEY_LENGTH:
101.             # factorsByCount is a list of tuples: (factor, factorCount)
102.             # factorsByCount has a value like: [(3, 497), (2, 487), ...]
103.             factorsByCount.append( (factor, factorCounts[factor]) )
```

For the second step of `getMostCommonFactors()`, we need to sort the values in the `factorCounts` dictionary by their count. But dictionaries do not have an order, so we must first convert the dictionary into a list of two-integer tuples. (We did something similar in Chapter

20 in the `getFrequencyOrder()` function of the *freqAnalaysis.py* module.) This list value will be stored in a variable named `factorsByCount`, which starts as an empty list on line 97.

The `for` loop on line 98 goes through each of the factors in `factorCounts` and appends this `(factor, factorCounts[factor])` tuple to the `factorsByCount` list as long as the factor is less than or equal to `MAX_KEY_LENGTH`.

vigenereHacker.py

```
105.     # Sort the list by the factor count.
106.     factorsByCount.sort(key=getItemAtIndexOne, reverse=True)
107.
108.     return factorsByCount
```

After the `for` loop finishes adding all the tuples to `factorsByCount`, the last step of `getMostCommonFactors()` is that the `factorsByCount` list is sorted on line 106. Because the `getItemAtIndexOne` function is passed for the `key` keyword argument and `True` is passed for the `reverse` keyword argument, the list is sorted in descending order by the factor counts.

After being sorted, the list in `factorsByCount` is returned on line 108.

The Kasiski Examination Algorithm

vigenereHacker.py

```
def kasiskiExamination(ciphertext):
    # Find out the sequences of 3 to 5 letters that occur multiple times
    # in the ciphertext. repeatedSeqSpacings has a value like:
    # {'EXG': [192], 'NAF': [339, 972, 633], ... }
    repeatedSeqSpacings = findRepeatSequencesSpacings(ciphertext)
```

The `kasiskiExamination()` function returns a list of the most likely key lengths for the given `ciphertext` argument. The key lengths are integers in a list, with the first integer in the list being the most likely key length, the second integer the second most likely, and so on.

The first step is to find the spacings between repeated sequences in the ciphertext. This is returned from `findRepeatSequencesSpacings()` as a dictionary with keys of the sequence strings and values of a list with the spacings as integers.

The `extend()` List Method

The `extend()` list method is very similar to the `append()` list method. While the `append()` method adds a single value passed to it to the end of the list, the `extend()` method will add every item in a list argument to the end of the list. Try typing the following into the interactive shell:

```
>>> spam = []
>>> eggs = ['cat', 'dog', 'mouse']
>>> spam.extend(eggs)
>>> spam
['cat', 'dog', 'mouse']
>>> spam.extend([1, 2, 3])
>>> spam
['cat', 'dog', 'mouse', 1, 2, 3]
>>>
```

Notice the difference if you pass a list to the `append()` list method. The *list itself* gets appended to the end instead of the values in the list:

```
>>> spam = []
>>> eggs = ['cat', 'dog', 'mouse']
>>> spam.append(eggs)
>>> spam
[['cat', 'dog', 'mouse']]
>>> spam.append([1, 2, 3])
>>> spam
[['cat', 'dog', 'mouse'], [1, 2, 3]]
>>>
```

vigenereHacker.py

```
117.     # See getMostCommonFactors() for a description of seqFactors.
118.     seqFactors = {}
119.     for seq in repeatedSeqSpacings:
120.         seqFactors[seq] = []
121.         for spacing in repeatedSeqSpacings[seq]:
122.             seqFactors[seq].extend(getUsefulFactors(spacing))
```

While `repeatedSeqSpacings` is a dictionary that maps sequence strings to lists of integer spacings, we actually need a dictionary that maps sequence strings to lists of factors of those integer spacings. Lines 118 to 122 do this.

Line 118 starts with an empty dictionary in `seqFactors`. The `for` loop on line 119 iterates over every key (which is a sequence string) in `repeatedSeqSpacings`. For each key, line 120 sets a blank list to be the value in `seqFactors`.

The `for` loop on line 121 iterates over all the spacing integers, which are each passed to a `getUsefulFactors()` call. The list returned from `getUsefulFactors()` has each of its items appended to `seqFactors[seq]`.

When all the `for` loops are finished, `seqFactors` is a dictionary that maps sequence strings to lists of factors of integer spacings.

vigenereHacker.py

```
123.     # See getMostCommonFactors() for a description of factorsByCount.
124.     factorsByCount = getMostCommonFactors(seqFactors)
```

The `seqFactors` dictionary is passed to `getMostCommonFactors()` on line 124. A list of two-integer tuples (the first integer in the tuple being the factor, the second integer being the count of how often that factor appeared in `seqFactors`) is returned and stored in `factorsByCount`.

vigenereHacker.py

```
126.     # Now we extract the factor counts from factorsByCount and
127.     # put them in allLikelyKeyLengths so that they are easier to
128.     # use later.
129.     allLikelyKeyLengths = []
130.     for twoIntTuple in factorsByCount:
131.         allLikelyKeyLengths.append(twoIntTuple[0])
132.
133.     return allLikelyKeyLengths
```

The `kasiskiExamination()` function doesn't return a list of two-integer tuples though, it returns a list of integer factors. These integer factors are in the first item of the two-integer tuples list in `factorsByCount`, so we need code to pull these integer factors out and put them in a separate list.

This separate list will be stored in `allLikelyKeyLengths`, which to begin with is set to an empty list on line 129. The `for` loop on line 130 iterates over each of the tuples in `factorsByCount`, and appends the tuple's index `0` item to the end of `allLikelyKeyLengths`.

After this `for` loop completes, the `allLikelyKeyLengths` variable contains all the factor integers that were in `factorsByCount`. This list is returned from `kasiskiExamination()`.

vigenereHacker.py

```
137. def getNthSubkeysLetters(n, keyLength, message):
138.     # Returns every Nth letter for each keyLength set of letters in text.
```

```
139.     # E.g. getNthSubkeysLetters(1, 3, 'ABCABCABC') returns 'AAA'
140.     #      getNthSubkeysLetters(2, 3, 'ABCABCABC') returns 'BBB'
141.     #      getNthSubkeysLetters(3, 3, 'ABCABCABC') returns 'CCC'
142.     #      getNthSubkeysLetters(1, 5, 'ABCDEFGHI') returns 'AF'
143.
144.     # Use a regular expression to remove non-letters from the message.
145.     message = NONLETTERS_PATTERN.sub('', message)
```

In order to pull out the letters from a ciphertext that were encrypted with the same subkey, we need a function that can create a string for the 1st, 2nd, or "N th" subkey's letters from a message. The first part of getting these letters is to remove the non-letter characters from `message` using a regular expression object and its `sub()` method on line 145. (Regular expressions were first discussed in Chapter 18's "A Brief Intro to Regular Expressions and the sub() Regex Method".) This letters-only string is stored as the new value in `message`.

vigenereHacker.py

```
147.     i = n - 1
148.     letters = []
149.     while i < len(message):
150.         letters.append(message[i])
151.         i += keyLength
152.     return ''.join(letters)
```

Next we will build up a string by appending the letter strings to a list and using the `join()` list method to create the final string value. This approach executes much faster than string concatenation with the + operator. (This approach was first discussed in Chapter 18's "Building Strings in Python with Lists" section.)

The `i` variable will point to the index of the letter in `message` that we want to append to our string-building list. This list is stored in a variable named `letters`. The `i` variable starts with the value `n - 1` on line 147 and the `letters` variable starts with a blank list on line 148.

The `while` loop on line 149 keeps looping while `i` is less than the length of `message`. On each iteration the letter at `message[i]` is appended to the list in `letters`. Then `i` is updated to point to the next of the subkey's letters by adding `keyLength` to `i` on line 151.

After this loop finishes, the code on line 152 joins the single-letter string values in the `letters` list together to form a single string, and this string is returned from `getNthSubkeysLetters()`.

vigenereHacker.py
```
def attemptHackWithKeyLength(ciphertext, mostLikelyKeyLength):
    # Determine the most likely letters for each letter in the key.
    ciphertextUp = ciphertext.upper()
```

Recall that our `kasiskiExamination()` function isn't guaranteed to return the one true integer length of the Vigenère key, but rather the function returns a list of several lengths sorted in order of most likely to be the key length. If our code has guessed the wrong key length, then it will have to try again with a different key length. The `attemptHackWithKeyLength()` function is passed the ciphertext and the key length guess. If successful, this function returns a string of the hacked message. If the hacking fails, the function returns `None`.

The hacking code works on uppercase letters but the original string will also be needed, so the uppercase form of the `ciphertext` string will be stored in a separate variable named `ciphertextUp`.

vigenereHacker.py
```
158.     # allFreqScores is a list of mostLikelyKeyLength number of lists.
159.     # These inner lists are the freqScores lists.
160.     allFreqScores = []
161.     for nth in range(1, mostLikelyKeyLength + 1):
162.         nthLetters = getNthSubkeysLetters(nth, mostLikelyKeyLength,
ciphertextUp)
```

If we assume the value in the `mostLikelyKeyLength` is the correct key length, the hack algorithm calls `getNthSubkeysLetters()` for each subkey and then brute-forces through the 26 possible letters for each subkey to find the one that produces decrypted text whose letter frequency closest matches the letter frequency of English.

First, an empty list is stored in `allFreqScores` on line 160. What this list stores will be explained a little later.

The `for` loop on line 161 sets the `nth` variable to each integer from `1` to the `mostLikelyKeyLength` value. (Remember, that when `range()` is passed two arguments, the range goes up to, but not including, the second argument. The `+ 1` is put into the code so that the integer value in `mostLikelyKeyLength` itself is included in the range object returned.)

The letters of the Nth subkey are returned from `getNthSubkeysLetters()` on line 162.

vigenereHacker.py
```
        # freqScores is a list of tuples like:
        # [(<letter>, <Eng. Freq. match score>), ... ]
        # List is sorted by match score. Higher score means better match.
```

```
167.         # See the englishFreqMatchScore() comments in freqAnalysis.py.
168.         freqScores = []
169.         for possibleKey in LETTERS:
170.             decryptedText = vigenereCipher.decryptMessage(possibleKey,
nthLetters)
171.             keyAndFreqMatchTuple = (possibleKey,
freqAnalysis.englishFreqMatchScore(decryptedText))
172.             freqScores.append(keyAndFreqMatchTuple)
```

Next, a list of English frequency match scores is stored in a list in a variable named `freqScores`. This variable starts as an empty list on line 168 and then the `for` loop on line 169 loops through each of the 26 uppercase letter from the `LETTERS` string. The `possibleKey` value is used to decrypt the ciphertext by calling `vigenereCipher.decryptMessage()` on line 170. The subkey in `possibleKey` is only one letter, but the string in `nthLetters` is made up of only the letters from `message` that would have been encrypted with that subkey if we've guessed the key length correctly.

The decrypted text is then passed to `freqAnalysis.englishFreqMatchScore()` to see how closely the frequency of the letters in `decryptedText` matches the letter frequency of regular English. (Remember from the last chapter that the return value will be an integer between `0` and `12`, with a higher number meaning a closer match.)

This frequency match score, along with the key used to decrypt, are put into a tuple that is stored in a variable named `keyAndFreqMatchTuple` on line 171. This tuple is appended to the end of `freqScores` on line 172.

vigenereHacker.py

```
173.         # Sort by match score
174.         freqScores.sort(key=getItemAtIndexOne, reverse=True)
```

After the `for` loop on line 169 completes, the `freqScores` list will contain 26 key-and-frequency-match-score tuples: one tuple for each of the 26 subkeys. We need to sort this so that the tuples with the largest English frequency match scores are first in the list.

This means that we want to sort by the value at index `1` of the tuples in `freqScores` and in reverse (that is, descending) order. We call the `sort()` method on the `freqScores` list, *passing the function value* `getItemAtIndexOne` (not *calling the function*: note the lack of parentheses) for the `key` keyword argument. The value `True` is passed for the `reverse` keyword argument to sort in reverse (that is, descending) order.

vigenereHacker.py
```
        allFreqScores.append(freqScores[:NUM_MOST_FREQ_LETTERS])
```

The `NUM_MOST_FREQ_LETTERS` constant was set to the integer value `3` on line 9. Once the tuples in `freqScores` are sorted, a list containing only the *first* 3 tuples (that is, the tuples with the three *highest* English frequency match scores) is appended to `allFreqScores`.

After the `for` loop on line 161 completes, `allFreqScores` will contain a number of list values equal to the integer value in `mostLikelyKeyLength`. (For example, since `mostLikelyKeyLength` was `3`, `allFreqScores` would be a list of three lists.) The *first list value* will hold the tuples for the top three highest matching subkeys for the *first subkey* of the full Vigenère key. The *second list value* will hold the tuples for the top three highest matching subkeys for the *second subkey* of the full Vigenère key, and so on.

Originally, if we wanted to brute-force through the full Vigenère key, there would be (26 ^ key length) number of possible keys. For example, if the key was ROSEBUD (with a length of 7) there would be 26 ^ 7 (that is, 8,031,810,176) possible keys.

But by checking the English frequency matching, we've narrowed it down to the 4 most likely letters for each subkey, meaning that there are now only (4 ^ key length) possible keys. Using the example of ROSEBUD (with a length of 7) for a Vigenère key, now we only need to check 4 ^ 7 (that is, 16,384) possible keys. This is a huge improvement over 8 billion!

The `end` Keyword Argument for `print()`

vigenereHacker.py
```
178.     if not SILENT_MODE:
179.         for i in range(len(allFreqScores)):
180.             # use i + 1 so the first letter is not called the "0th" letter
181.             print('Possible letters for letter %s of the key: ' % (i + 1), end='')
182.             for freqScore in allFreqScores[i]:
183.                 print('%s ' % freqScore[0], end='')
184.             print() # print a newline
```

At this point, the user might want to know which letters are in the top three most likely list for each subkey. If the `SILENT_MODE` constant was set to `False`, then the code on lines 178 to 184 will print out the values in `allFreqScores` to the screen.

Whenever the `print()` function is called, it will print the string passed to it on the screen along with a newline character. If we want something else printed at the end of the string instead of a newline character, we can specify the string for the `print()` function's `end` keyword argument. Try typing the following into the interactive shell:

```
>>> print('HEllo', end='\n')
HEllo
>>> print('Hello', end='\n')
Hello
>>> print('Hello', end='')
Hello>>> print('Hello', end='XYZ')
HelloXYZ>>>
```

(The above was typed into the *python.exe* interactive shell rather than IDLE. IDLE will always add a newline character before printing the >>> prompt.)

The `itertools.product()` Function

The `itertools.product()` function produces every possible combination of items in a list or list-like value, such as a string or tuple. (Though the `itertools.product()` function returns a "itertools product" object value, this can be converted to a list by passing it to `list()`.) This combination of things is called a **Cartesian product**, which is where the function gets its name. Try typing the following into the interactive shell:

```
>>> import itertools
>>> itertools.product('ABC', repeat=4)
<itertools.product object at 0x02C40170>
>>> list(itertools.product('ABC', repeat=4))
[('A', 'A', 'A', 'A'), ('A', 'A', 'A', 'B'), ('A', 'A', 'A', 'C'), ('A', 'A',
'B', 'A'), ('A', 'A', 'B', 'B'), ('A', 'A', 'B', 'C'), ('A', 'A', 'C', 'A'),
('A', 'A', 'C', 'B'), ('A', 'A', 'C', 'C'), ('A', 'B', 'A', 'A'), ('A', 'B',
'A', 'B'), ('A', 'B', 'A', 'C'), ('A', 'B', 'B', 'A'), ('A', 'B', 'B', 'B'),
   ...skipped for brevity...
('C', 'B', 'C', 'B'), ('C', 'B', 'C', 'C'), ('C', 'C', 'A', 'A'), ('C', 'C',
'A', 'B'), ('C', 'C', 'A', 'C'), ('C', 'C', 'B', 'A'), ('C', 'C', 'B', 'B'),
('C', 'C', 'B', 'C'), ('C', 'C', 'C', 'A'), ('C', 'C', 'C', 'B'), ('C', 'C',
'C', 'C')]
```

As you can see, by passing `'ABC'` and the integer `4` for the `repeat` keyword argument, `itertools.product()` returns an "itertools product" object that, when converted to a list, has tuples of four values with every possible combination of `'A'`, `'B'`, and `'C'`. (This results in a list with a total of 3 ^ 4 or 81 tuples in it.)

Since range objects returned from `range()` are also list-like, they can be passed to `itertools.product()` as well. Try typing the following into the interactive shell:

```
>>> import itertools
>>> list(itertools.product(range(8), repeat=5))
[(0, 0, 0, 0, 0), (0, 0, 0, 0, 1), (0, 0, 0, 0, 2), (0, 0, 0, 0, 3), (0, 0, 0,
0, 4), (0, 0, 0, 0, 5), (0, 0, 0, 0, 6), (0, 0, 0, 0, 7), (0, 0, 0, 1, 0), (0,
0, 0, 1, 1), (0, 0, 0, 1, 2), (0, 0, 0, 1, 3), (0, 0, 0, 1, 4),
    ...skipped for brevity...
(7, 7, 7, 6, 6), (7, 7, 7, 6, 7), (7, 7, 7, 7, 0), (7, 7, 7, 7, 1), (7, 7, 7,
7, 2), (7, 7, 7, 7, 3), (7, 7, 7, 7, 4), (7, 7, 7, 7, 5), (7, 7, 7, 7, 6), (7,
7, 7, 7, 7)]
```

When the range object returned from `range(8)` is passed to `itertools.product()` (along with `5` for the `repeat` keyword argument), the list that is generated has tuples of 5 values, and each value are from the integers `0` to `7`.

The `itertools.product()` function is an easy way to generate a list with every possible combination of some group of values. This is how our hacking program will create integer indexes to test every possible combination of possible subkeys.

vigenereHacker.py

```
    # Try every combination of the most likely letters for each position
    # in the key.
    for indexes in itertools.product(range(NUM_MOST_FREQ_LETTERS),
repeat=mostLikelyKeyLength):
```

The `allFreqScores` variable is a list of lists of tuples such that `allFreqScores[i]` will evaluate to a list of tuples of possible letters for a single subkey. That is, `allFreqScores[0]` has a list of tuples for the first subkey, `allFreqScores[1]` has a list of tuples for the second subkey, and so on.

Also, since the `NUM_MOST_FREQ_LETTERS` constant is set to `4`, `itertools.product(range(NUM_MOST_FREQ_LETTERS), repeat=mostLikelyKeyLength)` will cause the `for` loop to have a tuple of integers (from `0` to `3`) for the `indexes` variable. If `5` was passed for `mostLikelyKeyLength`, then the following values would be set to `indexes` for each iteration:

Table 21-4. Value of `indexes` on each iteration.

On the 1st iteration, `indexes` is set to:	`(0, 0, 0, 0, 0)`
On the 2nd iteration, `indexes` is set to:	`(0, 0, 0, 0, 1)`
On the 3rd iteration, `indexes` is set to:	`(0, 0, 0, 0, 2)`
On the 4th iteration, `indexes` is set to:	`(0, 0, 0, 1, 0)`
On the 5th iteration, `indexes` is set to:	`(0, 0, 0, 1, 1)`
And so on…	

vigenereHacker.py
```
189.         # Create a possible key from the letters in allFreqScores
190.         possibleKey = ''
191.         for i in range(mostLikelyKeyLength):
192.             possibleKey += allFreqScores[i][indexes[i]][0]
```

The full Vigenère key will be constructed from the subkeys in `allFreqScores` using the indexes supplied by `indexes`. The key starts off as a blank string on line 190, and the `for` loop on line 191 will iterate through the integers from `0` up to, but not including, `mostLikelyKeyLength`.

As the `i` variable changes for each iteration of the `for` loop, the value at `indexes[i]` will be the index of the tuple we want to use in `allFreqScores[i]`. This is why `allFreqScores[i][indexes[i]]` evaluates to the correct tuple we want (and the subkey we want is at index `0` in that tuple).

vigenereHacker.py
```
194.         if not SILENT_MODE:
195.             print('Attempting with key: %s' % (possibleKey))
```

If `SILENT_MODE` is `False`, the key created by the `for` loop on line 191 is printed to the screen.

vigenereHacker.py
```
197.         decryptedText = vigenereCipher.decryptMessage(possibleKey,
ciphertextUp)
198.
199.         if detectEnglish.isEnglish(decryptedText):
200.             # Set the hacked ciphertext to the original casing.
201.             origCase = []
202.             for i in range(len(ciphertext)):
203.                 if ciphertext[i].isupper():
204.                     origCase.append(decryptedText[i].upper())
205.                 else:
206.                     origCase.append(decryptedText[i].lower())
207.             decryptedText = ''.join(origCase)
```

Now that we have a complete Vigenère key, lines 197 to 208 will decrypt the ciphertext and check if the decrypted text is readable English. If it is, then it is printed to the screen for the user to confirm it is English (since `isEnglish()` might produce a false positive).

But `decryptedText` is in all uppercase letters. The code on lines 201 to 207 builds a new string by appending the `origCase` list with an uppercase or lowercase form of the letters in `decryptedText`. The `for` loop on line 202 goes through each of the indexes in the `ciphertext` string (which, unlike `ciphertextUp`, has the original casing of the `ciphertext`). If `ciphertext[i]` is uppercase, then the uppercase form of `decryptedText[i]` is appended to `origCase`. Otherwise, the lowercase form of `decryptedText[i]` is appended. The list in `origCase` is then joined together on line 207 to become the new value of `decryptedText`.

This table shows how the `ciphertext` and `decryptedText` values produce the strings that go into `origCase`:

```
        ciphertext  Adiz Avtzqeci Tmzubb wsa m Pmilqev halpqavtakuoi
     decryptedText  ALAN MATHISON TURING WAS A BRITISH MATHEMATICIAN
''.join(origCase)  Alan Mathison Turing was a British mathematician
```

vigenereHacker.py
```
209.             # Check with user to see if the key has been found.
210.             print('Possible encryption hack with key %s:' % (possibleKey))
211.             print(decryptedText[:200]) # only show first 200 characters
212.             print()
213.             print('Enter D for done, or just press Enter to continue hacking:')
214.             response = input('> ')
215.
216.             if response.strip().upper().startswith('D'):
217.                 return decryptedText
```

The correctly-cased decrypted text is printed to the screen for the user to confirm it is English. If the user enters `'D'` then the function returns the `decryptedText` string.

vigenereHacker.py
```
219.     # No English-looking decryption found, so return None.
220.     return None
```

Otherwise, after the `for` loop on line 188 iterates through all of the possible indexes to use and none of the decryptions look like English, the hacking has failed and the `None` value is returned.

vigenereHacker.py
```
223. def hackVigenere(ciphertext):
224.     # First, we need to do Kasiski Examination to figure out what the
225.     # length of the ciphertext's encryption key is.
226.     allLikelyKeyLengths = kasiskiExamination(ciphertext)
```

Now we define the `hackVigenere()` function, which calls all of the previous functions. We've already defined all the work it will do. Let's run through the steps it goes through to perform the hacking. The first step is to get the most likely lengths of the Vigenère key based on Kasiski Examination of `ciphertext`.

vigenereHacker.py

```
227.     if not SILENT_MODE:
228.         keyLengthStr = ''
229.         for keyLength in allLikelyKeyLengths:
230.             keyLengthStr += '%s ' % (keyLength)
231.         print('Kasiski Examination results say the most likely key lengths
are: ' + keyLengthStr + '\n')
```

The likely key lengths are printed to the screen if `SILENT_MODE` is `False`.

The `break` Statement

Similar to how the `continue` statement is used inside of a loop to continue back to the start of the loop, the `break` statement (which is just the `break` keyword by itself) is used inside of a loop to immediately exit the loop. When the program execution "breaks out of a loop", it immediately moves to the first line of code after the loop ends.

vigenereHacker.py

```
233.     for keyLength in allLikelyKeyLengths:
234.         if not SILENT_MODE:
235.             print('Attempting hack with key length %s (%s possible
keys)...' % (keyLength, NUM_MOST_FREQ_LETTERS ** keyLength))
236.         hackedMessage = attemptHackWithKeyLength(ciphertext, keyLength)
237.         if hackedMessage != None:
238.             break
```

For each possible key length, the code calls the `attemptHackWithKeyLength()` function on line 236. If `attemptHackWithKeyLength()` does not return `None`, then the hack was successful and the program execution should break out of the `for` loop on line 238.

vigenereHacker.py

```
240.     # If none of the key lengths we found using Kasiski Examination
241.     # worked, start brute-forcing through key lengths.
242.     if hackedMessage == None:
243.         if not SILENT_MODE:
244.             print('Unable to hack message with likely key length(s).
Brute-forcing key length...')
245.         for keyLength in range(1, MAX_KEY_LENGTH + 1):
246.             # don't re-check key lengths already tried from Kasiski
```

```
247.         if keyLength not in allLikelyKeyLengths:
248.             if not SILENT_MODE:
249.                 print('Attempting hack with key length %s (%s possible
keys)...' % (keyLength, NUM_MOST_FREQ_LETTERS ** keyLength))
250.             hackedMessage = attemptHackWithKeyLength(ciphertext,
keyLength)
251.             if hackedMessage != None:
252.                 break
```

If the hack had failed for all the possible key lengths that `kasiskiExamination()` returned, `hackedMessage` will be set to `None` when the `if` statement on line 242 executes. In this case, all the *other* key lengths up to `MAX_KEY_LENGTH` are tried. If Kasiski Examination failed to calculate the correct key length, then we can just brute-force through the key lengths.

Line 245 starts a `for` loop that will call `attemptHackWithKeyLength()` for each value of `keyLength` (which ranges from `1` to `MAX_KEY_LENGTH`) as long as it was not in `allLikelyKeyLengths`. (This is because the key lengths in `allLikelyKeyLengths` have already been tried in the code on lines 233 to 238.)

vigenereHacker.py

```
253.     return hackedMessage
```

Finally, the value in `hackedMessage` is returned on line 253.

vigenereHacker.py

```
256. # If vigenereHacker.py is run (instead of imported as a module) call
257. # the main() function.
258. if __name__ == '__main__':
259.     main()
```

Lines 258 and 259 call the `main()` function if this program was run by itself rather than imported by another program.

That's the full Vigenère hacking program. Whether it is successful or not depends on the characteristics of the ciphertext. Also, the closer the original plaintext's letter frequency is to regular English's letter frequency and the longer the plaintext, the more likely our hacking program will work.

Practice Exercises, Chapter 21, Set A

Practice exercises can be found at http://invpy.com/hackingpractice21A.

Modifying the Constants of the Hacking Program

There are a few things we can modify if the hacking program doesn't work though. There are three constants we set on lines 8 to 10 that affect how our hacking program runs:

vigenereHacker.py

```
 8. MAX_KEY_LENGTH = 16 # will not attempt keys longer than this
```

If the Vigenère key was longer than the integer in MAX_KEY_LENGTH, there is no possible way the hacking program will find the correct key. However, if we have MAX_KEY_LENGTH set very high and the kasiskiExamination() function mistakenly thinks that the key length could be a very large integer, the program could be spending hours (or days or months) attempting to hack the ciphertext with wrong key lengths.

Trying to hack the wrong key length that is small is not that big of a problem: it will only take seconds or minutes to go through the likely keys of that length. If the hacking program fails to hack the ciphertext, try increasing this value and running the program again.

vigenereHacker.py

```
 9. NUM_MOST_FREQ_LETTERS = 3 # attempts this many letters per subkey
```

The NUM_MOST_FREQ_LETTERS limits the number of possible letters tried for each subkey. By increasing this value, the hacking program tries many more keys (which is needed if the freqAnalysis.englishFreqMatchScore() was inaccurate for the original plaintext message), but this will also cause the program to slow down. And setting NUM_MOST_FREQ_LETTERS to 26 will cause the program to not narrow down the number of possible letters for each subkey at all!

Table 21-5. Tradeoffs for the MAX_KEY_LENGTH and NUM_MOST_FREQ_LETTERS.

Smaller value:	Larger value:
Faster to execute.	Slower to execute.
Less likely to hack.	More likely to hack.

vigenereHacker.py

```
10. SILENT_MODE = False # if set to True, program doesn't print attempts
```

While your computer can perform calculations very fast, displaying characters on the screen is relatively slow. If you want to speed up your program, you can set SILENT_MODE to True so that the program does not waste time printing information to the screen. On the downside, you will not know how the program is doing until it has completely finished running.

Summary

Hacking the Vigenère cipher requires several detailed steps to follow. There are also many parts where our hacking program could fail: perhaps the Vigenère key used for encryption was larger in length than `MAX_KEY_LENGTH`, or perhaps the English frequency matching function got inaccurate results because the plaintext doesn't follow normal letter frequency, or maybe the plaintext has too many words that aren't in our dictionary file and `isEnglish()` doesn't recognize it as English.

If you identify different ways that the hacking program could fail, you could change the code to become ever more sophisticated to handle these other cases. But the hacking program in this book does a pretty good job at reducing billions or trillions of possible keys to brute-force through to mere thousands.

However, there is one trick to make the Vigenère cipher mathematically impossible to break, no matter how powerful your computer or how clever your hacking program is. We'll learn about these "one-time pads" in the next chapter.

Chapter 22

The One-Time Pad Cipher

Topics Covered In This Chapter:

- The Unbreakable One-Time Pad Cipher
- The Two-Time Pad is the Vigenère Cipher

> "I've been over it a thousand times," Waterhouse says, "and the only explanation I can think of is that they are converting their messages into large binary numbers and then combining them with other large binary numbers —one-time pads, most likely —to produce the ciphertext."
>
> "In which case your project is doomed," Alan says, "because you can't break a one-time pad."
>
> "Cryptonomicon" by Neal Stephenson

The Unbreakable One-Time Pad Cipher

There is one cipher that is impossible to crack, no matter how powerful your computer is, how much time you have to crack it, or how clever of a hacker you are. We won't have to write a new program to use it either. Our Vigenère program can implement this cipher without any changes. But this cipher is so inconvenient to use on a regular basis that it is often only used for the most top-secret of messages.

The **one-time pad cipher** is an unbreakable cipher. It is a Vigenère cipher where:

1. The key is exactly as long as the message that is encrypted.
2. The key is made up of truly random symbols.
3. The key is used one time only, and never used again for any other message.

By following these three rules, your encrypted message will be invulnerable to any cryptanalyst's attack. Even with literally an infinite amount of computing power, the cipher cannot be broken.

The key for the one-time pad cipher is called a pad because they were printed on pads of paper. The top sheet of paper would be torn off the pad after it was used to reveal the next key to use.

Why the One-Time Pad is Unbreakable

To see why the one-time pad (OTP) cipher is unbreakable, let's think about why the regular Vigenère cipher is vulnerable to breaking. Our Vigenère cipher hacking program works by doing frequency analysis. But if the key is the same length as the message, then every possible ciphertext letter is equally probable to be for the same plaintext letter.

Say that we want to encrypt the message, "If you want to survive out here, you've got to know where your towel is." If we remove the spaces and punctuation, this message has 55 letters. So to encrypt it with a one-time pad, we need a key that is also 55 letters long. Let's use the key "kcqyzhepxautiqekxejmoretzhztrwwqdylbttvejmedbsanybpxqik". Encrypting the string looks like this:

Plaintext	`ifyouwanttosurviveouthereyouvegottoknowwhereyourtowelis`
Key	`kcqyzhepxautiqekxejmoretzhztrwwqdylbttvejmedbsanybpxqik`
Ciphertext	`shomtdecqtilchzssixghyikdfnnmacewrzlghraqqvhzguerplbbqc`

Now imagine a cryptanalyst got a hold of the ciphertext ("shomtdec..."). How could she attack the cipher? Brute-forcing through the keys would not work, because there are too many even for a computer. The number of keys is 26 ^ (number of letters in the message), so if the message has 55 letters, there would be a total of 26 ^ 55, or 666,091,878,431,395,624,153,823,182,526,730,590, 376,250,379,52 8,249,805,353,030,484,209,594,192,101,376 possible keys.

But it turns out that even if she had a computer that was powerful enough to try all the keys, it still would not break the one-time pad cipher. **This is because for any ciphertext, all possible plaintext messages are equally likely.**

For example, given the ciphertext "shomtdec...", we could easily say the original plaintext was "The myth of Osiris was of importance in ancient Egyptian religion." encrypted with the key "zakavkxolfqdlzhwsqjbzmtwmmnakwurwexdcuywksgorghnnedvtcp":

Plaintext	`themythofosiriswasofimportanceinancientegyptianreligion`
Key	`zakavkxolfqdlzhwsqjbzmtwmmnakwurwexdcuywksgorghnnedvtcp`
Ciphertext	`shomtdecqtilchzssixghyikdfnnmacewrzlghraqqvhzguerplbbqc`

The way we are able to hack encryption is because there is usually only one key that can be used to decrypt the message to sensible English. But we've just shown that the *same* ciphertext could have been made from two very *different* plaintext messages. For the one-time pad, the cryptanalyst has no way of telling which was the original message. In fact, **any** readable English plaintext message that is exactly 55 letters long **is just as likely** to be the original plaintext. **Just because a certain key can decrypt the ciphertext to readable English does not mean it was the original encryption key.**

Since any English plaintext could have been used to create a ciphertext with equal likelihood, it is completely impossible to hack a message encrypted with a one-time pad.

Beware Pseudorandomness

The `random` module that comes with Python does not generate truly random numbers. They are computed from an algorithm that creates numbers that only appear random (which is often good enough). If the pad is not generated from a truly random source, then it loses its mathematically-perfect secrecy.

The `os.urandom()` function can provide truly random numbers but is a bit more difficult to use. For more information about this function, see http://invpy.com/random.

Beware the Two-Time Pad

If you do use the same one-time pad key to encrypt two different messages, you have introduced a weakness into your encryption. Using the one-time pad cipher this way is sometimes called a "two-time pad cipher". It's a joke name though, the two-time pad cipher is really just using the one-time pad cipher incorrectly.

Just because a key decrypts the one-time pad ciphertext to readable English does not mean it is the correct key. However, if you use the same key for two different messages, now the hacker can know that if a key decrypts the first ciphertext to readable English, but that same key decrypts the second message to random garbage text, it must not be the original key. In fact, it is highly likely that there is only one key that will decrypt *both* messages to English.

If the hacker only had one of the two messages, then it is still perfectly encrypted. But, you must always assume that **all** of your encrypted messages are being intercepted by hackers and/or governments (otherwise, you wouldn't need to bother encrypting your messages.) Remember Shannon's Maxim: The enemy knows the system! This includes knowing the ciphertext.

The Two-Time Pad is the Vigenère Cipher

To see why the two-time pad is hackable just like the Vigenère Cipher, let's think about how the Vigenère cipher works when it encrypts a message that is longer than the key. Once we run out of characters in the key to encrypt with, we go back to the first character of the key and continue encrypting. So to encrypt a 20-character message like "AABBCCDDEEVVWWXXYYZZ" with a 10-character long key such as "PRECOCIOUS", the first ten characters (AABBCCDDEE) are encrypted with "PRECOCIOUS" and then the next ten characters (VVWWXXYYZZ) are also encrypted with "PRECOCIOUS".

Plaintext	AABBCCDDEEVVWWXXYYZZ
Vigenère Key	PRECOCIOUSPRECOCIOUS
Vigenère Ciphertext	PRFDQELRYWKMAYLZGMTR

We have already learned how to break Vigenère ciphers. If we can show that a two-time pad cipher is the same thing as a Vigenère cipher, then we can prove that it is breakable using the same techniques used to break Vigenère cipher.

Using the one-time pad cipher, let's say the 10-character message "AABBCCDDEE" was encrypted with the one-time pad key "PRECOCIOUS". Then the cryptographer makes the mistake of encrypting a second 10-character message "VVWWXXYYZZ" with the same one-time pad key, "PRECOCIOUS".

	Message 1	**Message 2**
Plaintext	AABBCCDDEE	VVWWXXYYZZ
One-Time Pad Key	PRECOCIOUS	PRECOCIOUS
One-Time Pad Ciphertext	PRFDQELRYW	KMAYLZGMTR

If we compare the ciphertext of the Vigenère cipher and the ciphertexts of the one-time pad cipher, we can see they are the exact same. The two-time pad cipher has the same properties as the Vigenère cipher, which means that the same techniques could be used to hack it!

This also tells us that if we do the Vigenère cipher but use a key that is as long as the message it is encrypting (and only use this key once for this message), then it will be perfectly unbreakable.

This is why we don't need to write a separate one-time pad cipher program. Our Vigenère cipher program already does it!

Practice Exercises, Chapter 22, Set A

Practice exercises can be found at http://invpy.com/hackingpractice22A.

Summary

In short, a one-time pad is just the Vigenère cipher with a key that is the same length as the message and is only used once. As long as these two conditions are followed, it is literally impossible to break the one-time pad. However, it is so inconvenient to use the one-time pad that it is not generally used except for the most top-secret of secrets. Usually a large list of one-time pad keys are generated and shared in person, with the keys marked for specific dates. This way, if you receive a message from your collaborator on October 31st, you can just look through the list of one-time pads to find the one for that day. But be sure this list doesn't fall into the wrong hands!

Chapter 23

Finding Prime Numbers

Topics Covered In This Chapter:

- Prime and Composite Numbers
- The Sieve of Eratosthenes
- The Rabin-Miller Primality Test

> "Mathematicians have tried in vain to this day to discover some order in the sequence of prime numbers, and we have reason to believe that it is a mystery into which the human mind will never penetrate."
>
> Leonhard Euler, 18th century mathematician

All of the ciphers described in this book so far have been around for hundreds of years, and all of them (with the exception of the one-time pad) are easily broken by computers. These ciphers worked very well when hackers had to rely on pencil and paper to hack them, but computers can now manipulate data trillions of times faster than a person with a pencil.

The RSA cipher has several improvements over these old ciphers, and it will be detailed in the next chapter. However, the RSA cipher will require us to learn about prime numbers first.

Prime Numbers

A prime number is an integer (that is, a whole number) that is greater than 1 and has only two factors: 1 and itself. Remember that the factors of a number are the numbers that can be multiplied to equal the original number. The numbers 3 and 7 are factors of 21. The number 12 has factors 2 and 6, but also 3 and 4.

Every number has factors of 1 and itself. The numbers 1 and 21 are factors of 21. The numbers 1 and 12 are factors of 12. This is because 1 times any number will always be that same number. But if no other factors exist for that number, then that number is **prime**.

Here's a list of prime numbers (note that 1 is not considered a prime number):

2, 3, 5, 7, 11, 13, 17, 19, 23, 29, 31, 37, 41, 43, 47, 53, 59, 61, 67, 71, 73, 79, 83, 89, 97, 101, 103, 107, 109, 113, 127, 131, 137, 139, 149, 151, 157, 163, 167, 173, 179, 181, 191, 193, 197, 199, 211, 223, 227, 229, 233, 239, 241, 251, 257, 263, 269, 271, 277, 281 …and so on, **FOREVER**.

There are an infinite number of prime numbers. This means there is no "largest" prime. They just keep getting bigger and bigger, just like regular numbers do. (See http://invpy.com/infiniteprimes for a proof of this.) The RSA cipher makes use of very large prime numbers in the keys it uses. Because of this, there will be far too many keys to brute-force through.

A **googol** is the number that has a one with a hundred zeros behind it:

10,000,000,000,000,000,000,000,000,000,000,000,000,000,000,000,000,000,000,000,000,000,000,000,00
0,000,000,000,000,000,000,000,000,000,000,000

(As a bit of history: the name of the search engine company Google came from misspelling "googol", but they decided they liked that spelling better and kept it.)

A **billion billion billion googols** has twenty-seven more zeros than a googol:

10,000,000,000,000,000,000,000,000,000,000,000,000,000,000,000,000,000,000,000,000,000,000,000,00
0,000,000,000,000,000,000,000,000,000,000,000,000,000,000,000,000,000,000,000,000,000,000

But these are tiny numbers. A typical prime number used in our RSA program will have hundreds of digits:

112,829,754,900,439,506,175,719,191,782,841,802,172,556,768,253,593,054,977,186,2355,84,9
79,780,304,652,423,405,148,425,447,063,090,165,759,070,742,102,132,335,103,295,947,000,71
8,386,333,756,395,799,633,478,227,612,244,071,875,721,006,813,307,628,061,280,861,610,153,
485,352,017,238,548,269,452,852,733,818,231,045,171,038,838,387,845,888,589,411,762,622,0
41,204,120,706,150,518,465,720,862,068,595,814,264,819

The above number is so big, I'm going to guess you didn't even read it to notice the typo in it.

Composite Numbers

Integers that are not prime numbers are called **composite** numbers, because they are composed of at least two factors besides 1 and the number itself. They are called composite numbers because these number are composed of prime numbers multiplied together, such as the composite number 1,386 being composed of the prime numbers in 2 × 3 × 3 × 7 × 11.

Here are four facts about prime numbers:

1. Prime numbers are integers greater than 1that have only 1 and themselves as factors.
2. Two is the only even prime number. (Though I guess that makes two a very odd prime number.)
3. There are an infinite number of prime numbers. There is no "largest prime number".
4. Multiplying two prime numbers will give a number that only has two pairs of factors, 1 and itself (like all numbers do), and the two prime numbers that were multiplied. For example, 3 and 7 are prime numbers. 3 times 7 is 21. The only factors for 21 are 1, 21, 3, and 7.

Source Code for The Prime Sieve Module

First we will create a module that has functions related to prime numbers:

- `isPrime()` will return either True or False if the number passed to it is prime or not. It will use the "divides test" algorithm.
- `primeSieve()` will use the "Sieve of Eratosthenes" algorithm (explained later) to generate numbers.

Like *cryptomath.py*, the *primeSieve.py* program is only meant to be imported as a module to our other programs. It does not do anything when run on its own.

Open a new file editor window by clicking on **File ► New Window**. Type in the following code into the file editor, and then save it as *primeSieve.py*.

Source code for primeSieve.py

```
# Prime Number Sieve
# http://inventwithpython.com/hacking (BSD Licensed)

import math


def isPrime(num):
```

```
    # Returns True if num is a prime number, otherwise False.

    # Note: Generally, isPrime() is slower than primeSieve().

    # all numbers less than 2 are not prime
    if num < 2:
        return False

    # see if num is divisible by any number up to the square root of num
    for i in range(2, int(math.sqrt(num)) + 1):
        if num % i == 0:
            return False
    return True


def primeSieve(sieveSize):
    # Returns a list of prime numbers calculated using
    # the Sieve of Eratosthenes algorithm.

    sieve = [True] * sieveSize
    sieve[0] = False # zero and one are not prime numbers
    sieve[1] = False

    # create the sieve
    for i in range(2, int(math.sqrt(sieveSize)) + 1):
        pointer = i * 2
        while pointer < sieveSize:
            sieve[pointer] = False
            pointer += i

    # compile the list of primes
    primes = []
    for i in range(sieveSize):
        if sieve[i] == True:
            primes.append(i)

    return primes
```

How the Program Works

primeSieve.py

```
# Prime Number Sieve
# http://inventwithpython.com/hacking (BSD Licensed)

import math
```

The only module *primeSieve.py* needs is the `math` module.

How to Calculate if a Number is Prime

primeSieve.py

```
def isPrime(num):
    # Returns True if num is a prime number, otherwise False.

    # Note: Generally, isPrime() is slower than primeSieve().

    # all numbers less than 2 are not prime
    if num < 2:
        return False
```

We will program the `isPrime()` function to return `False` if the `num` parameter is a composite number and `True` if the `num` parameter is a prime number. If `num` is less than `2` we know it is not prime and can simply return `False`.

primeSieve.py

```
    # see if num is divisible by any number up to the square root of num
    for i in range(2, int(math.sqrt(num)) + 1):
        if num % i == 0:
            return False
    return True
```

A prime number has no factors besides 1 and itself. So to find out if a given number is prime or not, we just have to keep dividing it by integers and see if any of them evenly divide the number with 0 remainder.

The `math.sqrt()` function will return a float value of the square root of the number it is passed. The square root of a number can be multiplied by itself to get the number. For example, the square root of 49 is 7, because 7 × 7 is 49.

For example, to find out if 49 is prime, divide it by the integers starting with 2:

$$49 \div 2 = 24 \text{ remainder } 1$$

$$49 \div 3 = 16 \text{ remainder } 1$$

$$49 \div 4 = 12 \text{ remainder } 1$$

$$49 \div 5 = 9 \text{ remainder } 4$$

$$49 \div 6 = 8 \text{ remainder } 1$$

49 ÷ 7 = 7 remainder 0

Actually, you only need to divide the number by prime numbers. For example, there's no reason to see if 6 divides 49, because if it did then 2 would have divided 49 since 2 is a factor of 6. *Any* number that 6 divides evenly can also be divided by 2 evenly:

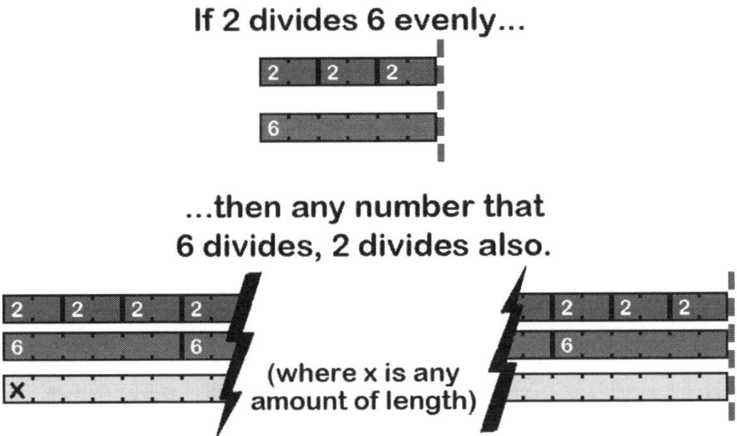

Figure 23-1. 2 divides 6, and 6 divides X, therefore 2 divides X.

Because there's an integer (that is not 1 or 49) that evenly divides 49 (that is, has a remainder of 0), we know that 49 is not a prime number. For another example, let's try 13:

13 ÷ 2 = 6 remainder 1

13 ÷ 3 = 4 remainder 1

13 ÷ 4 = 3 remainder 1

No integer divides 13 with a remainder of 0 (except for 1 and 13, which don't count). Actually, we don't even have to divide **all** the numbers up to 13. We only have to test the integers up to (and including) the square root of the number we are testing for primality. The **square root** of a number is the number that is multiplied by itself to get that first number. The square root of 25 is 5, because 5 × 5 = 25. The square root of 13 is about 3.6055512754639, because 3.6055512754639 × 3.6055512754639 = 13. This means that when we were testing 13 for primality, we only had to divide 2 and 3 because 4 is larger than the square root of 13.

Line 18 checks if the remainder of division is 0 by using the `%` mod operator. If line 17's `for` loop never returns `False`, the function will return `True` on line 20.

The Sieve of Eratosthenes

The sieve of Eratosthenes (pronounced "era, taws, thuh, knees") is an algorithm for calculating prime numbers. Imagine a bunch of boxes for each integer, all marked "prime":

Table 23-1. A blank sieve of Eratosthenes, with each number marked as "prime".

Prime 1	Prime 2	Prime 3	Prime 4	Prime 5	Prime 6	Prime 7	Prime 8	Prime 9	Prime 10
Prime 11	Prime 12	Prime 13	Prime 14	Prime 15	Prime 16	Prime 17	Prime 18	Prime 19	Prime 20
Prime 21	Prime 22	Prime 23	Prime 24	Prime 25	Prime 26	Prime 27	Prime 28	Prime 29	Prime 30
Prime 31	Prime 32	Prime 33	Prime 34	Prime 35	Prime 36	Prime 37	Prime 38	Prime 39	Prime 40
Prime 41	Prime 42	Prime 43	Prime 44	Prime 45	Prime 46	Prime 47	Prime 48	Prime 49	Prime 50

Mark 1 as "Not Prime" (since one is never prime). Then mark all the multiples of two (except for two itself) as "Not Prime". This means we will mark the integers 4 (2 × 2), 6 (2 × 3), 8 (2 × 4), 10, 12, and so on up to 50 (the largest number we have) are all marked as "Not Prime":

Table 23-2. The sieve with one and the multiples of 2 (except 2 itself) marked as "not prime".

Not Prime 1	Prime 2	Prime 3	Not Prime 4	Prime 5	Not Prime 6	Prime 7	Not Prime 8	Prime 9	Not Prime 10
Prime 11	Not Prime 12	Prime 13	Not Prime 14	Prime 15	Not Prime 16	Prime 17	Not Prime 18	Prime 19	Not Prime 20
Prime 21	Not Prime 22	Prime 23	Not Prime 24	Prime 25	Not Prime 26	Prime 27	Not Prime 28	Prime 29	Not Prime 30
Prime 31	Not Prime 32	Prime 33	Not Prime 34	Prime 35	Not Prime 36	Prime 37	Not Prime 38	Prime 39	Not Prime 40
Prime 41	Not Prime 42	Prime 43	Not Prime 44	Prime 45	Not Prime 46	Prime 47	Not Prime 48	Prime 49	Not Prime 50

Then repeat this with all the multiples of three, except for three itself: 6, 9, 12, 15, 18, 21, and so on are all marked "Not Prime". Then do this for all of the multiples of four (except for four itself), and all of the multiples of five (except for five itself), up until eight. We stop at 8 because it is larger than 7.071, the square root of 50). We can do this because all the multiples of 9, 10, 11, and so on will already have been marked.

The completed sieve looks like this:

Table 23-3. A completed sieve of Eratosthenes.

Not Prime 1	Prime 2	Prime 3	Not Prime 4	Prime 5	Not Prime 6	Prime 7	Not Prime 8	Not Prime 9	Not Prime 10
Prime 11	Not Prime 12	Prime 13	Not Prime 14	Not Prime 15	Not Prime 16	Prime 17	Not Prime 18	Prime 19	Not Prime 20
Not Prime 21	Not Prime 22	Prime 23	Not Prime 24	Not Prime 25	Not Prime 26	Not Prime 27	Not Prime 28	Prime 29	Not Prime 30
Prime 31	Not Prime 32	Not Prime 33	Not Prime 34	Not Prime 35	Not Prime 36	Prime 37	Not Prime 38	Not Prime 39	Not Prime 40
Prime 41	Not Prime 42	Prime 43	Not Prime 44	Not Prime 45	Not Prime 46	Prime 47	Not Prime 48	Not Prime 49	Not Prime 50

By using the sieve of Erastothenes, we've calculated that the prime numbers under 50 are 2, 3, 5, 7, 11, 13, 17, 19, 23, 29, 31, 37, 41, 43, and 47. This sieve algorithm is good when we want to quickly find out all the prime numbers *in a certain range* of numbers. It is much faster than using the previous "divides test" algorithm to test if 2 is prime, then test if 3 is prime, then test if 4 is prime, and so on.

The `primeSieve()` Function

```
23. def primeSieve(sieveSize):
24.     # Returns a list of prime numbers calculated using
25.     # the Sieve of Eratosthenes algorithm.
26.
27.     sieve = [True] * sieveSize
28.     sieve[0] = False # zero and one are not prime numbers
29.     sieve[1] = False
```

The `primeSieve()` function returns a list of all prime numbers between `1` and `sieveSize`. First, line 27 creates a list of Boolean `True` values that is the length of `sieveSize`. The `0` and `1` indexes are marked as `False` because `0` and `1` are not prime numbers.

```
31.     # create the sieve
32.     for i in range(2, int(math.sqrt(sieveSize)) + 1):
33.         pointer = i * 2
34.         while pointer < sieveSize:
35.             sieve[pointer] = False
36.             pointer += i
```

The `for` loop on line 32 goes through each integer from `2` up to the square root of `sieveSize`. The variable `pointer` will start at the first multiple of `i` after `i` (which will be `i * 2`). Then the `while` loop will set the `pointer` index in the `sieve` list to `False`, and line 36 will change `pointer` to point to the next multiple of `i`.

```
38.     # compile the list of primes
39.     primes = []
40.     for i in range(sieveSize):
41.         if sieve[i] == True:
42.             primes.append(i)
```

After the `for` loop on line 32 completes, the `sieve` list will contain `True` for each index that is a prime number. We can create a new list (which starts as an empty list in primes) and loop over the entire `sieve` list, and appends and numbers if `sieve[i]` is `True` (meaning `i` is prime).

```
44.     return primes
```

The list of prime numbers is returned on line 44.

Detecting Prime Numbers

The `isPrime()` function in *primeSieve.py* checks if the number can be divided evenly by a range of numbers from 2 to the square root of the number. But what about a number like 1,070,595,206,942,983? If you pass this integer to `isPrime()`, it takes several seconds to determine if it is prime or not. And if the number is hundreds of digits long (like the prime numbers in next chapter's RSA cipher program are), it would take over a trillion years to figure out if that *one* number is prime or not.

The `isPrime()` function in *primeSieve.py* is too slow for the large numbers we will use in the RSA cipher. Fortunately there is an algorithm called the Rabin-Miller Primality Test than can calculate if such large numbers are prime or not. We will create a new `isPrime()` function in *rabinMiller.py* that makes use of this better algorithm.

The code for this algorithm uses advanced mathematics, and how the algorithm works is beyond the scope of this book. Like the `gcd()` function in *cryptomath.py*, this book will just present the code for the algorithm for you to use without explanation.

Source Code for the Rabin-Miller Module

Open a new file editor window and type in the following code. Save this file as *rabinMiller.py*. This program will be a module that is meant to be imported by other programs.

Instead of typing out the list of numbers on line 43, just temporarily add the lines `import pyperclip` and `pyperclip.copy(primeSieve(1000))` in the *primeSieve.py* file and run it. This will copy the list of primes to the clipboard, and then you can paste it into the *rabinMiller.py* file.

Open a new file editor window by clicking on **File ► New Window**. Type in the following code into the file editor, and then save it as *rabinMiller.py*.

Source code for rabinMiller.py

```
 1. # Primality Testing with the Rabin-Miller Algorithm
 2. # http://inventwithpython.com/hacking (BSD Licensed)
 3.
 4. import random
 5.
 6.
 7. def rabinMiller(num):
 8.     # Returns True if num is a prime number.
 9.
10.     s = num - 1
11.     t = 0
12.     while s % 2 == 0:
13.         # keep halving s until it is even (and use t
14.         # to count how many times we halve s)
15.         s = s // 2
16.         t += 1
17.
18.     for trials in range(5): # try to falsify num's primality 5 times
19.         a = random.randrange(2, num - 1)
20.         v = pow(a, s, num)
21.         if v != 1: # this test does not apply if v is 1.
22.             i = 0
23.             while v != (num - 1):
24.                 if i == t - 1:
25.                     return False
26.                 else:
27.                     i = i + 1
```

```
                    v = (v ** 2) % num
    return True


def isPrime(num):
    # Return True if num is a prime number. This function does a quicker
    # prime number check before calling rabinMiller().

    if (num < 2):
        return False # 0, 1, and negative numbers are not prime

    # About 1/3 of the time we can quickly determine if num is not prime
    # by dividing by the first few dozen prime numbers. This is quicker
    # than rabinMiller(), but unlike rabinMiller() is not guaranteed to
    # prove that a number is prime.
    lowPrimes = [2, 3, 5, 7, 11, 13, 17, 19, 23, 29, 31, 37, 41, 43, 47, 53, 59, 61, 67, 71, 73, 79, 83, 89, 97, 101, 103, 107, 109, 113, 127, 131, 137, 139, 149, 151, 157, 163, 167, 173, 179, 181, 191, 193, 197, 199, 211, 223, 227, 229, 233, 239, 241, 251, 257, 263, 269, 271, 277, 281, 283, 293, 307, 311, 313, 317, 331, 337, 347, 349, 353, 359, 367, 373, 379, 383, 389, 397, 401, 409, 419, 421, 431, 433, 439, 443, 449, 457, 461, 463, 467, 479, 487, 491, 499, 503, 509, 521, 523, 541, 547, 557, 563, 569, 571, 577, 587, 593, 599, 601, 607, 613, 617, 619, 631, 641, 643, 647, 653, 659, 661, 673, 677, 683, 691, 701, 709, 719, 727, 733, 739, 743, 751, 757, 761, 769, 773, 787, 797, 809, 811, 821, 823, 827, 829, 839, 853, 857, 859, 863, 877, 881, 883, 887, 907, 911, 919, 929, 937, 941, 947, 953, 967, 971, 977, 983, 991, 997]

    if num in lowPrimes:
        return True

    # See if any of the low prime numbers can divide num
    for prime in lowPrimes:
        if (num % prime == 0):
            return False

    # If all else fails, call rabinMiller() to determine if num is a prime.
    return rabinMiller(num)


def generateLargePrime(keysize=1024):
    # Return a random prime number of keysize bits in size.
    while True:
        num = random.randrange(2**(keysize-1), 2**(keysize))
        if isPrime(num):
            return num
```

Sample Run of the Rabin Miller Module

If you run the interactive shell, you can import the *rabinMiller.py* module and call the functions in it. Try typing the following into the interactive shell:

```
>>> import rabinMiller
>>> rabinMiller.generateLargePrime()
1228811683422110410305236835154432390074842906007015553694882717483780547440094
6375131251147129101194573241337844666809140502037003673211052153493607681619999
0563076859566835016382556518967124921538212397036345815983641146000671635019637
218348455544435908428400192565849620509600312468757953899553441648428119
>>> rabinMiller.isPrime(45943208739848451)
False
>>> rabinMiller.isPrime(13)
True
>>>
```

How the Program Works

rabinMiller.py

```
1. # Primality Testing with the Rabin-Miller Algorithm
2. # http://inventwithpython.com/hacking (BSD Licensed)
3.
4. import random
```

The Rabin-Miller algorithm uses random numbers, so we import the `random` module on line 4.

The Rabin-Miller Primality Algorithm

rabinMiller.py

```
def rabinMiller(num):
    # Returns True if num is a prime number.

    s = num - 1
    t = 0
    while s % 2 == 0:
        # keep halving s until it is even (and use t
        # to count how many times we halve s)
        s = s // 2
        t += 1

    for trials in range(5): # try to falsify num's primality 5 times
        a = random.randrange(2, num - 1)
        v = pow(a, s, num)
        if v != 1: # this test does not apply if v is 1.
```

```
            i = 0
            while v != (num - 1):
                if i == t - 1:
                    return False
                else:
                    i = i + 1
                    v = (v ** 2) % num
    return True
```

The mathematics of the Rabin-Miller Primality algorithm are beyond the scope of this book, so the code in this function will not be explained.

The Rabin-Miller algorithm is also not a surefire test for primality; however, you can be extremely certain that it is accurate. (Although this is not good enough for commercial encryption software, it is good enough for the purposes of the programs in this book.) The main benefit of the Rabin-Miller algorithm is that it is a relatively simple primality test and only takes a few seconds to run on a normal computer.

If `rabinMiller()` returns `True`, then the `num` argument is extremely likely to be prime. If `rabinMiller()` returns `False`, then `num` is definitely composite.

The New and Improved `isPrime()` Function

rabinMiller.py

```
def isPrime(num):
    # Return True if num is a prime number. This function does a quicker
    # prime number check before calling rabinMiller().

    if (num < 2):
        return False # 0, 1, and negative numbers are not prime
```

All numbers that are less than two (such as one, zero, and negative numbers) are all not prime, so we can immediately return `False`.

rabinMiller.py

```
    # About 1/3 of the time we can quickly determine if num is not prime
    # by dividing by the first few dozen prime numbers. This is quicker
    # than rabinMiller(), but unlike rabinMiller() is not guaranteed to
    # prove that a number is prime.
    lowPrimes = [2, 3, 5, 7, 11, 13, 17, 19, 23, 29, 31, 37, 41, 43, 47,
53, 59, 61, 67, 71, 73, 79, 83, 89, 97, 101, 103, 107, 109, 113, 127, 131, 137,
139, 149, 151, 157, 163, 167, 173, 179, 181, 191, 193, 197, 199, 211, 223, 227,
229, 233, 239, 241, 251, 257, 263, 269, 271, 277, 281, 283, 293, 307, 311, 313,
317, 331, 337, 347, 349, 353, 359, 367, 373, 379, 383, 389, 397, 401, 409, 419,
```

```
421, 431, 433, 439, 443, 449, 457, 461, 463, 467, 479, 487, 491, 499, 503, 509,
521, 523, 541, 547, 557, 563, 569, 571, 577, 587, 593, 599, 601, 607, 613, 617,
619, 631, 641, 643, 647, 653, 659, 661, 673, 677, 683, 691, 701, 709, 719, 727,
733, 739, 743, 751, 757, 761, 769, 773, 787, 797, 809, 811, 821, 823, 827, 829,
839, 853, 857, 859, 863, 877, 881, 883, 887, 907, 911, 919, 929, 937, 941, 947,
953, 967, 971, 977, 983, 991, 997]
44.
45.     if num in lowPrimes:
46.         return True
```

The numbers in the `lowPrimes` list are primes. (Duh.) We can immediately return `True` if `num` is in the `lowPrimes` list.

rabinMiller.py

```
48.     # See if any of the low prime numbers can divide num
49.     for prime in lowPrimes:
50.         if (num % prime == 0):
51.             return False
```

Line 49 loops through each of the prime numbers in the `lowPrimes` list. The integer in `num` is modded with the `%` mod operator by each prime number on line 50, and if this evaluates to `0` then we know that `prime` divides `num` and so `num` is not prime. In that case, line 51 returns `False`.

Checking if `num` is divisible by all the primes under 1000 won't tell us if the number is prime, but it might tell us if the number is composite. About 30% of the random numbers that `generateLargePrime()` creates that are composite will be detected as composite by dividing by the low prime numbers. Dividing by the low prime numbers is much faster than executing the full Rabin-Miller algorithm on the number, so this shortcut can make our program execute much more quickly.

rabinMiller.py

```
53.     # If all else fails, call rabinMiller() to determine if num is a prime.
54.     return rabinMiller(num)
```

Those are all the quick tests to determine if a number is prime or not. But if `num` does not match any of those tests, then it is passed to the `rabinMiller()` function to check if it is prime or not. The return value of `rabinMiller()` will be returned by `isPrime()`.

The comment on line 53 means call the `rabinMiller()` *function* to determine if the number is prime. Please do not call Dr. Rabin or Dr. Miller personally to ask them if your number is prime.

rabinMiller.py

```
57. def generateLargePrime(keysize=1024):
```

```
58.     # Return a random prime number of keysize bits in size.
59.     while True:
60.         num = random.randrange(2**(keysize-1), 2**(keysize))
61.         if isPrime(num):
62.             return num
```

The `generateLargePrime()` function will return an integer that is prime. It does this by coming up with a large random number, storing it in `num`, and then passing `num` to `isPrime()`. The `isPrime()` function will then test to see if `num` is composite and then pass the `num` to `rabinMiller()` for a more thorough (and computationally expensive) primality test.

If the number `num` is prime, then line 62 returns `num`. Otherwise the infinite loop goes back to line 60 to try a new random number. This loop keeps trying over and over again until it finds a number that the `isPrime()` function says is prime.

Summary

Prime numbers have fascinating properties in mathematics. As you will learn in the next chapter, they are also the backbone of ciphers used in actual professional encryption software. The definition of a prime number is simple enough: a number that only has one and itself as factors. But determining which numbers are prime and which are composite (that is, not prime) takes some clever code.

Modding a number with all the numbers from two up to the square root of the number is how our `isPrime()` function determines if that number is prime or not. A prime number will never have a remainder of 0 when it is modded by any number (besides its factors, 1 and itself.) But this can take a while for the computer to calculate when testing large numbers for primality.

The sieve of Erastothenes can be used to quickly tell if a range of numbers is prime or not, but this requires a lot of memory.

The RSA cipher makes use of extremely large prime numbers that are hundreds of digits long. The Sieve of Erastothenes and the basic `isPrime()` function we have in *primeSieve.py* aren't sophisticated enough to handle numbers this large.

The Rabin-Miller algorithm uses some mathematics which has simple code (but the mathematical reasoning behind it is too complex for this book), but it allows us to determine if a number that is hundreds of digits long is prime.

In the next chapter, we will use the prime number code we developed for the *rabinMiller.py* module in our RSA Cipher program. At last, we will have a cipher easier to use than the one-time pad cipher but that cannot be hacked by the simple hacker techniques in this book!

Warning to Time Travelers:

Should you travel back to the early 1990's with this book, the contents of Chapter 24 would be illegal to possess in the United States. Strong crypto (that is, cryptography strong enough not to be hacked) was regulated at the same level as tanks, missiles, and flamethrowers and the export of encryption software would require State Department approval. They said that this was a matter of national security.

Daniel J. Bernstein, a student at the University of California, Berkeley at the time, wanted to publish an academic paper and associated source code on his "Snuffle" encryption system. He was told by the U.S. government that he would first need to become a licensed arms dealer before he could post his source code on the Internet. They also told him that they would deny him an export license if he actually applied for one, because his technology was too secure.

The Electronic Frontier Foundation, in its second major case as a young digital civil liberties organization, brought about the *Bernstein v. United States* court cases. The court ruled, for the first time ever, that written software code is speech protected by the First Amendment, and that the export control laws on encryption violated Bernstein's First Amendment rights by prohibiting his constitutionally protected speech.

Today, strong crypto is used to safeguard businesses and e-commerce used by millions of Internet shoppers everyday. Cryptography is at the foundation of a large part of the global economy. But in the 1990's, spreading this knowledge freely (as this book does) would have landed you in prison for arms trafficking.

A more detailed history of the legal battle for cryptography can be found in Steven Levy's book, *Crypto: How the Code Rebels Beat the Government, Saving Privacy in the Digital Age.*

The fears and predictions made by the "experts" of the intelligence community that encryption software would become a grave national security threat turned out to be… less than well-founded.

Chapter 24

Public Key Cryptography and the RSA Cipher

Topics Covered In This Chapter:

- Public key cryptography
- Man-in-the-middle attacks
- ASCII
- The `chr()` and `ord()` functions
- The bytes data type and `bytes()` function
- The `encode()` string and `decode()` bytes method
- The `min()` and `max()` functions
- The `insert()` list method
- The `pow()` function

> "Why shouldn't I work for the NSA? That's a tough one, but I'll take a shot. Say I'm working at the NSA and somebody puts a code on my desk, something no one else can break. Maybe I take a shot at it, and maybe I break it. I'm real happy with myself, 'cause I did my job well. But maybe that code was the location of some rebel army in North Africa or the Middle East and once they have that location they bomb the village where the rebels are hiding. Fifteen hundred people that I never met, never had no problem with, get killed.

Now the politicians are saying ‘Oh, send in the Marines to secure the area,’ ‘cause they don’t give a shit. It won’t be their kid over there getting shot just like it wasn’t them when their number got called ‘cause they were pulling a tour in the National Guard. It’ll be some kid from Southie over there taking shrapnel in the ass. He comes back to find that the plant he used to work at got exported to the country he just got back from, and the guy that put the shrapnel in his ass got his old job, ‘cause he’ll work for fifteen cents a day and no bathroom breaks.

Meanwhile he realizes that the only reason he was over there in the first place was so we could install a government that would sell us oil at a good price. And of course the oil companies use the little skirmish to scare up domestic oil prices, a cute little ancillary benefit for them, but it ain’t helping my buddy at two-fifty a gallon. They’re taking their sweet time bringing the oil back, of course, and maybe they took the liberty of hiring an alcoholic skipper who likes to drink martinis and fucking play slalom with the icebergs. It ain’t too long until he hits one, spills the oil, and kills all the sea life in the North Atlantic.

So now my buddy’s out of work, he can’t afford to drive, so he’s walking to the fucking job interviews which sucks because the shrapnel in his ass is giving him chronic hemorrhoids. And meanwhile he’s starving ‘cause any time he tries to get a bite to eat the only Blue Plate Special they’re serving is North Atlantic Scrod with Quaker State.

So what did I think? I’m holding out for something better.”

“Good Will Hunting”

Public Key Cryptography

All of the ciphers in this book so far have one thing in common: the key used for encryption is the same key used for decryption. This leads to a tricky problem: How do you share encrypted messages with someone you’ve never talked to before?

Say someone on the other side of the world wants to communicate with you. But you both know that spy agencies are monitoring all emails, letters, texts, and calls that you send. You could send them encrypted messages, however you would both have to agree on a secret key to use. But if one of you emailed the other a secret key to use, then the spy agency would be able to see this key and then decrypt any future messages you send with that key. Normally you would both secretly meet in person and exchange the key then. But you can't do this if the person is on the other side of the world. You could try encrypting the key before you send it, but then you would have to send the secret key for *that* message to the other person and it would also be intercepted.

This is a problem solved by public key cryptography. **Public key cryptography** ciphers have two keys, one used for encryption and one used for decryption. A cipher that uses different keys for encryption and decryption is called an **asymmetric cipher**, while the ciphers that use the same key for encryption and decryption (like all the previous ciphers in this book) are called **symmetric ciphers**.

The important thing to know is that **a message encrypted with one key can only be decrypted with the other key**. So even if someone got their hands on the encryption key, they would not be able to read an encrypted message because the encryption key can only encrypt; it cannot be used to decrypt messages that it encrypted.

So when we have these two keys, we call one the public key and one the private key. The **public key** is shared with the entire world. However, the **private key** must be kept secret.

If Alice wants to send Bob a message, Alice finds Bob's public key (or Bob can give it to her). Then Alice encrypts her message to Bob with Bob's public key. Since the public key cannot decrypt a message that was encrypted with it, it doesn't matter that everyone else has Bob's public key.

When Bob receives the encrypted message, he uses his private key to decrypt it. If Bob wants to reply to Alice, he finds her public key and encrypts his reply with it. Since only Alice knows her own private key, Alice will be the only person who can decrypt the encrypted message.

Remember that when sending encrypted messages using a public key cipher:

- The public key is used for encrypting.
- The private key is used for decrypting.

To go back to the example of communicating with someone across the world, now it doesn't matter if you send them your public key. Even if the spy agency has your public key, they cannot read messages that were encrypted with the public key. Only your private key can decrypt those messages, and you keep that key a secret.

The particular public key cipher that we will implement is called the RSA cipher, which was invented in 1977 and named after its inventors: Ron Rivest, Adi Shamir and Leonard Adleman.

The Dangers of "Textbook" RSA

While we don't write a hacking program for the RSA cipher program in this book, don't make the mistake of thinking the *rsaCipher.py* program featured in this chapter is secure. Getting cryptography right is very hard and requires a lot of experience to know if a cipher (and a program that implements it) is truly secure.

The RSA program in this chapter is known as **textbook RSA** because, while it does implement the RSA algorithm correctly using large prime numbers, there are several subtle faults with it that can lead to its encrypted messages being hacked. The difference between pseudorandom and truly random number generation functions is one such fault. But there are many others.

So while you might not be able to hack the ciphertext created by *rsaCipher.py*, don't think that no one else can. The highly accomplished cryptographer Bruce Schneier once said, "Anyone, from the most clueless amateur to the best cryptographer, can create an algorithm that he himself can't break. It's not even hard. What is hard is creating an algorithm that no one else can break, even after years of analysis. And the only way to prove that is to subject the algorithm to years of analysis by the best cryptographers around."

The program in this book is a fun example, but stick to professional encryption software to secure your files. You can find a list of (usually free) encryption software here: http://invpy.com/realcrypto.

A Note About Authentication

There is a slight problem with public key ciphers. Imagine you got an email that said this:

> "Hello. I am Emmanuel Goldstein, leader of the resistance. I would like to communicate secretly with you about very important matters. Attached is my public key."

Using the public key, you can be sure that the messages you send cannot be read by anyone other than "Emmanuel Goldstein". But how do you know the person who sent you this is actually Emmanuel Goldstein? Maybe it is Emmanuel Goldstein that you are sending encrypted messages to, or maybe it is a spy agency that is pretending to be Emmanuel Goldstein to lure you into a trap.

So while public key ciphers (and, in fact, all the ciphers in this book) can provide **confidentiality** (that is, keeping the message a secret), they don't provide **authentication** (that is, proof that who you are communicating with really is who they say they are).

Normally this isn't a problem with symmetric ciphers, because when you exchange keys with the person you can see them for yourself. However, you don't need to see a person in order to get their public key and begin sending them encrypted messages. This is something to keep in mind when using public key cryptography.

There is an entire field called PKI (Public Key Infrastructure) that deals with authentication so that you can match public keys to people with some level of security; however, PKI is beyond the scope of this book.

The Man-In-The-Middle Attack

Even more insidious than hacking our encrypted messages is a man-in-the-middle attack. Say Emmanuel Goldstein really did want to communicate with you and sent you the above message, but the spy agency intercepted it. They could then replace the public key Emmanuel attached to the email with their own public key, and then send it on to you. You would think the spy agency's key was Emmanuel's key!

Now when you encrypt a reply to Emmanuel, they intercept that message, decrypt it (since you really encrypted the message with the spy agency's public key, not Emmanuel's public key) and read it, and then they re-encrypt it with Emmanuel's actual public key and send it to him. They do the same thing with any messages that Emmanuel sends to you.

Figure 24-1. A man-in-the-middle attack.

To both you and Emmanuel, it looks like you are communicating secretly with each other. But actually, the spy agency is doing a **man-in-the-middle attack** and reading all of your messages. You and Emmanuel are actually encrypting your messages public keys generated by the spy agency! Again, this problem is caused by the fact that the public key cipher only provides *confidentiality*, but does not provide *authentication*.

Generating Public and Private Keys

A key in the RSA scheme is made of two numbers. There are three steps to creating the keys:

1. Create two random, very large prime numbers. These numbers will be called p and q. Multiply these numbers to get a number which we will call n.
2. Create a random number, called e, which is relatively prime with (p – 1) × (q – 1).
3. Calculate the modular inverse of e. This number will be called d.

The public key will be the two numbers n and e. The private key will be the two numbers n and d. (Notice that both keys have the number n in them.) We will cover how to encrypt and decrypt with these numbers when the RSA cipher program is explained. First let's write a program to generate these keys.

Source Code for the RSA Key Generation Program

Open a new file editor window by clicking on **File ▶ New Window**. Type in the following code into the file editor, and then save it as *makeRsaKeys.py*.

Source code for makeRsaKeys.py

```
# RSA Key Generator
# http://inventwithpython.com/hacking (BSD Licensed)

import random, sys, os, rabinMiller, cryptomath


def main():
    # create a public/private keypair with 1024 bit keys
    print('Making key files...')
    makeKeyFiles('al_sweigart', 1024)
    print('Key files made.')

def generateKey(keySize):
    # Creates a public/private key pair with keys that are keySize bits in
    # size. This function may take a while to run.

    # Step 1: Create two prime numbers, p and q. Calculate n = p * q.
    print('Generating p prime...')
```

```
    p = rabinMiller.generateLargePrime(keySize)
    print('Generating q prime...')
    q = rabinMiller.generateLargePrime(keySize)
    n = p * q

    # Step 2: Create a number e that is relatively prime to (p-1)*(q-1).
    print('Generating e that is relatively prime to (p-1)*(q-1)...')
    while True:
        # Keep trying random numbers for e until one is valid.
        e = random.randrange(2 ** (keySize - 1), 2 ** (keySize))
        if cryptomath.gcd(e, (p - 1) * (q - 1)) == 1:
            break

    # Step 3: Calculate d, the mod inverse of e.
    print('Calculating d that is mod inverse of e...')
    d = cryptomath.findModInverse(e, (p - 1) * (q - 1))

    publicKey = (n, e)
    privateKey = (n, d)

    print('Public key:', publicKey)
    print('Private key:', privateKey)

    return (publicKey, privateKey)


def makeKeyFiles(name, keySize):
    # Creates two files 'x_pubkey.txt' and 'x_privkey.txt' (where x is the
    # value in name) with the the n,e and d,e integers written in them,
    # delimited by a comma.

    # Our safety check will prevent us from overwriting our old key files:
    if os.path.exists('%s_pubkey.txt' % (name)) or os.path.exists('%s_privkey.txt' % (name)):
        sys.exit('WARNING: The file %s_pubkey.txt or %s_privkey.txt already exists! Use a different name or delete these files and re-run this program.' % (name, name))

    publicKey, privateKey = generateKey(keySize)

    print()
    print('The public key is a %s and a %s digit number.' % (len(str(publicKey[0])), len(str(publicKey[1]))))
    print('Writing public key to file %s_pubkey.txt...' % (name))
    fo = open('%s_pubkey.txt' % (name), 'w')
    fo.write('%s,%s,%s' % (keySize, publicKey[0], publicKey[1]))
```

```
    fo.close()

    print()
    print('The private key is a %s and a %s digit number.' % 
(len(str(publicKey[0])), len(str(publicKey[1]))))
    print('Writing private key to file %s_privkey.txt...' % (name))
    fo = open('%s_privkey.txt' % (name), 'w')
    fo.write('%s,%s,%s' % (keySize, privateKey[0], privateKey[1]))
    fo.close()


# If makeRsaKeys.py is run (instead of imported as a module) call
# the main() function.
if __name__ == '__main__':
    main()
```

Sample Run of the RSA Key Generation Program

When you run the *makeRsaKeys.py* program, the output will look something like this (of course, the numbers for your keys will be different since they are random numbers):

```
Making key files...
Generating p prime...
Generating q prime...
Generating e that is relatively prime to (p-1)*(q-1)...
Calculating d that is mod inverse of e...
Public key:
(210902406316700502401968491406579417405090396754616926135810621216116191338086
5678407459875355468897928072386270510720443827324671435893274858393749685062411
6776147241821152026946322876869404394483922202407821672864242478920813182699000
8473526711744296548563866768454251404951960805224682425498975230488955908086491
8521163487778495362706850854469709529156400505222122042218037444940658810103314
8646830531744960702788478777031572995978999471326531132766377616771007701834003
6668306612665759417207845823479903440572724068125211002329298338718615859542093
72109725826359561748245019920074018549204468791300114315056117093,
1746023076917516102173184545923683355383240391086912905495420037367858093524760
6622265764388235752176654737805849023006544732896308685513669509917451195822611
3980989513066766009588891895645995814564600702703936932776834043548115756816059
906591453170741270845572335375041024799371425300216777273298110097435989)
Private key:
(210902406316700502401968491406579417405090396754616926135810621216116191338086
5678407459875355468897928072386270510720443827324671435893274858393749685062411
6776147241821152026946322876869404394483922202407821672864242478920813182699000
8473526711744296548563866768454251404951960805224682425498975230488955908086491
8521163487778495362706850854469709529156400505222122042218037444940658810103314
```

```
8646830531744960702788478777031572995978999471326531132766377616771007701834003
6668306612665759417207845823479903440572724068125211002329298338718615859542093
7210972582635956174824501992007401854920446879130011431505611 7093,
4767673579813771041216688491698376504317312028941690434129597155228687099187466
6099933371008075948549008551224760695942666962465968168995404993934508399014283
0537106767608359489023128886399384026861870750523607730623641626642761449656525
5854533116668173598098138449334931305875025941768372702963348445191139635826000
8181223734862132564880771928931192572481077942568188460364002867327313529283117
0178614206817165802812291528319562200625082557261680470845607063596018339193179
7437503163601143217769616471700002543036826990539739057474642785416933878499897
0147774814073713280530018380853144435458452190872495446633985 89)

The public key is a 617 and a 309 digit number.
Writing public key to file al_sweigart_pubkey.txt...

The private key is a 617 and a 309 digit number.
Writing private key to file al_sweigart_privkey.txt...
```

These two keys are written out to two different files, *al_sweigart_pubkey.txt* and *al_sweigart_privkey.txt*. These filenames are used because the string `'al_sweigart'` was passed to the `makeKeyFiles()` function. You can specify a different filenames by passing a different string. These key files will be used by the RSA cipher program to encrypt and decrypt messages.

If you try to run *makeRsaKeys.py* again with the same string being passed to `makeKeyFiles()`, the output of the program will look like this:

```
Making key files...
WARNING: The file al_sweigart_pubkey.txt or al_sweigart_privkey.txt already
exists! Use a different name or delete these files and re-run this program.
```

This warning is here so you don't accidentally overwrite your key files, making any files you encrypted with them impossible to recover. Keep your keys safe!

How the Key Generation Program Works

makeRsaKeys.py

```
# RSA Key Generator
# http://inventwithpython.com/hacking (BSD Licensed)

import random, sys, os, rabinMiller, cryptomath
```

The program imports the `rabinMiller` and `cryptomath` modules that we created in the last chapter, along with a few others.

makeRsaKeys.py

```
 7. def main():
 8.     # create a public/private keypair with 1024 bit keys
 9.     print('Making key files...')
10.     makeKeyFiles('al_sweigart', 1024)
11.     print('Key files made.')
```

When *makeRsaKeys.py* is run, the `main()` function is called, which will create the key files. Since the keys might take a while for the computer to generate, we print a message on line 9 before the `makeKeyFiles()` call so the user knows what the program is doing.

The `makeKeyFiles()` call on line 10 passes the string `'al_sweigart'` and the integer `1024`. This will generate keys with a size of 1024 bits and store them in files named *al_sweigart_pubkey.txt* and *al_sweigart_privkey.txt*.

The Program's `generateKey()` Function

makeRsaKeys.py

```
13. def generateKey(keySize):
14.     # Creates a public/private key pair with keys that are keySize bits in
15.     # size. This function may take a while to run.
16.
17.     # Step 1: Create two prime numbers, p and q. Calculate n = p * q.
18.     print('Generating p prime...')
19.     p = rabinMiller.generateLargePrime(keySize)
20.     print('Generating q prime...')
21.     q = rabinMiller.generateLargePrime(keySize)
22.     n = p * q
```

The first step of creating keys is coming up with two random prime numbers which are called p and q. The `generateLargePrime()` function we wrote in the last chapter's *rabinMiller.py* program will return a prime number (as an integer value) of the size determined by the value in `keySize` on line 19 and line 21. These integer values are stored in variables named `p` and `q`.

On line 22, the number n is calculated by multiplying `p` and `q`, and stored in `n`.

makeRsaKeys.py

```
24.     # Step 2: Create a number e that is relatively prime to (p-1)*(q-1).
25.     print('Generating e that is relatively prime to (p-1)*(q-1)...')
26.     while True:
27.         # Keep trying random numbers for e until one is valid.
28.         e = random.randrange(2 ** (keySize - 1), 2 ** (keySize))
29.         if cryptomath.gcd(e, (p - 1) * (q - 1)) == 1:
30.             break
```

The second step is calculating a number e which is relatively prime to the product of `p - 1` and `q - 1`. The `while` loop on line 26 is an infinite loop. The `random.randrange()` call on line 28 returns a random integer (stored in the `e` variable) and line 29 tests if this random number is relatively prime to `(p - 1) * (q - 1)`. If it is, the `break` statement on line 30 breaks out of the infinite loop. Otherwise, the program execution jumps back to line 26 and will keep trying different random numbers until it finds one that is relatively prime with `(p - 1) * (q - 1)`.

This way we can guarantee that when the program execution gets past this `while` loop, the variable `e` will contain a number that is relatively prime to `(p - 1) * (q - 1)`.

makeRsaKeys.py

```
    # Step 3: Calculate d, the mod inverse of e.
    print('Calculating d that is mod inverse of e...')
    d = cryptomath.findModInverse(e, (p - 1) * (q - 1))
```

The third step is to find the mod inverse of `e`. The `findModInverse()` function that we wrote for our `cryptomath` module in Chapter 14 will do this calculation for us. The mod inverse of `e` is stored in a variable named `d`.

makeRsaKeys.py

```
36.     publicKey = (n, e)
37.     privateKey = (n, d)
```

In the RSA cipher, each key is made up of two numbers. The public key will be the integers stored in `n` and `e`, and the private key will be the integers stored in `n` and `d`. Lines 36 and 37 store these integers as tuples in the variables `publicKey` and `privateKey`.

There's no reason `e` has to be in the public key and `d` in the private key, and you could swap them. However, once you make the public key public, you must keep the private key a secret.

makeRsaKeys.py

```
39.     print('Public key:', publicKey)
40.     print('Private key:', privateKey)
41.
42.     return (publicKey, privateKey)
```

The remaining lines in the `generateKey()` function print the keys on the screen with `print()` calls on lines 39 and 40. Then line 42's `generateKey()` call returns a tuple with `publicKey` and `privateKey`.

makeRsaKeys.py

```
45. def makeKeyFiles(name, keySize):
46.     # Creates two files 'x_pubkey.txt' and 'x_privkey.txt' (where x is the
47.     # value in name) with the the n,e and d,e integers written in them,
48.     # delimited by a comma.
```

While the `generateKey()` function will generate the actual integers for the public and private keys, we need to store these numbers in a file so that our RSA cipher program can use them later to encrypt and decrypt. Each of the keys are made of two integers that are hundreds of digits long; that's too many to memorize or conveniently write down. The easiest way to store them is as text files on your computer.

This means that you have to be sure that nobody hacks your computer and copies these key files. It might be a good idea to store these files on a USB thumb drive instead of on your computer. However, this is also risky. If someone borrows the thumb drive then they could copy the key files, or if you accidentally break or lose the thumb drive then you will lose your own private key!

makeRsaKeys.py

```
50.     # Our safety check will prevent us from overwriting our old key files:
51.     if os.path.exists('%s_pubkey.txt' % (name)) or
os.path.exists('%s_privkey.txt' % (name)):
52.         sys.exit('WARNING: The file %s_pubkey.txt or %s_privkey.txt already
exists! Use a different name or delete these files and re-run this program.' %
(name, name))
```

To prevent us from accidentally deleting our key files by running the program again, line 51 checks to see if the public or private key files with the given name already exist. If they do, the program will exit with a warning message.

makeRsaKeys.py

```
54.     publicKey, privateKey = generateKey(keySize)
```

After the check, line 54 has a call to `generateKey()` to get the public and private keys using the multiple assignment trick. The `generateKey()` function returns a tuple of two tuples. The first tuple has two integers for the public key and the second tuple has two integers for the private key. These are stored in the variables `publicKey` and `privateKey`.

RSA Key File Format

makeRsaKeys.py

```
56.     print()
57.     print('The public key is a %s and a %s digit number.' %
(len(str(publicKey[0])), len(str(publicKey[1]))))
```

```
58.     print('Writing public key to file %s_pubkey.txt...' % (name))
59.     fo = open('%s_pubkey.txt' % (name), 'w')
60.     fo.write('%s,%s,%s' % (keySize, publicKey[0], publicKey[1]))
61.     fo.close()
```

Line 57 prints some information about the public key. It can tell how many digits are in the integer in `publicKey[0]` and `publicKey[1]` by converting those values to strings with the `str()` function, and then finding the length of the string with the `len()` function.

The key file's contents will be the key size, a comma, the n integer, another comma, and the e (or d) integer. The file's contents will look like: <key size integer>,<n integer>,<e or d integer>

Lines 59 to 61 open a file in write mode, as you can tell from the `'w'` string passed to `open()`.

makeRsaKeys.py

```
63.     print()
64.     print('The private key is a %s and a %s digit number.' %
(len(str(publicKey[0])), len(str(publicKey[1]))))
65.     print('Writing private key to file %s_privkey.txt...' % (name))
66.     fo = open('%s_privkey.txt' % (name), 'w')
67.     fo.write('%s,%s,%s' % (keySize, privateKey[0], privateKey[1]))
68.     fo.close()
```

Lines 63 to 68 do the exact same thing as lines 56 and 61, except for writing the private key out to a file.

makeRsaKeys.py

```
71. # If makeRsaKeys.py is run (instead of imported as a module) call
72. # the main() function.
73. if __name__ == '__main__':
74.     main()
```

Lines 73 and 74 are at the bottom of the program, and call `main()` if *makeRsaKeys.py* is being run as a program instead of imported as a module by another program.

Hybrid Cryptosystems

In real life, the complicated mathematics make RSA and public-key encryption slow to compute. This is especially true for servers that need to make hundreds or thousands of encrypted connections a second. Instead, the RSA cipher is often used to encrypt the key for a symmetric key cipher. The encrypted key is then sent to the other person, and that key is used to pass messages that are encrypted using the (faster) symmetric cipher. Using a symmetric key cipher and an asymmetric key cipher to securely communicate like this is called a **hybrid**

cryptosystem. More information about hybrid cryptosystems can be found at https://en.wikipedia.org/wiki/Hybrid_cryptosystem.

It's not recommended to use the *rsaCipher.py* program to encrypt the keys for, say, the *vigenereCipher.py* program. We've already proven that the Vigenère cipher is hackable. A strong symmetric key cipher isn't covered in this book, but you can still use *rsaCipher.py* to encrypt your files anyway.

Source Code for the RSA Cipher Program

Now that you can create key files, let's write the program that does encryption and decryption with the RSA cipher. Open a new file editor window by clicking on **File ► New Window**. Type in the following code into the file editor, and then save it as *rsaCipher.py*.

Source code for rsaCipher.py

```
# RSA Cipher
# http://inventwithpython.com/hacking (BSD Licensed)

import sys

# IMPORTANT: The block size MUST be less than or equal to the key size!
# (Note: The block size is in bytes, the key size is in bits. There
# are 8 bits in 1 byte.)
DEFAULT_BLOCK_SIZE = 128 # 128 bytes
BYTE_SIZE = 256 # One byte has 256 different values.

def main():
    # Runs a test that encrypts a message to a file or decrypts a message
    # from a file.
    filename = 'encrypted_file.txt' # the file to write to/read from
    mode = 'encrypt' # set to 'encrypt' or 'decrypt'

    if mode == 'encrypt':
        message = '''"Journalists belong in the gutter because that is where the ruling classes throw their guilty secrets." -Gerald Priestland "The Founding Fathers gave the free press the protection it must have to bare the secrets of government and inform the people." -Hugo Black'''
        pubKeyFilename = 'al_sweigart_pubkey.txt'
        print('Encrypting and writing to %s...' % (filename))
        encryptedText = encryptAndWriteToFile(filename, pubKeyFilename, message)

        print('Encrypted text:')
        print(encryptedText)

```

```
    elif mode == 'decrypt':
        privKeyFilename = 'al_sweigart_privkey.txt'
        print('Reading from %s and decrypting...' % (filename))
        decryptedText = readFromFileAndDecrypt(filename, privKeyFilename)

        print('Decrypted text:')
        print(decryptedText)


def getBlocksFromText(message, blockSize=DEFAULT_BLOCK_SIZE):
    # Converts a string message to a list of block integers. Each integer
    # represents 128 (or whatever blockSize is set to) string characters.

    messageBytes = message.encode('ascii') # convert the string to bytes

    blockInts = []
    for blockStart in range(0, len(messageBytes), blockSize):
        # Calculate the block integer for this block of text
        blockInt = 0
        for i in range(blockStart, min(blockStart + blockSize, len(messageBytes))):
            blockInt += messageBytes[i] * (BYTE_SIZE ** (i % blockSize))
        blockInts.append(blockInt)
    return blockInts


def getTextFromBlocks(blockInts, messageLength, blockSize=DEFAULT_BLOCK_SIZE):
    # Converts a list of block integers to the original message string.
    # The original message length is needed to properly convert the last
    # block integer.
    message = []
    for blockInt in blockInts:
        blockMessage = []
        for i in range(blockSize - 1, -1, -1):
            if len(message) + i < messageLength:
                # Decode the message string for the 128 (or whatever
                # blockSize is set to) characters from this block integer.
                asciiNumber = blockInt // (BYTE_SIZE ** i)
                blockInt = blockInt % (BYTE_SIZE ** i)
                blockMessage.insert(0, chr(asciiNumber))
        message.extend(blockMessage)
    return ''.join(message)


def encryptMessage(message, key, blockSize=DEFAULT_BLOCK_SIZE):
```

```
    # Converts the message string into a list of block integers, and then
    # encrypts each block integer. Pass the PUBLIC key to encrypt.
    encryptedBlocks = []
    n, e = key

    for block in getBlocksFromText(message, blockSize):
        # ciphertext = plaintext ^ e mod n
        encryptedBlocks.append(pow(block, e, n))
    return encryptedBlocks


def decryptMessage(encryptedBlocks, messageLength, key, blockSize=DEFAULT_BLOCK_SIZE):
    # Decrypts a list of encrypted block ints into the original message
    # string. The original message length is required to properly decrypt
    # the last block. Be sure to pass the PRIVATE key to decrypt.
    decryptedBlocks = []
    n, d = key
    for block in encryptedBlocks:
        # plaintext = ciphertext ^ d mod n
        decryptedBlocks.append(pow(block, d, n))
    return getTextFromBlocks(decryptedBlocks, messageLength, blockSize)


def readKeyFile(keyFilename):
    # Given the filename of a file that contains a public or private key,
    # return the key as a (n,e) or (n,d) tuple value.
    fo = open(keyFilename)
    content = fo.read()
    fo.close()
    keySize, n, EorD = content.split(',')
    return (int(keySize), int(n), int(EorD))


def encryptAndWriteToFile(messageFilename, keyFilename, message, blockSize=DEFAULT_BLOCK_SIZE):
    # Using a key from a key file, encrypt the message and save it to a
    # file. Returns the encrypted message string.
    keySize, n, e = readKeyFile(keyFilename)

    # Check that key size is greater than block size.
    if keySize < blockSize * 8: # * 8 to convert bytes to bits
        sys.exit('ERROR: Block size is %s bits and key size is %s bits. The RSA cipher requires the block size to be equal to or greater than the key size. Either decrease the block size or use different keys.' % (blockSize * 8, keySize))
```

```


    # Encrypt the message
    encryptedBlocks = encryptMessage(message, (n, e), blockSize)

    # Convert the large int values to one string value.
    for i in range(len(encryptedBlocks)):
        encryptedBlocks[i] = str(encryptedBlocks[i])
    encryptedContent = ','.join(encryptedBlocks)

    # Write out the encrypted string to the output file.
    encryptedContent = '%s_%s_%s' % (len(message), blockSize, encryptedContent)
    fo = open(messageFilename, 'w')
    fo.write(encryptedContent)
    fo.close()
    # Also return the encrypted string.
    return encryptedContent


def readFromFileAndDecrypt(messageFilename, keyFilename):
    # Using a key from a key file, read an encrypted message from a file
    # and then decrypt it. Returns the decrypted message string.
    keySize, n, d = readKeyFile(keyFilename)


    # Read in the message length and the encrypted message from the file.
    fo = open(messageFilename)
    content = fo.read()
    messageLength, blockSize, encryptedMessage = content.split('_')
    messageLength = int(messageLength)
    blockSize = int(blockSize)

    # Check that key size is greater than block size.
    if keySize < blockSize * 8: # * 8 to convert bytes to bits
        sys.exit('ERROR: Block size is %s bits and key size is %s bits. The RSA cipher requires the block size to be equal to or greater than the key size. Did you specify the correct key file and encrypted file?' % (blockSize * 8, keySize))

    # Convert the encrypted message into large int values.
    encryptedBlocks = []
    for block in encryptedMessage.split(','):
        encryptedBlocks.append(int(block))

    # Decrypt the large int values.
```

```
154.     return decryptMessage(encryptedBlocks, messageLength, (n, d),
blockSize)
155.
156.
157. # If rsaCipher.py is run (instead of imported as a module) call
158. # the main() function.
159. if __name__ == '__main__':
160.     main()
```

Sample Run of the RSA Cipher Program

Once you have a public and private key file, you can send anyone your public file (or post it somewhere online) so others can send you messages. If you want to send a secret message to someone, first get their public key file and place it in the same directory as the *rsaCipher.py* program. Set the `message` variable on line 19 to the string of the message to encrypt.

Make sure the `mode` variable is set to the string `'encrypt'` on line 16, and set the `pubKeyFilename` variable to the public key file's filename on line 20. The `filename` variable holds a string of the file that the ciphertext will be written to.

When you run the program, the output will look like this:

```
Encrypting and writing to encrypted_file.txt...
Encrypted text:
262_128_99261588918914129248869521413561361425429438626950729912505980066002708
9830015533870663668185646157509007528457226336261821873976954531347724960840148
5234147843064609273929706353514554444810285427183303767133366827434264155196422
0917826499299282445350219039270525853857169256807439317455881433369973441896615
9641434946805896304802494813292321784924727694126957902732539670170912919151008
4539012275457327046892059514600198713235394985023008043572425418307615110483262
2796568393228930000619315738939341534920563203314816419962044702016227849752350
4147024496499607512346485462995420751762074555090914356781544081543O367,6684261
3553841756289795361296785769122909029892643608575548034344009592725547265584325
2331933112765122922637923600156910575424723444966430139306688707256391991191466
4504822721492217530056774346964092597494522555496959638903763181124233744530745
2041948917261094688708004245747998030244635761849845611609053856921438831555343
2751213283486646600584040245146570901217502941710992503572482408074196762322544
6680099823178790059243202224297039960462494558200472899766913932921695002362188
1996217713713494770944644417894970293643840346744192412614346008019737829011867
0314427110407829483914429004322850863987919388388931l384,7277016624458973047704
0806680156575455285570435553143790299815533233656061333313422971390933175290260
5817773458688756774589737014227054621841244485285514206025269405528441594535085
0536174716382559790627193026256934316461174349640238168693204610463496242533658
4736211406286896178786120454116459075038688037119234659059503824465257190001591
```

```
9094263967757274610514128826270203357049019841335033192183418122067029417580137
3024013553583624428117568253845170657841567369678118510784447456725765265002966
2854459043617323327066630863887606386875040688709377112851144150781493772858323
2592297835889765112614355127753100385178O
```

At the start of the text is 262 (which is the original message length), followed by an underscore and then 128 (which is the "block size"; block sizes are explained later). If you look carefully at the long string of digits after that, you will find two commas. The message is encrypted into three very large integers, separated by commas. These integers are the encrypted form of the string in the `message` variable on line 19.

To decrypt, change the `mode` variable to `'decrypt'` and run the program again. Make sure `privKeyFilename` on line 28 is set to the filename of the private key file and that this file is in the same folder as *rsaCipher.py*. When you run the program, the output on the screen will look like this:

```
Reading from encrypted_file.txt and decrypting...
Decrypted text:
"Journalists belong in the gutter because that is where the ruling classes
throw their guilty secrets." -Gerald Priestland "The Founding Fathers gave the
free press the protection it must have to bare the secrets of government and
inform the people." -Hugo Black
```

Note that the way the RSA cipher program is implemented, it can only encrypt and decrypt **plaintext files**. A plaintext file (not to be confused with "plaintext" in the cryptography sense) is a file that only contains text characters (like the kind that you can type on your keyboard). For example, the .py files that you type for your Python programs are plaintext files. Plaintext files are the type created with text editor software such as Notepad (on Windows), TextMate (on OS X), or Gedit (on Ubuntu). Specifically, plaintext files are files that only contain ASCII values (which are described later in this chapter).

Files such as images, videos, executable programs, or word processor files are called **binary files**.(Word processor files are binary files because their text has font, color, and size information bundled with the text.) More information about plaintext files and binary files can be found at http://invpy.com/plainvsbinary.

Practice Exercises, Chapter 24, Set A

Practice exercises can be found at http://invpy.com/hackingpractice24A.

Digital Signatures

Digital signatures is a very large topic of its own, but we can cover a little of it here. Let's say Alice sent this email to Bob:

```
From: alice@inventwithpython.com
To: bob@coffeeghost.net
Subject: Our agreement.

Dear Bob,
I promise to buy your old broken laptop for one
million dollars.

Sincerely,
Alice
```

This is great news to Bob, who wants to get rid of his worthless laptop for any price. But what if Alice later claims that she didn't make this promise, and that the email Bob has is a forgery that didn't really come from her. The email just exists as some file on Bob's computer. Bob could have easily created this file himself.

If they had met in person, Alice and Bob could have signed a contract. The handwritten signature is not easy to forge and provides some proof that Alice really did make this promise. But even if Alice signed such a paper, took a photo of it with her digital camera, and sent Bob the image file, it is still believable for Alice to say that the image was photoshopped.

The RSA cipher (and any public key cipher) not only provides encryption, but it can also provide a way to *digitally sign* a file or string. Remember that RSA has a public key and a private key, and that any string that is encrypted with one key produces ciphertext that can only be decrypted with the other key. Normally we encrypt with the public key, so that only the owner of the private key can decrypt this ciphertext.

But we can also do the reverse. If Alice writes this message, and then "encrypts" it with her *private key*, this will produce "ciphertext" that only Alice's public key can decrypt. This "ciphertext" isn't really so secret since everyone in the world has access to Alice's public key to decrypt it. **But by encrypting a message with her own private key, Alice has digitally signed the message in a way that cannot be forged.** Everyone can decrypt this signed message with her public key, and since only Alice has access to her private key, only Alice could have produced this ciphertext. Alice has to stick to her digital signature; she can't say that Bob forged or photoshopped it!

This feature is called nonrepudiation. **Nonrepudiation** is where someone who has made a statement or claim cannot later refute that they made that statement or claim. Alice could always claim that her computer was hacked and somebody else had access to her private key, but this would mean that any other documents she signed could be called into question. (And it would be very suspicious if Alice's computer kept "getting hacked" each time she wanted to back out of a promise.)

Digital signatures can also provide authentication, which allows someone to prove they are who they say they are. If Alice gets an email claiming to be from the President but wants to be sure it really is the President, she could always respond with, "Prove you're the President! Encrypt the string 'SIMTAVOKXVAHXXSLBGZXVPKNMQMHOYGWFQMXEBCC' with the President's private key." and Alice would be able to decrypt the reply with the President's public key to see if it decrypted to her random string. This is called a **challenge-response authentication** system.

Digital signatures can be used to do many important things, including digital cash, authentication of public keys, or anonymous web surfing. If you'd like to find out more, go to http://invpy.com/digitalsignatures.

How the RSA Cipher Program Works

rsaCipher.py

```
# RSA Cipher
# http://inventwithpython.com/hacking (BSD Licensed)

import sys

# IMPORTANT: The block size MUST be less than or equal to the key size!
# (Note: The block size is in bytes, the key size is in bits. There
# are 8 bits in 1 byte.)
DEFAULT_BLOCK_SIZE = 128 # 128 bytes
BYTE_SIZE = 256 # One byte has 256 different values.
```

A single "byte" can hold a number between 0 and 255, that is, 256 different numbers. We will use this fact in some of the block-related math explained later. This is why the `BYTE_SIZE` constant is set to `256`. The `DEFAULT_BLOCK_SIZE` constant is set to `128` because we will be using block sizes of 128 bytes by default in our program. (Block sizes are explained later.)

rsaCipher.py

```
def main():
    # Runs a test that encrypts a message to a file or decrypts a message
    # from a file.
    filename = 'encrypted_file.txt' # the file to write to/read from
```

```
16.     mode = 'encrypt' # set to 'encrypt' or 'decrypt'
```

If `mode` is set to `'encrypt'` the program encrypts a message (and writes it to the file that is named in `filename`). If `mode` is set to `'decrypt'` the program reads the contents of an encrypted file (specified by the string in `filename`) to decrypt it.

rsaCipher.py

```
18.     if mode == 'encrypt':
19.         message = '''"Journalists belong in the gutter because that is
where the ruling classes throw their guilty secrets." -Gerald Priestland "The
Founding Fathers gave the free press the protection it must have to bare the
secrets of government and inform the people." -Hugo Black'''
20.         pubKeyFilename = 'al_sweigart_pubkey.txt'
21.         print('Encrypting and writing to %s...' % (filename))
22.         encryptedText = encryptAndWriteToFile(filename, pubKeyFilename,
message)
23.
24.         print('Encrypted text:')
25.         print(encryptedText)
```

The `message` variable contains the text to be encrypted, and `pubKeyFilename` contains the filename of the public key file. Line 22 calls the `encryptAndWriteToFile()` function, which will encrypt `message` using the key, and write the encrypted message to the file named in `filename`.

rsaCipher.py

```
27.     elif mode == 'decrypt':
28.         privKeyFilename = 'al_sweigart_privkey.txt'
29.         print('Reading from %s and decrypting...' % (filename))
30.         decryptedText = readFromFileAndDecrypt(filename, privKeyFilename)
31.
32.         print('Decrypted text:')
33.         print(decryptedText)
```

The code that handles calling the decryption function is similar to the code on lines 18 to 33. The filename of the private key file is set in `privKeyFilename`. The encrypted file's filename is stored in the `filename` variable. These two variables are passed to a call to `readFromFileAndDecrypt()`. The return value is stored in `decryptedText` and then printed to the screen.

ASCII: Using Numbers to Represent Characters

All data is stored on your computer as numbers. A code called the American Standard Code for Information Interchange, or ASCII (pronounced "ask-ee") maps numbers to characters. Table 24-1 shows how ASCII maps numbers and characters (only numbers 32 to 126 are used):

Table 24-1. The ASCII table.

32	(space)	48	0	64	@	80	P	96	`	112	p
33	!	49	1	65	A	81	Q	97	a	113	q
34	"	50	2	66	B	82	R	98	b	114	r
35	#	51	3	67	C	83	S	99	c	115	s
36	$	52	4	68	D	84	T	100	d	116	t
37	%	53	5	69	E	85	U	101	e	117	u
38	&	54	6	70	F	86	V	102	f	118	v
39	'	55	7	71	G	87	W	103	g	119	w
40	(	56	8	72	H	88	X	104	h	120	x
41	)	57	9	73	I	89	Y	105	i	121	y
42	*	58	:	74	J	90	Z	106	j	122	z
43	+	59	;	75	K	91	[	107	k	123	{
44	,	60	<	76	L	92	\	108	l	124	|
45	-	61	=	77	M	93	]	109	m	125	}
46	.	62	>	78	N	94	^	110	n	126	~
47	/	63	?	79	O	95	_	111	o		

A single ASCII character uses one byte of memory to store. A byte is enough memory to store a number from 0 to 255 (for a total of 256 different values.) So the string `'Hello'` is actually stored on your computer as the numbers 72, 101, 108, 108, and 111. These numbers take up 5 bytes. ASCII provides a standard way to convert string characters to numbers and back.

ASCII works fine for English messages, but not so much for other European languages that have special characters such as the è in "Vigenère", or languages such as Chinese and Arabic. ASCII doesn't even work well outside of America, since ASCII includes the $ dollar sign but not the € euro or £ pound signs. If you want to learn about Unicode, the international system of character encoding, go to http://invpy.com/unicode. But this book will use ASCII for simplicity.

The `chr()` and `ord()` Functions

Remember from the first chapter where a code was a publicly-known way of translating information from one format to another format? For example, Morse code was a way of translating English letters into electric pulses of dots and dashes. ASCII is just a code. We can encode characters into ASCII numbers and decode ASCII numbers back to characters.

The `chr()` function (pronounced "char", short for "character") takes an integer ASCII number as the argument and returns a single-character string. The `ord()` function (short for "ordinal") takes a single-character string as the argument, and returns the integer ASCII value for that character. Try typing the following into the interactive shell:

```
>>> chr(65)
'A'
>>> ord('A')
65
>>> chr(73)
'I'
>>> chr(65+8)
'I'
>>> chr(52)
'4'
>>> chr(ord('F'))
'F'
>>> ord(chr(68))
68
>>>
```

But if you have a string with many letters, it may be easier to use the `encode()` and `decode()` string methods explained later in this chapter.

Practice Exercises, Chapter 24, Set B

Practice exercises can be found at http://invpy.com/hackingpractice24B.

Blocks

In cryptography, a "block" is a fixed length of bits. In our RSA cipher program, a block is represented by an integer. We've set the block size to 128 bytes, or 1024 bits (since there are 8 bits in 1 byte). Our message string value will be converted into several integer values (i.e. several blocks).

- It is important to note that the RSA encryption algorithm requires that **the block size be equal or less than the key size**. Otherwise, the math doesn't work and you won't be able to decrypt the ciphertext the program produced.

So a cryptographic block is really just a very large integer. Since our block size is 128 bytes, it can represent any integer between 0 and up to (but not including) 256 ^ 128, which is 179,769,313,486,231,590,772,930,519,078,902,473,361,797,697,894,230,657,273,430,081,157,732,675,805,500,963,132,708,477,322,407,536,021,120,113,879,871,393,357,658,789,768,814,41

6,622,492,847,430,639,474,124,377,767,893,424,865,485,276,302,219,601,246,094,119,453,082,952,085,005,768,838,150,682,342,462,881,473,913,110,540,827,237,163,350,510,684,586,298,239,947,245,938,479,716,304,835,356,329,624,224,137,216.

(You might have noticed that the RSA cipher uses a lot of big numbers.)

The reason RSA needs to work on a block (which represents multiple characters) is because if we used the RSA encryption algorithm on a single character, the same plaintext characters would always encrypt to the same ciphertext characters. In that case, the RSA cipher just becomes a simple substitution cipher with fancy mathematics, kind of like the affine and Caesar ciphers.

The RSA cipher works by encrypting an integer that is hundreds of digits long (that is, a block) into a new integer that is hundreds of digits long (that is, a new block). The mathematics of encrypting a large plaintext integer to a large ciphertext integer are simple enough. But first we will need a way to convert between a string and a large integer (that is, a block).

We can use ASCII as a system to convert between a single character and a small integer (between 0 and 255). But we will also need a way to combine several small integers into a large integer that we perform RSA encryption on.

Remember how the affine cipher in Chapter 15 had two keys, Key A and Key B, but they were combined by multiplying Key A by the symbol set size (which was 95) and then adding Key B? This was how we combined two small key integers into one larger key integer.

This worked because the ranges of both Key A and Key B were from 0 to 94. In the RSA program, each character's ASCII integer ranges from 0 to 255. To combine ASCII integers together into one large number we use the following formula:

Take the ASCII integer of the character at index `0` of the string and multiply it by 256 ^ 0 (but since 256 ^ 0 is 1, and multiplying by 1 leaves you with just the original number, this one is easy). Take the ASCII integer of the character at index `1` and multiply it by 256 ^ 1. Take the ASCII integer of the character at index `2` and multiply it by 256 ^ 2, and so on and so on. To get the final large integer, add all of these products together. This integer is the ciphertext's block.

Table 24-2 has an example using the string, `'Hello world!'`:

Table 24-2. Encoding a string into a block.

Index	Character	ASCII Number	Multiplied By	Number
0	H	72	× 256 ^ 0	= 72
1	e	101	× 256 ^ 1	= 25,856
2	l	108	× 256 ^ 2	= 7,077,888
3	l	108	× 256 ^ 3	= 1,811,939,328
4	o	111	× 256 ^ 4	= 476,741,369,856
5	(space)	32	× 256 ^ 5	= 35,184,372,088,832
6	w	119	× 256 ^ 6	= 33,495,522,228,568,064
7	o	111	× 256 ^ 7	= 7,998,392,938,210,000,896
8	r	114	× 256 ^ 8	= 2,102,928,824,402,888,884,224
9	l	108	× 256 ^ 9	= 510,015,580,149,921,683,079,168
10	d	100	× 256 ^ 10	= 120,892,581,961,462,917,470,617,600
11	!	33	× 256 ^ 11	= 10,213,005,324,104,387,267,917,774,848
			SUM:	10,334,410,032,606,748,633,331,426,632

(You might have noticed that the RSA cipher does a lot of math with big numbers.)

So the string `'Hello world!'` when put into a single large integer "block" becomes the integer 10,334,410,032,606,748,633,331,426,632. This integer uniquely refers to the string `'Hello world!'`. By continuing to use larger and larger powers of 256, any string possible has exactly one large integer. For example, 2,175,540 is the integer for `'42!'` and 17,802,628,493,700,941 is the integer for `'Moose??'` and 23,071,981,395,336,227,453,293,155,570,939,985,398,502,658,016,284,755,880,397,214,576,110,064,091,578,359,739,349,325 is the integer for `'My cat's breath smells like cat food.'`.

Because our block size is 128 bytes, we can only encrypt up to 128 characters in a single block. But we can just use more blocks if the message is longer than 128 characters. The RSA cipher program will separate the blocks it outputs with commas so we can tell when one block ends and the next one begins.

As an example, here's a message that is split into blocks, and the integer that represents each block (calculated using the same method in Table 24-2.). Each block has at most 128 characters of the message.

Table 24-3. A message split into blocks, with each block's integer.

	Message	Block Integer
1st Block (128 characters)	Alan Mathison Turing was a British mathematician, logician, cryptanalyst, and computer scientist. He was highly influential in t	81546931218178010029845817915569188970228 63503588092404856861189798874246340656702 38839432215827478831941988018897629951268 20043055718365161172430048774726604180301 48768604258244651074200425332013985856895 55969506391783606289711328048889254351125 31133886746309774148590001157056903849858 716430520524535327809
2nd Block (128 characters)	he development of computer science, providing a formalisation of the concepts of "algorithm" and "computation" with the Turing m	76631289268154712859022451851447083030531 65677349319343558638588471345037404319956 45932085093160422349968619052225062492420 68799766044149679741160521638235464390814 93343748091892111084834682008279498952509 54725768834415584340223896902248947030025 14434767442075089828357797890134106785932 701869224970151814504
3rd Block (128 characters)	achine. Turing is widely considered to be the father of computer science and artificial intelligence. During World War II, Turin	77533874832922662837221187157031815413218 69665618828947923728504232931792998759025 56568632161704130179292825376098664640739 13897327838474709028475738093888688583459 78166272494460147358283858671447396525449 89137517820478280435270940014295674175014 93130489686652467441331220556610652015232 230994266943673361249
4th Block (107 characters)	g worked for the Government Code and Cypher School (GCCS) at Bletchley Park, Britain's codebreaking centre.	87080208891262703930798322686594857958157 73519113112470129994578811890430257029137 88108716196921960428416274796671334547332 64625727703476738415017881880631980435061 77034123161704448596151119133333044771426 77343891157354079822547964726407323487308 38206586983

Converting Strings to Blocks with `getBlocksFromText()`

rsaCipher.py

```
def getBlocksFromText(message, blockSize=DEFAULT_BLOCK_SIZE):
    # Converts a string message to a list of block integers. Each integer
    # represents 128 (or whatever blockSize is set to) string characters.
```

The `getBlocksFromText()` function takes the message and returns a list of blocks (that is, a list of very large integer values) that represents the message. It is trivially easy to convert between strings to blocks and blocks to strings, so this step isn't encrypting anything. The encryption will be done later in the `encryptMessage()` function.

The `encode()` String Method and the Bytes Data Type

rsaCipher.py

```
40.     messageBytes = message.encode('ascii') # convert the string to bytes
```

First, we need to convert the characters in the message string into ASCII integers. The `encode()` string method will return a "bytes" object. Because a byte is represented as a number from 0 to 255, a bytes value is like a list of integers (although these integers have a very limited range of 0 to 255). The `len()` function and indexing work with a bytes object in the same way a list of integers would. A bytes value can be turned into a list value of integer values by passing it to the `list()` function. Try typing the following into the interactive shell:

```
>>> spam = 'hello'.encode('ascii')
>>> spam
b'hello'
>>> list(spam)
[104, 101, 108, 108, 111]
>>> len(spam)
5
>>> spam[2]
108
>>>
```

Note that a single bytes value is a collection of values, just like a single list value can contain multiple values. If you try to get a single "byte" from a bytes object (like `spam[2]` does above), this just evaluates to an integer value.

Line 140 places the bytes form of the `message` string in a variable named `messageBytes`.

The `bytes()` Function and `decode()` Bytes Method

Just like you can create a list by calling the `list()` function, you can also create a bytes object by calling the `bytes()` function. The `bytes()` function is passed a list of integers for the byte values. Try typing the following into the interactive shell:

```
>>> spam = bytes([104, 101, 108, 108, 111])
>>> spam
b'hello'
>>> list(spam)
[104, 101, 108, 108, 111]
```

```
>>>
```

You can also directly type a bytes object into your source code just like you type a string or list. A bytes object has the letter b right before what looks like an ordinary string value. But remember, the letter b right before the quotes means that this is a bytes value, not a string value. Try typing the following into the interactive shell, making sure that there is no space between the b and the quote characters:

```
>>> spam = b'hello'
>>> list(spam)
[104, 101, 108, 108, 111]
>>>
```

We don't use the `decode()` bytes method in this program, but you should know about it. It does the opposite of the `encode()` string method. When called on a bytes object, the `decode()` method returns a string made from the values stored in the bytes object. Try typing the following into the interactive shell:

```
>>> spam = bytes([104, 101, 108, 108, 111])
>>> spam.decode('ascii')
'hello'
>>>
```

Practice Exercises, Chapter 24, Set C

Practice exercises can be found at http://invpy.com/hackingpractice24C.

Back to the Code

rsaCipher.py

```
42.     blockInts = []
43.     for blockStart in range(0, len(messageBytes), blockSize):
```

The `blockInts` list will contain the large integer "blocks" form of the characters in `message`. The `blockSize` parameter is set to `DEFAULT_BLOCK_SIZE` by default, and the `DEFAULT_BLOCK_SIZE` constant was set to `128` (meaning, 128 bytes) on line 9. This means that each large integer block can only store 128 string characters at most (since 1 ASCII character takes up 1 byte). See Table 24-3 for an example of a message split into 128-character blocks.

Line 43's `for` loop will set the value in `blockStart` so that on each iteration it will be set to the index of the block being created. For example, if `blockSize` is set to `128`, then the index of the start of the first block will be `0`, the index of the start of the second block will be `128`, the index of the start of the third block will be `256`, and so on as long as the index is less than `len(messageBytes)`.

The `min()` and `max()` Functions

The `min()` function returns the smallest (that is, the minimum) value of its arguments. Try typing the following into the interactive shell:

```
>>> min(13, 32, 13, 15, 17, 39)
13
>>> min(21, 45, 18, 10)
10
```

You can also pass `min()` a single argument if the argument is a list or tuple value. In this case, `min()` returns the smallest value in that list or tuple. Try typing the following into the interactive shell:

```
>>> min([31, 26, 20, 13, 12, 36])
12
>>> spam = (10, 37, 37, 43, 3)
>>> min(spam)
3
>>>
```

The `max()` function will return the largest (that is, the maximum) value of its arguments:

```
>>> max(18, 15, 22, 30, 31, 34)
34
>>>
```

rsaCipher.py

```
44.         # Calculate the block integer for this block of text
45.         blockInt = 0
46.         for i in range(blockStart, min(blockStart + blockSize,
len(messageBytes))):
```

The code inside line 43's `for` loop will create the very large integer for a single block. Recall from earlier in this chapter that this is done by multiplying the ASCII value of the character by (256 ^ index-of-character).

The very large integer will eventually be stored in `blockInt`, which starts at `0` on line 45. (This is much like how our previous cipher programs had a `translated` variable that started as a blank string but eventually held the encrypted or decrypted message by the end of the program.)

Line 46's `for` loop sets `i` to be the index of all the characters in `message` **for this block**. This index should start at `blockStart` and go up to `blockStart + blockSize` (that is, `blockSize` characters after `blockStart`) *or* `len(messageBytes)`, whichever is smaller. The `min()` call on line 46 will return the smaller of these two expressions.

The second argument to `range()` on line 46 should be the smaller of these values because each block will always be made up of 128 (or whatever value is in `blockSize`) characters, *except* for the last block. The last block might be exactly 128 characters, but more likely it is less than the full 128 characters. In that case we want `i` to stop at `len(messageBytes)` because that will be the last index in `messageBytes`.

```
rsaCipher.py
47.             blockInt += messageBytes[i] * (BYTE_SIZE ** (i % blockSize))
```

The value that is added to the block integer in `blockInt` is the ASCII value of the character (which is what `messageBytes[i]` evaluates to) multiplied by (256 ^ index-of-character).

The variable `i` cannot directly be used for the index-of-character part of the equation, because it is the index in the entire `messageBytes` object which has indexes from `0` up to `len(messageBytes)`. We only want the index relative to the *current iteration's block*, which will always be from `0` to `blockSize`. This table shows the difference between these indexes:

Table 24-4. The indexes of the full message on top, and indexes relative to the block on bottom.

1st Block's Indexes						2nd Block's Indexes					3rd Block's Indexes				
0	1	2	…	127	128	129	130	…	255	256	257	258	…	511	512
0	1	2	…	127	128	0	1	…	127	128	0	1	…	127	128

By modding `i` by `blockSize`, we can get the position relative to the block. This is why line 47 is `BYTE_SIZE ** (i % blockSize)` instead of `BYTE_SIZE ** i`.

```
rsaCipher.py
48.         blockInts.append(blockInt)
49.     return blockInts
```

After line 46's `for` loop completes, the very large integer for the block has been calculated. We want to append this block integer to the `blockInts` list. The next iteration of line 43's `for` loop will calculate the block integer for the next block of the message.

After line 43's `for` loop has finished, all of the block integers have been calculated and are stored in the `blockInts` list. Line 49 returns `blockInts` from `getBlocksFromText()`.

rsaCipher.py

```
52. def getTextFromBlocks(blockInts, messageLength,
blockSize=DEFAULT_BLOCK_SIZE):
53.     # Converts a list of block integers to the original message string.
54.     # The original message length is needed to properly convert the last
55.     # block integer.
56.     message = []
57.     for blockInt in blockInts:
```

The `getTextFromBlocks()` function does the opposite of `getBlocksFromText()`. This function is passed a list of block integers (as the `blockInts` parameter) and returns the string value that these blocks represent. The function needs the length of the message encoded in `messageLength`, since this information is needed to get the string from the last block integer if it is not a full 128 characters in size.

Just as before, `blockSize` will default to `DEFAULT_BLOCK_SIZE` if no third argument is passed to `getTextFromBlocks()`, and `DEFAULT_BLOCK_SIZE` was set to `128` on line 9.

The `message` list (which starts as blank on line 56) will contain a string value for each character that was computed from each block integer in `blockInts`. (This list of strings will be joined together to form the complete string at the end of `getTextFromBlocks()`.) The `message` list starts off empty on line 56. The `for` loop on line 57 iterates over each block integer in the `blockInts` list.

rsaCipher.py

```
58.         blockMessage = []
59.         for i in range(blockSize - 1, -1, -1):
```

Inside the `for` loop, the code from lines 58 to 65 calculates the letters that are in the current iteration's block. Recall from Chapter 15's affine cipher program how one integer key was split into two integer keys:

```
def getKeyParts(key):
    keyA = key // len(SYMBOLS)
    keyB = key % len(SYMBOLS)
    return (keyA, keyB)
```

The code in `getTextFromBlocks()` works in a similar way, except the single integer (i.e. the block integer) is split into 128 integers (and each is the ASCII value for a single character). The way the ASCII numbers are extracted from `blockInt` has to work backwards, which is why the `for` loop on line 59 starts at `blockSize - 1`, and then subtracts `1` on each iteration down to (but not including) `-1`. This means the value of `i` on the last iteration will be `0`.

rsaCipher.py

```
60.             if len(message) + i < messageLength:
61.                 # Decode the message string for the 128 (or whatever
62.                 # blockSize is set to) characters from this block integer.
63.                 asciiNumber = blockInt // (BYTE_SIZE ** i)
64.                 blockInt = blockInt % (BYTE_SIZE ** i)
```

The length of the `message` list will be how many characters have been translated from blocks so far. The `if` statement on line 60 makes sure the code does not keep computing text from the block after `i` has reached the end of the `message`.

The ASCII number of the next character from the block is calculated by integer dividing `blockInt` by `(BYTE_SIZE ** i)`. Now that we have calculated this character, we can "remove" it from the block by setting `blockInt` to the remainder of `blockInt` divided by `(BYTE_SIZE ** i)`. The `%` mod operator is used to calculate the remainder.

The `insert()` List Method

While the `append()` list method only adds values to the end of a list, the `insert()` list method can add a value *anywhere* in the list. The arguments to `insert()` are an integer index of where in the list to insert the value, and the value to be inserted. Try typing the following into the interactive shell:

```
>>> spam = [2, 4, 6, 8]
>>> spam.insert(0, 'hello')
>>> spam
['hello', 2, 4, 6, 8]
>>> spam.insert(2, 'world')
>>> spam
['hello', 2, 'world', 4, 6, 8]
>>>
```

rsaCipher.py

```
65.                 blockMessage.insert(0, chr(asciiNumber))
```

Using the `chr()` function, the character that `asciiNumber` is the ASCII number of is inserted to the beginning of the list at index `0`.

rsaCipher.py

```
66.         message.extend(blockMessage)
```

After the `for` loop on line 59 completes, `blockMessage` will be a list of single-character strings that were computed *from the current block integer*. The strings in this list are appended to the end of the `message` list with the `extend()` method.

rsaCipher.py
```
67.     return ''.join(message)
```

After the `for` loop on line 57 completes, the single-character strings in `message` are joined together into a single string which is the complete message. This string is then returned from the `getTextFromBlocks()` function.

The Mathematics of RSA Encrypting and Decrypting

With the numbers for e, d, and n from the public and private keys, the mathematics done on the block integers to encrypt and decrypt them can be summarized as follows:

- Encrypted Block = Plaintext Block ^ e mod n
- Decrypted Block = Ciphertext Block ^ d mod n

rsaCipher.py
```
70. def encryptMessage(message, key, blockSize=DEFAULT_BLOCK_SIZE):
71.     # Converts the message string into a list of block integers, and then
72.     # encrypts each block integer. Pass the PUBLIC key to encrypt.
73.     encryptedBlocks = []
74.     n, e = key
```

The `encryptMessage()` function is passed the plaintext string along with the two-integer tuple of the private key. The function returns a list of integer blocks of the encrypted ciphertext. First, the `encryptedBlocks` variable starts as an empty list that holds the integer blocks and the two integers in `key` are assigned to variables `n` and `e`.

The `pow()` Function

While the `**` operator does exponents, the `pow()` function handles exponents and mod. The expression `pow(a, b, c)` is equivalent to `(a ** b) % c`. However, the code inside the `pow()` function knows how to intelligently handle very large integers and is **much** faster than typing the expression `(a ** b) % c`. Try typing the following into the interactive shell:

```
>>> pow(2, 8)
256
>>> (2 ** 8)
256
>>> pow(2, 8, 10)
```

```
6
>>> (2 ** 8) % 10
6
>>>
```

rsaCipher.py

```
76.     for block in getBlocksFromText(message, blockSize):
77.         # ciphertext = plaintext ^ e mod n
78.         encryptedBlocks.append(pow(block, e, n))
79.     return encryptedBlocks
```

While creating the public and private keys involved a lot of math, the actual math of the encryption is simple. The very large integer of the block created from the string in `message` is raised to `e` and then modded by `n`. This expression evaluates to the encrypted block integer, and is then appended to `encryptedBlocks` on line 78.

After all the blocks have been encrypted, the function returns `encryptedBlocks` on line 79.

rsaCipher.py

```
82. def decryptMessage(encryptedBlocks, messageLength, key, blockSize=DEFAULT_BLOCK_SIZE):
83.     # Decrypts a list of encrypted block ints into the original message
84.     # string. The original message length is required to properly decrypt
85.     # the last block. Be sure to pass the PRIVATE key to decrypt.
86.     decryptedBlocks = []
87.     n, d = key
```

The math used in the `decryptMessage()` function is also simple. The `decryptedBlocks` variable will store a list of the decrypted integer blocks, and the two integers of the `key` tuple are placed in `n` and `d` respectively using the multiple assignment trick.

rsaCipher.py

```
88.     for block in encryptedBlocks:
89.         # plaintext = ciphertext ^ d mod n
90.         decryptedBlocks.append(pow(block, d, n))
```

The math of the decryption on line 90 is the same as the encryption's math, except the integer block is being raised to `d` instead of `e`.

rsaCipher.py

```
91.     return getTextFromBlocks(decryptedBlocks, messageLength, blockSize)
```

The decrypted blocks along with the `messageLength` and `blockSize` parameters are passed `getTextFromBlocks()` so that the decrypted plaintext as a string is returned from `decryptMessage()`.

Reading in the Public & Private Keys from their Key Files

rsaCipher.py

```
94. def readKeyFile(keyFilename):
95.     # Given the filename of a file that contains a public or private key,
96.     # return the key as a (n,e) or (n,d) tuple value.
97.     fo = open(keyFilename)
98.     content = fo.read()
99.     fo.close()
```

The key files that *makeRsakeys.py* creates look like this:

<key size as an integer>,<big integer for N>,<big integer for E or D>

The `readKeyFile()` function is called to read the key size, n, and e (for the public key) or d (for the private key) values from the key file. Lines 97 to 99 open this file and read in the contents as a string into the `content` variable.

rsaCipher.py

```
100.     keySize, n, EorD = content.split(',')
101.     return (int(keySize), int(n), int(EorD))
```

The `split()` string method splits up the string in content along the commas. The list that `split()` returns will have three items in it, and the multiple assignment trick will place each of these items into the `keySize`, `n`, and `EorD` variables respectively on line 100.

Remember that `content` was a string when it was read from the file, and the items in the list that `split()` returns will also be string values. So before returning the `keySize`, `n`, and `EorD` values, they are each passed to `int()` to return an integer form of the value. This is how `readKeyFile()` returns three integers that were read from the key file.

The Full RSA Encryption Process

rsaCipher.py

```
104. def encryptAndWriteToFile(messageFilename, keyFilename, message,
blockSize=DEFAULT_BLOCK_SIZE):
105.     # Using a key from a key file, encrypt the message and save it to a
106.     # file. Returns the encrypted message string.
107.     keySize, n, e = readKeyFile(keyFilename)
```

The `encryptAndWriteToFile()` function is passed three string arguments: a filename to write the encrypted message in, a filename of the public key to use, and a message to be encrypted. This function handles not just encrypting the string with the key, but also creating the file that contains the encrypted contents. (The `blockSize` parameter can also be specified, but it will be set to `DEFAULT_BLOCK_SIZE` by default, which is `128`.)

The first step is to read in the values for `keySize`, `n`, and `e` from the key file by calling `readKeyFile()` on line 107.

rsaCipher.py

```
109.     # Check that key size is greater than block size.
110.     if keySize < blockSize * 8: # * 8 to convert bytes to bits
111.         sys.exit('ERROR: Block size is %s bits and key size is %s bits. The RSA cipher requires the block size to be equal to or greater than the key size. Either decrease the block size or use different keys.' % (blockSize * 8, keySize))
```

In order for the mathematics of the RSA cipher to work, the key size must be equal to or greater than the block size. The `blockSize` value is in bytes, while the key size that was stored in the key file was in bits, so we multiply the integer in `blockSize` by 8 on line 110 so that both of these values represent number of bits.

If `keySize` is less than `blockSize * 8`, the program exits with an error message. The user will either have to decrease the value passed for `blockSize` or use a larger key.

rsaCipher.py

```
114.     # Encrypt the message
115.     encryptedBlocks = encryptMessage(message, (n, e), blockSize)
```

Now that we have the `n` and `e` values for the key, we call the `encryptMessage()` function which returns a list of integer blocks on line 115. The `encryptMessage()` is expecting a two-integer tuple for the key, which is why the `n` and `e` variables are placed inside a tuple that is then passed as the second argument for `encryptMessage()`.

rsaCipher.py

```
117.     # Convert the large int values to one string value.
118.     for i in range(len(encryptedBlocks)):
119.         encryptedBlocks[i] = str(encryptedBlocks[i])
120.     encryptedContent = ','.join(encryptedBlocks)
```

The `join()` method will return a string of the blocks separated by commas, but `join()` only works on lists with string values, and `encryptedBlocks` is a list of integers. These integers will have to first be converted into strings.

The `for` loop on line 118 iterates through each index in `encryptedBlocks`, replacing the integer at `encryptedBlocks[i]` with a string form of the integer. When the loop completes, `encryptedBlocks` now contains a list of string values instead of a list of integer values.

The list of string values is passed to the `join()` method, which returns a single string of the list's strings joined together with commas. Line 120 stores this string in a variable named `encryptedContent`.

rsaCipher.py

```
122.     # Write out the encrypted string to the output file.
123.     encryptedContent = '%s_%s_%s' % (len(message), blockSize,
encryptedContent)
```

We want to write out more than just the encrypted integer blocks to the file though, so line 123 changes the `encryptedContent` variable to include the size of the message (as an integer), followed by an underscore, followed by the `blockSize` (which is also an integer), followed by another underscore, and then followed by the encrypted integer blocks.

rsaCipher.py

```
124.     fo = open(messageFilename, 'w')
125.     fo.write(encryptedContent)
126.     fo.close()
```

The last step is to write out the contents of the encrypted file. The filename provided by the `messageFilename` parameter is created with the call to `open()` on line 124. (The `'w'` argument tells `open()` to open the file in "write mode".) Note that if a file with this name already exists, then it will be overwritten by the new file.

The string in `encryptedContent` is written to the file by calling the `write()` method on line 125. Now that we are done writing the file's contents, line 126 closes the file object in `fo`.

rsaCipher.py

```
127.     # Also return the encrypted string.
128.     return encryptedContent
```

Finally, the string in `encryptedContent` is returned from the `encryptAndWriteToFile()` function on line 128. (This is so that the code that calls the function can use this string to, for example, print it on the screen.)

The Full RSA Decryption Process

rsaCipher.py

```
131. def readFromFileAndDecrypt(messageFilename, keyFilename):
132.     # Using a key from a key file, read an encrypted message from a file
133.     # and then decrypt it. Returns the decrypted message string.
134.     keySize, n, d = readKeyFile(keyFilename)
```

The `readFromFileAndDecrypt()` function, like `encryptAndWriteToFile()`, has parameters for the encrypted message file's filename and the key file's filename. (Be sure to pass the filename of the private key for `keyFilename`, not the public key.)

The first step is the same as `encryptAndWriteToFile()`: the `readKeyFile()` function is called to get the values for the `keySize`, `n`, and `d` variables.

rsaCipher.py

```
137.     # Read in the message length and the encrypted message from the file.
138.     fo = open(messageFilename)
139.     content = fo.read()
140.     messageLength, blockSize, encryptedMessage = content.split('_')
141.     messageLength = int(messageLength)
142.     blockSize = int(blockSize)
```

The second step is to read in the contents of the file. The `messageFilename` file is opened for reading (the lack of a second argument means `open()` will use "read mode") on line 138. The `read()` method call on line 139 will return a string of the full contents of the file.

Remember that the encrypted file's format has an integer of the message length, an integer for the block size used, and then the encrypted integer blocks (all separated by underscore characters). Line 140 calls the `split()` method to return a list of these three values, and the multiple assignment trick places the three values into the `messageLength`, `blockSize`, and `message` variables respectively.

Because the values returned by `split()` will be strings, lines 141 and 142 will set `messageLength` and `blockSize` to their integer form, respectively.

rsaCipher.py

```
144.     # Check that key size is greater than block size.
145.     if keySize < blockSize * 8: # * 8 to convert bytes to bits
146.         sys.exit('ERROR: Block size is %s bits and key size is %s bits.
The RSA cipher requires the block size to be equal to or greater than the key
size. Did you specify the correct key file and encrypted file?' % (blockSize *
8, keySize))
```

The readFromFileAndDecrypt() function also has a check that the block size is equal to or greater than the key size. This should always pass, because if the block size was too small, then it would have been impossible to create this encrypted file. Most likely the wrong private key file was specified for the keyFilename parameter, which means the key would not have decrypted the file correctly anyway.

rsaCipher.py

```
148.     # Convert the encrypted message into large int values.
149.     encryptedBlocks = []
150.     for block in encryptedMessage.split(','):
151.         encryptedBlocks.append(int(block))
```

The encryptedMessage string contains many integer characters joined together with commas. Line 150's for loop iterates over the list returned by the split() method. This list contains strings of individual blocks. The integer form of these strings is appended to the encryptedBlocks list (which starts as an empty list on line 149) each time line 151 is executed. After the for loop on line 150 completes, the encryptedBlocks list contains integer values of the numbers that were in the encryptedMessage string.

rsaCipher.py

```
153.     # Decrypt the large int values.
154.     return decryptMessage(encryptedBlocks, messageLength, (n, d),
blockSize)
```

The list in encryptedBlocks is passed to decryptMessage(), along with messageLength, the private key (which is a tuple value of the two integers in n and d), and the block size. The decryptMessage() function returns a single string value of the decrypted message, which itself is returned from readFileAndDecrypt() on line 154.

rsaCipher.py

```
157. # If rsaCipher.py is run (instead of imported as a module) call
158. # the main() function.
159. if __name__ == '__main__':
160.     main()
```

Lines 159 and 160 call the main() function if this program was run by itself rather than imported by another program.

Practice Exercises, Chapter 24, Set D

Practice exercises can be found at http://invpy.com/hackingpractice24D.

Why Can't We Hack the RSA Cipher

All the different types of cryptographic attacks we've used in this book can't be used against the RSA cipher:

1. The brute-force attack won't work. There are too many possible keys to go through.
2. A dictionary attack won't work because the keys are based on numbers, not words.
3. A word pattern attack can't be used because the same plaintext word can be encrypted differently depending on where in the block it appears.
4. Frequency analysis can't be used. Since a single encrypted block represents several characters, we can't get a frequency count of the individual characters.

There are no mathematical tricks that work, either. Remember, the RSA decryption equation is:

M = C^d mod n

Where M is the message block integer, C is the ciphertext block integer, and the private key is made up of the two numbers (d, n). Everyone (including a cryptanalyst) has the public key file, which provides (e, n), so the n number is known. If the cryptanalyst can intercept the ciphertext (which we should always assume is possible), then she knows C as well. But without knowing d, it is impossible to do the decryption and calculate M, the original message.

A cryptanalyst knows that d is the inverse of e mod $(p - 1) \times (q - 1)$ and also knows e from the public key. But there's no way she knows what $(p - 1) \times (q - 1)$ is. There are some hints to figure it out though.

The key sizes are known (it's in the public key file), so the cryptanalyst knows that p and q are less than 2 ^ 1024 and that e is relatively prime with $(p - 1) \times (q - 1)$. But e is relatively prime with *a lot* of numbers, and with a range of 0 to 2 ^ 1024 possible numbers, it is too large to brute-force.

The cryptanalyst has another hint from the public key, though. The public key is two numbers (e, n). And from the RSA algorithm she knows that $n = p \times q$. And since p and q are both prime numbers, for the given n number there can be only two numbers for p and q.

(Remember, prime numbers have no factors besides 1 and themselves. If you multiply two prime numbers, that new number will only have the factors of 1 and itself, and also the two prime numbers.)

So to solve everything and hack the RSA cipher, all we need to do is figure out what the factors are for n. Since there are two and only two numbers that multiply to n, we won't have several different numbers to choose from. Then we can calculate $(p - 1) \times (q - 1)$ and then calculate d.

This seems pretty easy. We already have code that finds factors in *primeSieve.py*'s `isPrime()` function:

Source code from primeSieve.py

```
def isPrime(num):
    # Returns True if num is a prime number, otherwise False.

    # Note: Generally, isPrime() is slower than primeSieve().

    # all numbers less than 2 are not prime
    if num < 2:
        return False

    # see if num is divisible by any number up to the square root of num
    for i in range(2, int(math.sqrt(num)) + 1):
        if num % i == 0:
            return False
    return True
```

We can just modify this code to return the first factors it finds (since we know that there can be only two factors for n besides 1 and n):

```
def isPrime(num):
    # Returns (p,q) where p and q are factors of num

    # see if num is divisible by any number up to the square root of num
    for i in range(2, int(math.sqrt(num)) + 1):
        if num % i == 0:
            return (i, num / i)
    return None # no factors exist for num, num must be prime
```

We can just call this function, pass it n (which we get from the public key file), and wait for it to find our factors, p and q. Then we can know what $(p - 1) \times (q - 1)$ is, which means we can calculate the mod inverse of e mod $(p - 1) \times (q - 1)$, which is d, the decryption key. Then it would be easy to calculate M, the plaintext message.

There's a problem, though. Remember that n is a number that is around 600 digits long. In fact, Python's `math.sqrt()` function can't even handle a number that big (it will give you an error message). But even if it could, Python would be executing that `for` loop for a very, very long time.

Our Sun doesn't have enough mass to eventually go supernova, but in 5 billion years it will expand into a red giant star and utterly destroy the Earth. Even if your computer was still running then, there's still no chance that 5 billion years is long enough to find the factors of n. That is how big the numbers we are dealing with are.

And here's where the strength of the RSA cipher comes from: **Mathematically, there is no shortcut to finding the factors of a number.** It's easy to look at a small number like 15 and say, "Oh, 5 and 3 are two numbers that multiply to 15. Those are factors of 15." But it's another thing entirely to take a (relatively small) number like 178,565,887,643,607,245,654,502,737 and try to figure out the factors for it. The only way we can try is by brute-forcing through numbers, but there are too many numbers.

It is really easy to come up with two prime numbers p and q and multiply them together to get n. But it is reasonably impossible to take a number n and figure out what p and q are. These facts make the RSA cipher usable as a cryptographic cipher.

Summary

That's it! This is the last chapter of the book! There is no "Hacking the RSA Cipher" chapter because there's no straightforward attack on the mathematics behind the RSA cipher. And any brute-force attack would fail, because there are far too many possible keys to try: the keys are literally hundreds of digits long. If you had a trillion buildings each with a trillion computers that each tried a trillion keys every nanosecond, it would still take longer than the universe as been in existence to go through a fraction of the possible keys. (And the electric bill for all those computers would bankrupt every industrialized nation on the planet.)

That's a lot of possible keys.

The RSA algorithm is a real encryption cipher used in professional encryption software. When you log into a website or buy something off the Internet, the RSA cipher (or one like it) is used to keep passwords and credit card numbers secret from anyone who may be intercepting your network traffic.

Actually, while the basic mathematics used for professional encryption software are the same as described in this chapter, you probably don't want to use this program for your secret files. The hacks against an encryption program like *rsaCipher.py* are pretty sophisticated, but they do exist. (For example, the "random" numbers returned from `random.randint()` aren't truly random and can be predicted, meaning that a hacker could figure out which "random" numbers were used for the prime numbers of your private key.)

You've seen how all the previous ciphers in this book have each been hacked and rendered worthless. In general, you don't want to write your own cryptography code for things you want to keep secret, because you will probably make subtle mistakes in the implementation of these programs. And hackers and spy agencies use these mistakes to hack your encrypted messages.

A cipher is only secure if everything but the key can be revealed but still keep the message a secret. You cannot rely on a cryptanalyst not having access to the same encryption software or knowing what cipher you used. Remember Shannon's Maxim: The enemy knows the system!

Professional encryption software is written by cryptographers who have spent years studying the mathematics and potential weaknesses of various ciphers. Even then, the software they write is inspected by other cryptographers to check for mistakes or potential weaknesses. You are perfectly capable of learning about these cipher systems and cryptographic mathematics too. It's not about being the smartest hacker, but spending the time to study to become the most knowledgeable hacker.

I hope you've found this book to be a helpful start on becoming an elite hacker and programmer. There is a lot more to learn about programming and cryptography than what is in this book, but I encourage you explore and learn more! One great book about the general history of cryptography that I highly recommend is "The Code Book" by Simon Singh. You can go to http://invp.com/morehacking for a list of other books and websites to learn more about cryptography. Feel free to email me your programming or cryptography questions at al@inventwithpython.com.

Good luck!

About the Author

Albert Sweigart (but you can call him Al), is a software developer in San Francisco, California who enjoys haunting coffee shops and making useful software. *Hacking Secret Ciphers with Python* is his third book.

His first two books, *Invent Your Own Computer Games with Python* and *Making Games with Python & Pygame* can be read online for free at http://inventwithpython.com.

He is originally from Houston, Texas. He laughs out loud when watching park squirrels, which makes people think he's a simpleton. He almost ended up working at the NSA after college, but then again we all do dumb things when we are young.

- Email: al@inventwithpython.com
- Twitter: @AlSweigart

Made in the USA
San Bernardino, CA
16 January 2014